THE GRILL-ING BOOK

THE DEFINITIVE GUIDE FROM

bon appétit

EDITED BY **ADAM RAPOPORT**

PHOTOGRAPHY BY **PEDEN + MUNK**

**Andrews McMeel
Publishing, LLC**

Kansas City • Sydney • London

Andrews McMeel Publishing, LLC
an Andrews McMeel Universal company
1130 Walnut Street, Kansas City, Missouri 64106

www.andrewsmcmeel.com

13 14 15 16 17 TEN 10 9 8 7 6 5 4 3 2 1

ISBN: 978-1-4494-2752-8

Library of Congress Control Number: 2012952341

Design: Joe Shouldice, YesYesYes Design
Photography: Peden + Munk
Photography Assistant: Jaesung Lee
Food Stylist: Rebecca Jurkevich
Food Stylist Assistant: Tina DeGraff
Meats: DeBragga and Spitler
Seafoods: Browne Trading Company
Surfaces and Props: Dawn Hill Antiques
Prop Stylist: Lucy Attwater
Prop Stylist Assistant: Maya Rossi
Food Stylist (page 67): Alison Attenborough
Prop Stylist (page 67): Kaitlyn Du Ross
Illustrations: Joe McKendry

www.bonappetit.com

ATTENTION: SCHOOLS AND BUSINESSES
Andrews McMeel books are available at quantity discounts with
bulk purchase for educational, business, or sales promotional use.
For information, please e-mail the Andrews McMeel Special Sales
Department: specialsales@amuniversal.com

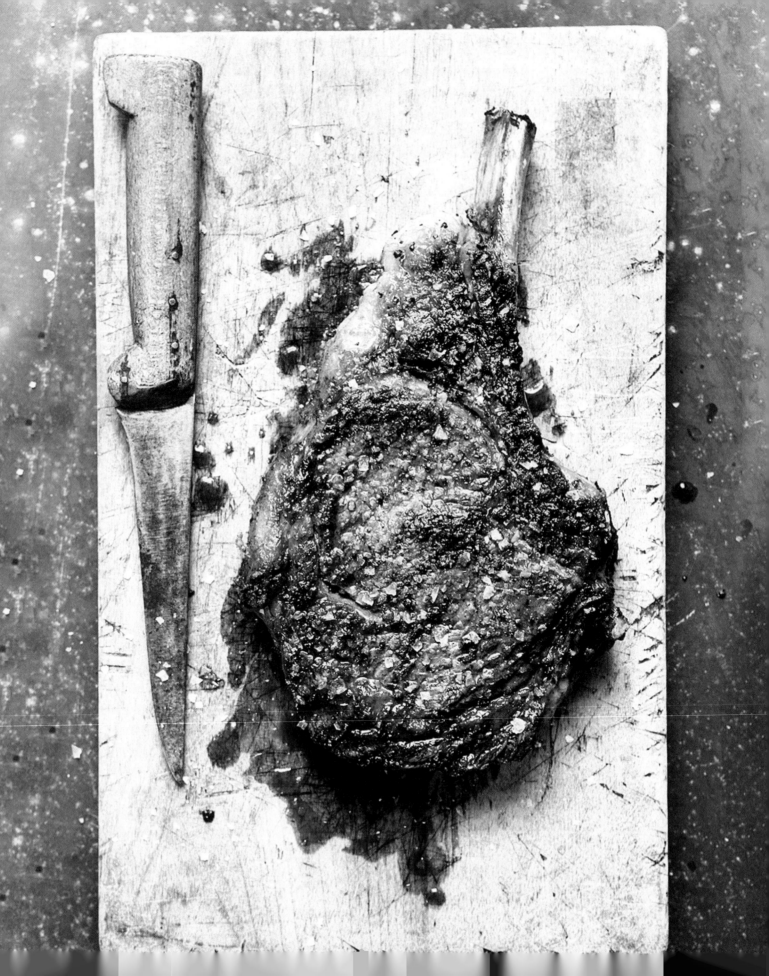

CONTENTS

"LET'S FIRE UP THE GRILL."

You hear those words and you can't help but smile.

There's something about grilling—something that suggests that everything is about to get a lot better. That you won't be cooped up in a house or apartment, but that you'll be outside under an open sky. Your friends or family will be joining you, you'll soon have a cold beer or glass of wine in your hand, and, of course, you'll be laying something absolutely delicious on that soon-to-be blazing-hot grill.

At *Bon Appétit*, we love all types of cuisines, but when it comes to *forms* of cooking, nothing gets us more revved up than grilling. Hands down. It is an art form (or is it a science?) that's as challenging as it is rewarding, as primal as it is complex, and, to be honest, at times as maddening as it is fun.

In short, it's about knowledge—knowledge that we want to pass on to you. When I was a kid, my father used to drench charcoal briquettes in lighter fluid, and he'd engulf our black kettle grill in a tower of flames. He'd then grill a big slab of cheap steak until it was blackened and overcooked. Sure, it wasn't exactly the worst scenario on earth—it was summertime, there were hot dogs involved, and it was my dad cooking, after all—but I'm pretty sure that I knew my dad was doing nearly everything wrong. If he was trying to pass on any important lessons, I wasn't absorbing them. And yet I cherish those memories of my family on our back deck, hanging out together, laughing, eating, and watching the sun dip below the neighborhood trees.

With *The Grilling Book*, we want to help you make grilling with your friends and family not just fun, but also delicious. These pages won't just tell you *what* to grill, but they'll also teach you *how* to grill. You'll learn about equipment (gas vs. charcoal), cedar planks, the best techniques for working with different meats, fish, and vegetables. So whether you've got a porterhouse or a rib eye, a rack of lamb or a couple of chops, a side of salmon or a whole striped bass, you'll know how to prep and grill it the right way, every time.

There are more than 380 recipes in the book, all of which were at some point published in the pages of *Bon Appétit*. And just like the recipes that appear in our pages, many are internationally oriented, like grilled clams with lemon-ginger butter (page 259), flatbreads with charmoula and ancho chile oil (page 298), and Cambodian-style ginger-honey baby back ribs (page 157). Because if there's one form of cooking that unites the cultures of the world, it's grilling.

Some of the recipes you'll encounter in the coming pages call for techniques that might be new to you. Others feature herbs and spices you'll want to add to your pantry. But all of them are written with clear, precise instructions that will arm you with confidence.

So whether you use this book to savor the flavors of Carolina or California, Jamaica or Malaysia, the important thing is that you go ahead and fire up that grill.

ADAM RAPOPORT
Editor in Chief

GRILL PREP

LIGHTING UP A GRILL

isn't so different from cooking inside your kitchen. Once you gather the essential tools and fire up your major appliance (that is, the grill), it's pretty easy to prepare a delicious meal. In the beginning, you'll need to learn a few basic techniques. Then, as with any type of cooking, the more often you grill, the more intuitive it'll become.

In this chapter, we outline everything you need to get started, from the right size tongs to the best type of charcoal. You'll also get fail-safe rules for seasoning steaks, chicken, and fish, and tips on how to master the fire. Sound good? **NOW, LET'S DO THIS.**

I. CHOOSE YOUR FUEL

One of the most important questions in grilling is, of course: gas or charcoal? There are pros and cons to both approaches. It just depends on what works best for you.

the case for: CHARCOAL

AT *BON APPÉTIT*, we love a charcoal grill. Sure, this method is a temperamental art that takes patience, practice, and, well... patience. But for us, the results it produces are unparalleled. First, a bed of glowing orange coals generates a level of heat that's steadier and more intense than a gas burner could ever create.

Second, there's the char. Do you want juicy burgers and steaks with a crisp, mahogany brown crust? If so, you need the type of heat that charcoal delivers.

Finally, there's just something romantic and iconically American about hoisting a bag of charcoal, lighting a fire, and watching flames build and fade to perfectly glowing, grill-ready coals.

the case for: GAS

THERE ARE LOTS OF REASONS why two-thirds of Americans use gas grills instead of charcoal. Reason No. 1? Convenience. It's great to walk outside, flip a switch, and instantly have a hot grill at the ready.

But gas grills do have a couple of drawbacks. First, most of them just don't get as hot as a charcoal grill. Second, they don't deliver the same authentic, smoky flavor that charcoal provides. When you're dealing with gas, you're essentially grilling over an outdoor stove burner as opposed to an open fire. Make no mistake: You *will* taste the difference.

That said, there are ways to optimize a gas grill to make it as powerful as possible. See the tips below.

HOW TO: Pick Your Coals

There are many different kinds of charcoal out there, and not all of them are created equal.

1 Lump hardwood charcoal
These charred pieces of real hardwood are, hands down, our top choice for grilling. That's because they burn the hottest and cleanest of any fuel option. They're more expensive than briquettes, but we think the extra cost is worth it.

2 Pressed charcoal briquettes
Made from wood fragments and other materials, these offer long-lasting heat. Use a charcoal chimney (see page 14) to get them started.

3 Instant charcoal briquettes
These are soaked in lighter fluid and other chemicals. Use them only in a pinch.

HOW TO: Get the Most from Gas

To help a gas grill get really hot, and keep it operating at peak performance, always:

1 Keep it clean
Use a toothpick to make sure all burner holes are clear of debris or other matter. If the burner holes are clogged, the flame will be low or non-existent, and heat levels will drop dramatically.

2 Put a lid on it
You wouldn't preheat your oven with its door open, right? So close the lid on your gas grill and preheat it for 10 minutes for maximum intensity. And if you want a nice crust on a steak, keep the lid closed during cooking. Don't worry, you won't "steam" the food. A closed lid keeps things hot and lets the heat work its magic.

2. GO FOR THE CHAR

Ultimately, grilling is all about heat—how to manage it, and how to embrace it. If you know what you're doing, you'll get crispy chicken, crusty steak, and beautifully caramelized vegetables. The key is understanding how to grill over *direct* heat (as in, right over coals or gas flames). Here's what you need to know.

cooking with DIRECT HEAT

DON'T BE AFRAID OF INTENSE HEAT. Whether you're grilling over gas or charcoal, the aim is to create high heat in one area and lower heat in another. This allows you to sear quick-cooking foods (with a safe zone for flare-ups), or to develop a nice char or crust on your food, before sliding it to the calmer section of the grill, where it cooks through. Gas and charcoal grills require different approaches to achieve this.

CHARCOAL

1 Use *lots* of coals
There's nothing worse than a small fire that can't support all the great food above it.

2 Then, let 'em mellow
Once the coals are engulfed in flames, allow those flames to die down until there's a bed of glowing orange embers. You want to cook over intense *heat,* not flames that will blacken your food.

3 Get in the zone
In order to avoid flare-ups, a 2-zone fire is a must. To master one, see facing page.

4 Use your hands
For a hot fire, you should be able to hold your hand over the grate for no more than 2 seconds. For a medium fire, 4 seconds.

GAS

1 Be patient—let it heat up
Crank up the burners on your gas grill to high and close the lid. Do this at least 5 or 10 minutes before you're ready to start grilling. This will get the grill as hot as possible—which is exactly what you want when grilling steaks and burgers. However, if you want a mellower fire (say, if you're barbecuing chicken), preheat the closed grill with the knobs turned to medium.

2 Create two levels of heat
If your gas grill has an upper-tier warming rack, use that as your safe zone whenever you need to slide food away from direct heat that's too fiery. If your grill doesn't have a warming rack, just leave one burner unlit and use that as your safe zone.

GETTING IT RIGHT: Use a Charcoal Chimney

1. Stuff newspaper in the bottom. Place on the bottom grate of your grill. **2. Fill the top** with charcoal. **3. Light the paper**, and let the chimney work its magic. **4. Wait** until the flames have died down and the coals are orange. **5. Empty out the coals** and start grilling.

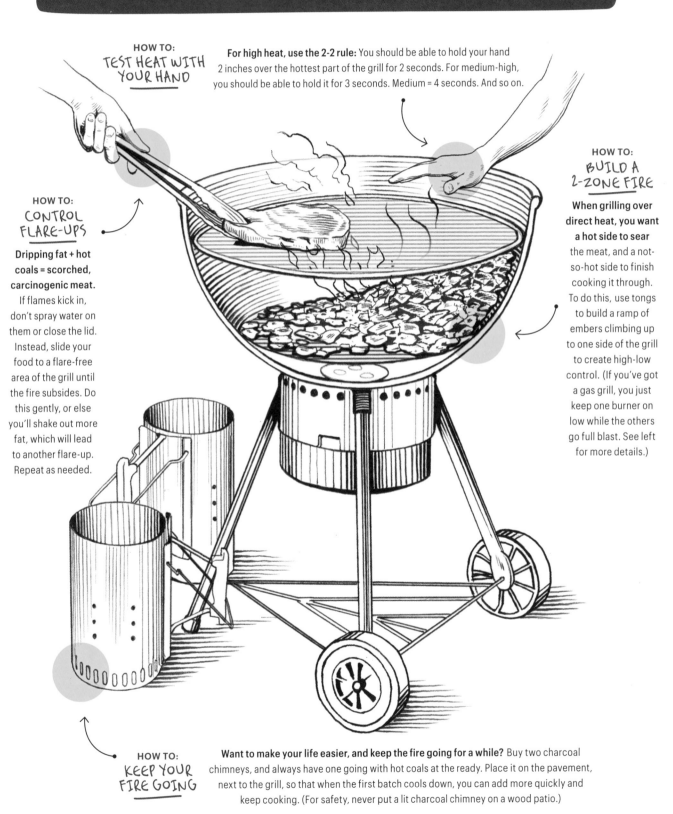

HOW TO:
TEST HEAT WITH YOUR HAND

For high heat, use the 2-2 rule: You should be able to hold your hand 2 inches over the hottest part of the grill for 2 seconds. For medium-high, you should be able to hold it for 3 seconds. Medium = 4 seconds. And so on.

HOW TO:
BUILD A 2-ZONE FIRE

When grilling over direct heat, you want a hot side to sear the meat, and a not-so-hot side to finish cooking it through. To do this, use tongs to build a ramp of embers climbing up to one side of the grill to create high-low control. (If you've got a gas grill, you just keep one burner on low while the others go full blast. See left for more details.)

HOW TO:
CONTROL FLARE-UPS

Dripping fat + hot coals = scorched, carcinogenic meat. If flames kick in, don't spray water on them or close the lid. Instead, slide your food to a flare-free area of the grill until the fire subsides. Do this gently, or else you'll shake out more fat, which will lead to another flare-up. Repeat as needed.

HOW TO:
KEEP YOUR FIRE GOING

Want to make your life easier, and keep the fire going for a while? Buy two charcoal chimneys, and always have one going with hot coals at the ready. Place it on the pavement, next to the grill, so that when the first batch cools down, you can add more quickly and keep cooking. (For safety, never put a lit charcoal chimney on a wood patio.)

4. GRILL IT SLOW AND LOW

Cooking with INDIRECT HEAT

WHEN SHOULD YOU SLOW COOK? When you want to grill food for a long time without charring it. Use this technique for whole chicken, or to make a fall-apart tender pork shoulder or a bone-in leg of lamb. In short, you want the heat of the fire to gently envelop the meat and slowly cook it through, but not sear it.

With low and slow cooking, keep the grill lid closed and never place meat directly over the fire. Here's a step-by-step guide to getting it right, for both kinds of grills:

CHARCOAL

1 Fire up your coals—then divide them
When coals are hot, push half of them to either side of the grill, leaving space in the middle.

2 Position your drip pan
Place a foil baking pan in between the two coal piles. This is used to collect drippings during cooking. Add water to the drip pan as directed in the recipe.

3 Close the lid
Unless the recipe says otherwise, keep lid closed during cooking. If things are cooking too quickly, close the vents to deprive the fire of oxygen until the flames die down.

4 Keep the fire fueled
After every hour of cooking, add hot coals from the charcoal chimney to keep the fire going.

GAS

1 Turn on the grill—but not all burners
If there are two burners, heat one to the temperature specified in the recipe and leave the other unlit. If there are three or four burners, light the ones on the outside or front and rear.

2 Position your drip pan
Arrange the drip pan directly on top of the unlit burner(s). It's important to note that many gas grills have built-in drip pans; if yours has one, make sure to keep it clean. Add water to the pan as directed in the recipe.

3 Cook meat over the drip pan
If you find that food is cooking too quickly, just lower the temperature on the grill.

5. ADD SOME WOOD-SMOKED FLAVOR

Cooking over wood chips is a fantastic way to infuse food with a delicious, unmistakably smoky flavor. Different kinds of wood—mesquite, hickory, maple, or fruitwoods—have different accents. Soak your chips well (at least an hour) in water, beer, juice, or wine for 30 minutes to 1 hour before grilling. This allows them to smoke without burning up. Then drain them well.

ON A CHARCOAL GRILL

After you soak them, sprinkle a few handfuls of well-drained chips **directly onto hot coals**. Just be careful not to douse the coals.

ON A GAS GRILL

Put drained wood chips in **a foil broiler pan** or wrap them loosely in 2 layers of heavy-duty foil, leaving the packet open slightly. Place the pan or the packet directly over flames.

+

Meat gets infused with delicious smoky flavor when you **cook it over wood chips.**

6. YOUR GRILLING TOOLBOX

Before you light a match or turn a knob, organize your gear so it's within arm's reach. Here are the tools you'll need on a regular basis.

METAL SKEWERS

Keep meat kebabs or a row of vegetable pieces in place. Long and strong is what you want.

TONGS

Sturdy stainless-steel tongs are indispensable when grilling. Make sure the handle is long enough to reach all the way to the back of your grill.

GRILL BASKET/ FISH BASKET

Using baskets isn't cheating, it's common sense. There's no easier way to cook small vegetables or a whole fish or fillets than with one of these handy wire contraptions.

CHARCOAL CHIMNEY

Use this to start your fire with ease—coals are glowing hot and ready within 20 to 30 minutes. Plus, it eliminates the need for lighter fluid. In fact, buy two so that you can prepare a lot of coals at once.

STAINLESS-STEEL SPATULA

Get one with a head that's strong and broad enough to flip anything from a burger to a whole fish, and make sure it's got sharp edges to cleanly lift food from the grate.

BASTING BRUSH

Whether you want to shellac ribs with barbecue sauce or glaze salmon with marinade, this is the ultimate flavor-enhancing tool.

GRILLING FORK

Just like your tongs, this should be long and sturdy. It's key for flipping large, family-friendly cuts of meat like flank steak or butterflied leg of lamb. Be careful to avoid stabbing meat with it any more than necessary or you'll lose the juices.

INSTANT-READ THERMOMETER

Experienced grillers can determine doneness by look and feel—and we'll show you how to do it that way. But to prevent disaster with that pricey rack of lamb or filet mignon, nothing beats a digital thermometer.

OVERSIZE BARBEQUE MITT

Grills get hot—**really hot**. And the more confidently you can manipulate what you're cooking, the smoother things will go.

GRILL BRUSH

Your grill grate doesn't fit in the dishwasher, but it still needs to be cleaned—often. Before and after you use the grill each time, give it a good scrape with a stiff metal wire brush. Invest in a new one whenever the bristles start to wear down or come loose.

7. ALWAYS SEASON IT WELL

Brines, rubs, marinades, and sauces are worthwhile and tasty ways to add flavor to food before and after it's grilled (see page 373). But when it comes down to it, when you're grilling with high-quality meat, fish, and vegetables, all you *really* need is a hot fire and some salt and pepper. That basic-as-can-be preparation lets the food's inherent flavors shine.

SALT

It's crucial to salt the meat both before and after it cooks.

To season **before** cooking, we use kosher salt. We recommend Diamond Crystal brand; its porous, evenly sized crystals are easy to sprinkle and are full of pure flavor.

1 **For thick cuts** of steak, lamb, or pork, season 20 minutes before grilling: 1 tsp. per 1 lb. of meat. Once the meat is salted, let it rest on a wire rack.

2 **For thinner filets**, cutlets, fish fillets, and vegetables, season just before they go on the grill.

3 **When seasoning**, sprinkle salt all over the piece of meat—don't forget the edges and ends.

After cooking, slice the meat and top with sea salt. Our favorite is Maldon—the crunch of the delicate flakes punctuates and accentuates the protein's flavor.

PEPPER

A few cranks of a peppermill can add kick to pretty much anything you throw on the grill. However, for thick cuts of meat like steak, coarsely cracked peppercorns bring another dimension of bracing flavor.

To **crack your own**, place peppercorns in either a large skillet or a resealable plastic bag on a counter, and apply a little elbow grease to crush them with the flat bottom of a small skillet. Just before grilling, coat your rib eye or strip steak generously with the freshly cracked pepper.

SECRET WEAPON: Do-It-Yourself Herb Basting Brush

One of our favorite ways to add layers of flavor to grilled meat is with an herb basting brush. It's easy to make one at home: **Take a big bunch of hardy herb sprigs** (we recommend a combination of rosemary, oregano, and thyme) and **tie them together** at the stems with kitchen twine. Dip herbs in olive oil and brush the meat continuously as it cooks. The aromatic oils from the herbs mix with the caramelizing meat to create unexpected, incredible flavor.

Salt and Pepper 101:
Yes, you want this much seasoning.

It all adds up:
butterflied chicken
grilled to perfection.

5 KEYS to GRILLING SUCCESS

You now have the tools and the essential know-how to tackle everything from whole sea bass to bone-in rib eye. But things can get intense at a cookout once the food is on the grill.
To keep your cool, remember these guidelines when the heat is on:

1 PRACTICE, PRACTICE

Every grill is different, and grilling isn't a precise science. But trust us: **The more you grill, the better you'll understand the fire**, the more organized you'll be, and the better your food will taste.

So grill a lot (what could be bad about that?) and learn from your mistakes—and from your successes.

2 KEEP IT CLEAN

Before and after you use your grill, clean it. Yes—every time. When you're done cooking, and **while the grill's still hot, use the grill brush to scrape the grate** clean. When you fire up the grill the next time, brush the grate again. If you have a gas grill with a built-in drip pan, clean that, too.

3 OIL THE GRATE

To help food release easily from the grill, **oil the grate thoroughly**. Unless the recipe specifies otherwise, use vegetable oil. (And never, ever use nonstick spray cans around a heated grill—they can explode.) If you don't have a brush at the ready, crumple a piece of aluminum foil and use that.

4 KEEP IT MOVING

Both gas and charcoal grills have some spots that are hotter and cooler than others. Get to know yours, and **move food around on the grill for even cooking**. Place food at an angle to increase the surface area that's exposed to the heat.

5 LOVE THE CHAR

We write a lot about char in this book—it's nirvana in grilling. More than just turning food black, **it's a chemical process that happens at high temperatures in dry-heat cooking**, changing food's molecular structure and creating deep brown color and intense flavor. So yes, that rib-eye steak really *does* taste better straight off a grill.

Got all that? Okay. Now turn the page...
Let's get started!

CHICKEN

CHICKEN—IT'S WHAT'S FOR DINNER.

At least that's true for so many of us in America. When we're finalizing each issue of *Bon Appétit,* we always double check to make sure that we've included enough chicken recipes. Because let's face it, chicken is a great, all-purpose protein that adapts easily to countless cuisines and skill levels.

And rarely is it as satisfying as when prepared on a fiery-hot grill—whether crispy and juicy and dripping with a sweet-and-spicy glaze, or redolent of a fragrant spice rub.

The question is: What kind of chicken are you grilling? Are you talking about skin-on, bone-in pieces, which require a gentle dance between direct and indirect heat so that they develop a caramelized crust on the outside and are thoroughly cooked through, yet still moist, inside? Or are you thinking more of a weeknight preparation—like pounded-thin cutlets marinated in a ginger-yogurt purée and then seared for a few minutes over intense heat?

Whichever you choose, chicken on the grill is ever versatile and endlessly delicious. No other chapter in this book offers as much variety and as many possibilities. So start reading, and, more important, start grilling.

CHICKEN KEBABS
with Aleppo Pepper

1½ Tbsp. Aleppo pepper, or 2 tsp. crushed red pepper flakes plus 2 tsp. Hungarian sweet paprika, plus more Aleppo pepper or paprika for sprinkling

1 cup plain whole-milk Greek yogurt

3 Tbsp. extra-virgin olive oil, plus more for brushing

2 Tbsp. red wine vinegar

2 Tbsp. tomato paste

2 tsp. kosher salt, more as needed

1 tsp. freshly ground black pepper, more as needed

6 garlic cloves, crushed

2 lemons, 1 thinly sliced into rounds, 1 cut into wedges

2¼ lb. skinless, boneless chicken thighs, cut into 1¼-inch pieces

INGREDIENT INFO Aleppo pepper is a slightly sweet Syrian pepper with a moderate heat level that is sold finely ground or crushed into small flakes; either variety will work well in this recipe. It can be found at specialty foods stores or wholespice.com.

SPECIAL EQUIPMENT 6 metal skewers

The combination of creamy yogurt, pungent garlic, and smoky Aleppo pepper results in the sort of chicken that has made Turkish cooks the Near East's undisputed grill masters for centuries.

Place 1½ Tbsp. Aleppo pepper and 1 Tbsp. warm water in a large bowl and let stand until a thick paste forms, about 5 minutes. If using red pepper flakes and paprika combination, place in a large bowl and stir in 2 Tbsp. warm water; let stand until a paste forms, about 5 minutes. Whisk in yogurt, 3 Tbsp. oil, vinegar, tomato paste, 2 tsp. salt, and 1 tsp. black pepper. Stir in garlic and lemon rounds, then chicken. Cover and chill for at least 1 hour. **DO AHEAD:** Can be made 1 day ahead. Keep chilled.

Build a medium fire in a charcoal grill, or heat a gas grill to medium-high. Thread chicken pieces on metal skewers, dividing equally. Discard marinade in bowl. Season chicken with salt and black pepper and sprinkle with Aleppo pepper. Brush grill grate with oil. Grill chicken, turning skewers occasionally, until golden brown and cooked through, 10 to 12 minutes total. Transfer skewers to a platter. Surround with lemon wedges.

CHICKEN SKEWERS
with Coriander Marinade and Lemon Salsa

photo, right

8 Meyer lemons

½ cup finely chopped cucumber, preferably English hothouse

3 Tbsp. thinly sliced scallions, divided

1 serrano chile, finely chopped
Pinch of sugar
Kosher salt

1½ lb. skinless, boneless chicken thighs, cut into 1½-inch pieces
Freshly ground black pepper

¼ cup plus 2 Tbsp. chopped fresh cilantro

¼ cup plain whole-milk yogurt

1 Tbsp. vegetable oil, plus more for brushing

2 garlic cloves, coarsely chopped

1 tsp. cracked coriander seeds

1 tsp. turmeric (optional)

SPECIAL EQUIPMENT 12 metal skewers

Chicken and lemon are ideal partners. Here, Meyer lemons give a sweet and fruity note to the salsa; if you're using regular lemons, which are more tart, use fewer.

Using a sharp knife, cut all peel and white pith from lemons; discard. Cut between membranes to release lemon segments into a medium bowl; squeeze juice from membranes into bowl and discard membranes. Strain juice into a clean bowl; reserve lemon segments and juices separately.

Mix segments, 1 Tbsp. lemon juice (set aside remaining juice for another use), cucumber, 2 Tbsp. scallions, and chile in a small bowl. Stir in sugar; season salsa to taste with salt and set aside.

Place chicken in a medium bowl and season with salt and pepper. Purée ¼ cup cilantro, yogurt, 1 Tbsp. oil, garlic, coriander, and turmeric, if using, in a mini food processor or blender until smooth. Pour marinade over chicken; toss to coat. Let marinate at room temperature for 20 minutes. **DO AHEAD:** Can be made 1 day ahead. Cover and refrigerate. Let stand at room temperature for 30 minutes before continuing.

Build a medium fire in a charcoal grill, or heat a gas grill to medium-high. Brush grill grate with oil. Thread 4 pieces of chicken on each skewer. Grill, turning once and watching closely to prevent burning, until browned and an instant-read thermometer inserted into the thickest part of the meat registers 165°F, about 8 minutes. Transfer chicken to plates. Spoon lemon salsa over chicken. Garnish with remaining 2 Tbsp. cilantro and 1 Tbsp. scallions.

Kitchen Wisdom

BETTER CHICKEN = BETTER FLAVOR The flavor in grilled chicken doesn't start with herbs, spices, marinade, or brine. **It starts with the chicken.** When you're shopping, buy the best-quality bird you can find. In the Bon Appétit Test Kitchen, we use chickens that are raised without the use of antibiotics or growth hormones. Two brands we like to go back to again and again are Bell & Evans (bellandevans.com) and Murray's (murrayschicken.com).

The bright, **citrus-spiked salsa** that accompanies these skewers also pairs nicely with roasted fish or seared scallops.

CHICKEN SKEWERS
WITH CORIANDER MARINADE
AND LEMON SALSA

THAI-STYLE CHICKEN THIGHS

⅓ cup chopped fresh basil
⅓ cup chopped fresh cilantro
⅓ cup chopped fresh mint
3 Tbsp. chopped peeled ginger
4 garlic cloves, chopped
1½ Tbsp. (packed) dark brown sugar
1½ Tbsp. fish sauce (such as nam pla or nuoc nam)
1½ Tbsp. reduced-sodium soy sauce
1½ Tbsp. vegetable oil, plus more for brushing
1 serrano chile, with seeds, chopped
12 skinless, boneless chicken thighs (about 2¼ lb.)

INGREDIENT INFO Fish sauce can be found in the Asian foods section of most supermarkets, at some specialty foods stores, and at Asian markets.

A strong blend of sweet, sour, salty, and spicy aromatics infuses these chicken thighs with exotic Thai flavor. As for fish sauce, it's a key ingredient in Thai cookery. If you don't have any in your pantry, get some—every serious griller should have a bottle. The recipe only calls for a splash, but a little goes a long way, so don't skip it.

Blend basil, cilantro, mint, ginger, garlic, brown sugar, fish sauce, soy sauce, 1½ Tbsp. oil, and chile in a food processor, stopping occasionally to scrape down sides of bowl, until a coarse purée forms.

Arrange chicken in a 13x9x2-inch glass baking dish. Spoon herb mixture over chicken; turn to coat. Cover dish and chill, turning chicken occasionally, for at least 2 hours. **DO AHEAD:** Can be made 1 day ahead. Keep chilled.

Build a medium fire in a charcoal grill, or heat a gas grill to medium-high. Brush grill grate with oil. Grill chicken, turning once, until an instant-read thermometer inserted into the thickest part of the thigh registers 165°F, about 6 minutes per side. Let rest for 5 minutes before serving.

WHY WE LOVE: Chicken Thighs

Bone-in or boneless, thighs are juicier and more versatile than any other cut. In fact, if you ask the cooks in the Bon Appétit Test Kitchen to name their favorite chicken part, this is their pick. Here's why:

GOOD VALUE

Pound for pound, thighs cost less than the boneless breasts you find at the supermarket—which makes them the ideal choice when you're planning a big backyard cookout.

FULL OF FLAVOR

Because of their higher fat content, thighs pack so much flavor on their own that all they really need in the way of seasonings is **kosher salt** and **freshly ground pepper**.

THEY'RE FORGIVING

Unlike chicken breasts, **thighs won't dry up on you** if you happen to leave them on the grill for a bit too long. Instead, they come off the grill with crisp skin and succulent meat.

CHICKEN BREASTS
with Tomato, Olive, and Feta Relish

4 servings

1½ cups coarsely chopped cherry
    tomatoes (about 10 oz.)
½ cup pitted Kalamata olives,
    chopped
3 Tbsp. extra-virgin olive oil,
    divided, plus more for brushing
2 Tbsp. chopped fresh mint
1 Tbsp. red wine vinegar
¾ cup crumbled feta (about 3½ oz.)
    Kosher salt and freshly ground
    black pepper
4 skinless, boneless chicken
    breasts (about 6 oz. each)

If you're counting calories but don't want to feel deprived, get your fill of the fresh, robust flavors in these boneless, skinless chicken breasts. During summer, look for Sweet 100's or any other kind of small, sweet cherry tomato. The relish is a delicious showcase for them.

Mix cherry tomatoes, olives, 2 Tbsp. oil, mint, and vinegar in a medium bowl. Gently stir in feta. Season relish to taste with salt and pepper.

Build a medium fire in a charcoal grill, or heat a gas grill to medium-high. Brush grill grate with oil. Brush chicken on both sides with remaining 1 Tbsp. oil; season with salt and pepper. Grill chicken about 5 minutes per side, turning once, or until an instant-read thermometer inserted into the thickest part of the breast registers 165°F. Transfer chicken to plates and slice, if desired. Top with relish.

CHICKEN BREASTS
with Edamame Hummus

4 servings

1 16-oz. bag frozen shelled
    edamame (soybeans)
½ cup coarsely chopped fresh basil
⅓ cup extra-virgin olive oil, plus
    more for brushing
3 garlic cloves
6 Tbsp. finely grated Parmesan
2 Tbsp. fresh lemon juice
    Kosher salt and freshly ground
    black pepper
4 skinless, boneless chicken
    breasts (about 6 oz. each)

This clever take on hummus uses edamame instead of chickpeas. It's perfect with the grilled chicken and also makes a great dip for toasted pita chips or crudités. Serve with bread or pita and a green salad for a simple weeknight meal.

Cook edamame in a large saucepan of boiling salted water until just tender, about 10 minutes. Drain, reserving 1 cup cooking liquid for hummus.

Meanwhile, pulse basil, ⅓ cup oil, and garlic in a food processor until basil and garlic are finely chopped. Transfer 2 Tbsp. basil oil to a small bowl and reserve.

Add cooked edamame, ½ cup reserved cooking liquid, Parmesan, and lemon juice to remaining basil oil in processor; purée, adding more cooking liquid by tablespoonfuls if mixture is dry, until almost smooth. Season hummus generously with salt and pepper and set aside.

Build a medium fire in a charcoal grill, or heat a gas grill to medium-high. Brush grill grate with oil. Brush chicken breasts on both sides with reserved basil oil; season with salt and pepper. Grill, turning once, until an instant-read thermometer inserted into the thickest part of the breast registers 165°F, about 6 minutes per side. Transfer to a cutting board and slice chicken breasts crosswise.

Spoon warm or room-temperature hummus onto plates. Top with chicken.

Save a portion of the herbed yogurt sauce to **serve at the table as a dip** for grilled flatbread or pita.

YOGURT-MARINATED CHICKEN BREASTS

YOGURT-MARINATED CHICKEN BREASTS

photo, left

8 skinless, boneless chicken breasts (about 6 oz. each)
⅓ cup extra-virgin olive oil, plus more for brushing
2 tsp. kosher salt, more as needed
2 cups plain whole-milk yogurt
1 cup coarsely chopped fresh cilantro
½ large onion, coarsely chopped
6 garlic cloves, coarsely chopped
1 Tbsp. fresh lime juice
1 Tbsp. garam masala or curry powder
1 tsp. freshly ground black pepper
1 2-inch piece ginger, peeled, chopped

INGREDIENT INFO Garam masala, an Indian spice blend, is sold in the spice section of many supermarkets and at Indian markets.

This recipe is a weeknight favorite among the staff at *Bon Appétit*. Boneless breasts make for quick, simple grilling, while an Indian-inspired herb-and-yogurt marinade adds bright, zesty flavors.

Working with 1 chicken breast at a time, place chicken between 2 sheets of waxed paper and pound to ½-inch thickness. Transfer chicken breasts to a resealable plastic bag. Blend ⅓ cup oil, 2 tsp. salt, and all remaining ingredients in a food processor until smooth. Pour yogurt mixture over chicken (reserving about ½ cup), seal bag, and turn chicken to coat. Marinate chicken in the refrigerator for at least 3 hours or overnight.

Build a medium fire in a charcoal grill, or heat a gas grill to medium-high. Brush grill grate with oil. Scrape excess marinade off chicken; season with salt. Grill chicken, turning once, until browned and an instant-read thermometer inserted into the thickest part of the breast registers 165°F, 3 to 4 minutes per side.

Serve with reserved marinade as a dipping sauce.

GARLICKY LEMON CHICKEN

2 small heads of garlic, separated into cloves
¼ cup minced flat-leaf parsley
Kosher salt and freshly ground black pepper
4 skin-on, boneless chicken breasts (about 6 oz. each)
Vegetable oil, for brushing
2 Tbsp. (¼ stick) unsalted butter
2 Tbsp. fresh lemon juice

Garlic is good—you don't need us to tell you that. In this recipe, we use two full heads of it, some of which gets rubbed under the chicken's skin and the rest of which is incorporated into a garlic-lemon sauce that gets spooned over the finished dish. It may sound like an outrageous amount, but the cloves are boiled in water before grilling, which reduces their pungency and brings out sweetness.

Build a medium-low fire in a charcoal grill, or heat a gas grill to medium. Cook garlic in a large pot of boiling water for 1 minute; drain. Thinly slice garlic cloves and place in a small bowl. Add parsley; season with salt and pepper. Set aside 2 Tbsp. garlic mixture for sauce. Run your fingers under skin along 1 long side of each chicken breast to loosen skin from meat, creating pockets. Fill pockets with remaining garlic mixture, dividing equally. Season chicken with salt and pepper.

Brush grill grate with oil. Grill chicken, turning once, about 6 minutes per side, until skin is crisp or an instant-read thermometer inserted into the thickest part of the breast registers 165°F. Transfer chicken to plates and tent with foil to keep warm.

Melt butter in a small saucepan over medium heat. Add reserved garlic mixture and sauté until garlic is tender, about 5 minutes. Stir in lemon juice; season to taste with salt and pepper. Remove foil and spoon lemon sauce over chicken.

PARTS of the CHICKEN

The various parts of a chicken don't require techniques as wildly distinct as those for, say, a pork tenderloin and a whole ham. But they do need to be handled a bit differently on the grill.

THE PART	BEST FOR ...	THE TECHNIQUE ...
BONELESS BREASTS	• Quick grilling • Using with **marinades**	• Pound to uniform thickness for even cooking, then grill **briefly over high heat** to avoid drying out.
SKIN-ON, BONE-IN BREASTS	• When you want **juicier, more flavorful meat** and you have more time • A less expensive alternative to boneless	• Use **lower/indirect heat**, so the skin doesn't burn. Keep in mind that these cuts take a bit longer to cook.
BONELESS THIGHS	• **Rich flavor** on a weeknight schedule • Easy to grill	• Cook over **medium heat**, but move to a cooler part of the grill if it's browning too quickly.
BONE-IN LEGS AND THIGHS	• Big, juicy flavor and **crunchy skin**	• Cook over **medium heat** to allow time for skin to crisp and meat to cook through.
WINGS	• Combining with all kinds of flavors and sauces • **Low-maintenance grilling**	• Cook over **low to medium-low heat** all the way.

MEDITERRANEAN CHICKEN
with Za'atar

2 heads of garlic, top third cut off each

6 Tbsp. extra-virgin olive oil, divided

1 3- to 4-lb. chicken, cut in half lengthwise, backbone removed

4 Tbsp. za'atar, divided (recipe follows)

1½ tsp. lemon zest

3 Tbsp. fresh lemon juice

1 Tbsp. chopped fresh rosemary

1 small serrano chile, seeded, minced

2 tsp. dried marjoram

Kosher salt and freshly ground black pepper

INGREDIENT INFO If you don't have time to make your own za'atar, it can be found at Middle Eastern markets, specialty foods stores, and wholespice.com.

Za'atar (pronounced ZAH-tahr) is an eastern Mediterranean spice blend traditionally made with dried herbs, such as marjoram and thyme. The updated version used in the marinade gains vibrancy from fresh oregano and helps create an intensely aromatic and flavorful dish. The marinated chicken halves are grilled over medium heat so that the skin slowly crisps as the meat gently cooks through.

Preheat oven to 400°F. Place garlic on a large sheet of foil. Drizzle with 1 Tbsp. oil and wrap tightly in foil. Roast until tender and golden brown, 45 to 50 minutes. Let cool.

Place chicken in a 13x9x2-inch glass baking dish. Sprinkle 2½ Tbsp. za'atar over chicken. Squeeze roasted garlic cloves out of skins and into a small bowl; mash into a paste with the back of a fork. Whisk in 4 Tbsp. oil, lemon zest and juice, rosemary, chile, and marjoram. Pour over chicken; turn to coat. Cover; chill overnight.

Season chicken with salt and pepper; let stand at room temperature for 30 minutes. Build a medium-low fire in a charcoal grill, or heat a gas grill to medium. Brush grill grate with remaining 1 Tbsp. oil. Grill chicken, turning occasionally, until skin is crisp and browned and an instant-read thermometer inserted into the thickest part of the thigh registers 165°F, about 35 minutes.

Transfer chicken to a cutting board, sprinkle with remaining 1½ Tbsp. za'atar, and let rest for 10 minutes. Cut each chicken half into 4 pieces; serve on a platter.

makes about ¼ cup

ZA'ATAR

use with
Mediterranean chicken

1 Tbsp. chopped fresh oregano

1 Tbsp. ground cumin

1 Tbsp. sesame seeds

1 Tbsp. sumac

1 tsp. freshly ground black pepper

1 tsp. kosher salt

INGREDIENT INFO You can find sumac at Middle Eastern markets, specialty foods stores, and wholespice.com.

Combine all ingredients in a small bowl. **DO AHEAD:** Can be made 2 weeks ahead. Store airtight at room temperature.

BEER-CAN CHICKEN

photo, right

Spice rub (optional), store-bought or use the Ultimate Dry Rub (see recipe on page 375)
1   3- to 4-lb. chicken
Kosher salt and freshly ground black pepper
1   12-oz. can of beer, half full

SPECIAL EQUIPMENT A foil baking pan (for drip pan)

There's a reason why backyard grillers obsess over this creative technique. It's easy to master and reliably delicious. First up, slather a chicken with your favorite spice rub (we like our Ultimate Dry Rub, but check out all the options on pages 375–378). Then lower it over an open beer can. As the chicken cooks, the beer steams and imparts flavor and moisture. The result is an amber bird that's crisp on the outside and wonderfully succulent on the inside. (For a few variations, take a look below.)

Prepare grill for indirect heat with a drip pan (see page 16 for instructions), building a medium-low fire in a charcoal grill or heating a gas grill to medium. Add enough water to drip pan to reach a depth of ½ inch.

Apply your favorite spice rub, if desired, under and on skin of chicken. Season with salt and pepper.

Place chicken on open beer can so that can is inside the cavity. Place upright on grill. Grill, covered, over drip pan until an instant-read thermometer inserted into the thickest part of the thigh registers 165°F, 45 minutes to 1 hour (add more charcoal to charcoal grill as needed during cooking time).

VARIATIONS ON A THEME: Beer-Can Chicken

Want another reason to love Beer-Can Chicken? It's endlessly adaptable. Instead of beer in a can, you can use wine or water, enhanced with any herbs, spices, and flavorings you like. Once you've tried the basic recipe above, experiment with these internationally inspired riffs.

SPANISH

Rub a mixture of extra-virgin olive oil, minced garlic, and smoked paprika (use the Spanish version, Pimentón de La Vera), under the skin, in the chicken's cavity, and all over the outside of the bird. Then tuck paper-thin slices of Spanish chorizo sausage under the skin.

CREOLE

Add hot pepper sauce and a few rosemary and thyme sprigs to the half-full beer can. Then rub the bird all over with a blend of melted butter, Creole seasoning, minced garlic, and Worcestershire sauce (don't forget inside the cavity).

ASIAN

Make a mixture of toasted sesame oil, reduced-sodium soy sauce, honey, minced ginger, garlic, Chinese five-spice powder, and crushed red pepper flakes; rub all over the chicken. Once the bird is done cooking, sprinkle with chopped scallions and cilantro. Serve with hoisin sauce.

+

Don't be fooled by the name ... this technique yields one of the **most flavorful and moist** chickens that you'll ever make.

BEER-CAN CHICKEN

DIXIE CHICKEN
with Cayenne Spice Rub

8 servings

2 Tbsp. kosher salt

1 Tbsp. coarsely ground black pepper

1 Tbsp. (packed) light brown sugar

2 tsp. garlic powder

1½ tsp. cornstarch

1½ tsp. onion powder

1 tsp. cayenne pepper

1 tsp. chili powder

1 tsp. lemon-pepper with garlic and onion seasoning

½ cup (1 stick) unsalted butter, room temperature

2 4-lb. chickens, quartered, or 8 lb. skin-on, bone-in chicken thighs, legs, and breasts

Vegetable oil, for brushing

1 sourdough baguette, cut on a diagonal into ¾-inch-thick slices

A cayenne pepper–accented spice rub seasons both the chicken and the butter that gets slathered over the grilled baguette slices and brushed atop the chicken. Meanwhile, a touch of cornstarch in the rub creates an extra-crisp coating by soaking up moisture on the surface of the skin. Try this spice mix over chicken wings for a grilled version of traditional fried hot wings.

Whisk first 9 ingredients in a small bowl. Transfer 1 Tbsp. spice mixture to a medium bowl; add butter and mix well. **DO AHEAD:** Rub and seasoned butter can be made 2 days ahead. Cover separately. Chill butter. Bring butter to room temperature before using.

Rub spice mixture all over chicken pieces. Arrange chicken pieces on 2 large rimmed baking sheets. Cover with plastic wrap and let stand at room temperature for at least 1 hour and up to 2 hours.

Build a medium-low fire in a charcoal grill, or heat a gas grill to medium. Brush grill grate with oil. Reserve ¼ cup seasoned butter. Spread remaining ¼ cup seasoned butter on 1 side of baguette slices; set aside. Place chicken on grill, skin side up. Grill for 20 minutes. Turn chicken over; grill until skin is deep golden brown, about 15 minutes longer. Turn chicken again and grill, skin side up, until an instant-read thermometer inserted into the thickest part of the thigh registers 165°F, about 5 minutes longer. Transfer chicken to a platter. Brush chicken with reserved seasoned butter.

Grill bread, turning once, until just golden, about 2 minutes per side. Arrange toasts around chicken.

DIJON-TARRAGON CHICKEN

6 servings

⅓ cup chopped fresh tarragon

¼ cup Dijon mustard

¼ cup dry white wine

1 Tbsp. honey

1 Tbsp. extra-virgin olive oil, plus more for brushing

2 3¼-lb. chickens, each cut into 8 pieces, or 6½ lb. skin-on, bone-in chicken thighs, legs, and breasts

Kosher salt and freshly ground black pepper

This marinade features the French pairing of tarragon and mustard and is sweetened with a bit of honey. Keep an eye on the chicken as it cooks, as the sugar in the honey may cause the flames to flare up.

Purée tarragon, mustard, wine, honey, and 1 Tbsp. oil in a food processor until smooth. Arrange chicken in a 15x10x2-inch glass baking dish. Season chicken with salt and pepper and pour tarragon-mustard mixture over; turn to coat. Let stand, turning occasionally, at room temperature for 1 hour or chill for 2 to 4 hours.

Build a medium-low fire in a charcoal grill, or heat a gas grill to medium. Brush grill grate with oil. Remove chicken from marinade, leaving some still clinging. Cover and grill, turning occasionally, until an instant-read thermometer inserted into the thickest part of the thigh registers 165°F, about 30 minutes. Serve chicken hot, warm, or at room temperature.

Steps to perfect Chicken on the BONE

When done right—meaning, cooked slowly over medium-low heat—grilled bone-in chicken is an ever-so-smoky, crackly-crisp revelation. There are many different preparations, but here's a technique that'll work for all types of skin-on, bone-in chicken, from whole bird to parts.

❶ SEASON IT

Before you do anything else, drizzle extra-virgin olive oil over your chicken. Use 2 Tbsp. for a whole, butterflied chicken; a generous 1 Tbsp. for a half chicken; or 2 tsp. each for individual parts (thighs, breasts, or legs). Then, season it generously with salt and pepper.

❷ START SLOW

Place the chicken, skin side down, on the grill grate over a medium-low charcoal fire or medium gas heat for 15 minutes. You want the fat to render slowly from the skin. If you try and cook it at too high a temperature too quickly, you'll end up battling flare-ups and scorch the skin.

❸ TURN IT OVER

Once the skin has begun to take on a golden hue and is getting crisp, turn the chicken over and let it cook on the bone side for 10 more minutes. If you're grilling chicken parts, keep turning them until an instant-read thermometer inserted into the thickest part of the thigh registers 165°F.

❹ HIT THE SIDES

If you're grilling half a chicken, turn the chicken on its side (if necessary, use a brick or a potato to prop it up), and render out the fat on one edge for 5 minutes. Then turn it onto the other side for 5 more minutes to cook the meat through. (Note: This doesn't apply to whole chickens or chicken pieces.)

❺ GIVE IT A REST

Once it's done, let the chicken rest on a platter for at least 5 or 10 minutes before you carve and serve it. This gives the juices a chance to reabsorb—and you can use the time to grill some quick-cooking veggies to serve alongside.

MARINATED CHICKEN
with Garlic, Chiles, and Citrus Juices

6 servings

½ cup extra-virgin olive oil, plus more for brushing
⅓ cup fresh orange juice
¼ cup fresh lime juice
⅓ cup ancho, pasilla, or guajillo chile powder
1 Tbsp. minced canned chipotle chiles in adobo
6 garlic cloves, crushed
1 onion, chopped
3 3-lb. chickens, halved, backbone removed (or 3 lb. each chicken breasts, thighs, and legs)
Kosher salt and freshly ground black pepper

INGREDIENT INFO Pasilla, ancho, and guajillo chile powders can be found in the spice section of some supermarkets and Latin markets.

This recipe calls for three small whole chickens, which, when halved, make for ideal serving amounts. Ask your butcher to cut the chicken in half and remove the backbone—the chickens cook quicker without it—or see "How to Butterfly a Chicken" (page 54) for instructions on doing it yourself. (Of course, you can also make life simple and use chicken parts instead.)

Whisk ½ cup oil, orange and lime juices, chile powder, chipotle chiles, and garlic in a 15x10x2-inch glass baking dish. Mix in onion. Add chicken halves and turn to coat. Cover and chill, turning occasionally, for at least 4 hours or overnight.

Build a medium-low fire in a charcoal grill, or heat a gas grill to medium. Brush grill grate with oil. Remove chicken halves from marinade and season with salt and pepper. Grill, turning occasionally, until an instant-read thermometer inserted into the thickest part of the thigh registers 165°F, about 40 minutes.

JERK CHICKEN

4 servings

1 4-lb. chicken, cut into 8 pieces
1 medium red onion, chopped
12 garlic cloves
10 Scotch bonnet or 15 small habanero chiles, stemmed, seeded
8 scallions, white and pale green parts only, chopped
1 3-inch piece ginger, peeled, sliced
2 Tbsp. chopped fresh thyme
1½ Tbsp. ground cinnamon
1½ Tbsp. whole allspice
1 Tbsp. kosher salt
1 Tbsp. powdered adobo seasoning
½ tsp. Maggi Liquid Seasoning
Vegetable oil, for brushing

INGREDIENT INFO Look for powdered adobo seasoning at Latin markets.

When done right, this iconic roadside dish from Jamaica delivers crisp skin over tender, smoky meat and complex flavors, courtesy of a wet rub that's heavy on herbs and spices. Scotch bonnet chiles are extremely hot, but also add a touch of fruitiness. Be sure to let the chicken marinate for at least 24 hours for the paste to infuse the meat.

Pierce chicken all over with the tip of a small knife; transfer to a large bowl. Purée onion, next 10 ingredients, and ¾ cup water in a blender until smooth. Reserve 1 cup for dipping sauce, if desired. Pour remaining marinade over chicken; massage into chicken. (Wear food-handling gloves, if desired.) Cover; chill for at least 1 day and up to 2 days.

Let chicken sit at room temperature for 1 hour before cooking. Build a medium-low fire in a charcoal grill, or heat a gas grill to medium. Brush grill grate with oil. Place chicken on grill, skin side up. Cover grill and cook, turning occasionally, until skin is crisp and nicely charred and an instant-read thermometer inserted into the thickest parts of the chicken registers 165°F, 30 to 45 minutes.

Transfer chicken to a platter and tent loosely with foil; let stand for 10 minutes. Serve with reserved marinade as a sauce, if desired.

ALL-AMERICAN BARBECUED CHICKEN

3 lb. chicken pieces, such as wings, legs, and breasts (or one 3¼-lb. chicken, cut up)
Kosher salt and freshly ground black pepper
Vegetable oil, for brushing
1 cup All-American Barbecue Sauce (page 389) or your favorite barbecue sauce, plus more for serving

SPECIAL EQUIPMENT A foil baking pan (for drip pan)

Here is the classic barbecued chicken—with just the right sweet-sour sauce—that you'll be making for your very happy friends and family all summer. What's the secret to getting juicy meat and crispy skin without over-charring it? Cooking the chicken over indirect heat, keeping the grill covered, and brushing on the sauce during the last 5 minutes of grilling. See below for more tips on perfect barbecued birds.

Season chicken with salt and pepper. Let sit for at least 30 minutes before cooking or chill for up to 1 day.

Prepare grill for indirect heat with a drip pan (see page 16), building a medium-low fire in a charcoal grill or heating a gas grill to medium. Brush grill grate with oil. Arrange chicken on grate over drip pan, cover, and cook, turning every 5 minutes, until skin is crisp and an instant-read thermometer inserted into the thickest piece registers 165°F, about 25 minutes. Uncover grill and brush chicken with sauce. Cook, turning chicken and brushing it often and moving pieces over direct heat if needed, until chicken is glazed, about 5 minutes (do not let it burn).

Transfer to a cutting board and let chicken rest for 10 minutes. Serve with more sauce alongside.

GETTING IT RIGHT: Barbecued Chicken

We've all had them. Those pieces of barbecued chicken that turn out black on the outside and raw on the inside. It's easy to avoid that scenario, though. Here's how.

ALWAYS

- **Season meat in advance** so that the chicken can soak up the flavors.
- **Apply sauce with a brush so that you can get it into every little part of the chicken** (this is much more thorough than using a spoon, trust us).
- **Cook wings for same amount of time** as you do larger pieces. Don't worry—they won't dry out. Done right, they'll be crispy and tender.

NEVER

- **Never put chicken directly over flames**. This is what leads to BBQ tragedy: burnt yet raw chicken. Instead, use indirect heat. It lets the meat cook through without charring the skin too quickly.
- **Never apply sauce** until the last 5 minutes of cooking. If you do it too soon, all those sugars in the sauce will burn long before the meat is cooked.

CHICKEN THIGHS
with Rhubarb-Cucumber Salsa

4 servings

1 habanero, Scotch bonnet, or
   Thai chile, with seeds, stemmed
2 garlic cloves
2 scallions, thinly sliced, white and
   green parts divided
1 Tbsp. soy sauce
¼ cup extra-virgin olive oil,
   plus more for brushing
6 large skin-on, bone-in chicken
   thighs (about 2½ lb.)
   Kosher salt
1½ cups ¼-inch cubes rhubarb
1 cup ¼-inch cubes unpeeled
   seeded cucumber, preferably
   English hothouse
½ cup coarsely chopped fresh
   cilantro
1 Tbsp. honey
1 Tbsp. vegetable oil
1 tsp. fresh lime juice
   Freshly ground black pepper

Here's a great way to serve chicken thighs alongside some of the tastiest flavors of summertime. Scoring the thighs is the trick for encouraging quicker cooking in this dish and also helps deliver more spice and flavor to the meat when it's slathered with a spicy chile sauce. The piquant and crunchy rhubarb salsa offers a refreshing counterpoint to the heat of the chiles.

Pulse chile, garlic, and white parts of scallions in a food processor until finely chopped. With machine running, drizzle in soy sauce, then ¼ cup olive oil; process until emulsion forms. Transfer sauce to a bowl.

Place chicken thighs, skin side up, on a work surface and slash each crosswise at ¾-inch intervals down to the bone. Season lightly with salt and then slather all over with the sauce. Let sit at room temperature while you prepare the grill.

Build a medium fire in a charcoal grill, or heat a gas grill to medium-high. Brush grill grate with olive oil. Grill chicken, turning occasionally, until skin is crisp and an instant-read thermometer inserted into thickest part of thigh registers 165°F, 20 to 25 minutes. Let rest for 5 to 10 minutes.

Meanwhile, toss rhubarb, next 5 ingredients, and green parts of scallions in a medium bowl to coat. Season to taste with salt and pepper and let stand for at least 10 minutes to allow flavors to meld. Serve chicken with rhubarb salsa alongside.

CILANTRO-LIME CHICKEN THIGHS

8 servings

1 cup fresh lime juice
⅔ cup fresh orange juice
½ cup chopped fresh cilantro
½ cup extra-virgin olive oil, plus
   more for brushing
4 garlic cloves, thinly sliced
2 tsp. crushed red pepper flakes
2 tsp. hot pepper sauce
   Kosher salt and freshly ground
   black pepper
16 large skin-on, bone-in chicken
   thighs (about 6 lb.)
16 scallions, trimmed
8 ears of corn, husked

A combination of freshly squeezed lime and orange juice is the base of this bright and rustic-feeling dish. Look for limes with smooth skin that feel heavy for their size; both are good indicators that the limes are juicy. Serve the chicken on a large platter with the charred corn and scallions so guests can help themselves.

Whisk both juices, cilantro, ½ cup oil, garlic, red pepper flakes, and hot pepper sauce in a medium bowl. Season marinade to taste with salt and pepper.

Place chicken thighs in a large resealable plastic bag. Place scallions and corn in 1 or 2 extra-large resealable plastic bags. Divide marinade equally between bags; seal bags and turn chicken thighs and corn to coat. Chill chicken, corn, and scallions, turning bags occasionally, for 4 hours.

Build a medium-low fire in a charcoal grill, or heat a gas grill to medium. Brush grill grate with oil. Remove chicken and vegetables from marinade; discard marinade. Grill chicken, turning occasionally and rearranging on grill for even cooking, until charred and an instant-read thermometer inserted into the thickest part of the thigh registers 165°F, about 25 minutes. Grill scallions and corn until charred on all sides, about 6 minutes for scallions and 13 minutes for corn. Transfer chicken, scallions, and corn to a platter.

TANDOORI-STYLE CHICKEN THIGHS

2 cups plain whole-milk yogurt, divided
2 Tbsp. fresh lemon juice
2 Tbsp. minced peeled ginger
4 garlic cloves, minced
1 tsp. ground coriander
1 tsp. turmeric
1 tsp. kosher salt
½ tsp. cayenne pepper
½ tsp. freshly ground black pepper
½ tsp. ground cumin
½ tsp. saffron threads, crumbled (optional)
8 skinless, bone-in leg-thigh chicken pieces (about 3 lb.)
Vegetable oil, for brushing
3 Tbsp. unsalted butter, melted
1 small red onion, thinly sliced crosswise, separated into rings
¼ cup chopped fresh cilantro

Traditional Indian tandoori chicken is cooked at high temperatures in a cylindrical clay oven called a tandoor. This recipe has been adapted for the grill yet stil maintains the authentic tandoori flavors—starting with yogurt, a great meat tenderizer. Unlike most marinades, which just add flavor, yogurt contains enzymes that gently break down tough meat fibers. The chicken tastes excellent if you marinate it for only an hour or two, but it is ideal if you can let everything marinate overnight, allowing the flavors to thoroughly meld and penetrate the meat.

Purée 1 cup yogurt, lemon juice, ginger, garlic, coriander, turmeric, salt, cayenne, black pepper, cumin, and saffron in a food processor until smooth. Transfer to a large bowl. Mix in remaining 1 cup yogurt. Add chicken and turn to coat. Cover and chill overnight.

Build a medium-low fire in a charcoal grill, or heat a gas grill to medium. Brush grill grate with oil. Remove chicken from marinade, leaving some still clinging, and grill for about 12 minutes per side, turning once and occasionally basting with melted butter during last 2 minutes. If you're using an instant-read thermometer, insert it into the thickest part of the thigh—you want it to register 165°F. Transfer chicken to a platter. Top with onion and cilantro.

MUSTARDY THIGHS
with Fresh Corn Polenta

CHICKEN
6 scallions, finely chopped
¼ cup Dijon mustard
1 Tbsp. fresh lemon juice
1 large garlic clove, minced
6 large skin-on, bone-in chicken thighs (about 2½ lb.)
Kosher salt and freshly ground black pepper
Vegetable oil, for brushing

POLENTA
1 cup polenta
2 cups fresh corn kernels (cut from about 3 large ears)
½ cup mascarpone
Kosher salt and freshly ground black pepper

A scallion–Dijon mustard mixture is gently spread under the chicken skin before the thighs are grilled, and gives wonderful flavor to the meat.

CHICKEN
Whisk scallions, mustard, lemon juice, and garlic in a medium bowl. Gently loosen skin on each chicken thigh, leaving it attached. Spoon the mustard seasoning atop thighs; spread to cover meat and use your fingertips to work some of the seasoning under the skin. Season thighs with salt and pepper on both sides. Turn thighs to coat with mustard seasoning; transfer to a small baking sheet. **DO AHEAD:** Chicken can be prepared 6 hours ahead. Cover and chill.

Build a medium-low fire in a charcoal grill, or heat a gas grill to medium. Preheat oven to 250°F. Brush grill grate with oil. Grill chicken, turning occasionally and moving to a cooler spot on the grill if browning too quickly, until golden brown and an instant-read thermometer inserted into the thickest part of the thigh registers 165°F, 40 to 50 minutes. Transfer grilled chicken to another baking sheet; keep warm in oven while preparing polenta.

POLENTA
Prepare polenta per package instructions; add corn kernels and cook, stirring constantly over medium-low heat, until corn is tender, about 5 minutes. Mix in mascarpone. Season with salt and pepper. Spoon onto plates; top with chicken.

ULTIMATE CRISPY CHICKEN WINGS

makes about 60 pieces

5 lb. chicken wings
2 Tbsp. vegetable oil, plus more for brushing
1 Tbsp. kosher salt
½ tsp. freshly ground black pepper

Once you try this master recipe for grilling wings, you'll never fry another chicken wing again. Once the wings are done, toss them with one or more of the sauces on these two pages. (Each recipe will make enough for about 20 wings.)

Combine wings, 2 Tbsp. oil, salt, and pepper in a large bowl; toss to coat.

Build a 2-zone medium-low/low fire in a charcoal grill (see page 15 for instructions), or heat a gas grill to medium, leaving one burner unlit. Brush grill grate with oil. Grill wings over higher heat, turning occasionally and moving to low heat if skin is browning too quickly or flare-ups occur, until cooked through and skin is crisp and charred in spots, 30 to 35 minutes. Toss with one or more of the sauces, if desired; or if using glaze, coat wings with glaze and return to grill (see instructions below).

makes enough for about 20 wings

Ginger-Soy Glaze

photo, page 46

Ultimate Crispy Chicken Wings (recipe above)
3 large garlic cloves, crushed
1 2x1-inch piece ginger, peeled, sliced
¼ cup honey
2 Tbsp. reduced-sodium soy sauce

Coat grilled wings with this glaze and return them to the heat for a few minutes over low/medium-low heat to give them a delicious caramelized char.

Prepare Ultimate Crispy Chicken Wings.

Place a fine-mesh sieve over a small bowl. Bring all ingredients and ¼ cup water to a boil in a small saucepan, stirring to dissolve honey. Simmer, stirring occasionally, until thickened and reduced to ¼ cup, 7 to 8 minutes. Strain glaze; discard solids in sieve. **DO AHEAD:** Can be made 5 days ahead. Cover and chill. Rewarm before continuing.

Brush grilled wings with glaze and return to grill, turning and brushing wings occasionally, until wings are lightly charred and the glaze has thickened and caramelized, 8 to 10 minutes.

GETTING IT RIGHT: Chicken Wings 101

Wings are great for grilling. They boast the perfect ratio of skin to meat to bone, so they get crispy skin on the outside and juicy meat on the inside. Here's what to keep in mind:

GO LOW

Always cook wings over **low/medium-low** heat. Any higher leads to uneven cooking.

TAKE YOUR TIME

They'll need about **20 minutes** if wings and drumettes are separated, and 30 to 40 minutes if attached.

KEEP IT TOGETHER

Leave **wings and drumettes attached** when grilling, if possible. Larger pieces are easier to turn.

CONSIDER THE SKEWER

For particularly even cooking and easy handling, grill wings on **metal skewers**.

Roasted Garlic, Lemon and Herb Sauce

makes enough for about 20 wings

Ultimate Crispy Chicken Wings
(see recipe, left)
1 head of garlic
2 tsp. extra-virgin olive oil
1 Tbsp. plus 1 tsp. fresh lemon juice
1 tsp. finely chopped flat-leaf
parsley
2 tsp. finely chopped fresh chives,
divided
Kosher salt and freshly ground
black pepper

This sauce gets its flavor from a whole head of garlic—first mellowed by roasting, then combined with lemon and fresh herbs.

Prepare Ultimate Crispy Chicken Wings.
　　Preheat oven to 450°F. Cut ½ inch off top of garlic, place garlic on a sheet of foil, and drizzle with oil. Wrap up in foil and bake until completely tender, about 45 minutes. Unwrap garlic and let cool.
　　Squeeze garlic cloves into a medium bowl and mash with the back of a spoon until smooth. Stir in lemon juice, parsley, and 1 tsp. chives. Season with salt and pepper. Add one-third of grilled wings and toss to evenly coat. Sprinkle remaining 1 tsp. chives over.

Classic Buffalo Sauce

makes enough for about 20 wings

Ultimate Crispy Chicken Wings
(see recipe, left)
1 Tbsp. unsalted butter, melted
¼ tsp. cayenne pepper
¼ tsp. freshly ground black pepper
¼ tsp. kosher salt
¼ cup hot pepper sauce (such as
Frank's or Texas Pete)

Like the original, created in Buffalo, New York, this recipe starts with melted butter and hot pepper sauce (use Frank's for ultimate authenticity).

Prepare Ultimate Crispy Chicken Wings.
　　Combine butter and next 3 ingredients in a medium bowl and let infuse for 5 minutes. Whisk in hot pepper sauce. Add one-third of grilled wings and toss evenly to coat. **DO AHEAD:** Can be made 1 week ahead. Cool; cover and chill. Rewarm before using.

Sriracha-Lime Sauce

makes enough for about 20 wings

Ultimate Crispy Chicken Wings
(see recipe, left)
¼ cup fresh lime juice
¼ cup Sriracha
2 Tbsp. honey
1 Tbsp. unsalted butter, melted

INGREDIENT INFO Sriracha is available in the Asian foods section of many supermarkets and Asian markets.

This spicy wings sauce gets an Asian spin with Sriracha and lime, plus a touch of honeyed sweetness.

Prepare Ultimate Crispy Chicken Wings.
　　Combine remaining ingredients in a medium bowl and whisk to combine. Add one-third of grilled wings and toss evenly to coat. **DO AHEAD:** Can be made 1 day ahead. Cover and chill. Rewarm before using.

Wings require **low to medium-low heat**. This renders fat from the skin and **crisps it slowly.**

ULTIMATE CRISPY CHICKEN WINGS WITH GINGER-SOY GLAZE
(PAGE 44)

MALAYSIAN WINGS
with Turmeric and Lemongrass

1 cup canned unsweetened
  coconut milk
3 shallots, chopped
3 garlic cloves
2 lemongrass stalks (bottom
  third only, tough outer layers
  removed), finely chopped
2 jalapeños, stemmed
1 1-inch piece ginger, peeled,
  chopped
2 Tbsp. fresh lime juice
2 Tbsp. tamarind juice concentrate
  (not paste or pulp) or 1 Tbsp.
  fresh lime juice
1 Tbsp. fish sauce (such as
  nuoc nam or nam pla)
2 tsp. kosher salt
1 tsp. turmeric
3 lb. whole chicken wings
  Vegetable oil, for brushing
  Lime wedges

INGREDIENT INFO Fish sauce can
be found in the Asian foods section
of most supermarkets, at some
specialty foods stores, and at
Asian markets.

There's a lot going on in this unique marinade: Coconut milk sweetens and tenderizes, tamarind juice adds tang, lemongrass gives a floral aroma, and turmeric provides a golden-orange hue indicative of South Asian food. For best results, start a day ahead so that the flavors can infuse the chicken as it marinates overnight.

Combine coconut milk, shallots, garlic, lemongrass, jalapeños, ginger, lime juice, tamarind juice, fish sauce, kosher salt, turmeric, and 1 cup water in a blender. Purée mixture until a smooth marinade forms.

Place chicken wings in a large baking dish. Pour marinade over; turn wings to coat evenly. Cover chicken and chill overnight.

Remove chicken from marinade, shaking any excess marinade back into dish. Transfer to a large platter. Let chicken stand at room temperature for 15 minutes.

Transfer marinade to a large saucepan and bring to a boil over medium heat. Reduce heat to medium-low and simmer, stirring occasionally, until marinade thickens, 10 to 15 minutes. Pour half of marinade into a small bowl; set aside for basting chicken while it grills. Keep remaining marinade in saucepan; cover and keep warm until ready to serve the chicken.

Build a 2-zone medium-low/low fire in a charcoal grill (see page 15), or heat a gas grill to medium, leaving one burner unlit. Brush grill grate with oil. Grill chicken wings over higher heat, turning every 5 minutes and basting occasionally with marinade in small bowl, until fat is rendered and skin is nicely charred in spots, 30 to 35 minutes. (The key here is to turn the wings often so the skin doesn't burn. Move wings to low-heat side of the grill if the skin is browning too quickly or if flare-ups occur.)

Continue cooking chicken without basting (so skin will get crisp) until wings are cooked through, about 10 minutes longer.

Transfer chicken to a large platter and let it rest for 5 minutes. Squeeze lime wedges over wings. Transfer marinade in saucepan to a small bowl. Serve warm marinade alongside chicken as a dipping sauce.

SPICY TEXAS DRUMSTICKS

3 Tbsp. chili powder
2 tsp. ground cumin
1 cup ketchup-style chili sauce
¼ cup robust-flavored (dark)
   molasses
3 Tbsp. apple cider vinegar
2 Tbsp. fresh orange juice
2 tsp. finely grated orange zest
   Vegetable oil, for brushing
4 chicken drumsticks
   Kosher salt and freshly ground
   black pepper

Make a quick barbecue sauce by doctoring chili sauce (the tomato-based sauce that looks a lot like cocktail sauce or ketchup, not Asian chili sauce) with toasted spices, a touch of vinegar, and a bit of molasses. When you brush the sauce over the chicken as it grills, the flames caramelize the sugars in the sauce, resulting in chicken with a crisp and golden brown coating. But don't add the sauce too soon, or it will over-caramelize and burn.

Stir chili powder and cumin in a small heavy saucepan over medium heat until toasted and fragrant, about 1 minute. Mix in chili sauce, molasses, vinegar, orange juice, and orange zest. Reduce heat to medium-low and simmer until sauce thickens slightly, about 6 minutes. Transfer half of sauce to a small bowl.

Build a medium-low fire in a charcoal grill, or heat a gas grill to medium. Brush grill grate with oil. Season drumsticks with salt and a generous amount of pepper. Grill drumsticks, turning occasionally, for 15 minutes.

Brush sauce in small saucepan all over chicken; continue to grill, occasionally turning and brushing with sauce, until crisp and brown and an instant-read thermometer inserted into drumstick registers 165°F, about 12 minutes longer. Serve chicken with reserved sauce in small bowl.

Is It Done Yet?

TAKE THE TEMPERATURE To find out if your chicken is done, insert an instant-read thermometer into the thickest part of the meat without letting it touch bone. You want it to register **165°F**.

GRILL-ROASTED CHICKEN

6 to 8 servings

with Lemons, Artichokes, and Eggplant

SALMORIGLIO

- 1 large garlic clove
- 2 tsp. kosher salt
- 2 Tbsp. fresh lemon juice
- 6 Tbsp. extra-virgin olive oil

CHICKEN

- ½ cup chopped flat-leaf parsley
- ½ cup fresh lemon juice
- ¼ cup extra-virgin olive oil, plus more for brushing
- 6 garlic cloves, minced
- 1 tsp. kosher salt, more as needed
- ½ tsp. freshly ground black pepper, more as needed
- 2 3½- to 4-lb. chickens
  Grilled Lemons, Artichokes, and Eggplants (recipe follows)

SPECIAL EQUIPMENT A foil baking pan (for drip pan)

The prized Sicilian sauce *salmoriglio*, made with lemon juice, garlic, and olive oil, enhances slowly grill-roasted whole chickens.

SALMORIGLIO

Smash garlic with the side of a knife and finely chop with salt to make a paste. Transfer to a small bowl. Whisk in lemon juice, then oil. Set salmoriglio aside.

CHICKEN

Whisk parsley, lemon juice, ¼ cup oil, garlic, 1 tsp. salt, and ½ tsp. pepper in a medium bowl for marinade. Place chickens in two extra-large resealable plastic bags. Divide marinade between bags. Seal bags, releasing excess air, and turn to coat chicken. Chill chicken, turning bags occasionally, for at least 1 hour and up to 1 day.

Prepare grill for indirect heat with a drip pan (see page 16), building a medium-low fire in a charcoal grill or heating a gas grill to medium. Remove chickens from marinade; season all over with salt and pepper. Tie legs together.

Brush grill grate with oil. Place chickens, breast side down, over drip pan. Cover and grill, adjusting vents and adjusting gas levels or adding more charcoal as needed to maintain grill temperature between 350° and 400°F, for 45 minutes.

Turn chickens breast side up. Cover and continue to grill, maintaining temperature between 350° and 400°F, until an instant-read thermometer inserted into the thickest part of the thigh registers 165°F, about 35 minutes longer. Let rest for 10 minutes. Carve chicken; surround with Grilled Lemons, Artichokes, and Eggplant. Spoon salmoriglio over and serve.

Grilled Lemons, Artichokes, and Eggplant

6 to 8 servings

use with grill-roasted chicken

- 12 baby artichokes, stems trimmed, dark outer leaves removed
  Kosher salt
  Extra-virgin olive oil, for brushing
- 12 Japanese eggplants, halved lengthwise, or 2 medium eggplants cut crosswise into ½-inch-thick rounds
- 4 lemons, halved
  Freshly ground black pepper

The vegetables and lemons cook so quickly (the artichokes are precooked in boiling water) that you can grill them while the chickens are resting.

Cook baby artichokes in a large saucepan of boiling salted water until tender when bottom is pierced with a sharp knife, about 8 minutes. Drain and run under cold water to cool. Cut artichokes in half through stem; pat dry. **DO AHEAD:** Can be made 2 days ahead. Cover and chill.

Build a medium fire in a charcoal grill, or heat a gas grill to medium-high. Brush cooked artichokes, eggplants, and cut side of lemons with oil and season with salt and pepper. Brush grill grate with oil. Grill vegetables, turning once, until tender and slightly charred, about 2 minutes per side. Grill lemons, cut side down, until charred, about 2 minutes. Transfer vegetables to platter with chicken; garnish with grilled lemons for squeezing over chicken.

— 49 —

HERBES DE PROVENCE CHICKEN

2 Tbsp. (¼ stick) unsalted butter, room temperature
2 Tbsp. herbes de Provence
1 Tbsp. kosher salt
2 3½-lb. chickens
Vegetable oil, for brushing

INGREDIENT INFO Look for herbes de Provence, a dried herb mixture, in the spice section of most supermarkets and at specialty foods stores. If it's unavailable, use a mixture of dried thyme, basil, savory, and fennel seeds.

SPECIAL EQUIPMENT A foil baking pan (for drip pan)

This dish has all the satisfying elements of a perfectly cooked rotisserie chicken. The simple yet flavorful herb butter deepens the flavor of the meat and the skin.

Place butter, herbes de Provence, and salt in a small bowl; mash with a fork until blended to thick granular paste. Starting at the neck end of each chicken, carefully run your fingers under the skin of the breasts to loosen. Starting at each side of the main cavity, carefully run your fingers under the skin of the thighs to loosen. Rub the herb butter on chickens under loosened skin and on the outside of each bird. Truss chickens by tying legs together and tying wings flush to sides with kitchen twine. Enclose chickens in extra-large resealable plastic bags. Chill for at least 6 hours. **DO AHEAD:** Chickens can be prepared 1 day ahead. Keep chilled. Let chickens stand at room temperature for about 30 minutes before cooking.

Prepare grill for indirect heat with a drip pan (see page 16), building a medium-low fire in a charcoal grill or heating a gas grill to medium. Close grill and insert an instant-read thermometer into top vent. Bring temperature to between 350° and 400°F.

Brush grill grate with oil and place chickens above pan. Close grill. Adjust vents or heat setting or add more charcoal from chimney starter as needed to maintain temperature. Cook chickens until instant-read thermometer inserted into the thickest part of the thigh registers 165°F, about 45 minutes. Turn off grill (if using gas grill), but do not open. Let chickens rest in covered grill for 10 minutes.

GETTING IT RIGHT: Roasting Chicken on the Grill

Want the hearty flavor of roast chicken, minus the overheated kitchen? Try grill-roasting. Basically, you treat the grill like an oven—lid closed, so the heat trapped inside cooks the bird. Here are the key steps.

1

PREP & PLACE

Prepare your grill for indirect heat (see page 16). Place a **whole bird** in the middle of the unlit portion. Or, if grilling parts, place **legs and thighs** closest to the heat, **breasts** farthest from it.

2

CLOSE LID & CHECK TEMPERATURE

Insert an instant-read thermometer through the top vent of the grill to make sure that the inside temperature stays **between 350° and 400°F.**

3

MAINTAIN THE HEAT

Open the vents to let in more oxygen and increase the heat; close the vents to reduce the temperature. For a charcoal grill, have extra charcoal at the ready and **use the chimney starter** to keep hot coals coming.

4

LET IT REST

Once the chicken is cooked to desired doneness (test it with an instant-read thermometer to make sure), **let it rest for at least 10 minutes** before carving and serving.

GLAZED CHICKEN
with Tangerine, Honey, and Chipotle

4 servings

GLAZE

2 cups fresh tangerine or
   orange juice

5 Tbsp. honey

¼ cup reduced-sodium soy sauce

2 Tbsp. finely grated tangerine zest
   or orange zest

2 tsp. minced canned chipotle chile
   in adobo

CHICKEN

1 cup fresh tangerine or
   orange juice

⅓ cup chopped flat-leaf parsley

⅓ cup chopped fresh cilantro

3 Tbsp. chopped fresh thyme

3 Tbsp. minced peeled ginger

3 Tbsp. rice vinegar

2 Tbsp. finely grated tangerine zest
   or orange zest

2 Tbsp. extra-virgin olive oil, plus
   more for brushing

1 tsp. kosher salt, more as needed

1 3-lb. chicken, quartered,
   backbone removed

INGREDIENT INFO Canned chipotle
chiles are dried, smoked jalapeños
in a spicy tomato sauce called
adobo. They can be found at some
supermarkets and at specialty foods
stores and Latin markets.

The bright citrus flavors in the marinade and the glaze really come through in this
dish—as long as you don't let the skin get over-charred on the grill. Reposition the
chicken from hot spots to cooler areas to maintain fresh flavors and ensure a
beautiful golden-brown color.

GLAZE

Bring tangerine juice, honey, and soy sauce to a boil in a medium heavy
saucepan and cook until reduced to ⅔ cup, about 20 minutes. Mix in tangerine
zest and chile.

CHICKEN

Whisk tangerine juice, parsley, cilantro, thyme, ginger, vinegar, tangerine zest,
2 Tbsp. oil, and 1 tsp. salt in a 13x9x2-inch glass baking dish. Add chicken; turn to
coat. Cover; chill, turning occasionally, for at least 2 hours and up to 1 day.

Build a medium-low fire in a charcoal grill, or heat a gas grill to medium. Brush
grill rack with oil. Remove chicken from marinade; discard marinade. Season
chicken lightly with salt and grill, turning and repositioning occasionally for even
cooking, until an instant-read thermometer inserted into the thickest part of the
thigh registers 165°F, about 30 minutes. Brush chicken all over with glaze; grill
for 2 minutes longer on each side. Transfer chicken to a platter. Let rest for 10
minutes. Serve, passing remaining glaze alongside.

+

Grilling a flattened chicken under **the weight of a brick ensures even, quick cooking**— and irresistibly crispy skin.

CHICKEN UNDER A BRICK
WITH GRILLED AVOCADOS AND CHILES

CHICKEN UNDER A BRICK
with Grilled Avocados and Chiles

photo, left

1 3½- to 4-lb. chicken, backbone removed
1 Tbsp. kosher salt, more as needed
½ tsp. freshly ground black pepper, more as needed
¼ tsp. cayenne pepper
1 Tbsp. extra-virgin olive oil, plus more for brushing
2 Tbsp. finely grated lemon zest
3 Tbsp. fresh rosemary leaves
  Grilled Avocados and Chiles (recipe follows)

SPECIAL EQUIPMENT A brick wrapped in foil or a cast-iron skillet wrapped in foil

This straightforward preparation can serve as the foundation for any number of sauces or accompaniments, such as the fresh, colorful side dish featured below.

Open chicken and place on a work surface, skin side up. Using your palms, firmly press on breastbone to flatten the breast (see page 54 for tips on butterflying a chicken). Season chicken all over with 1 Tbsp. salt, ½ tsp. black pepper, and cayenne. Place in a baking dish; rub with 1 Tbsp. oil, sprinkle with lemon zest, and scatter rosemary over. Let stand at room temperature for 1 hour.

Build a medium-low fire in a charcoal grill, or heat a gas grill to medium. Brush grill grate with oil. Place chicken, skin side down, on grill and place a foil-wrapped brick or heavy skillet on top of chicken to weigh it down. Cook until skin is crispy and golden brown, about 15 minutes.

Using tongs, set brick aside. Turn chicken, cover grill, and cook for 10 more minutes. Continue cooking and turning chicken every 10 minutes, covering grill between turns, until an instant-read thermometer inserted into the thickest part of the thigh registers 165°F, about 50 minutes total.

Transfer to a cutting board; let chicken rest for 10 minutes (resting will make for juicier meat). Serve with Grilled Avocados and Chiles.

Grilled Avocados and Chiles

serve with chicken under a brick

3 Tbsp. extra-virgin olive oil, divided, plus more for brushing
1 large poblano chile, quartered, seeded
1 large red bell pepper, quartered, seeded
1 red onion, cut into ½-inch slices
  Kosher salt and freshly ground black pepper
¼ cup red wine vinegar, more as needed
2 garlic cloves, sliced
1 cup fresh basil leaves
4 avocados, halved and pitted
¼ tsp. chili powder

INGREDIENT INFO Poblano chiles are available at specialty foods stores, farmers' markets, Latin markets, and some supermarkets.

The interplay of charred poblano chile, bell pepper, and onion—combined with sautéed garlic and basil—make for a rich, flavorful accompaniment to Chicken Under a Brick. And for the record, you haven't lived until you've eaten a grilled avocado.

Build a medium fire in a charcoal grill, or heat a gas grill to medium-high. Brush grill grate with oil. Season chile, bell pepper, and onion with salt and pepper. Grill, turning occasionally, until softened and charred in spots, about 12 minutes. Transfer onion to a medium bowl. Transfer chiles and peppers to a work surface and cut lengthwise into 1-inch slices. Add to bowl with onion. Add ¼ cup vinegar and toss to coat.

Heat 2 Tbsp. oil in a small skillet over medium-low heat. Add garlic and cook until soft but not browned, about 4 minutes. Add basil and stir to wilt. Transfer basil mixture to bowl with onion. Season vegetables to taste with salt and more vinegar, if desired.

Rub cut side of avocados with remaining 1 Tbsp. oil, season with salt, and sprinkle with chili powder. Grill, cut side down, until avocado is gently warmed and flesh is golden brown, about 3 minutes. Serve with chicken and vegetables.

Working with a whole chicken on the grill becomes very simple when you remove the backbone and flatten the bird—a technique also known as "butterflying" or "spatchcocking." Here's the secret to this handy skill.

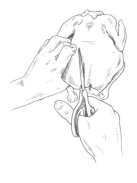

1

Place the chicken, breast side down, on a work surface. Using poultry shears or kitchen shears, **cut down one side of the backbone**.

2

Cut down the other side and **remove the backbone**. You can save it to make stock later.

3

Grab the legs and thighs and bend them back. Turn the chicken over; lay it flat. Use your palms to **firmly press down on the breastbone** (you'll hear it crack).

TEQUILA-JALAPEÑO GLAZED CHICKEN

4 servings

1½ Tbsp. whole coriander seeds
1¾ tsp. kosher salt
½ tsp. crushed red pepper flakes
1 3½- to 4-lb. chicken, cut into 8 pieces, or 4 lb. skin-on, bone-in thighs, legs (thigh and drumstick), and breasts
⅓ cup fresh orange juice or pineapple juice
¼ cup gold or silver tequila
2 Tbsp. honey
2 Tbsp. (packed) light brown sugar
1 to 2 red jalapeños, with seeds, finely chopped
1 shallot, minced
Vegetable oil, for brushing

This dish packs great flavor with a minimum of effort. Rub the spices on the chicken at least six hours ahead, then turn the pieces every six to eight minutes.

Place coriander seeds in a heavy-duty resealable plastic bag, seal, and crush with a mallet. Mix ground coriander, salt, and red pepper flakes in a small bowl. Rub mixture all over chicken. Arrange chicken, skin side up, on a baking sheet; cover and chill for at least 6 hours or overnight.

Bring orange juice, tequila, honey, brown sugar, 1 jalapeño, and shallot to a boil in a small saucepan and cook, stirring until sugar dissolves. Reduce heat to medium-low; simmer until mixture thickens slightly, about 10 minutes. Add remaining jalapeño, if desired. Let glaze cool. Transfer 3 Tbsp. glaze to a small bowl and set aside.

Build a medium-low fire in a charcoal grill, or heat a gas grill to medium. Brush grill grate with oil. Place chicken, skin side up, on grill. Grill, turning occasionally, for 15 minutes. Brush chicken with glaze in saucepan. Turn chicken over; brush with glaze. Grill, turning and brushing occasionally with glaze, until an instant-read thermometer inserted into the thickest part of the thigh registers 165°F, about 10 minutes longer. Transfer to a platter; spoon reserved glaze over.

ROSEMARY-BASTED CHICKEN

2 3- to 4-lb. chickens, each cut into
  4 pieces, backbones removed
  (or 6 to 8 lb. chicken breasts,
  thighs, and legs)
¾ cup extra-virgin olive oil, divided,
  plus more for brushing
¼ cup fresh lemon juice
12 sprigs rosemary, divided
10 garlic cloves, coarsely chopped
  Kosher salt and freshly ground
  black pepper
  Large pinch of smoked paprika
1 lemon

This lemony, garlicky chicken gains even more flavor when basted with rosemary branches dipped in olive oil. Serve with grilled potatoes and one of the slaws on pages 321–325.

Arrange chicken in a large glass baking dish. Drizzle with ½ cup oil and lemon juice. Coarsely chop leaves from 10 rosemary sprigs. Add chopped rosemary and garlic to chicken and toss to coat; season with salt and pepper and sprinkle with paprika. Cover; chill for 3 hours or overnight.

Build a medium-low fire in a charcoal grill, or heat a gas grill to medium. Let chicken come to room temperature. Brush grill grate with oil. Remove chicken from marinade; grill chicken, turning occasionally, until browned and an instant-read thermometer inserted into the thickest part of the thigh registers 165°F, 20 to 22 minutes. Pour remaining ¼ cup oil into a small bowl. Dip remaining 2 rosemary sprigs in oil; occasionally baste chicken with sprigs until cooked through, about 5 minutes longer.

Let chicken rest for 10 to 15 minutes. Transfer to a bowl. Cut lemon in half lengthwise, then cut thinly crosswise into half-moons. Add to chicken with any leftover basting oil; toss to coat. Serve chicken on a platter.

SPICE-RUBBED CHICKEN
with Hickory Barbecue Sauce

CHILI RUB
¾ cup chili powder (about 3½ oz.)
3 Tbsp. (packed) light brown sugar
2 tsp. cayenne pepper

SAUCE AND CHICKEN
1 cup purchased hickory barbecue
  sauce
¾ cup ketchup
⅓ cup fresh orange juice
1 Tbsp. reduced-sodium soy sauce
1 tsp. hot pepper sauce
8 lb. skin-on, bone-in chicken
  thighs, legs, and breasts
  Kosher salt and freshly ground
  black pepper
  Vegetable oil, for brushing

SPECIAL EQUIPMENT A foil baking pan
(for drip pan)

These chicken pieces have twice the firepower because they're dry-rubbed before grilling and then served with a quick, doctored barbecue sauce for added flavor.

CHILI RUB
Mix all ingredients in a small bowl.

SAUCE AND CHICKEN
Mix barbecue sauce, ketchup, orange juice, soy sauce, and hot pepper sauce in a medium bowl. Reserve sauce.

Arrange chicken in a single layer on a large baking sheet. Season with salt and pepper. Rub chili mixture generously all over chicken. Let stand at room temperature for 1 hour.

Prepare grill for indirect heat with a drip pan (see page 16 for instructions), building a medium-low fire in a charcoal grill or heating a gas grill to medium. Brush grill grate with oil.

Place chicken, skin side down, on grill grate over drip pan. Cover grill and cook chicken, turning every 10 minutes, until an instant-read thermometer inserted into the thickest part of the thigh registers 165°F, 35 to 40 minutes (chili rub may look slightly burned). Serve hot or warm, passing reserved sauce.

CHICKEN YAKITORI
with Basting Sauce

photo, right

2 lb. ground chicken, preferably dark meat, divided
1 cup minced scallions (about 6)
2 Tbsp. red miso (fermented soybean paste)
2 Tbsp. sesame oil (not toasted), plus more for hands
Vegetable oil, for brushing
Tare (Soy Basting Sauce; recipe follows)

INGREDIENT INFO Red miso, also known as aka miso, is available in the refrigerated Asian foods section of some supermarkets and at natural foods stores and Japanese markets.

SPECIAL EQUIPMENT Thirty-two 6-inch flat wooden skewers; 2 bricks; square mesh grill grate or wire rack

For a taste of Tokyo at home, try these yakitori-style Japanese meatballs. To achieve and preserve the proper texture, blend the chicken mixture by hand for about 5 minutes before skewering (wear disposable plastic or latex gloves and coat them with oil) and place the skewers on a square mesh grate or wire rack set on bricks above the regular grate. The meatballs are too delicate to cook directly on the grill's grate, and the skewers need to be kept away from the heat.

Heat a small nonstick skillet over medium heat. Cook ⅔ lb. (1½ cups) ground chicken, stirring frequently, until it is opaque and just cooked through, about 2 minutes. Transfer to a plate. Combine cooked chicken, remaining 1⅓ lb. chicken, scallions, miso, and 2 Tbsp. oil in a large bowl. Knead until a homogenized, sticky mixture forms, about 5 minutes. Clean hands; lightly coat with oil to prevent meat mixture from sticking. Divide mixture into 16 equal portions. Roll each into a ball, then form each ball into a 4-inch-long cylinder. Insert 2 skewers into each cylinder. Press meat gently to flatten slightly. Repeat with remaining skewers and meat.

Build a medium-hot fire in a charcoal grill, or heat a gas grill to high. Set two bricks on top grill grate; place square mesh grate on bricks so that the mesh grate rests just above the rim of the grill. Brush mesh grate with vegetable oil. Place yakitori on mesh grate, keeping wooden skewers away from direct heat. Working in batches, grill yakitori, turning every minute, for 4 minutes. Brush with Tare and continue cooking, turning once, for 2 minutes. Brush again with Tare and grill, turning once, until cooked through, about 2 minutes longer. Serve immediately.

Tare
(Soy Basting Sauce)

use with chicken yakitori

½ cup low-salt chicken broth
¼ cup mirin
¼ cup reduced-sodium soy sauce
2 Tbsp. sake
¾ tsp. (packed) light brown sugar
¼ tsp. freshly ground black pepper
1 garlic clove, crushed
1 scallion, chopped
1 1-inch piece ginger, peeled, sliced

INGREDIENT INFO Mirin is available in the Asian foods section of some supermarkets and at Japanese markets.

Try this basting sauce on more than yakitori: Brush it on grilled vegetables, tofu, or pork.

Place a fine-mesh sieve over a small bowl. Bring all ingredients to a boil in a small heavy saucepan, stirring until sugar dissolves. Reduce heat to medium-low and simmer until reduced to a generous ½ cup, about 20 minutes. Strain sauce, discarding solids in sieve. Let cool. **DO AHEAD:** Can be made 2 weeks ahead. Cover and chill.

CHICKEN YAKITORI WITH BASTING SAUCE

PIRI-PIRI CHICKEN

GLAZE

3 Tbsp. unsalted butter

3 Tbsp. chopped fresh cilantro

2 garlic cloves, minced

2 Tbsp. fresh lemon juice

2 Tbsp. piri-piri sauce or other hot pepper sauce

CHICKEN

¼ cup chopped fresh cilantro

1 2-inch piece ginger, peeled, thinly sliced

1 large shallot, quartered

3 garlic cloves

½ cup piri-piri sauce or other hot pepper sauce

¼ cup extra-virgin olive oil, plus more for brushing

¼ cup fresh lemon juice

1 tsp. kosher salt

1 tsp. freshly ground black pepper

1 3½- to 4-lb. chicken, butterflied, backbone removed

INGREDIENT INFO Piri-piri sauce can be found at specialty foods stores and online from africantradingco.com. Choose the heat level that suits you, keeping in mind that the mild version still has a nice kick to it.

SPECIAL EQUIPMENT A foil baking pan (for drip pan)

Piri-piri **chicken is a spicy dish originally created in Angola and Mozambique when Portuguese settlers arrived with the small, very spicy chile pepper known as African bird's eye—*piri-piri* in Swahili. This recipe uses the easier-to-find bottled *piri-piri* sauce (though any hot pepper sauce will do) and calls for the chicken to marinate for at least 4 hours, so it will pack some punch. See page 54 for tips on butterflying a chicken.**

GLAZE

Melt butter in a small saucepan over medium-high heat. Add cilantro and garlic; cook until garlic begins to brown, about 2 minutes. Add lemon juice and piri-piri sauce. Reduce heat to medium-low; simmer for 2 minutes. **DO AHEAD:** Glaze can be made up to 1 day ahead. Cover and chill. Rewarm before using.

CHICKEN

Finely chop cilantro, ginger, shallot, and garlic in a food processor. Add piri-piri sauce, ¼ cup oil, lemon juice, salt, and pepper; pulse marinade to blend.

Pour half of marinade into an 11x7x2-inch glass baking dish. Place butterflied chicken, skin side down, in a single layer in dish. Pour remaining marinade over. Cover; chill, turning occasionally, for at least 4 hours or overnight.

Prepare grill for indirect heat with a drip pan (see page 16 for instructions), building a medium-low fire in a charcoal grill or heating a gas grill to medium. Place drip pan on indirect heat side of grill. Place upper grate on grill; brush with oil.

Remove chicken from marinade. Arrange, skin side up, on grill grate above drip pan. Cover; grill, turning often, until skin is browned and an instant-read thermometer inserted into the thickest part of the thigh registers 165°F, about 40 minutes. Transfer to a platter and pour warm glaze over.

CHICKEN SANDWICHES
with Onions, Watercress, and Paprika Aioli

½ cup mayonnaise

1 Tbsp. fresh lime juice

1 tsp. hot smoked Spanish paprika

1 garlic clove, minced

2 Tbsp. extra-virgin olive oil, plus more for brushing

Kosher salt and freshly ground black pepper

2 Tbsp. vegetable oil

2 lb. onions, halved lengthwise, thinly sliced crosswise (about 7 cups)

3 8-oz. skinless, boneless chicken breasts, halved crosswise

6 sourdough sandwich rolls or twelve ½-inch-thick slices sourdough bread

3 cups (lightly packed) watercress or arugula

Pounding the chicken into thinner pieces helps reduce the time they spend on the grill and encourages more even cooking. The zingy condiment of paprika, lime, and mayonnaise brilliantly marries all of the elements of this delicious sandwich (it's also useful to have on hand for sprucing up everything from grilled steak to pork tenderloin).

Whisk mayonnaise, lime juice, paprika, and garlic in a small bowl. Gradually whisk in 2 Tbsp. olive oil and season to taste with salt and pepper. **DO AHEAD:** Aioli can be made 2 days ahead. Cover and chill.

Heat vegetable oil in a large heavy skillet over medium-high heat. Add onions; season with salt and cook, stirring often, until onions are beginning to brown, about 10 minutes. Reduce heat to medium and continue to cook, stirring often, until onions are soft and deep golden brown, about 20 minutes longer. Season to taste with salt and pepper. **DO AHEAD:** Caramelized onions can be made 2 hours ahead. Let stand at room temperature.

Build a medium fire in a charcoal grill, or heat a gas grill to medium-high. Place chicken breast pieces between 2 sheets of waxed paper. Pound with a mallet to ⅓-inch thickness. Season with salt and pepper. Brush grill grate with oil. Grill chicken, turning once, until an instant-read thermometer inserted into the thickest part of the breast registers 165°F, about 3 minutes per side. Transfer to a work surface. Brush cut side of rolls with olive oil. Grill rolls, cut side down, until grill marks appear, about 1 minute. Spread rolls with some aioli. Assemble sandwiches with chicken, caramelized onions, and watercress, dividing evenly. Serve warm.

CHICKEN PAN BAGNAT

6 skinless, boneless chicken breasts (4 to 6 oz. each)
⅓ cup plus ¾ cup extra-virgin olive oil; additional for brushing
6 Tbsp. fresh lemon juice, divided
1 Tbsp. herbes de Provence
2 garlic cloves, minced, divided
   Kosher salt and freshly ground black pepper
2 tsp. anchovy paste
2 16-oz. round sourdough bread loaves
4 Tbsp. drained capers
2 large tomatoes, thinly sliced
1 small red onion, thinly sliced
4 large romaine lettuce leaves

INGREDIENT INFO Herbes de Provence is a dried herb mixture sold in the spice section of most supermarkets and at specialty foods stores. A combination of dried thyme, basil, savory, and fennel seeds may be substituted.

A Provençal specialty, *pan bagnat* is literally a sandwich with "bathed bread"—that is, the loaf of bread is split and drizzled with olive oil and/or a vinaigrette before being filled with other ingredients. In this version, grilled chicken breast (first pounded thin so that it cooks evenly) stands in for the traditional tuna. These are the perfect sandwiches to take on a picnic, because they should be made at least 2 hours before serving to allow all the flavors to blend.

Using a mallet, pound chicken breasts between sheets of waxed paper to ¾-inch thickness. Combine ⅓ cup oil, 2 Tbsp. lemon juice, herbes de Provence, and 1 garlic clove in a large resealable plastic bag. Add chicken to bag; seal and turn to coat. Chill for at least 2 hours and up to 6 hours.

Build a medium fire in a charcoal grill, or heat a gas grill to medium-high. Brush grill grate with oil. Remove chicken from marinade, shaking off excess. Season chicken with salt and pepper. Grill chicken, turning once, until an instant-read thermometer inserted into the thickest part of the breast registers 165°F, about 4 minutes per side. Let cool and then cut chicken on a diagonal into ½- to ¾-inch-thick slices.

Whisk remaining 4 Tbsp. lemon juice, remaining garlic, and anchovy paste in a small bowl. Gradually whisk in remaining ¾ cup oil. Season dressing to taste with salt and pepper.

Cut bread loaves in half horizontally. Pull out and discard soft interior crumbs from top halves, leaving ½-inch-thick shell; drizzle ¼ cup dressing over inside of each top. Drizzle ¼ cup dressing over inside of each bottom half; sprinkle 2 Tbsp. capers over each bottom half. Layer chicken, tomatoes, onion, then lettuce on each sandwich, dividing evenly. Cover with tops, pressing to compact. Wrap sandwiches in foil, then place a heavy skillet or food cans on top to weigh down. Chill for at least 2 hours. **DO AHEAD:** Can be made 1 day ahead. Keep chilled.

Cut each sandwich into quarters and serve cold or at room temperature.

CHICKEN SANDWICHES
with Sage Pesto and Apples

¾ cup (lightly packed) fresh sage
    leaves (from 2 large bunches)

¾ cup pine nuts, walnuts, or
    almonds (about 4 oz.)

¼ cup (packed) flat-leaf parsley
    leaves

1 garlic clove

¾ cup plus 3 Tbsp. extra-virgin
    olive oil; additional for brushing

6 Tbsp. finely grated Parmesan
    Kosher salt and freshly ground
    black pepper

6 skinless, boneless chicken
    breasts (4 to 6 oz. each)

6 5x4-inch rectangles focaccia,
    ciabatta, or long French rolls,
    split horizontally
    Mayonnaise, for spreading

3 medium apples (such as Fuji,
    Granny Smith, or Pink Lady),
    halved, cored, thinly sliced

Once grilled, the chicken is combined with thin apple slices and a sage-parsley pesto in sandwiches with the flavors of fall. Try adding slices of white cheddar or Gruyère, then wrap the sandwiches in foil and warm them on the top shelf of the grill until the cheese melts.

Pulse sage, pine nuts, parsley, and garlic in a food processor until mixture is finely chopped. With processor running, add ¾ cup oil and blend until a thick paste forms. Pulse in cheese. Transfer pesto to a small bowl; season to taste with salt and pepper. **DO AHEAD:** Can be made 1 day ahead. Press plastic wrap directly onto surface of pesto and chill. Bring to room temperature before using.

Using a mallet, pound chicken breasts between sheets of waxed paper to ¾-inch thickness. Brush chicken with 3 Tbsp. oil; season with salt and pepper. Let chicken stand for 30 minutes.

Build a medium fire in a charcoal grill, or heat a gas grill to medium-high. Brush grill grate with oil. Grill chicken, turning once, until an instant-read thermometer inserted into the thickest part of the breast registers 165°F, about 5 minutes per side. Transfer chicken to a platter. Grill focaccia, turning once, until just beginning to brown, about 1 minute per side.

Arrange bottom halves of focaccia on a work surface. Spread each cut side with mayonnaise. Top each with overlapping layer of apple slices, then 1 chicken breast. Drizzle each chicken breast with pesto. Spread pesto on cut side of bread tops. Place tops on chicken, pesto side down. Cut sandwiches in half on a diagonal.

CHICKEN SALAD
with Tarragon Pesto

photo, right

¼ cup (packed) fresh tarragon leaves plus 2 tsp. chopped fresh tarragon

¼ cup (packed) flat-leaf parsley

4 Tbsp. pine nuts, divided

5 tsp. fresh lemon juice, divided

2 tsp. chopped shallot

6 Tbsp. extra-virgin olive oil, more as needed, divided; additional for brushing

Kosher salt and freshly ground black pepper

4 skin-on, boneless chicken breasts (about 6 oz. each)

4 ½-inch-thick slices country-style French or sourdough bread

5 oz. mixed baby greens

1 cup thinly sliced radishes (from 1 large bunch)

1 cup thinly sliced Japanese cucumbers (about 1½)

In this alternative to classic pesto, the anise-like flavor of tarragon is balanced with the fresh taste of parsley and paired with boneless chicken breasts (it would also complement grilled lobster and shrimp). You can easily double the amount of pesto and save half to toss with pasta later in the week.

Coarsely chop ¼ cup tarragon leaves, parsley, 2 Tbsp. pine nuts, 1 tsp. lemon juice, and shallot in a mini food processor. With processor running, gradually add 3 Tbsp. oil, adding more oil by teaspoonfuls to thin, if needed. Season pesto to taste with salt and pepper.

Whisk 2 tsp. chopped tarragon, remaining 4 tsp. lemon juice, and 3 Tbsp. oil in a small bowl. Season dressing to taste with salt and pepper.

Build a medium fire in a charcoal grill, or heat a gas grill to medium-high. Brush grill grate with oil. Brush chicken breasts on both sides with oil. Season with salt and pepper. Grill chicken, turning once, until grill marks form, skin is crisp, and an instant-read thermometer inserted into the thickest part of the breast registers 165°F, 7 to 8 minutes per side. Transfer to a cutting board; let rest for 5 minutes. Using a clean brush, brush both sides of bread with oil and season with salt and pepper. Grill bread, turning once, until dark brown grill marks appear on both sides, 2 to 3 minutes per side.

Place greens, radishes, and cucumbers in a large bowl; drizzle with dressing and toss to coat. Season to taste with salt and pepper. Divide salad among plates.

Cut grilled chicken breasts crosswise into ⅓-inch-thick slices. Arrange 1 sliced chicken breast atop salad on each plate. Spoon tarragon pesto over chicken. Sprinkle remaining 2 Tbsp. pine nuts over salads and serve with grilled bread slices alongside.

This spin on pesto **swaps in tarragon and parsley** for the traditional basil. Slices of **radish and cucumber** add crunch.

CHICKEN SALAD WITH TARRAGON PESTO

CHICKEN AND ROMAINE
with Caper Dressing

4 servings

3 Tbsp. Sherry vinegar
½ cup extra-virgin olive oil, plus
    more for brushing
¼ cup minced shallots
2 Tbsp. drained capers
1 Tbsp. Dijon mustard
    Kosher salt and freshly ground
    black pepper
4 skinless, boneless chicken
    breasts (about 6 oz. each)
2 hearts of romaine lettuce, halved
    lengthwise, core left intact
    Shaved Manchego cheese or
    Parmesan, for garnish

INGREDIENT INFO Manchego cheese,
a sheep's milk cheese from Spain, is
available at some supermarkets and
at specialty foods stores.

Both the chicken and romaine hearts hit the grill in this quick and addictive dish. Keep the core of the lettuce intact so it holds together while cooking. The romaine will char and wilt slightly but will remain crisp and take on a delicious grilled flavor that goes well with the tangy caper vinaigrette. Parmesan or Manchego cheese (use a vegetable peeler to shave it) adds a slightly salty finishing touch.

Build a medium fire in a charcoal grill, or heat a gas grill to medium-high. Purée vinegar, ½ cup oil, shallots, capers, and mustard in a mini food processor until almost smooth. Season dressing to taste with salt and pepper.

Place chicken and ¼ cup dressing in a medium bowl. Season with salt and pepper. Let stand at room temperature for 15 minutes. Place romaine, cut side up, on a baking sheet. Drizzle with ¼ cup dressing; turn to coat.

Brush grill grate with oil. Grill chicken, turning once, until an instant-read thermometer inserted into the thickest part of the breast registers 165°F, about 5 minutes per side. Transfer to a plate. Grill romaine, turning, until charred and slightly wilted on all sides, about 2 minutes.

Place 1 chicken breast and 1 romaine spear on each plate. Drizzle chicken with remaining dressing and top generously with cheese.

PEACHY CHICKEN SALAD

4 servings

5 Tbsp. extra-virgin olive oil,
    divided, plus more for brushing
2 Tbsp. fresh lime juice
1½ tsp. fleur de sel or fine sea salt,
    divided
1 tsp. freshly ground black pepper,
    divided
4 skinless, boneless chicken
    breasts (about 6 oz. each)
2 scallions, minced
1 shallot, finely chopped
1½ Tbsp. Sherry vinegar
2 tsp. fresh thyme leaves
1 tsp. honey-Dijon mustard
2 ripe peaches, halved, pitted, diced
1 small avocado, halved, pitted, diced
½ cup thinly sliced radicchio
2½ oz. mixed baby greens

This recipe makes full use of fresh peaches and teams them with avocado, Sherry wine vinaigrette, and citrusy grilled chicken for a summery main-course salad. You can use either yellow or white peaches, as there's not a huge difference in flavor— yellow peaches have a nice acidic tang; white ones are sweeter and more fragile. The important thing is to make sure they're ripe but not too soft.

Whisk 1 Tbsp. oil, lime juice, 1 tsp. fleur de sel, and ½ tsp. pepper in an 11x7x2-inch glass baking dish. Add chicken and turn to coat. Let marinate, turning occasionally, for 30 minutes.

Build a medium fire in a charcoal grill, or heat a gas grill to medium-high. Whisk 4 Tbsp. oil, remaining ½ tsp. fleur de sel and ½ tsp. pepper, scallions, shallot, vinegar, thyme, and mustard in a large bowl. Add peaches, avocado, and radicchio and toss to coat.

Brush grill grate with oil. Grill chicken, turning once, until an instant-read thermometer inserted into the thickest part of the breast registers 165°F, about 5 minutes per side. Transfer to a cutting board; cut crosswise into thin slices.

Add baby greens to salad and toss gently to coat. Divide salad among plates; arrange chicken alongside.

CRUNCHY CHICKEN SALAD
with Sesame Dressing

DRESSING
- ½ cup plus 1 Tbsp. seasoned rice vinegar
- 1½ Tbsp. Dijon mustard
- ½ cup plus 1 Tbsp. vegetable oil
- ¼ cup plus 1½ tsp. toasted sesame oil
- 2½ Tbsp. reduced-sodium soy sauce
- 12 scallions, chopped
- 1 tsp. crushed red pepper flakes
  Kosher salt and freshly ground black pepper

SALAD
- 1 1½-lb. head of Napa cabbage, sliced
- 1½ cucumbers, preferably English hothouse, sliced on a diagonal
- 1½ bunches carrots, peeled, sliced on a diagonal
- 1 cup chopped fresh mint
- 6 skinless, boneless chicken breasts (about 6 oz. each)
- 12 shiitake mushrooms, stemmed
  Vegetable oil, for brushing
  Kosher salt and freshly ground black pepper
- 1 cup lightly salted, dry-roasted peanuts, coarsely chopped

Fresh vegetables and a robust dressing team up for a satisfying main-course salad that's similar to a classic Chinese chicken salad, but with a more distinctive sesame flavor. Remove woody stems from the shiitake mushrooms, and toss this salad with the dressing just moments before you eat it so that the vegetables stay crunchy.

DRESSING
Whisk vinegar and mustard in a medium bowl. Gradually whisk in both oils, then soy sauce. Stir in scallions and red pepper flakes and season to taste with salt and pepper.

SALAD
Combine cabbage, cucumbers, carrots, and mint in a large bowl. **DO AHEAD:** Dressing and salad can be made 4 hours ahead. Cover separately and chill. Bring to room temperature before using.

Place chicken and mushrooms in a 13x9x2-inch glass baking dish. Pour ½ cup plus 2 Tbsp. dressing over and turn to coat. Cover; chill for at least 30 minutes and up to 1 hour.

Build a medium fire in a charcoal grill, or heat a gas grill to medium-high. Brush grill grate with oil. Remove chicken and mushrooms from marinade; season with salt and pepper. Grill chicken, turning once, until an instant-read thermometer inserted into the thickest part of the breast registers 165°F, about 5 minutes per side. Transfer to a cutting board. Grill mushrooms, turning once, until tender, about 2 minutes per side.

Drizzle some dressing over salad and toss gently to coat; season with salt and pepper. Transfer to a large platter. Slice chicken on a diagonal and arrange around edge of platter. Halve mushrooms and tuck in among chicken slices. Drizzle chicken with remaining dressing and garnish salad with peanuts.

GRILL-ROASTED TURKEY
with Simple Brine

photo, right

1 12–14-lb. turkey, giblets and neck removed, brined (see recipe), at room temperature for 1 hour
1 apple, cored, quartered
1 orange, quartered
1 red onion, peeled, quartered
2 Tbsp. unsalted butter, room temperature
Kosher salt and freshly ground black pepper

SPECIAL EQUIPMENT A large foil baking pan (for drip pan); charcoal chimney; 2 cups wood chips, soaked in water for at least 2 hours (optional)

This recipe for grilled turkey, from Sam Sifton of *The New York Times*, requires a charcoal grill—gas grills just can't duplicate the heat or the smoky flavor you're going for. A few important notes to keep in mind: First, use high-quality hardwood charcoal and wood chips for maximum flavor; oak, cherry, apple, and hickory work well. And second, don't stuff the bird. Smoky turkey is excellent. Smoky stuffing isn't.

Prepare grill for smoking (see page 161). Add 2 cups water to drip pan.

Pat turkey dry with paper towels. Place apple, orange, and onion in cavity. Tie legs with kitchen twine. Rub bird inside and out with butter. Season skin lightly with salt and pepper.

Place turkey on grate over drip pan (do not allow any part of turkey to sit over coals). Cover grill. Insert stem of an instant-read thermometer through the top vent. Maintain temperature as close as possible to 350°F by opening vents to increase temperature and closing vents to reduce it, lifting grate with turkey to replenish coals as needed using charcoal chimney. If using wood chips, scatter a handful of drained chips over charcoal every 30 minutes.

Cook turkey, rotating every hour for even browning (lift the grate with the turkey on it; rotate grate 180 degrees), until an instant-read thermometer inserted into thickest part of the thigh without touching bone registers 165°F (juices should run clear when thermometer is removed), about 2¾ hours.

Transfer turkey to a platter. Tent with foil and let rest for 1 hour before carving.

Simple Brine

use with
grill-roasted
turkey

¾ cup plus 2 Tbsp. kosher salt
¾ cup sugar
1 carrot, peeled, diced
1 large onion, peeled, diced
¼ cup diced celery
2 large sprigs thyme
2 bay leaves
1 Tbsp. whole black peppercorns
¼ tsp. crushed red pepper flakes
¼ tsp. fennel seeds

Bring salt, sugar, and 4 cups water to a boil in a very large (16-qt.) pot, stirring until salt and sugar are dissolved.

Turn off heat. Add remaining ingredients to brine base. Refrigerate, uncovered, until cold.

Add 6 quarts cold water to pot. Add turkey. Place a plate on top of turkey to keep submerged. Cover; chill for up to 72 hours. (The turkey will be moister and more flavorful if allowed to brine the full 72 hours.)

**GRILL-ROASTED TURKEY
WITH SIMPLE BRINE**

TEA-BRINED TURKEY
with Tea-and-Lemon Gravy

5 lemons, divided
18 tea bags, preferably Earl Grey
11 4-inch-long sprigs rosemary, divided
2 cups kosher salt
1½ cups (packed) light brown sugar
1 22-lb. turkey, neck, heart, and gizzard reserved for gravy
1 celery stalk, cut crosswise into 3-inch pieces
1 medium onion, quartered
¼ cup extra-virgin olive oil, plus more for brushing
Tea-and-Lemon Gravy (recipe follows)

SPECIAL EQUIPMENT 2 large plastic turkey roasting bags; one large foil baking pan (for drip pan)

Lemons and Earl Grey tea in the brine and gravy result in bright citrusy flavor. We like Diamond Crystal kosher salt for the brine; it dissolves quickly and has a pure taste.

Bring 6½ quarts water to a boil in a large pot. Remove from heat. Remove zest from 3 lemons and squeeze juice to measure ½ cup; set aside. Add zest, tea bags, and 6 rosemary sprigs to water; let steep for 20 minutes. Remove tea bags. Add salt and brown sugar; stir to dissolve. Stir in reserved lemon juice. Let cool to lukewarm. Add 12 cups ice to reduce temperature to below 45°F.

Place 1 roasting bag inside the second, forming 2 layers. Place inside a large pot. Place turkey in roasting bags, breast side up. Pour brine over turkey. Tie bags tightly, eliminating any air pockets. Chill for 36 to 48 hours.

Prepare grill for indirect heat with a drip pan (see page 16), building a medium-low fire in a charcoal grill or heating a gas grill to medium. Drain turkey and pat dry. Pierce remaining 2 lemons all over with a fork. Place lemons, remaining 5 rosemary sprigs, celery, and onion in turkey's cavity. Tie legs together; brush turkey all over with ¼ cup oil.

Brush grill grate with oil. Place turkey on grill above drip pan; close grill. Insert an instant-read thermometer through the top vent. Add more charcoal from a chimney every 30 minutes or adjust temperature on gas grill to maintain 350°F. Roast turkey until instant-read thermometer inserted into the thickest part of the thigh registers 165°F, about 3 hours. Transfer turkey to a platter; tent with foil. Let rest for 30 minutes. Serve with Tea-and-Lemon Gravy.

Tea-and-Lemon Gravy

use with tea-brined turkey

8 cups low-salt chicken broth
2 celery stalks, coarsely chopped
2 carrots, peeled, coarsely chopped
1 medium onion, halved
1 sprig rosemary
Neck, heart, and gizzard, reserved from 22-lb. turkey
1 lemon
1 tea bag, preferably Earl Grey
5 Tbsp. unsalted butter
5 Tbsp. all-purpose flour
½ cup heavy cream
1 Tbsp. finely grated lemon zest
Kosher salt and freshly ground black pepper

Combine broth, celery, carrots, onion, rosemary sprig, neck, heart, and gizzard in a large saucepan. Using a vegetable peeler, remove zest from lemon and add to broth mixture. Bring mixture to a boil; reduce heat and simmer until neck and gizzard are tender, about 45 minutes.

Remove neck, heart, and gizzard from broth; finely chop heart and gizzard. Pull meat from neck and chop. Strain broth into a large bowl. Return broth to pan; bring to a boil and cook until reduced to 3 cups, about 10 minutes. Remove from heat; add tea bag. Cover; let steep for 10 minutes. Discard tea bag.

Melt butter in a medium heavy saucepan over medium heat. Whisk in flour and cook, stirring often, until light brown, about 5 minutes. Whisk in seasoned broth and cream. Bring to a boil; reduce heat to medium and simmer, stirring often, until slightly thickened and smooth, about 8 minutes. Stir in finely grated lemon zest and neck, heart, and gizzard pieces. Season to taste with salt and pepper.

ROSEMARY-LEMON
TURKEY CUTLETS

¼ cup extra-virgin olive oil,
   plus more for brushing
3 Tbsp. fresh lemon juice
2 tsp. minced fresh rosemary
2 garlic cloves, minced
   Kosher salt and freshly ground
   black pepper
1¼ lb. red-skinned potatoes,
   unpeeled, cut into ½-inch-thick
   wedges
1¼ to 1½ lb. ⅓-inch-thick turkey cutlets

If you're craving a turkey dinner in the middle of summer (or any other time of year), try these easy turkey fillets and potato wedges. If the cutlets are thicker than ⅓ inch, place them into a heavy-duty resealable plastic bag or between sheets of wax paper and pound them with a mallet or rolling pin.

Whisk ¼ cup oil, lemon juice, rosemary, and garlic in a small bowl. Season dressing to taste with salt and pepper.

Place potatoes in a medium bowl; add 2 Tbsp. dressing. Place turkey in another medium bowl; add 2 Tbsp. dressing. Let potatoes and turkey marinate at room temperature, turning occasionally, for 15 to 30 minutes.

Build a medium fire in a charcoal grill, or heat a gas grill to medium-high. Brush grill grate with oil. Place turkey cutlets and potatoes on separate rimmed baking sheets; season with salt and pepper. Grill turkey and potatoes, turning once, until charred, cooked through, and an instant-read thermometer inserted into cutlets registers 165°F, 3 to 4 minutes per side. Grill potatoes for about 10 minutes per side. Divide turkey and potatoes among plates and drizzle with remaining dressing.

Kitchen Wisdom

A COOLER WAY TO BRINE Using a cooler to brine a whole turkey saves space in your refrigerator. (1) **Buy a food-grade resealable brining bag.** Fold down the sides of the bag for a contamination-free seal, then place the turkey in the bag, breast side up. (2) **Transfer the bag to a large cooler** filled halfway with ice, snuggling the bag into the cubes. Spread open the top of the folded bag, then carefully pour the brine over the turkey. (3) Fold up the sides, press out any excess air, then seal the bag. Fold over top of bag and **completely cover bag with ice.** (4) Insert a digital thermometer into the ice and make sure it registers **40°F or lower at all times.** Keep the cooler shut, and refill with ice as necessary.

TURKEY SHAWARMA
with Tomato Relish and Tahini Sauce

2½ lb. ¼-inch-thick turkey cutlets

2 onions, cut into ¼-inch-thick rounds

1 Tbsp. turmeric

2 tsp. kosher salt

2 tsp. ground coriander

1 tsp. ground cumin

1 tsp. freshly ground black pepper

1 tsp. freshly ground white pepper

1 tsp. Hungarian hot paprika or cayenne pepper

8 Tbsp. extra-virgin olive oil, divided, plus more for brushing

8 whole pita breads

Tomato Relish (recipe follows)

Tahini Sauce (recipe follows)

1 cup thinly sliced dill pickles

Direct-grilling turkey cutlets offers a simpler way to create the taste and texture of *shawarma,* **which is traditionally cooked on a vertical rotisserie. The tomato relish and tahini sauce are classic accompaniments to** *shawarma.*

Arrange turkey cutlets in a 15x10x2-inch glass baking dish. Spread onion slices in a 13x9x2-inch glass baking dish. Mix turmeric, salt, coriander, cumin, black pepper, white pepper, and paprika in a small bowl. Sprinkle onion slices with 1 Tbsp. spice mixture, then drizzle 2 Tbsp. oil over; turn onions to coat. Rub remaining spice mixture all over both sides of turkey cutlets and drizzle 4 Tbsp. oil over turkey; turn cutlets to coat. Cover and chill onions and turkey for at least 4 hours and up to 8 hours.

Build a medium fire in a charcoal grill, or heat a gas grill to medium-high. Brush grill grate with oil. Brush pita breads with remaining 2 Tbsp. oil. Grill onion slices, turning once, until tender, about 4 minutes per side. Grill turkey cutlets, turning once, until an instant-read thermometer inserted into cutlets registers 165°F, 3 to 4 minutes per side. Grill pita breads, turning once, until grill marks appear, about 2 minutes per side.

Transfer turkey cutlets and onion slices to a cutting board and tent pita breads with foil to keep warm. Working in batches, stack several turkey slices and cut thinly crosswise. Repeat stacking and cutting with onion slices. Mix turkey and onion in a large bowl. Place 1 pita bread on each plate and top with turkey-onion mixture, then Tomato Relish, Tahini Sauce, and pickle slices.

Tomato Relish

makes about 2½ cups

use with
turkey shawarma

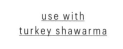

1 lb. ripe tomatoes, finely chopped (with seeds and juices)

⅔ cup finely chopped red onion

¼ cup chopped flat-leaf parsley

¼ cup extra-virgin olive oil

3 Tbsp. fresh lemon juice

3 serrano chiles, seeded, finely chopped (about 2 Tbsp.)

Kosher salt and freshly ground black pepper

This would also be delicious spooned over grilled lamb, chicken, or fish.

Combine first 6 ingredients in a medium bowl. Season relish to taste with salt and pepper. **DO AHEAD:** Can be made 4 hours ahead. Cover and chill.

Tahini Sauce

1 cup tahini (sesame seed paste)
½ cup fresh lemon juice
Kosher salt

INGREDIENT INFO Tahini is sold at some supermarkets and at natural foods stores and Middle Eastern markets.

You can also add this sauce to puréed chickpeas for homemade hummus or drizzle it over grilled fish.

Spoon tahini into a medium bowl; whisk in lemon juice until smooth. Add ½ cup hot water and whisk until well blended, adding more hot water by tablespoonfuls if mixture is too thick. Season to taste with salt. **DO AHEAD:** Can be made 1 day ahead. Cover and chill.

BURGERS & DOGS

IF YOU SPEND ENOUGH TIME GRILLING

(or reading books like this one), you might think a lot about intricate rubs, brines, and marinades, eight-hour smoked briskets, and the merits of hickory vs. walnut wood chips. But what you might forget is just how good a perfectly grilled burger or charred-just-so hot dog can taste.

So, in this chapter, we're focusing on the basics. You'll learn our thoughts on what makes the ultimate burger (start with quality ground beef with the right amount of fat)—while recognizing that the "ultimate burger" might also be made with turkey, chicken, tuna, salmon, lamb, or veggies. The next 20 pages are filled with the essential tips, techniques, and seasonings for each type.

What about hot dogs and sausages? We've got them covered, too—from when (and why) you should parboil a fresh sausage before you throw it on the grate to a four-pack of pickled-condiments that covers every base.

Everybody loves a good burger or dog—and these days, the possibilities for how to make one at home are nearly endless.

THE PERFECT CHEESEBURGER

photo, page 76

makes 4

1½ lb. ground beef, preferably chuck (20% fat)
Vegetable oil, for brushing
1¼ tsp. kosher salt
½ tsp. freshly ground black pepper
4 slices American cheese
4 potato rolls (such as Martin's or Oroweat), sliced

There are plenty of ways to gussy up a burger—and you'll find several on the next few pages. But to make one that's as mouthwatering as it is classic, all you *really* need is good old American cheese and just the right amount of fat in your ground beef. (Turn the page for our five-step primer on how to make it right.)

Divide meat into 4 equal portions (about 6 oz. each). Place 1 portion on a work surface. Cup your hands around the meat and begin to gently shape it into a rounded mound. (Use light pressure as you shape so that you don't pack the meat too tightly.) Lightly press down on the top of the meat with your palm to gently flatten it. Continue rotating and cupping the meat, patting the top of it occasionally, until you've formed a 4-inch diameter, ¾-inch-thick patty. Using your thumb, make a small indentation in the center to help keep the burger flat as it cooks. Repeat with remaining portions. Transfer to a plate, cover with plastic wrap, and chill until ready to cook.

Build a medium-hot fire in a charcoal grill, or heat a gas grill to high. Brush grill grate with oil. Season patties on one side with salt and pepper; place on grill, seasoned side down, then season other side. Grill until lightly charred on bottom, 3 to 4 minutes. Turn and top with cheese. Grill to desired doneness, 3 to 4 minutes longer for medium-rare burgers. Transfer to rolls and let stand for 3 minutes before serving.

LEMON BUTTER–STUFFED BURGERS

makes 4

6 Tbsp. (¾ stick) unsalted butter, room temperature
1 Tbsp. finely chopped flat-leaf parsley
1 Tbsp. finely chopped fresh basil
1 Tbsp. finely chopped fresh tarragon
1 tsp. finely grated lemon zest
1 tsp. fresh lemon juice
Kosher salt and freshly ground black pepper
1½ lb. ground beef (preferably chuck)
Vegetable oil, for brushing
4 sesame seed hamburger buns, sliced
1 large tomato, thinly sliced crosswise
1 bunch arugula

A pat of slightly tangy compound butter—made with fresh herbs and lemon—is tucked into the center of each of these burgers. As the patties cook, the butter melts, giving the meat an especially tender texture.

Mix butter, all herbs, lemon zest, and lemon juice in a small bowl. Season with salt and pepper. Measure ⅓ cup herb butter; transfer to a sheet of plastic wrap (reserve remaining butter in bowl for spreading on buns). Using plastic wrap as aid, form butter into a 3-inch-long log; wrap plastic around to seal. Freeze until firm, about 30 minutes. Cut crosswise into 4 rounds. Flatten rounds into 2-inch-diameter disks.

Divide meat into 4 pieces. With wet hands, form each piece into a ball. Using your thumb, make a deep, wide indentation in the center of each. Press 1 butter round flatly into indentation, then press meat securely over to enclose. Flatten each burger into a 3½-inch diameter patty. **DO AHEAD:** Burgers can be made 6 hours ahead. Place on a baking sheet, cover with plastic wrap, and chill.

Build a medium-hot fire in a charcoal grill, or heat a gas grill to high. Brush grill grate with oil. Season both sides of burgers with salt and pepper. Spread remaining butter over cut sides of buns. Grill burgers for 3 to 5 minutes per side for medium-rare. Grill buns until slightly charred, about 1 minute per side.

Assemble burgers with tomato slices and arugula leaves.

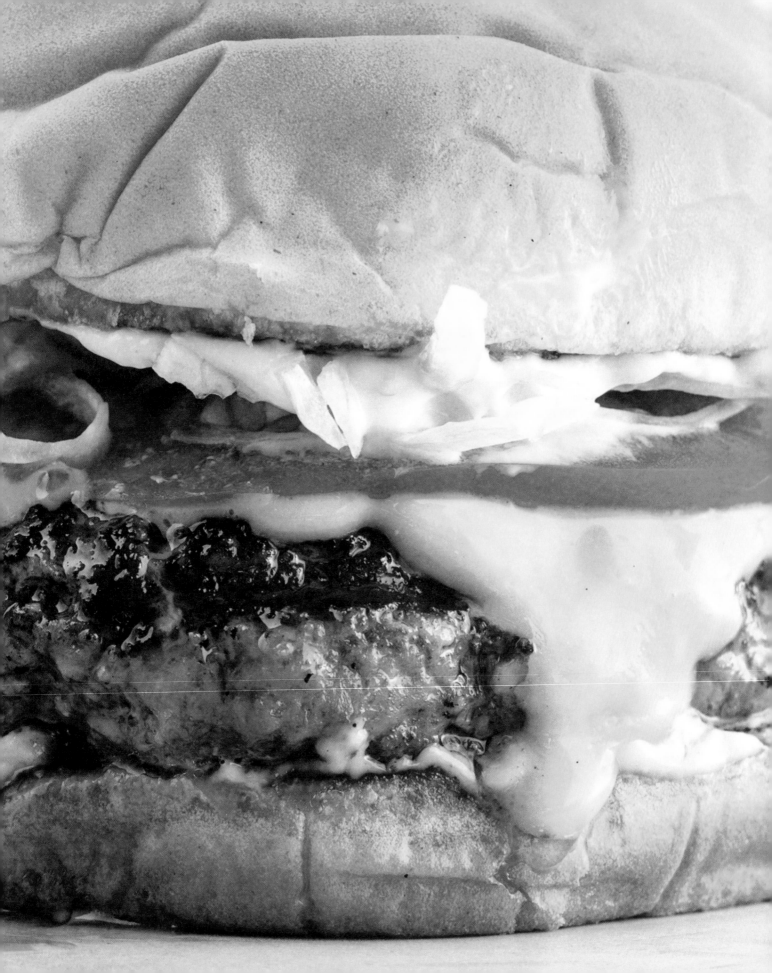

Steps to a Better BURGER

① GREAT MEAT EQUALS GREAT FLAVOR

It all starts with the meat. Look for freshly ground chuck with a ratio of **80 percent meat to 20 percent fat.** This magic formula will yield you a juicy, delicious burger—but not one that's so fatty you'll start a bonfire on the grill.

Why 20 percent? Because fat equals flavor. It's that simple.

② MAKE THE PATTY— GENTLY

Pack the meat *loosely*, just enough that it holds together.

Press the meat gently between your palms to **form a patty about ¾ inch thick.** This results in a nice char on the outside, and makes a burger sturdy enough to shore up the toppings but not so tall that it won't fit in your mouth.

Before placing it on the grill, make a small indentation in the center with your thumb. This prevents it from contracting and forming a bulge in the middle.

③ GRILL OVER MEDIUM TO HIGH HEAT

Three to 4 minutes per side is all it should take to cook a ¾-inch-thick burger to medium-rare.

Use a 2-zone fire (see page 15) so that you can slide the burger over to the cooler side of the grill if you get flare-ups.

While the burger is cooking, resist the urge to press it with your spatula. That does nothing for your burger except squeeze out the juices that make it so tasty. Turn the burger once, and no more.

④ GOING FOR CHEESE? GO ALL-AMERICAN

There's nothing we like better on a burger than **a slice of plain old American cheese,** straight out of the cellophane wrapper. It's fine if you want to get creative here—with cheddar, Swiss, Gorgonzola. But for classic melty, gooey goodness, seeping into the crags of the patty and merging with the special sauce, nothing beats American.

Whichever cheese you use, add it *after* you flip the patty.

⑤ THE BUN: WE SAY POTATO

You want a bun that's moist, soft, and—okay, we'll say it—squishy.

We love **potato rolls, because they complement the beefy flavor** of the burger without getting in the way. They make the burger the star and add a touch of sweetness that is a great foil for salty, savory beef.

There you have it: the classic burger. On the following pages, you'll find plenty of variations—because sometimes you want a little burger razzle-dazzle. And when you don't, you know what to do.

JALAPEÑO CHEESEBURGERS
with Bacon

SPICY RANCH SAUCE

- 4 scallions, finely chopped
- 1 cup mayonnaise
- 1 cup sour cream
- ½ cup chopped fresh cilantro
- 6 Tbsp. fresh lime juice
- 2 Tbsp. minced seeded jalapeño
- ½ tsp. cayenne pepper
  Kosher salt and freshly ground black pepper

BURGERS

- 2 lb. ground beef (20% fat)
- 1 small onion, chopped (about 1¼ cups)
- ¼ cup chopped flat-leaf parsley
- 2 Tbsp. Worcestershire sauce
- 1 Tbsp. chopped seeded jalapeño
- 1 tsp. freshly ground black pepper
- 1 tsp. kosher salt
- ¼ tsp. cayenne pepper

WORCESTERSHIRE-COFFEE GLAZE

- ⅓ cup light corn syrup
- 2 Tbsp. ketchup
- 2 Tbsp. Worcestershire sauce
- 2 tsp. (packed) light brown sugar
- 1 tsp. instant coffee powder
- 3 Tbsp. unsalted butter
  Kosher salt and freshly ground black pepper
- 16 slices bacon
  Vegetable oil, for brushing
- 8 hamburger buns or 3- to 4-inch square focaccia rolls, split horizontally
- 8 lettuce leaves
- 2 cups coarsely shredded sharp white cheddar (about 8 oz.)
  Assorted additional toppings (such as tomato and grilled onion slices)

If you're a chile hound, here's one for you. Chopped jalapeño is blended straight into the burgers (if you want to amp up the heat even more, include some of the seeds) and gives spice to the spicy ranch sauce. The burgers gain another layer of flavor from a Worcestershire-coffee glaze that gets brushed on while they grill.

SAUCE

Whisk first 7 ingredients in a medium bowl to blend. Season sauce with salt and pepper.

BURGERS

Gently mix all ingredients in a large bowl. Form mixture into eight ½- to ¾-inch-thick patties. Using your thumb, make a small indentation in the center of each. Place on a small baking sheet. Cover and chill for at least 2 hours and up to 1 day.

GLAZE

Stir first 5 ingredients in a small saucepan over medium heat until coffee is dissolved. Remove from heat. Whisk in butter. Season glaze to taste with salt and pepper.

Working in batches if necessary, cook bacon in a large skillet over medium-high heat until crisp and brown. Transfer bacon to paper towels to drain.

Build a medium-hot fire in a charcoal grill, or heat a gas grill to high. Brush grill grate with oil. Toast buns until golden, about 2 minutes per side. Transfer buns, cut side up, to plates. Place lettuce on each bun bottom. Grill burgers for 2 to 3 minutes, basting with glaze. Turn burgers and baste with glaze. Press cheese atop each burger. Grill until cooked to desired doneness, 2 to 3 minutes longer for medium-rare. Spread some sauce on buns and assemble burgers, topping each with 2 slices bacon and additional toppings as desired.

ROQUEFORT BURGERS

with Cabernet Reduction

CABERNET REDUCTION

- 6 oz. applewood-smoked bacon, cut crosswise into thin slices
- 2 large onions, chopped
- 4 cups Cabernet Sauvignon
- 4 cups low-sodium beef broth
- 1 cup ruby Port
- 2 tsp. finely chopped fresh thyme

BURGERS

- 3 lb. coarsely ground high-quality boneless beef chuck roast
- 2 tsp. freshly cracked black pepper, more as needed
- 2 tsp. kosher salt, more as needed
- 2 tsp. minced fresh thyme
  Vegetable oil, for brushing
- 4 oz. crumbled Roquefort (about 1 cup)
- 4 oz. grated Gruyère (about 1 cup)
  Butter
- 8 round ciabatta rolls, country-style buns, or focaccia squares, split horizontally
- 3 cups arugula (about 2 oz.)

This over-the-top creation features haute French components—Roquefort, Gruyère, and a jam-like Cabernet reduction rich with bacon, onions, and red wine. It's all balanced out nicely with peppery arugula.

CABERNET REDUCTION

Cook bacon in a large heavy saucepan over medium heat until crisp, about 8 minutes. Using a slotted spoon, transfer bacon to a small bowl. Add onions to pan drippings and cook over low heat, stirring often, until caramelized, about 45 minutes. Add wine and all remaining ingredients and simmer, stirring occasionally, until mixture is very thick and almost jam-like and reduced to 1½ cups, about 1 hour. Stir in reserved crisped bacon. **DO AHEAD:** Can be made 2 days ahead. Cover and refrigerate; rewarm before using.

BURGERS

Build a medium-hot fire in a charcoal grill, or heat a gas grill to high. Gently mix first 4 ingredients in a large bowl. Shape beef mixture into eight ¾-inch-thick patties. Using your thumb, make a small indentation in the center of each.Season patties with additional salt and pepper, if desired. Brush grill grate with oil. Grill patties until brown on bottom and almost halfway cooked through, about 3 minutes. Turn over and top each patty with crumbled Roquefort and grated Gruyère. Grill until cheeses melt and burgers are cooked to desired doneness, about 3 minutes for medium-rare.

Meanwhile, lightly butter cut sides of rolls. Grill rolls, cut side down, until lightly toasted and golden, about 2 minutes. Assemble burgers, spooning 3 Tbsp. Cabernet reduction over each and topping with arugula.

HOW TO: TAKE YOUR TOPPINGS OVER THE TOP

When planning toppings for your burgers, you'll never go wrong with a platter of stand-bys: peak-season tomatoes, slices of onion, and some relish. But sometimes, you want to get creative. When that time comes, here's what to make.

Sweet Cucumber Relish

makes about 7 cups

⅓ cup kosher salt
2½ cups ¼-inch cubes seeded peeled cucumbers (from 2 large)
¾ lb. pickling cucumbers, scrubbed, cut into ¼-inch cubes
3 cups finely chopped onions
3 cups sugar
1½ cups distilled white vinegar
1 cup finely chopped cored unpeeled Granny Smith apple
¾ cup finely chopped celery
¼ cup chopped red bell pepper
¼ cup mustard seeds
6 Tbsp. dry mustard
¼ cup all-purpose flour
2½ tsp. turmeric

Relish takes on unexpected and delicious notes with the addition of apple, celery, mustard, and turmeric. Note that the cucumbers need to brine overnight. Besides adding oomph to burgers, this relish also pairs well with hot dogs, ham, deviled eggs, and meatloaf.

Mix salt and 3 cups boiling water in a large heatproof glass bowl. Stir in cucumbers and onions. Cover; refrigerate overnight.

Drain cucumber mixture. Rinse; drain again. Place in a large heavy nonreactive pot. Add sugar, vinegar, apple, celery, bell pepper, and mustard seeds. Bring to a boil over medium-high heat, stirring until sugar dissolves. Simmer, stirring often, until cucumbers are crisp-tender and liquid is reduced to syrup, about 10 minutes.

Mix dry mustard, flour, and turmeric in a small bowl. Gradually add ¾ cup water, whisking until smooth. Whisk mustard paste into cucumber mixture; return to a boil, stirring often. Boil gently, stirring often, until cucumbers are translucent and relish thickens, about 15 minutes. Let cool for 1 hour. Cover; chill. **DO AHEAD:** Can be made up to 2 months ahead. Store in refrigerator.

Balsamic-Marinated Tomatoes

8 servings

4 large tomatoes, cut into ½-inch-thick slices
Kosher salt and freshly ground black pepper
1½ Tbsp. balsamic vinegar
¼ cup chopped fresh basil

The richness of balsamic vinegar intensifies the sweet flavor of thick-cut tomatoes.

Arrange tomato slices in a single layer in a 13x9x2-inch glass dish. Season sliced tomatoes with salt and pepper, then balsamic vinegar and chopped basil. Let stand for at least 1 hour and up to 3 hours, turning tomato slices once.

Caramelized Onions

3 Tbsp. extra-virgin olive oil
3 large onions, thickly sliced
   Kosher salt and freshly ground
   black pepper

Onion slices are sautéed in olive oil until silky and tender. We recommend making a double batch while you're at it, to store in the fridge and add to sandwiches or pastas, or mix into rice the next day.

Heat oil in a large heavy skillet over medium-low heat. Add onions and cook, stirring occasionally, until tender and pale golden, about 35 minutes. Continue to cook, stirring often and adding a splash of water if onions begin to burn, until deeply caramelized, about 10 minutes more. Season onions to taste with salt and pepper. **DO AHEAD:** Can be made 1 day ahead. Cover and chill. Rewarm before serving.

Special Sauce

makes about 1 cup

½ cup mayonnaise
2 Tbsp. ketchup
1 Tbsp. finely grated onion
1 Tbsp. sweet relish or dill
   pickle relish
2 tsp. adobo sauce from canned
   chipotle chiles in adobo
⅛ tsp. celery salt
⅛ tsp. kosher salt

When ketchup meets mayonnaise—and adobo sauce—magic happens. Earn bonus points by bringing a jar of this sauce to the next cookout you attend. If your supermarket doesn't carry chipotle chiles in adobo, look for them at Latin markets.

Combine all ingredients in a medium bowl and serve with burgers. **DO AHEAD:** Can be made 3 days ahead. Store in refrigerator.

BUILD A BETTER BURGER
Turkey and Chicken

Turkey and chicken are ideal choices when you're hungry for a healthy burger. There's a world of flavor options, because they go with just about everything. The challenge here is keeping them moist—they need to be cooked through for food safety reasons but you don't want them to dry out. To make sure you're getting the most of them, keep these three things in mind:

❶ GO DARK. Always use ground dark meat. Lean white turkey or chicken tends to get dry when cooked through. **❷** If ground dark meat isn't available, **ADD SOME FAT** by mixing in chopped bacon or a spoonful of rendered chicken fat or mayonnaise with ground white meat. **❸ WATCH THE CLOCK.** A ¾-inch-thick burger needs just 4 to 5 minutes per side over medium-high to high heat.

TURKEY BURGERS
with Cheddar and Aioli

makes 4

½ tsp. coriander seeds
½ tsp. cumin seeds
½ cup mayonnaise
2 Tbsp. extra-virgin olive oil, plus more for brushing
2 tsp. fresh lemon juice
1½ tsp. smoked paprika
1 garlic clove, pressed
    Kosher salt and freshly ground black pepper
1 lb. ground dark-meat turkey
4 ⅓-inch-thick slices red onion
1 large or 2 small red bell peppers, quartered
4 slices white cheddar or Monterey Jack
4 sesame seed hamburger buns, sliced
    Arugula leaves
    Pickle wedges
    Corn chips

A simple aioli, made with store-bought mayonnaise and given complexity with toasted spices and smoked paprika, works two ways here: It's mixed with the ground meat to create a moist and juicy patty, then spooned atop the burger to add great flavor.

Toast coriander seeds and cumin seeds in a small skillet over medium-high heat until aromatic and slightly darker in color, shaking skillet often, about 1½ minutes. Let cool. Finely grind toasted seeds in a spice mill or clean coffee grinder, or with a mortar and pestle. Whisk mayonnaise, 2 Tbsp. extra-virgin olive oil, lemon juice, smoked paprika, garlic, and ground spices in a small bowl. Season aioli to taste with salt and pepper. **DO AHEAD:** Aioli can be made 1 day ahead. Cover and refrigerate.

   Place turkey in a medium bowl. Add 2 Tbsp. aioli; mix gently. With wet hands, divide turkey mixture into 4 equal portions, then form each into a scant ¾-inch-thick patty, about 3½ inches in diameter. Using your thumb, make a small indentation in the center of each patty. **DO AHEAD:** Can be made 4 hours ahead. Cover and refrigerate.

   Build a medium-hot fire in a charcoal grill, or heat a gas grill to high. Brush grill grate with oil. Season burgers with salt and pepper. Brush onion slices and bell pepper pieces with oil; season with salt and pepper. Grill onions and bell peppers until soft and charred, about 4 minutes per side.

   Grill turkey burgers for 5 minutes. Turn over; grill until almost cooked through, about 4 minutes. Top each burger with 1 cheese slice and grill until meat is cooked through and cheese is melted, about 1 minute longer. Assemble burgers, topping each with grilled red pepper pieces and grilled onion slices, a dollop of aioli, and some arugula. Serve with pickle wedges and corn chips.

BOMBAY SLIDERS
with Garlic Curry Sauce

makes 12

GARLIC-CURRY SAUCE
- ¾ cup mayonnaise
- 2¼ tsp. curry powder
- 1½ Tbsp. plain yogurt
- 1½ Tbsp. ketchup
- 1 garlic clove, minced

SLIDERS
- 2 lb. ground dark-meat turkey
- ¼ cup mayonnaise
- 6 Tbsp. chopped fresh cilantro
- ¼ cup minced scallions
- 2 Tbsp. minced peeled ginger
- 4 tsp. curry powder
- 2 tsp. ground cumin
- ¾ tsp. hot chili powder or Hungarian hot paprika
- 1 tsp. kosher salt
  Vegetable oil, for brushing
- 12 small dinner rolls, sliced

These little burgers pack a punch. Cilantro, cumin, chili powder, and fresh ginger go right into the patties, and the grilled burgers are topped with a vibrant garlic-curry sauce. Though the flavors are complex, the burgers are quick to make—and to eat. Plan on three sliders per person for a main course, and serve them with toppings like fresh tomato, red onion, and cucumber slices.

SAUCE
Combine all ingredients in a small bowl. Let stand at room temperature while preparing sliders.

SLIDERS
Place first 9 ingredients in a large bowl. Mix with a fork or your hands until just blended (do not overmix). Divide mixture into 12 equal portions. With wet hands, form each portion into a patty about ½ inch thick. Using your thumb, make a small indentation in center of each patty.

Build a medium-hot fire in a charcoal grill, or heat a gas grill to high. Brush grill grate with oil. Grill patties until cooked through, about 3 minutes per side. Grill rolls, cut side down, for about 1 minute.

Assemble sliders, topping each with sauce. Place 3 sliders on each of 4 plates.

CHICKEN BURGERS
with Basil Mayonnaise

makes 4

- 1 cup mayonnaise
- 1¼ cups chopped fresh basil, plus 8 large leaves, divided
- 3 Tbsp. chopped drained cornichons or dill pickle, plus 1½ Tbsp. brine from jar
- 2 scallions, finely chopped
  Kosher salt and freshly ground black pepper
- 1¼ lb. ground chicken, preferably dark meat
- 4 hamburger buns, sliced
  Extra-virgin olive oil, for brushing
- 4 ⅓-inch-thick slices large red or orange heirloom tomato

Chopped basil, cornichons, and scallions turn store-bought mayonnaise into a fragrant basil mayo in these chicken-burger sandwiches.

Build a medium fire in a charcoal grill, or heat a gas grill to medium-high. Mix mayonnaise, 1 cup chopped basil, cornichons, brine, and scallions in a small bowl. Season basil mayonnaise to taste with salt and pepper.

Mix chicken and ½ cup basil mayonnaise in a large bowl. With wet hands, shape chicken mixture into four ½-inch-thick patties. Using your thumb, make a small indentation in center of each patty. Season with salt and pepper. Brush cut sides of buns with oil.

Brush grill grate with oil. Grill buns until crisp and golden, about 1 minute. Transfer to plates. Grill burgers until firm to the touch and cooked through, about 5 minutes per side.

Spread bottom halves of buns thickly with basil mayonnaise. Assemble burgers, topping each with tomato, 2 basil leaves, and a dollop of basil mayonnaise. Garnish with remaining ¼ cup chopped basil.

For the juiciest, most flavorful turkey burger, **always start with ground dark meat.**

TURKEY BURGERS
WITH TOMATO JAM, OLIVES, AND FETA

TURKEY BURGERS

With Tomato Jam, Olives, and Feta

makes 4

photo, left

- 1 lb. ground dark-meat turkey
- ⅔ cup finely chopped red onion
- ⅓ cup crumbled feta (about 2 oz.), plus more for topping
- 3 Tbsp. coarsely chopped pitted Kalamata olives (about 6), plus more for topping
- 1½ tsp. extra-virgin olive oil, plus more for brushing
- 1 small garlic clove, minced
- ½ tsp. chopped fresh rosemary
- ½ tsp. (generous) kosher salt, more as needed
- ½ tsp. (generous) freshly ground black pepper, more as needed
- 4 hamburger buns, sliced
  Tomato Jam (recipe follows)

Adding feta to the ground turkey patties here enhances the meat's texture and adds zing. Try this with lamb burgers, too.

Build a medium-hot fire in a charcoal grill, or heat a gas grill to high. Gently mix turkey, onion, ⅓ cup feta, 3 Tbsp. olives, 1½ tsp. olive oil, garlic, rosemary, generous ½ tsp. salt, and generous ½ tsp. pepper in a medium bowl. Form into 4 patties, each about 1 inch thick. Using your thumb, make a small indentation in the center of each patty. Brush with oil and season with salt and pepper.

Brush grill grate with oil. Grill burgers until charred on both sides and cooked through, about 5 minutes per side. Grill cut side of buns until toasted, about 2 minutes. Assemble burgers with Tomato Jam and additional feta and chopped olives.

Tomato Jam

makes 2 ¼ cups

use with
turkey burgers

- 1 Tbsp. extra-virgin olive oil
- 1 cup (scant) finely chopped onion
- 1 garlic clove, minced
- 2 14-oz. cans diced tomatoes with juices
- 1 Tbsp. sugar
- ½ tsp. dried thyme
- ½ tsp. kosher salt
- ¼ tsp. freshly ground black pepper

This recipe makes more jam than you'll need for the burgers. We recommend using whatever you have left over as a sandwich spread or as a condiment with grilled or roast meat.

Heat oil in a medium saucepan over medium heat. Add onion and garlic; cook, stirring often, until onion is soft and translucent, about 4 minutes. Add diced tomatoes with juices, sugar, thyme, salt, and pepper. Cook over medium-high heat, stirring occasionally, until almost all liquid has evaporated and mixture is reduced to about 2¼ cups, about 10 minutes. Let cool. **DO AHEAD:** Can be made 2 weeks ahead. Cover and chill.

BUILD A BETTER BURGER
Lamb and Pork

To make great **lamb burgers**, start with good-quality ground lamb—leg of lamb or lamb shoulder work best. The assertive flavor of this protein calls for bold seasonings, so be generous with the salt and pepper. As you'll see in this section, lamb also benefits from Middle Eastern and Indian spices, such as cumin, coriander, and curry, and herbs like rosemary and oregano.

Thanks to a healthy fat content, **pork burgers** are packed with natural flavor. Using ground pork from the supermarket is fine, but if you want to elevate things, ask the butcher for ground pork shoulder.

CURRIED LAMB BURGERS
with Mint Raita

makes 6

A refreshing mint *raita*, the Indian yogurt-based sauce, is a cool counterpoint to these curry-spiced burgers. Thinly sliced grilled zucchini and scallions offer a nice texture contrast—but you can skip the veggies if you want, and focus on the burger.

RAITA

- 1 cup plain whole-milk yogurt (preferably Greek)
- 3 Tbsp. chopped fresh mint
- 2 Tbsp. chopped fresh cilantro
- 1¼ tsp. finely grated lime zest
  Kosher salt and freshly ground black pepper

BURGERS

- 4 Tbsp. extra-virgin olive oil, divided, plus more for brushing
- 1¼ cups chopped onion
- 2 Tbsp. minced peeled ginger
- 2 tsp. kosher salt, divided
- 2 tsp. Madras curry powder
- 1¾ lb. ground lamb
- 3 Tbsp. chopped fresh cilantro
- 1½ tsp. freshly ground black pepper, divided
- 3 medium zucchini (about 12 oz.), cut lengthwise into ¼-inch-thick slices (optional)
- 6 scallions, trimmed (optional)
- 6 small naans (Indian flatbreads; about 6 inches long) or pita breads
- 1 large tomato, thinly sliced

RAITA

Mix yogurt, mint, cilantro, and lime zest in a small bowl. Season to taste with salt and pepper. Cover; chill until cold, at least 30 minutes and up to 4 hours.

BURGERS

Heat 2 Tbsp. oil in a large skillet over medium heat. Add onion, ginger, and ½ tsp. salt. Sauté until onion is tender, about 8 minutes. Mix in curry powder and stir for 30 seconds. Remove from heat. Let onion mixture cool to room temperature, at least 15 minutes.

Place lamb in a large bowl. Add onion mixture, 1 tsp. salt, cilantro, and 1 tsp. cracked pepper. Blend mixture gently; shape into six ½-inch-thick patties. Using your thumb, make a small indentation in the center of each patty.

Build a medium-hot fire in a charcoal grill, or heat a gas grill to high. If using, combine zucchini and scallions in another large bowl. Add 2 Tbsp. oil, remaining ½ tsp. salt, and ½ tsp. cracked pepper; toss to coat. Brush grill grate with oil. Place vegetables and burgers on grill. Cook until grill marks appear, about 4 minutes. Turn vegetables and burgers over. Cook vegetables until tender, about 3 minutes. Cook burgers to desired doneness, 3 to 4 minutes longer for medium-rare. Brush naan with olive oil; grill briefly. Cut zucchini and scallions crosswise into 2-inch-long pieces.

Place naans on plates; top with burgers and tomato slices. Mound vegetables on burgers; spoon a dollop of raita over each. Fold naan up around burgers and serve with remaining raita.

PORK-MUSHROOM BURGER
LETTUCE WRAPS

makes 18

BURGERS AND SAUCE

- 2 Tbsp. canola oil or peanut oil
- 2 Tbsp. minced lemongrass (from bottom 3 inches of about 4 stalks)
- 2 garlic cloves, minced
- 4 oz. fresh shiitake mushrooms, stemmed, caps chopped
- 1 tsp. kosher salt, divided
- 1¾ lb. ground pork shoulder (preferably Boston butt)
- 2 Tbsp. soy sauce, divided
- 3 tsp. toasted sesame oil, divided
- ¾ tsp. coarsely cracked black peppercorns
- ½ cup hoisin sauce
- 1 Tbsp. minced peeled ginger
- 1 Tbsp. unseasoned rice vinegar
- 1 tsp. Sriracha
  Vegetable oil, for brushing

TOPPINGS

- 2 heads of Bibb lettuce, cored, leaves separated
- 1 cup matchstick-size strips red bell pepper
- 1 cup matchstick-size strips peeled carrot
- ⅓ cup fresh cilantro leaves

INGREDIENT INFO Lemongrass is sold in the produce section of some supermarkets and at Asian markets. Hoisin sauce and Sriracha are available in the Asian foods section of many supermarkets and at Asian markets.

These mushroom-studded pork patties are flavored with soy, Sriracha, and lemongrass, and are served in the manner of Asian lettuce wraps. The recipe yields 18 burgers, or about 3 per person. Encourage your guests to wrap their burgers in the lettuce leaves and then doctor as desired with hoisin-ginger sauce and thin strips of bell pepper and carrot for extra crunch.

BURGERS AND SAUCE

Heat canola oil in a large skillet over medium-high heat. Add lemongrass and garlic; sauté for 2 minutes. Add mushrooms. Sprinkle with ½ tsp. salt; sauté until mushrooms are tender, about 4 minutes. Remove from heat; let cool in skillet.

Place pork in a large bowl. Mix in 1 Tbsp. soy sauce, 1 tsp. sesame oil, cracked pepper, and remaining ½ tsp. salt, then fold in mushroom mixture. Using 2 generous tablespoonfuls for each, shape into 18 patties, each about 2¼ inches in diameter. Using your thumb, make a small indentation in the center of each patty. Arrange on a plastic-lined baking sheet.

Whisk hoisin sauce, ginger, vinegar, Sriracha, remaining 1 Tbsp. soy sauce, and remaining 2 tsp. sesame oil in a small bowl for sauce. **DO AHEAD:** Burgers and sauce can be made 6 hours ahead. Cover separately; chill.

Build a medium-hot fire in a charcoal grill, or heat a gas grill to high. Brush grill grate with vegetable oil. Grill burgers until cooked through, about 3 minutes per side. Arrange burgers on a platter; set out sauce.

TOPPINGS

Place lettuce, bell pepper, carrot, and cilantro in separate bowls. Have guests wrap burgers in lettuce and add sauce and vegetables as desired.

+

Regular hamburgers
just need salt and
pepper. But **lamb
burgers love assertive
seasonings,** via fresh
herbs and spices.

LAMB BURGERS
WITH MOROCCAN SPICES AND ORANGE SALSA

LAMB BURGERS
with Moroccan Spices and Orange Salsa

photo, left

Subtly spiced with cumin, paprika, jalapeño, and cilantro, these tender lamb burgers get a nice boost from a bright-tasting salsa made with beets instead of tomatoes.

SALSA

- 2 Tbsp. fresh lemon juice
- 2 Tbsp. extra-virgin olive oil
- 1 Tbsp. honey
- 2 beets, boiled, peeled, cut into ⅓-inch cubes
- 1 large orange, peel and pith cut away, flesh cut into ⅓-inch cubes
- 1 cup chopped red onion
- ¼ cup chopped pitted green Greek olives

  Kosher salt and freshly ground black pepper

BURGERS

- 1 large shallot, minced
- 2 Tbsp. chopped fresh cilantro
- 1 jalapeño, seeded, minced
- 1 garlic clove, minced
- 1¼ tsp. kosher salt
- ¾ tsp. freshly ground black pepper
- ½ tsp. paprika
- ½ tsp. ground cumin
- 1¾ lb. ground lamb

  Vegetable oil, for brushing
- 4 large cracked-wheat or sesame seed hamburger buns, sliced
- 1⅓ cups thinly sliced Bibb lettuce

  Mayonnaise

SALSA

Whisk first 3 ingredients in a medium bowl to blend. Mix in next 4 ingredients. Season salsa to taste with salt and pepper. **DO AHEAD:** Can be made 8 hours ahead. Cover and chill.

BURGERS

Stir shallot, cilantro, jalapeño, garlic, salt, pepper, paprika, and cumin in a large bowl to blend. Add lamb and mix gently to combine. Shape mixture into four ½-inch-thick patties. Using your thumb, make a small indentation in the center of each patty. Arrange on a small baking sheet. **DO AHEAD:** Can be made 8 hours ahead. Cover and chill.

Build a medium-hot fire in a charcoal grill, or heat a gas grill to high. Brush grill grate with oil. Grill buns, cut side down, until golden, about 2 minutes; transfer to a work surface. Grill burgers until slightly charred and cooked to desired doneness, 3 to 4 minutes per side for medium-rare. Place lettuce and a large spoonful of salsa on each bun bottom. Top each with burger, mayonnaise, and bun top. Serve with remaining salsa.

BUILD A BETTER BURGER
Salmon and Tuna

The perfect fish burgers start with **super-fresh, super-cold fish** that you've chopped yourself at home. Look for the freshest skinless fillets you can find. When they're fresh, they won't smell like fish, but rather sweet and of the sea. If you like your seafood rare, buy sushi-grade fish.

To chop fish, **freeze it for 15 minutes first.** This will make it easier to work with. If you're using a food processor or the grinding attachment on a stand mixer, cut the fish into 1-inch cubes and freeze them in a single layer; freeze the grinding attachments, too. The fish should be chopped finely, but not to a paste. Then grill the burgers on a clean, well-oiled grill—otherwise, seafood will stick to the grate.

SALMON BURGERS
with Dill Tartar Sauce

makes 2

photo, right

10 oz. chilled skinless salmon fillets, cut into 1-inch pieces
3 Tbsp. plus ½ cup store-bought tartar sauce
2 Tbsp. chopped fresh dill, divided
¼ tsp. kosher salt
¼ tsp. freshly ground black pepper
    Vegetable oil, for brushing
1 tsp. finely grated lemon zest
2 sesame seed buns, sliced
    Red onion slices
4 Bibb lettuce leaves

Tartar sauce, particularly when enlivened with fresh dill and lemon zest, is just the thing to create succulent, flavorful salmon burgers. To make the burgers easy to handle, chill them for at least an hour before putting them on the grill.

Pulse salmon fillets, 3 Tbsp. tartar sauce, 1 Tbsp. dill, salt, and pepper in a food processor until coarsely ground. Form into two ½-inch-thick patties. **DO AHEAD:** Can be made 6 hours ahead. Cover and refrigerate.

Build a medium-hot fire in a charcoal grill, or heat a gas grill to high. Brush grill grate with oil. Whisk remaining ½ cup tartar sauce, 1 Tbsp. dill, and zest in a medium bowl to blend.

Grill buns, cut side down, until toasted, about 1 minute. Transfer to plates and spread bottom halves generously with sauce. Grill patties until fish is cooked through, about 2 minutes per side. Place burgers atop sauce on rolls. Top each with onion slices, 2 lettuce leaves, and the top half of roll. Serve, passing remaining sauce separately.

+

Unlike other kinds of protein, **fish needs to be kept cold** until the moment you put it on the grill. This helps hold it together while cooking.

SALMON BURGERS
WITH DILL TARTAR SAUCE

SALMON BURGERS
with Lemon and Capers

makes 10

¼ cup extra-virgin olive oil, plus
    more for brushing
1 cup chopped shallots (about
    3 large)
1 cup dry white wine
½ cup fresh lemon juice
1 4-oz. jar capers, drained, chopped
2 lb. chilled skinless salmon fillets,
    cut into 1-inch pieces, any bones
    removed
3 cups fresh breadcrumbs made
    from French bread
2 large eggs, beaten
3 Tbsp. chopped fresh dill
1½ tsp. kosher salt
¾ tsp. freshly ground black pepper
10 hamburger buns, sliced
    Mayonnaise
    Lettuce leaves
    Tomato slices

Classic salmon accompaniments—shallots, white wine, lemon juice, capers, and dill—are blended into this burger. Egg and breadcrumbs bind the mix to ensure that the patties hold together on the grill.

Heat ¼ cup oil in a medium heavy skillet over medium heat. Add shallots and sauté until translucent, about 4 minutes. Increase heat to medium-high. Add wine, lemon juice, and drained capers and cook until almost all liquid evaporates, about 12 minutes. Transfer shallot mixture to a large bowl. Refrigerate until well chilled, about 1 hour.

Pulse salmon fillets in a food processor until coarsely ground. Add ground salmon to shallot mixture. Mix in fresh breadcrumbs, beaten eggs, dill, salt, and pepper. Form salmon mixture into 10 patties, dividing equally. **DO AHEAD:** Salmon patties can be prepared 6 hours ahead. Transfer to a baking sheet, then cover with plastic wrap and refrigerate.

Build a medium-hot fire in a charcoal grill, or heat a gas grill to high. Brush grill grate with oil. Grill patties until golden brown and cooked through, about 2 minutes per side. Grill buns for about 1 minute. Serve salmon burgers on buns with mayonnaise, lettuce leaves, and tomato slices.

TUNA BURGERS
with Tapenade and Tomatoes

makes 6

TAPENADE
1 cup pitted Kalamata olives
3 Tbsp. extra-virgin olive oil
2 Tbsp. chopped shallot
2 Tbsp. chopped fresh mint
2 tsp. chopped fresh thyme
2 tsp. fresh lemon juice
    Kosher salt and freshly ground
      black pepper
BURGERS
2 lb. chilled tuna steaks, finely diced
2 Tbsp. chopped drained capers
2 Tbsp. chopped shallot
1 Tbsp. Dijon mustard
1 tsp. freshly ground black pepper
1 tsp. minced fresh thyme
¾ tsp. kosher salt
    Vegetable oil, for brushing
6 hamburger buns
6 slices heirloom tomato

Think of this as *salade niçoise* in burger form. Tuna patties are stuffed with capers, shallot, mustard, and thyme; the olives appear as an herby tapenade that's spread on the buns. Thin red onion slices and some arugula would be good, too. Refrigerating the patties before cooking them keeps them super fresh and prevents the burgers from falling apart on the grill.

TAPENADE
Blend first 6 ingredients in a mini food processor to a coarse purée. Season tapenade to taste with salt and pepper. Transfer to a small bowl. **DO AHEAD:** Can be made 3 days ahead. Cover and chill.

BURGERS
Gently mix diced tuna and next 6 ingredients in a large bowl. With wet hands, shape tuna mixture into six ¾-inch-thick patties (each about 4 inches in diameter). Place burgers on a plate. Cover and refrigerate for at least 1 hour and up to 1 day.

Build a medium-hot fire in a charcoal grill, or heat a gas grill to high. Brush grill grate with oil. Grill burgers until almost cooked through, about 4 minutes per side. Grill buns for about 1 minute.

Spread tapenade on bun bottoms. Assemble burgers, topping each with tomato slice.

BUILD A BETTER BURGER
veggie

Black beans, chickpeas, corn—there are lots of different ways to create moist, flavorful homemade veggie burgers. Here are a few things to keep in mind for foolproof cooking. First, mix all the ingredients thoroughly so they'll stick together in burger form. Second, veggie burgers have almost no fat to speak of—and they *will* stick to the grill if the grate isn't cleaned thoroughly and oiled generously. Finally, after you place the burger over the flames, leave it alone for a while. Don't touch it or try to flip it over until it begins to release from the grill grate on its own.

JALAPEÑO-BEAN BURGERS

makes 4

These satisfying vegetarian patties don't pretend to be beef. Instead, with their combination of bold ingredients—jalapeño, kidney beans, onion, garlic—they are reminiscent of vegetarian chili.

BURGERS

- 1 tsp. vegetable oil, plus more for brushing
- ½ cup finely chopped onion
- ½ cup chopped seeded plum tomato
- 1 tsp. minced jalapeño
- 1 garlic clove, minced
- 1 tsp. chili powder
- 1 15- to 16-oz. can kidney beans, rinsed, well drained
- ¼ cup dry breadcrumbs
- 2 Tbsp. store-bought barbecue sauce, divided
- 1 large egg white, beaten
- 4 whole grain hamburger buns, sliced

TOPPINGS

- 4 Tbsp. store-bought barbecue sauce
- 4 Tbsp. grated cheddar
- 4 lettuce leaves
- 4 tomato slices

BURGERS

Heat 1 tsp. oil in a medium nonstick skillet over medium heat. Add next 5 ingredients; sauté for 5 minutes. Let cool slightly. Using a fork, coarsely mash beans in a medium bowl. Mix in onion mixture, breadcrumbs, barbecue sauce, and egg white. Shape mixture into four ½-inch-thick patties.

DO AHEAD: Can be prepared 4 hours ahead. Cover and chill.

Build a medium fire in a charcoal grill, or heat a gas grill to medium-high. Brush grill grate with oil. Lightly brush patties on both sides with oil. Place patties on grill and cook until golden brown and heated through, about 3 minutes per side. Grill buns, cut side down, for about 1 minute.

TOPPINGS

Assemble burgers, topping each with 1 Tbsp. barbecue sauce, cheese, lettuce, and tomatoes.

CHICKPEA AND TAHINI BURGERS

This meatless chickpea burger is a close cousin to the falafel sandwich, all the way down to the spiced yogurt sauce that's drizzled over the top. The ingredients don't require any precooking, so the patties are quick to make. Serve them in pita pockets or on their own with a salad alongside.

BURGERS

- 1 15- to 16-oz. can chickpeas (garbanzo beans), rinsed, drained, divided
- 3 Tbsp. minced red onion
- 3 Tbsp. chopped fresh dill
- 2½ Tbsp. dry breadcrumbs
- 1½ Tbsp. fresh lemon juice
- 1 large egg white
- 1 Tbsp. tahini (sesame seed paste)
- 2 garlic cloves
  Kosher salt and freshly ground black pepper
  Vegetable oil, for brushing

TOPPINGS

- ⅓ cup plain nonfat yogurt
- ½ tsp. hot pepper sauce
- ¼ tsp. ground cumin
- 2 pita bread rounds, warmed, sliced horizontally
- 2 cups shredded romaine lettuce
- 1 cup chopped tomatoes

INGREDIENT INFO Tahini is available at Middle Eastern and natural foods stores and at some supermarkets.

BURGERS

Using a fork, coarsely mash ¾ cup chickpeas in a medium bowl. Mix in onion and next 3 ingredients. Purée remaining chickpeas, egg white, tahini, and garlic in a food processor until almost smooth. Stir into mashed chickpea mixture. Season with salt and pepper. Shape mixture into four ½-inch-thick patties. **DO AHEAD:** Can be made 4 hours ahead. Cover and chill.

Build a medium fire in a charcoal grill, or heat a gas grill to medium-high. Brush grill grate with oil. Lightly brush patties on both sides with oil. Place patties on grill and cook until golden brown and heated through, about 3 minutes per side.

TOPPINGS

Meanwhile, mix yogurt, hot pepper sauce, and cumin in a small bowl. Assemble burgers in pita halves with lettuce, tomatoes, and yogurt sauce.

PORTOBELLO BURGERS
with Piquillo Pepper Aioli and Watercress

AIOLI

½ cup chopped drained piquillo peppers or roasted red peppers from jar

1 Tbsp. Sherry vinegar

2 tsp. finely chopped fresh thyme

1 garlic clove, minced

½ cup mayonnaise

Kosher salt and freshly ground black pepper

Cayenne pepper

BURGERS

6 large portobello mushrooms, stemmed, dark gills scraped out

1 sweet onion (such as Vidalia or Walla Walla), cut into ⅓-inch-thick slices

Extra-virgin olive oil, for brushing

Kosher salt and freshly ground black pepper

2 tsp. chopped fresh thyme

1 large garlic clove, minced

8 oz. Idiazábal or smoked Gouda, rind trimmed, thinly sliced

6 sourdough rolls (each about 4 inches in diameter), sliced horizontally

1 bunch watercress, stems trimmed

A few years back, grilled portobello mushrooms doused with balsamic vinegar overstayed their welcome. But this fantastic Spanish-influenced spin is something completely different. Hearty portobellos provide a great base for aioli made spicy-sweet with roasted piquillo peppers from northern Spain, and for the smoky Basque sheep's-milk cheese, Idiazábal.

AIOLI

Purée first 4 ingredients in a mini food processor. Transfer to a small bowl. Whisk in mayonnaise; season with salt, black pepper, and cayenne. **DO AHEAD:** Can be made 3 days ahead. Cover; chill.

BURGERS

Arrange mushroom caps and onion slices on a baking sheet; brush both sides with oil, then sprinkle with salt, pepper, and thyme. Turn mushrooms gill side up and top with garlic. Let stand for at least 30 minutes and up to 2 hours.

Build a medium-hot fire in a charcoal grill, or heat a gas grill to high. Brush grill grate with oil. Place mushrooms, gill side up, and onion slices on grate. Cook until grill marks appear, about 4 minutes. Turn vegetables over, transferring to the cooler part of grill. Cover and cook until mushrooms are very tender and onion slices still retain some texture, about 8 minutes. Turn mushrooms gill side up; top with cheese. Arrange rolls, cut side down, on grill. Cover; cook until cheese on mushrooms melts and cut sides of rolls are golden, about 1 minute longer.

Spread aioli on grilled rolls and assemble burgers, topping each mushroom with onion slice and watercress.

HOT DOGS + SAUSAGES
Go for the Grilled

Biting into a grilled **hot dog** is one of our favorite rituals of summer. With its split skin and burst of juice, a fresh-off-the-grill dog trumps the watery blandness of a boiled hot dog every time. And then there are **sausages,** which come in so many different varieties now—from the traditional (bratwurst and kielbasa) to the contemporary (sun-dried tomato and basil).

Preparing hot dogs is about as easy as it gets: a few minutes over direct high heat and you're done. Fresh sausages need a little more care—see page 99 for tips.

HOT DOGS
with Mango Chutney Relish

makes 8

1 9-oz. jar mango chutney (such as Major Grey's), any large pieces chopped
½ cup chopped red onion
¼ cup chopped fresh cilantro
1 Tbsp. Dijon mustard, plus more for serving
   Vegetable oil, for brushing
8 all-beef hot dogs
8 hot dog buns

A classic combo—hot dogs and relish—is taken to new heights by creating a zesty relish with red onion, cilantro, and Dijon mustard and adding sweet mango chutney to the mix.

Mix chutney, onion, cilantro, and mustard in a bowl for relish. **DO AHEAD:** Can be made 1 day ahead. Cover; chill.

Build a medium-hot fire in a charcoal grill, or heat a gas grill to high. Brush grill grate with oil. Grill hot dogs and buns until heated through and grill marks form, 2 to 3 minutes per side for hot dogs and about 1 minute per side for buns. Serve hot dogs with mustard and relish.

BEER-BRAISED HOT DOGS
with Sauerkraut

SAUERKRAUT

- 3 cups store-bought refrigerated sauerkraut, rinsed, drained
- ½ cup lager or Pilsner beer
- 1 Tbsp. dark brown sugar
  Freshly ground black pepper

HOT DOGS

- 1 12-oz. bottle lager or Pilsner beer
- 2 Tbsp. sugar
- 6 all-beef hot dogs
  Vegetable oil, for brushing
- 6 hot dog buns
  Mustard

Giving hot dogs a pre-grill bath in a sweetened beer syrup imparts extra flavor— as does adding another dose of beer to the sauerkraut.

SAUERKRAUT
Simmer sauerkraut, beer, and sugar in a large heavy skillet over medium-high heat for 5 minutes. Season to taste with pepper.

HOT DOGS
Build a medium-hot fire in a charcoal grill, or heat a gas grill to high. Bring beer and sugar to a simmer in a medium skillet over medium-low heat. Add hot dogs; simmer until dogs are plump and lightly coated with beer syrup, about 8 minutes. Brush grill grate with oil. Transfer dogs to grill; reserve syrup. Grill hot dogs for 2 to 3 minutes per side and buns for about 1 minute per side.

Top hot dogs with sauerkraut; drizzle with reserved beer syrup. Serve with mustard.

GARLIC MOJO HOT DOGS

- ¼ cup extra-virgin olive oil, plus more for brushing
- 6 garlic cloves, chopped
- 1 tomato, halved, seeded, chopped
- ⅓ cup fresh lime juice
- ⅓ cup fresh orange juice
- ½ tsp. ground cumin
  Kosher salt and freshly ground black pepper
- 6 all-beef hot dogs
- 6 hot dog buns
- 2 avocados, halved, pitted, diced
- ⅔ cup finely chopped peeled cored pineapple

Mojo (pronounced MO-ho) is a popular Cuban sauce that's traditionally made with sour orange juice and garlic. In this recipe, a mixture of orange and lime juices replaces the sour orange. It's often used as a marinade for meat and fish; here we use it as a condiment for the dogs, along with avocado and pineapple.

Heat ¼ cup oil in a medium heavy skillet over medium heat. Add garlic; stir for 30 seconds. Add next 4 ingredients; bring to a simmer. Remove from heat. Season mojo sauce to taste with salt and pepper.

Build a medium-hot fire in a charcoal grill, or heat a gas grill to high. Brush grill grate with oil. Grill hot dogs and buns until heated through and grill marks form, 2 to 3 minutes per side for hot dogs and about 1 minute per side for buns.

Top hot dogs with avocado, pineapple, and mojo sauce. Serve with remaining mojo on the side.

To get a nice crispy char on fresh sausages without making them explode, **parcook them first** in beer or water.

BRATWURST AND ONION SANDWICHES

makes 2

¼ cup beer
3 Tbsp. coarse-grained Dijon
   mustard
1 Tbsp. vegetable oil, plus more for
   brushing
1 Tbsp. chopped fresh thyme or
   1 tsp. dried thyme
2 ½-inch-thick slices red onion
4 links fully cooked bratwurst (about
   10 oz. each), halved lengthwise
2 slices caraway rye bread (each
   about 5x3 inches)

A mustardy dressing made with beer and thyme accentuates the meaty flavors in this German-style open-face sandwich. Use your favorite brew for the dressing—and to wash down the brats.

Build a medium fire in a charcoal grill, or heat a gas grill to medium-high. Whisk beer, mustard, 1 Tbsp. oil, and thyme in a small bowl to blend. Brush both sides of onion slices with some of Dijon mustard dressing, keeping slices intact.

Brush grill grate with oil. Grill onion and bratwurst until onion is tender and slightly charred at edges and bratwurst is golden brown, turning twice, about 10 minutes for onion and 6 minutes for bratwurst. Grill bread until lightly toasted, about 1 minute.

Place toasted bread on plates. Brush with some of mustard dressing. Top bread with bratwurst and onion and drizzle with remaining dressing.

GETTING IT RIGHT: How to Grill Fresh Sausages

Due to their high fat content, fresh sausages can be a bit more challenging to handle on a grill than regular hot dogs (which only need a few minutes over high heat). You've got two choices:

PARCOOK

By precooking sausages before you put them on the grill, you can avoid flare-ups or geysers of fat shooting out when the casing ruptures. To do it, **simmer sausages in water—or better, beer—for 8 to 10 minutes** to keep them plump and juicy. Then move them to the grill for a final browning.

GRILL 'EM STRAIGHT

To cook fresh sausages entirely on the grill: Use a 2-zone fire (see page 15 for the details), and **start the sausages out on the cooler part of the grill** to allow the inside to cook fully. Then use tongs to move them over to the hotter side of the grill to give them a final char.

MANCHEGO CHEESE AND GARLIC DOGS

RELISH

- 2 large heads of garlic, top ½ inch cut off
- 5 tsp. extra-virgin olive oil, divided
- ½ cup diced drained roasted red peppers from a jar
- 1 Tbsp. chopped flat-leaf parsley

  Kosher salt and freshly ground black pepper

HOT DOGS

- Vegetable oil, for brushing
- 6 all-beef hot dogs
- 6 hot dog buns, opened, or 2½-inch-wide pieces ciabatta or pain rustique, cut to length of hot dogs and split lengthwise
- 2 oz. Manchego cheese, grated

  Sherry vinegar or balsamic vinegar, for drizzling

INGREDIENT INFO Manchego is a Spanish cheese made from sheep's milk; it's available at some supermarkets and at specialty foods stores.

Like burgers, hot dogs love cheese. We top these dogs with the most famous of Spanish cheeses, Manchego, then add a relish of roasted garlic and red peppers, plus a finishing drizzle of Sherry vinegar.

RELISH

Preheat oven to 400°F. Place each head of garlic, cut side up, in the center of a square of foil; drizzle each with 1 tsp. oil. Enclose garlic in foil. Place packets on oven rack; roast until garlic is tender, about 45 minutes. Open packets; let garlic cool for 15 minutes.

Squeeze garlic cloves into a small bowl. Mash enough roasted garlic to measure ¼ cup; transfer to a medium bowl. Mix in remaining 3 tsp. oil, red peppers, and parsley. Season to taste with salt and pepper.

HOT DOGS

Build a medium-hot fire in a charcoal grill, or heat a gas grill to high. Brush grill grate with oil. Grill hot dogs and buns until heated through and grill marks form, 2 to 3 minutes per side for hot dogs and about 1 minute per side for buns. Top hot dogs with cheese, garlic relish, and a drizzle of vinegar.

Brands we Love

YOU WOULDN'T SKIMP on the steak or fish, so when it comes to choosing your hot dog, likewise look for the good stuff. There's a slew of new varieties on the market that are made with more natural ingredients and less filler. They also taste great. We especially like **Niman Ranch Fearless Uncured Franks** and **Wellshire Farms Old Fashioned Uncured Franks**.

This collection of tasty, colorful pickles is a quick, easy way to spruce up a weeknight dinner or a party, and they're simple to make ahead of time. They also keep well in the fridge.

Pickled Peppers

makes 1 quart

4 cups assorted chiles (such as serrano, jalapeño, and Thai)
1½ cups distilled white vinegar
3 garlic cloves
2 Tbsp. whole black peppercorns
2 Tbsp. kosher salt
2 Tbsp. sugar
2 Tbsp. coriander seeds

The pickling process tames the heat of the peppers a bit, making these more like pickles with bite.

Cut large chiles into ¼-inch rings. Pierce small chiles 3 or 4 times with a skewer. Pack all chiles in a clean 1-qt. jar.

Bring vinegar, all remaining ingredients, and 1½ cups water to a boil in a medium saucepan. Reduce heat to medium and simmer for 5 minutes. Pour hot brine over peppers; seal jar. Let cool, then refrigerate. Serve within 1 month.

Pickled Baby Squash

makes 1 quart

1 lb. baby squash or zucchini
6 sprigs dill, divided
6 garlic cloves, smashed
1 cup apple cider vinegar
1 Tbsp. whole black peppercorns
1 Tbsp. kosher salt
1 tsp. sugar

The classic dill pickle gets extra heft and crunch when made with baby squash.

Thinly slice squash into coins. Place squash, 3 dill sprigs, and garlic in a clean 1-qt. jar.

Bring vinegar, peppercorns, salt, sugar, remaining 3 dill sprigs, and 1 cup water to a boil in a small saucepan, stirring to dissolve salt and sugar. Pour into jar with squash mixture. Cover and let cool slightly; chill. Serve within 2 weeks.

+

We love yellow mustard too, but an array of pickles is, hands down, the **best way to jazz up hot dogs, sausages, and brats**.

THE BA HOT DOG CONDIMENT BAR
(PAGES 101 AND 103)

Cauliflower Chowchow

4 cups ½-inch cauliflower florets (cut from 1 large head)
Kosher salt
1 cup apple cider vinegar
⅔ cup finely chopped onion
5½ Tbsp. sugar
4 tsp. yellow mustard seeds
1¼ tsp. (generous) dry mustard
1¼ tsp. (generous) celery seeds

Cauliflower is a tasty addition to the traditional Southern relish.

Cook cauliflower florets in a large pot of boiling salted water until just crisp-tender, about 2 minutes. Drain cauliflower. Transfer to a rimmed baking sheet and set aside.

Meanwhile, combine vinegar, onion, sugar, mustard seeds, dry mustard, and celery seeds in a large saucepan. Stir over medium heat until sugar dissolves.

Add cauliflower to saucepan; bring to a boil. Reduce heat to medium and simmer until cauliflower is tender, about 3 minutes. Transfer mixture and pickling juices to a clean 1-qt. jar. Cover and let cool slightly; chill. Serve within 1 month.

Tricolor Pepper Relish

makes 1¼ cups

3 large bell peppers (1 red, 1 orange, 1 yellow), cored, seeded
¾ cup white wine vinegar
½ cup sugar
1½ tsp. yellow mustard seeds
¾ tsp. kosher salt
¼ tsp. celery seeds

Use a combination of different colored bell peppers for visual pop.

Cut peppers into ¼-inch dice; transfer to a medium heatproof bowl. Pour 4 cups boiling water over; let steep for 5 minutes. Drain.

Stir all remaining ingredients in a medium saucepan over medium-high heat until sugar dissolves. Add peppers; simmer until almost dry, 13 to 14 minutes. Transfer to a clean jar. Cover and let cool slightly; chill. Serve within 2 weeks.

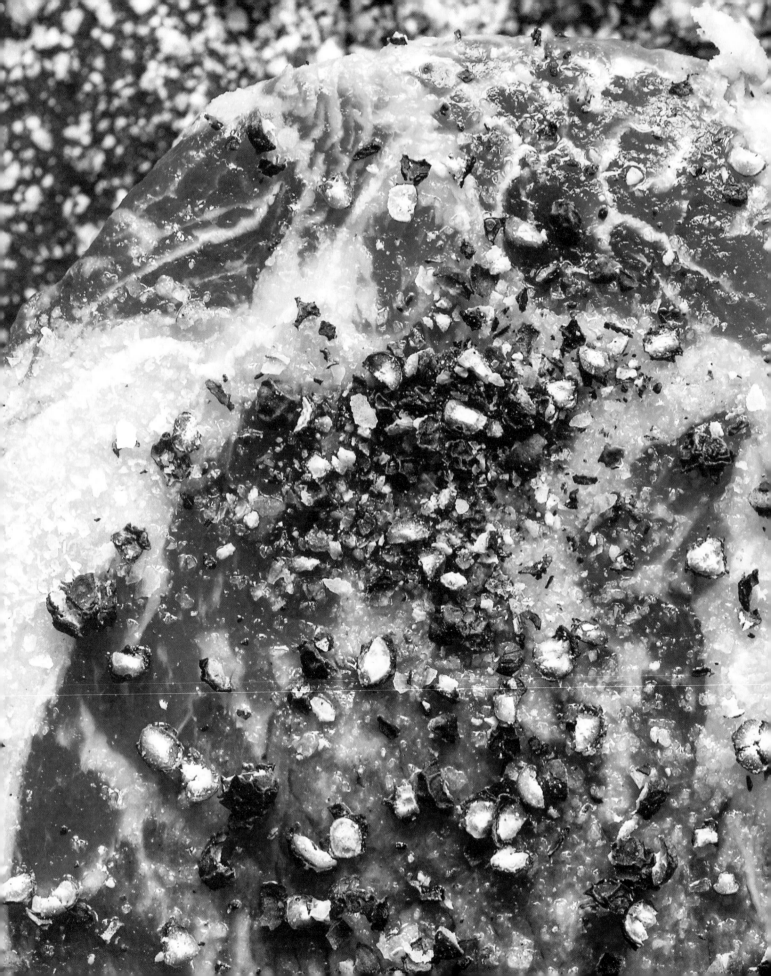

BEEF

OUR ULTIMATE MEAL?

That's easy. For the grilling diehards at *Bon Appétit*, it starts by unwrapping a thick-cut, bone-in, dry-aged steak from our butcher. This might be a rib eye, or maybe a porterhouse, or perhaps a neatly trimmed strip. Whatever the case, it is richly marbled with flecks of clean, white fat. We shower it liberally with flakes of kosher salt and pack it firmly with plenty of cracked black pepper. Finally, it hits a blazing-hot charcoal grill, immediately producing that mesmerizing *tsssssssssss.* . . .

At this point, of course, we raise a glass (or a can) to our lips and stand back to admire our handiwork, while eagerly awaiting the magnificence that we'll soon be sitting down to enjoy.

Nothing says grilling quite like steak. This is cooking at its most primal, its most satisfying. And once you know what you're doing, nothing is more rewarding. It starts with choosing the right cut of beef. As you'll learn in this chapter, certain premium cuts require nothing more than salt and pepper. And, of course, there are more affordable steaks that have intense flavor and take well to any number of marinades. This chapter outlines which cuts fall into which category, from a filet mignon to a chimichurri-sauced skirt steak. We'll tell you how to season your cuts and, finally, how to grill to a perfect medium-rare (which, in our minds, is the ideal doneness for nearly every cut of beef).

In short, if you want to be a grillmaster, you need to master steak. Here's how.

SALT-AND-PEPPER RIB EYE

photo page 108

1 2-lb. bone-in rib-eye steak (1½ to 2 inches thick)
2 tsp. kosher salt, divided
1 tsp. coarsely cracked black peppercorns
Vegetable oil, for brushing
Coarse sea salt

A well-marbled rib eye is so rich and flavorful on its own that it requires nothing more than salt, pepper, and fire. Build a 2-zone fire (see page 15) so you can sear it over hot embers then finish cooking it slowly over medium-low heat to develop a crispy, crunchy steakhouse crust and a juicy interior. If you're working with a boneless rib eye, lower the cooking time by a few minutes. (For more tips on grilling a steak, see page 109.)

Put steak on a wire rack set on a rimmed baking sheet. Pat dry with paper towels. Season with ½ tsp. kosher salt per side. Let stand at room temperature for at least 1 hour. Pat dry with paper towels. Season again with ½ tsp. salt per side; press in ½ tsp. cracked peppercorns per side so pieces adhere.

Build a 2-zone medium-hot/medium-low fire in a charcoal grill (see page 15), or heat a gas grill to high just before cooking, leaving one burner on low. Brush grill grate with oil. Sear steak over higher heat, flipping once, until nicely charred, 3 to 4 minutes per side. (If a flare-up occurs, use tongs to gently slide the steak to a cooler part of grill.) Move steak to lower heat and continue grilling, flipping once, 3 to 4 minutes per side. Using tongs, lift steak and sear both edges (the bone side and the fat-cap side) for 1 to 2 minutes per side to render out some of the fat. Grill steak to desired temperature, 14 to 18 minutes total or until instant-read thermometer registers 120°F for rare (steak will carry over to 125°F, or medium-rare, as it rests).

Transfer steak to work surface; let rest for 10 minutes. Slice against the grain, season with coarse sea salt.

COWBOY STEAKS

1 Tbsp. kosher salt
1 tsp. Hungarian sweet paprika
1 tsp. garlic powder
1 tsp. coarsely cracked black peppercorns
1 tsp. dried thyme
1 tsp. finely ground coffee
4 1 lb. bone-in rib-eye steaks (each about 1½ inches thick)
Vegetable oil, for brushing

SPECIAL EQUIPMENT 1 cup mesquite or hickory wood chips, soaked in cold water for at least 30 minutes; a foil broiler pan (for wood chips if using gas grill)

Texas-size bone-in rib eyes take on an incredible smokiness from a coffee-spiked dry rub and mesquite-enhanced grilling. If you're using a charcoal grill, you can amp up the flavor even more by using mesquite charcoal.

Mix first 6 ingredients in a small bowl. Sprinkle spice rub over both sides of steaks, pressing to adhere. Let steaks stand at room temperature for 1 hour.

Build a 2-zone medium-hot/medium-low fire in a charcoal grill (see page 15), or heat a gas grill to high. Brush grill grate with oil. Grill steaks over higher heat until brown on both sides, about 2 minutes per side. Transfer steaks to a platter. If using gas grill, reduce heat to medium. Drain wood chips. Scatter over charcoal if using charcoal grill; or place wood chips in foil broiler pan and set directly on flame if using gas grill. Return steaks to a cooler part of the grill. Cover grill with lid; grill steaks until an instant-read thermometer registers 120°F for rare (steaks will carry over to 125°F, or medium-rare, as they rest), about 9 minutes. Let steaks rest for 10 minutes before serving.

The ideal doneness for a bone-in rib eye is **medium rare**—rosy pink on the inside, with a crunchy **steakhouse crust** on the outside.

SALT AND PEPPER RIB EYE

Steps to a PERFECT STEAK

Grilling steak isn't a science, but it *is* an art that requires practice. You can achieve a perfect mahogany crust, juicy pink interior, and irresistibly tender texture, but always remember that the path to success starts long before the steak hits the grill.

① SIZE MATTERS

When it comes to hefty cuts like rib eye or New York strip, most *Bon Appétit* recipes call for a thickness of **1½ to 2 inches**.

This is not an arbitrary measurement: A steak of this thickness will achieve the perfect char on the outside just as the interior reaches the ideal temperature. Thinner steaks will require shorter cooking times.

② LET IT WARM UP

Never throw a piece of steak on the grill when it's still cold. For a steak that cooks evenly and has a juicy, rosy center, you must let the meat sit at room temperature for **at least 1 hour before grilling**. If you're working with a thicker cut or a roast, you'll need even more time.

Why the wait? Because if the center is still cold when you put the steak on the grill, you'll end up with a charred outside and mostly gray meat inside.

③ ONE WORD: SALT

Salt early and salt often. This adds flavor, keeps meat juicy, and intensifies the browning process to yield a dark, crisp crust.

● Use **kosher salt**. The larger flakes make for a superior crust.

● At least **1 hour before grilling**, sprinkle both sides of the steak with salt; put it on a wire rack.

● At the table, pass good-quality sea salt like **Maldon or fleur de sel** for more flavor and crunch.

④ HOT AND COOL ZONES

Use a **2-zone fire** (see page 15). The **hot zone is for searing**. The cooler zone is for gently cooking the inside. **Move the steak to the cool zone if it looks like the crust is burning**, or if flames leap up and envelop that well-marbled rib eye. (Nudge the steak back to the hot zone once the flames subside.)

Check the underbelly regularly, till you have a crisp, deep brown (but not charred black) crust. Then flip it, and do the same dance on the other side until they match.

⑤ LET IT STAND

The hardest thing about grilling a steak? Letting that perfectly cooked porterhouse **stand for 10 minutes before you cut into it**. The temptation to pick up your knife right away may be strong. Resist it. The rest period is crucial. It gives the meat time to reabsorb all of its flavorful juices.

To preserve the steak's crisp crust, we recommend resting it on a wire cooling rack set above a plate.

RIB-EYE STEAKS
with Mediterranean Rub

2 Tbsp. ground cumin
1 Tbsp. paprika
1½ tsp. ground ginger
1½ tsp. ground coriander
1 tsp. freshly ground black pepper
¼ tsp. cayenne pepper
2 Tbsp. extra-virgin olive oil, plus more for brushing
4 1-lb. boneless rib-eye steaks (each about 1½ inches thick), trimmed
Kosher salt and freshly ground black pepper
8 lemon wedges

Apply this simple, spice-based rub well in advance—even the night before, if possible. It doesn't contain any salt, though, so make sure to generously salt the steaks about an hour before grilling.

Whisk first 6 ingredients in a small bowl. Mix in 2 Tbsp. oil to form a smooth paste. Rub mixture over steaks. Transfer to a baking dish. Cover and chill for at least 3 hours or overnight.

Season steaks with salt and let stand at room temperature for 1 hour. Build a medium-hot fire in a charcoal grill, or heat a gas grill to high. Brush grill grate with oil. Grill steaks until an instant-read thermometer registers 120°F for rare (steaks will carry over to 125°F, or medium-rare, as they rest), about 4 minutes per side. Transfer to work surface; let stand for 10 minutes.

Cut steaks on a diagonal into ½-inch-thick slices. Transfer to a platter. Season to taste with salt and pepper. Serve with lemon wedges for squeezing over.

Kitchen Wisdom

THE BEAUTY OF MARBLING The best cuts of beef—rib eye, T-bone, Porterhouse—are well marbled. This means they're streaked through with flecks of rich fat within the muscle, and they'll be supremely tender once cooked. **The more marbling, the better the flavor.** These cuts are also perfect for grilling, and they should all be cooked the same way: seared over a hot fire and then finished over medium-low heat. (See page 15 for information on how to build a 2-zone fire.)

HICKORY RIB-EYE STEAKS
with Bacon-Molasses Butter

6 servings

6 slices thick-cut bacon
⅓ cup mild-flavored (light) molasses
   Freshly ground black pepper
6 Tbsp. (¾ stick) unsalted butter, room temperature
   Kosher salt
   Vegetable oil, for brushing
6 rib-eye steaks (each about 1 inch thick)

SPECIAL EQUIPMENT 2 cups hickory or other wood chips, soaked in water for 1 hour, drained; a foil broiler pan (for wood chips if using gas grill)

If you can resist eating the molasses-coated bacon long enough to mix it into the butter, you'll discover that these few simple ingredients create something delicious. The hickory wood chips are one of the other crucial "ingredients": They give the steaks a wonderful smoky flavor.

Position rack in top third of oven and preheat to 375°F. Line a small baking sheet with foil. Arrange bacon slices on foil; brush bacon with molasses, then season with pepper. Bake until bacon is cooked through but not crisp, about 15 minutes. Transfer bacon to a work surface; let cool. Chop bacon; transfer to a small bowl. Add butter and stir to blend. Season to taste with salt and pepper. **DO AHEAD:** Bacon-molasses butter can be made 1 day ahead. Cover and chill. Bring to room temperature before using.

Season steaks with salt and pepper; let stand at room temperature for 1 hour. Build a medium-hot fire in a charcoal grill, or heat a gas grill to high. Scatter drained wood chips over charcoal if using charcoal grill; or place wood chips in foil broiler pan and set directly on flame if using gas grill. Brush grill grate with oil. When chips are smoking, place steaks on grill grate. Cover grill and cook steaks until an instant-read thermometer registers 120°F for rare (steaks will carry over to 125°F, or medium-rare, as they rest), about 3 minutes per side. Transfer steaks to plates. Spoon bacon-molasses butter atop each.

T-BONE STEAKS
with Lemon and Rosemary

6 servings

1 cup extra-virgin olive oil, plus more for brushing
⅓ cup fresh lemon juice
⅓ cup coarsely chopped fresh rosemary or 1½ Tbsp. dried
   Freshly ground black pepper
6 12- to 14-oz. T-bone steaks (each about 1 inch thick)
   Kosher salt

When a recipe calls for only six simple ingredients (including salt and pepper), it's best to use the finest ingredients available. Always use freshly squeezed lemon juice and kosher salt, and grind black pepper from your pepper mill. Give the fresh rosemary just a rough chop—any finer and it could overpower the other flavors.

Combine 1 cup oil, lemon juice, rosemary, and a generous amount of pepper in a large glass baking dish. Add steaks and turn to coat. Cover and chill for 4 to 6 hours.

Remove steaks from marinade and season with salt; let stand at room temperature for 1 hour. Build a medium-hot fire in a charcoal grill, or heat a gas grill to high. Brush grill grate with oil. Grill steaks until an instant-read thermometer registers 120°F for rare (steaks will carry over to 125°F, or medium-rare, as they rest), about 4 minutes per side. Let rest for 5 to 10 minutes before serving.

CAVEMAN PORTERHOUSE
with Poblano Pan-Fry

4 servings

photo, right

4   1¼-inch-thick porterhouse steaks
    Coarse sea salt
    Coarsely cracked black
        peppercorns
⅓   cup extra-virgin olive oil
2   fresh poblano chiles, seeded, cut
        into strips
2   red bell peppers, cut into strips
1   yellow bell pepper, cut into strips
1   cup coarsely chopped fresh
        cilantro
2   large shallots, thinly sliced

SPECIAL EQUIPMENT Natural-bristle
pastry brush

INGREDIENT INFO Poblano chiles are
available at some supermarkets and
at specialty foods stores, farmers'
markets, and Latin markets.

This recipe is a *Bon Appétit* favorite for two good reasons: flavor and drama. You'll need a charcoal grill and a 12-inch cast-iron skillet; the steaks and the pan-fry are cooked right on hot coals. We recommend hardwood lump charcoal, which burns cleaner, hotter, and faster than processed charcoal briquettes. Note that you want to cook the steaks over the intense, even heat of glowing embers, not leaping flames.

Season steaks generously with coarse sea salt and cracked peppercorns; let stand at room temperature for 1 hour. Build a hot fire in a charcoal grill using hardwood lump charcoal. When charcoal is orange, spread out in an even layer on lower grill grate. Use newspaper to fan excess ash from coals. Arrange steaks in a single layer directly atop hot embers and grill until an instant-read thermometer registers 120°F for rare (steaks will carry over to 125°F, or medium-rare, as they rest), about 4 minutes per side. Using long tongs, transfer steaks to a plate. Using natural-bristle brush, remove any embers and loose ash from steaks. Tent steaks with foil and let rest for 10 minutes.

Add oil to 12-inch cast-iron skillet. Place skillet directly atop embers in grill. When oil begins to smoke, add chiles and all remaining ingredients to skillet. Sauté until vegetables begin to brown, 2 to 5 minutes, depending on heat remaining from embers. Using oven mitts as your aid, carefully lift skillet from grill. Season pan-fry to taste with salt and pepper. Serve over steaks.

GETTING IT RIGHT: How to Choose Beef

Why does it matter how your meat was raised? Because an animal's diet and lifestyle has a huge effect on how it will taste and how it should be prepared.

GRAIN-FED

The majority of the meat sold in the U.S. is grain-fed. There are huge variations in quality, but at its best, **grain-fed beef is richly marbled** with the sweet flavor that you get at top steakhouses. All that fat is what gives the meat so much flavor.

100 PERCENT GRASS-FED

It takes more time to raise cows that are purely grass-fed, which means that the meat is pricier. But since it takes less energy to grow grass than grain, grass-fed beef is an **eco-friendly choice**. It lacks the richness that grain-fed beef delivers, and because it's lean, it can overcook quickly on the grill. Cook it with care.

GRASS-FED, GRAIN-FINISHED

Choosing meat that has been primarily grass-fed but finished on a diet of grains is a tasty compromise that gives you the best of both worlds. This meat has a **deep, complex flavor** with more marbling than purely grass-fed meat, so it's less prone to overcooking.

+

The dramatic, flavor-packed preparation for these porterhouses calls for steaks to be **cooked directly**—yes, directly—**on hot coals**.

CAVEMAN PORTERHOUSE

PORTERHOUSE STEAK
with Paprika-Parmesan Butter

PAPRIKA-PARMESAN BUTTER
- 3 Tbsp. unsalted butter, room temperature
- 2 tsp. finely grated Parmesan
- 1 anchovy fillet packed in oil, drained, minced
- 1 tsp. paprika
- ½ tsp. Dijon mustard
- ½ tsp. Worcestershire sauce
- ¼ tsp. freshly ground black pepper
- ¼ tsp. hot pepper sauce

STEAK
- 1 2¾- to 3-inch-thick porterhouse steak (about 2¾ lb.)
- ¼ cup extra-virgin olive oil, plus more for brushing
- 7 large garlic cloves, minced
- 1 Tbsp. chopped fresh thyme
- 1 Tbsp. kosher salt, more as needed
- 2 tsp. freshly ground black pepper, more as needed
- 1 tsp. chopped fresh rosemary

About 3 inches thick and weighing in at nearly 3 lb., this is no ordinary steak—you'll need to ask your butcher to cut the meat this specific thickness for you. Because this is such a big cut, treat it like a roast: Grill-roast it slowly over medium heat with the grill lid closed (see page 50 for more on grill-roasting).

PAPRIKA-PARMESAN BUTTER
Mash all ingredients in a small bowl until blended. **DO AHEAD:** Can be made 2 days ahead. Cover and chill. Return to room temperature before using.

STEAK
Place steak in a glass baking dish. Whisk ¼ cup oil, garlic, thyme, 1 Tbsp. salt, 2 tsp. pepper, and rosemary in a small bowl to blend. Pour marinade over steak; turn to coat. Cover and chill for at least 2 hours and up to 1 day, turning occasionally. Let stand at room temperature for 1 hour before grilling.

Build a medium fire in a charcoal grill, or heat a gas grill to medium-high. Brush grill grate with oil. Remove steak from marinade, shaking off excess. Season with salt and pepper. Place steak on grill; cover grill. Grill steak, occasionally moving steak to a cooler part of the grate if burning, until an instant-read thermometer registers 120°F for rare (steak will carry over to 125°F, or medium-rare, as it rests) about 15 minutes per side. Transfer steak to a platter; cover to keep warm. Let rest for 10 minutes.

Using a sharp knife, cut meat off of the bone, then cut into ⅓-inch-thick slices. Spread Paprika-Parmesan Butter over top of slices.

Kitchen Wisdom

THE DRY-AGED ADVANTAGE If you want an exceptional steak, you want one that has been dry-aged. This kind of beef hangs in a carefully controlled cooler for a period of days or weeks before it goes to market. Water evaporates (concentrating the flavor) and enzymes break down the connective tissue inside the muscles, making the meat more tender. It costs about 25 percent more than regular beef—but you get a **pure beef flavor that's worth every penny** and a mineral top note steak lovers crave.

FILET MIGNON
with Red Wine-Horseradish Sauce

4 servings

1 Tbsp. unsalted butter
1 cup chopped shallots
1 tsp. coarsely cracked black
   peppercorns
2 sprigs thyme
2 cups dry red wine
½ cup heavy cream
1 Tbsp. prepared white horseradish
   Kosher salt and freshly ground
   black pepper
4 6- to 8-oz. filet mignon steaks
   (each about 1 inch thick)
   Vegetable oil, for brushing

You'll forget all about bottled steak sauce the minute you taste this homemade version made with horseradish, shallots, thyme, black pepper, cream, and, of course, red wine. Reduction is the secret here—a 3-cup mixture is reduced to 1 cup. This intensifies all the flavors and thickens the sauce to a luxurious consistency.

Melt butter in a medium heavy saucepan over medium heat. Add shallots, peppercorns, and thyme sprigs; sauté until shallots are tender, about 5 minutes. Add red wine. Increase heat and boil until liquid is reduced to 1 cup, about 10 minutes. Strain sauce and return to same saucepan. Add cream and boil until reduced to a sauce consistency, about 7 minutes. Stir in horseradish. Season sauce to taste with salt and pepper. **DO AHEAD:** Can be prepared 1 day ahead. Cover and refrigerate. Bring to a simmer before using.

Season steaks generously with salt and pepper and let stand at room temperature for 1 hour. Build a medium-hot fire in a charcoal grill, or heat a gas grill to high. Brush grill grate with oil. Grill until an instant-read thermometer registers 120°F for rare (steaks will carry over to 125°F, or medium-rare, as they rest), about 4 minutes per side. Let rest for 10 minutes.

Transfer steaks to plates. Spoon horseradish sauce around.

MEXICAN FILET MIGNON
with Rajas

4 servings

4 6-oz. filet mignon steaks
   (each 1½ to 2 inches thick)
   Kosher salt
3 fresh poblano chiles
1 Tbsp. vegetable oil, plus more for
   brushing
1 Tbsp. extra-virgin olive oil
½ small white onion, thinly sliced
½ cup heavy cream
2 Tbsp. chopped fresh oregano

INGREDIENT INFO Poblano chiles can be found at some supermarkets and at specialty foods stores, farmers' markets, and Latin markets.

Rich *rajas con crema*, a traditional Mexican dish of roasted poblano strips simmered in cream, revs up filet mignon. Poblanos don't have nearly the heat level of other fresh green chiles such as jalapeños and serranos, but they're richly flavored and take on a slight sweetness when roasted. Try serving the steak, sliced, and the rajas in warm corn tortillas for some truly decadent tacos.

Season steaks with salt and let stand at room temperature for 1 hour.

Char chiles over a gas flame or in the broiler until blackened on all sides. Enclose in a paper bag. Let stand for 10 minutes. Peel and seed chiles; slice thinly. Heat 1 Tbsp. vegetable oil and olive oil in a large skillet over medium heat. Add onion and sauté until translucent, about 2 minutes. Add poblanos, cream, and oregano; simmer until rajas thicken slightly, about 3 minutes. Season to taste with salt.

Meanwhile, build a medium-hot fire in a charcoal grill, or heat a gas grill to high. Brush grill grate with vegetable oil. Grill steaks until an instant-read thermometer registers 120°F for rare (steaks will carry over to 125°F, or medium-rare, as they rest), about 5 minutes per side. Let rest for 10 minutes. Transfer steaks to plates; top with rajas.

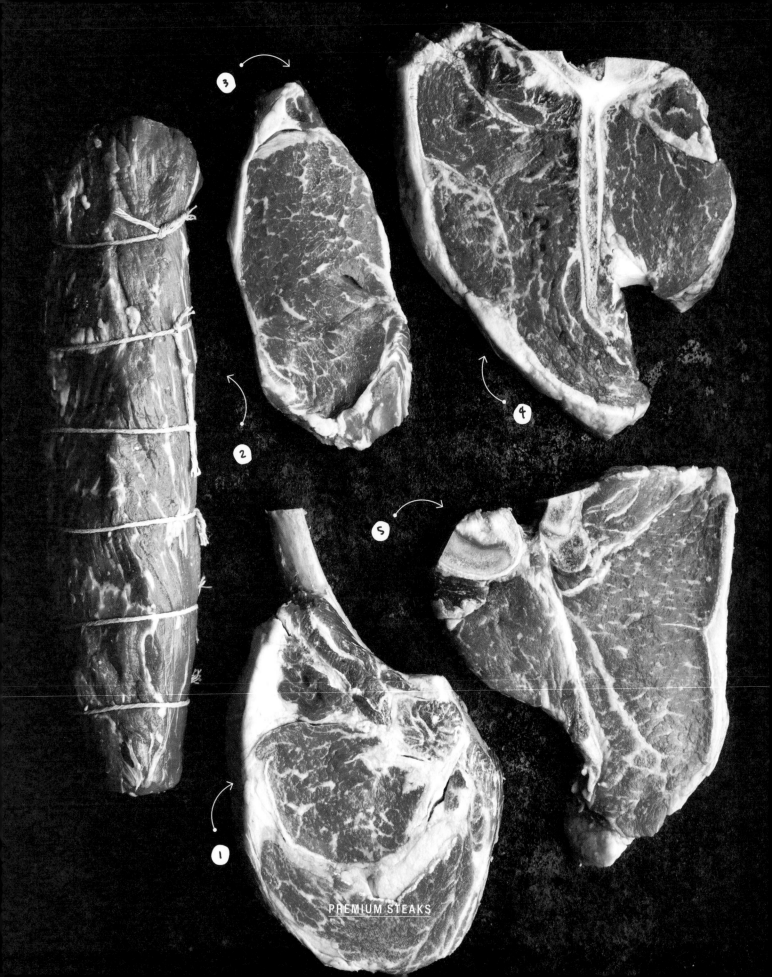

PREMIUM STEAKS

FILET MIGNON
with Tomato-Herb Butter

½ cup (1 stick) unsalted butter, room temperature
2 Tbsp. chopped drained oil-packed sun-dried tomatoes
2 Tbsp. chopped fresh basil
2 garlic cloves, minced
1 tsp. chopped fresh rosemary
1 tsp. chopped fresh thyme
¾ tsp. freshly ground black pepper, more as needed
Kosher salt
6 6- to 8-oz. filet mignon steaks (each 1¼ to 1½ inches thick)
Vegetable oil, for brushing

An easy and delicious compound butter melts over the hot filet mignon, creating its own sauce. (For more compound butters, see pages 396–398.) If you're in a hurry, skip the process of forming the butter mixture into a log and wrapping it with plastic wrap—that's just a great way to store it, yielding even, coin-shaped slices. Simply mix it up and drop a spoonful atop the grilled steaks.

Combine first 6 ingredients and ¾ tsp. black pepper in a medium bowl to blend. Season to taste with salt. Lay a sheet of plastic wrap on a work surface. Transfer mixture to plastic and use plastic as your aid to form into 6-inch-long log. Roll up in plastic, twisting ends to enclose. Freeze until firm, at least 1 hour and up to 1 week.

Season steaks with salt and pepper and let stand at room temperature for 1 hour. Build a medium-hot fire in a charcoal grill, or heat a gas grill to high. Brush grill grate with oil. Grill until an instant-read thermometer registers 120°F for rare (steaks will carry over to 125°F, or medium-rare, as they rest), about 5 minutes per side. Transfer steaks to plates and let rest for 10 minutes. Serve each steak with 3 butter slices on top.

KNOW YOUR CUTS: Premium Steaks

The steaks listed here are on the expensive side—but they're also the most tender and flavorful.

RIB EYE

1 For many meat lovers, a bone-in rib eye is the ultimate steak. Ask your butcher to cut it **1½ inches thick**—the magic measurement that results in a **nice dark crust** on the outside without overcooking the center. You'll want to cook this steak to **at least medium-rare**, because all that pretty marbling means it's got too much fat to be served rare.

FILET MIGNON

2 The **most tender steak** of all doesn't have a very complex taste—which is why it's often served wrapped in bacon or topped with a compound butter. Serve **rare** or **medium-rare**.

NEW YORK STRIP

3 This **moderately marbled, boneless** cut is one of our favorites: It's so **easy to cook consistently**. Don't grill beyond medium-rare; it can get tough.

PORTERHOUSE

4 This **large, bone-in cut** offers a substantial piece of tender filet mignon on one side of the bone, juicy New York strip on the other.

T-BONE

5 Similar to the porterhouse, in terms of being a **hefty cut** with two types of meat. But the T-bone has a **smaller piece of filet**.

STRIP STEAK
with Blue Cheese Butter and Salsa Verde

¼ cup chopped flat-leaf
 parsley
2 Tbsp. chopped fresh basil
2 Tbsp. chopped fresh tarragon
2 small garlic cloves, minced
2 tsp. finely grated lemon zest
1 tsp. anchovy paste
1 tsp. drained capers, minced
7 Tbsp. extra-virgin olive oil, plus
 more for brushing
 Kosher salt and freshly ground
 black pepper
1 cup blue cheese (about 4 oz.)
½ cup (1 stick) unsalted butter, room
 temperature
4 large heirloom tomatoes, cut
 into ⅓-inch-thick slices
4 12- to 16-oz. bone-in New York
 strip steaks or 8- to 10-oz.
 boneless New York strip steaks

The salsa verde that accompanies this steak is delicious on heirloom tomatoes, and excellent with other grilled vegetables, fish, and bread. Use a creamy blue cheese (we like St. Agur) for the compound butter; it will blend more easily. Using different colored tomatoes would make the presentation particularly eye-catching.

Mix first 7 ingredients in a small bowl. Gradually whisk in 7 Tbsp. oil. Season salsa verde to taste with salt and pepper. Mix blue cheese and butter in another small bowl to blend. Season to taste with salt and pepper. **DO AHEAD:** Salsa verde and blue cheese butter can be made 1 day ahead. Cover separately and chill.

Let steaks stand at room temperature for 1 hour. Build a medium-hot fire in a charcoal grill, or heat a gas grill to high. Arrange tomato slices in a single layer on a rimmed baking sheet. Season with salt and pepper. Drizzle salsa verde over tomatoes.

Brush grill grate with oil. Grill steaks until charred and an instant-read thermometer registers 120°F for rare (steaks will carry over to 125°F, or medium-rare, as they rest), about 3 minutes per side. Let rest for 10 minutes.

Stack seasoned tomatoes on each plate and place steaks alongside tomatoes. Place a generous dollop of blue cheese butter atop each steak.

SIRLOIN STEAK
with Chopped Salad

2 large garlic cloves, minced
1¾ tsp. coarsely cracked black
 peppercorns
1¼ tsp. kosher salt, more as needed
1 2-lb. 1½-inch-thick top sirloin steak
 Vegetable oil, for brushing
1 cup baby arugula or chopped
 regular arugula (about 1 oz.)
1 cup diced tomatoes
½ cup crumbled feta
½ cup (generous) diced red onion
3 Tbsp. chopped pitted Kalamata
 olives
1½ Tbsp. extra-virgin olive oil
1 jalapeño, seeded, finely chopped
 (about 4 tsp.)
 Freshly ground black pepper

To get the perfect combination of spice and crunch on these steaks, crack whole peppercorns by placing them in a resealable plastic bag and crushing with the bottom of a heavy skillet.

Mix garlic, peppercorns, and 1¼ tsp. salt in a small bowl; rub all over steak. Let stand at room temperature for 1 hour.

Build a medium-hot fire in a charcoal grill, or heat a gas grill to high. Brush grill grate with oil. Grill steak until charred and an instant-read thermometer registers 120°F for rare (steak will carry over to 125°F, or medium-rare, as it rests), about 6 minutes per side. Transfer to a work surface; let rest for 10 minutes.

Mix arugula and all remaining ingredients in a medium bowl. Season to taste with salt and pepper. Slice steak thinly against the grain; arrange on a plate. Spoon salad over steak.

SOY-GINGER FLANK STEAK
with Sweet Slaw

4 servings

¼ cup reduced-sodium soy sauce
5 Tbsp. vegetable oil, plus more for brushing
5 tsp. minced peeled ginger, divided
1 garlic clove, minced
1 1½-lb. flank steak
3 Tbsp. sugar
3 Tbsp. seasoned rice vinegar
2 red jalapeños, seeded, thinly sliced into rounds
5 cups thinly sliced Napa cabbage (about 9 oz.)
¾ cup chopped scallions, divided
Kosher salt and freshly ground black pepper

The Asian marinade for the steak finds its partner in a zesty slaw. The sweet and sour flavors of vinegar, sugar, chile, and garlic are reminiscent of Vietnamese dipping sauces.

Mix soy sauce, 5 Tbsp. oil, 3 tsp. ginger, and garlic in a resealable plastic bag. Add flank steak and seal bag; turn to coat. Let stand at room temperature, turning occasionally, for 30 minutes.

Stir sugar and vinegar in a small saucepan over medium heat until sugar dissolves; remove from heat. Add jalapeños and remaining 2 tsp. ginger. Transfer to freezer and let chill for 15 minutes.

Place cabbage and ½ cup scallions in a medium bowl. Pour chilled vinegar mixture over and toss to coat. Season to taste with salt and pepper. Let stand while grilling steak, tossing occasionally.

Build a medium fire in a charcoal grill, or heat a gas grill to medium-high. Brush grill grate with oil. Grill steak until cooked to desired doneness, about 6 minutes per side for medium-rare. Transfer to a work surface and let rest for 10 minutes.

Slice steak thinly against the grain. Sprinkle remaining ¼ cup scallions over slaw and serve alongside steak.

BUTCHER FAVORITES: Skirt Steak, Flank Steak, Hanger Steak

Skirt steak, flank steak, and hanger steak are thin, flat, relatively affordable cuts with a rich, beefy taste. These are the steaks you see at French bistros and Latin American steakhouses—and they're most likely the ones your butcher is grilling at home. When prepared properly, they are deeply flavorful.

TENDERIZE

Soak these cuts in a **strong, acidic marinade or coat with a dry rub** (see pages 379–383 for ideas). These steaks can stand up to bold flavors, so don't be shy.

FAST AND HOT

Grill these steaks **over direct heat to just medium-rare** (our preferred doneness for most steaks). These cuts are thin and they can overcook easily—so you want to sear them quickly over a hot fire.

SLICE AGAINST THE GRAIN

Most meat should be sliced against the grain to avoid shredding. That's especially true for these muscular cuts; **slice them thinly**. And you can't go wrong if you serve them with a zingy salsa or sauce, like the Chimichurri Sauce on page 390.

FLATIRON STEAKS
with Tapenade and Tomatoes

An assertive wet rub gives these steaks a nice crust on the grill. And the spice from the meat pairs with the pungency of the tapenade to play deliciously against the tomatoes and watercress. (Bonus: The tapenade is great on fish, chicken—really, anything savory.)

TAPENADE

- ⅓ cup extra-virgin olive oil, more as needed
- ¼ cup vegetable oil
- 1 cup pitted olives (such as Niçoise or Kalamata), chopped
- 1 Tbsp. minced capers
- 1 garlic clove, minced
- 1 anchovy fillet packed in oil, drained, minced (optional)

STEAK

- 2 lb. flatiron, flank, hanger, or skirt steak
- Kosher salt
- Zest and juice of 1 orange
- ¼ cup thinly sliced shallots
- 2 Tbsp. chopped fresh oregano
- 2 Tbsp. minced garlic
- 2 Tbsp. smoked paprika
- 2 Tbsp. vegetable oil, plus more for brushing
- 1 Tbsp. crushed red pepper flakes

TOMATOES

- 4 large tomatoes (about 3 lb.), sliced ¼ inch thick
- 1 shallot, thinly sliced into rings
- ¼ cup (loosely packed) flat-leaf parsley
- 1 Tbsp. extra-virgin olive oil, plus more for drizzling
- Sea salt and freshly ground black pepper
- 1 bunch watercress, tough stems removed (about 4 cups)
- 1 Tbsp. fresh lemon juice

TAPENADE

Stir ⅓ cup olive oil, next 4 ingredients, and anchovy, if using, in a small bowl. Add more olive oil for a thinner tapenade, if desired. (For a smoother sauce, purée tapenade in a food processor or blender.) Set aside.

STEAK

Place steak in a large baking dish and season generously with salt. Stir orange zest and juice, shallots, oregano, garlic, paprika, 2 Tbsp. oil, and crushed red pepper flakes in a small bowl to combine. Spread mixture evenly over both sides of steak and let marinate at room temperature for 1 hour.

Build a medium-hot fire in a charcoal grill, or heat a gas grill to high. Brush grill grate with oil. Grill steak, turning once, until nicely charred, about 5 minutes on each side for medium-rare. Transfer steak to a work surface; let rest for 5 to 10 minutes.

TOMATOES

Arrange tomatoes on a serving platter. Scatter shallot and parsley over; drizzle with oil and season with salt and pepper. In a medium bowl, toss watercress with 1 Tbsp. each oil and lemon juice. Season watercress to taste with salt. Mound watercress on platter.

Slice steaks thinly against the grain; transfer to platter with tomatoes and watercress. Spoon some tapenade over steak and serve the rest alongside.

STEAK AND EGGS
with Kimchi Rice

STEAKS
- ¼ cup mirin
- 2 Tbsp. finely grated cored peeled Granny Smith apple
- 2 Tbsp. reduced-sodium soy sauce
- 2 Tbsp. light corn syrup
- 1½ Tbsp. finely chopped scallion (white and pale green parts)
- 1 Tbsp. (scant) gochujang (Korean chili paste)
- 1 Tbsp. (scant) minced peeled ginger
- 2 garlic cloves, minced
- 1½ tsp. toasted sesame oil
- 1½ tsp. unseasoned rice vinegar
- 4 5-oz. pieces skirt steak

KIMCHI RICE
- 1 cup sushi rice (or other short-grain rice)
- 1 tsp. kosher salt, more as needed
- 2 Tbsp. plus 1 tsp. vegetable oil, divided, plus more for brushing
- 1½ cups Napa cabbage kimchi, coarsely chopped
- 2 Tbsp. unseasoned rice vinegar
  Freshly ground black pepper
- 4 large eggs
  Chopped scallions, for garnish

INGREDIENT INFO Mirin is available in the Asian foods section of some supermarkets and at Japanese markets. Korean chili paste (gochujang or kochujang) is made with puréed fermented soybeans (miso) and hot chiles. Kimchi is a spicy and pungent fermented vegetable mixture; this recipe calls for the version made with Napa cabbage (it may be identified as Korean cabbage). Both are available at Korean markets and online at koamart.com.

This dish is an entire meal, and it embraces the unique flavors of the Korean kitchen. Skirt steak is marinated in the traditional sweet-and-salty style, then grilled and paired with rice mixed with tangy kimchi. Add two fried eggs and you've got brunch, lunch, or dinner. Of course, the marinated steak is also delicious on its own.

STEAKS
Whisk first 10 ingredients in a bowl. Add steaks; turn to coat. Cover and chill overnight. Let stand at room temperature for 1 hour before grilling.

KIMCHI RICE
Bring 2 cups water to a boil in a small saucepan. Add rice and 1 tsp. salt. Return to boil; reduce heat to low, cover, and cook until water is absorbed, about 18 minutes.

Meanwhile, build a medium-hot fire in a charcoal grill, or heat a gas grill to high. Brush grill grate with oil. Grill steaks until slightly charred but still pink in center, about 3 minutes per side. Transfer to a work surface; let rest for 5 minutes.

Heat 2 Tbsp. oil in a large skillet over medium heat. Add kimchi and vinegar. Stir until heated. Fold in rice. Season to taste with salt and pepper. Keep warm.

Heat remaining 1 tsp. oil in a large nonstick skillet over medium heat. Crack eggs into skillet, being careful not to break yolks. Season with salt and pepper. Cook until whites are set, about 3 minutes.

Divide kimchi rice among plates. Slice steaks thinly against the grain; arrange over rice. Top each with egg; sprinkle with scallions.

SKIRT STEAK
with Chimichurri Sauce

photo, right

1 1½-lb. skirt steak (about ½ inch thick), cut in half crosswise
Kosher salt and freshly ground black pepper
Vegetable oil, for brushing
½ cup Chimichurri Sauce (page 390)

Tart, herbaceous, and absolutely addictive, Argentinean *chimichurri* sauce is the perfect match for the rich beefy flavor of skirt steak—or any cut of steak. Cook the steak over intense heat quickly to sear the outside while cooking the inside just to medium-rare. Then slice it thinly and serve with generous amounts of sauce.

Season skirt steak lightly with salt and let sit at room temperature for 30 minutes. Pat dry with paper towels and season again with salt and pepper.

Build a medium-hot fire in a charcoal grill, or heat a gas grill to high. Brush grill grate with oil. Cook until meat is nicely charred and medium-rare, 3 to 4 minutes per side.

Transfer steak to a work surface; let rest for 5 to 10 minutes. Slice thinly against the grain and serve with Chimichurri Sauce.

ADOBO-MARINATED HANGER STEAKS

4 10- to 12-oz. hanger steaks, trimmed of fat and center connective tissue
4 tsp. powdered adobo seasoning
½ cup fresh orange juice
¼ cup fresh lemon juice
2 Tbsp. white wine vinegar
Vegetable oil, for brushing
Kosher salt and freshly ground black pepper

INGREDIENT INFO Powdered adobo seasoning is available at Latin markets.

This flat steak with long grains of muscle is prized for its deep beef flavor, and it's terrific when marinated, then grilled to medium-rare and thinly sliced against the grain. Here we season it with citrus, vinegar, and the Latin spice mixture adobo. Since some hanger steaks are sold in doubles, you (or your butcher) will need to separate them and trim away the tough central membrane that connects them (a sharp paring knife is the right tool for the job). If you can't find hanger steak, use flank or skirt steak instead.

Sprinkle steaks with adobo seasoning. Place in a single layer in a glass baking dish. Mix orange juice, lemon juice, and vinegar in a bowl; pour over steaks. Let marinate at room temperature for 1 hour.

Build a medium-hot fire in a charcoal grill, or heat a gas grill to high. Brush grill grate with oil. Remove steaks from marinade; season with salt and pepper. Grill steaks to desired doneness, about 5 minutes per side for medium-rare. Transfer to a work surface; let rest for 5 to 10 minutes. Slice thinly against the grain.

This **sensational chimichurri** also makes a great topping for fish, roasted vegetables, or poached eggs and toast.

SKIRT STEAK WITH CHIMICHURRI SAUCE

FLANK STEAK
with Bloody Mary Tomato Salad

STEAK

- 2 1½-lb. flank steaks
   Kosher salt
- 2 tsp. (packed) light brown sugar
- 1 tsp. paprika
- ¼ tsp. cayenne pepper
- ¼ tsp. freshly ground black pepper
   Vegetable oil, for brushing

SALAD

- 1 cup finely chopped red onion
- 3 Tbsp. Sherry vinegar, divided
- 2 lb. cherry or grape tomatoes, halved
- 1 cup chopped celery hearts (inner stalks and leaves from 1 bunch)
- ½ cup chopped brined green olives, plus 2 Tbsp. olive brine
- 2 Tbsp. prepared horseradish
- 1 Tbsp. Worcestershire sauce
- 1 tsp. Tabasco
- ½ tsp. celery seeds
- ¼ cup extra-virgin olive oil
   Kosher salt and freshly ground black pepper

Fresh tomatoes and celery, briny green olives, and chopped red onion are tossed in a horseradish- and Tabasco-infused vinaigrette, creating a new interpretation of a Bloody Mary for your next Sunday brunch or summer picnic. You can serve the salad immediately, but it's even juicier after marinating for a few hours.

STEAK

Place steaks on a large rimmed baking sheet; season with salt. Mix sugar and next 3 ingredients in a small bowl; rub all over steaks. Cover; refrigerate for 1 to 3 hours.

Let steaks stand at room temperature for 1 hour. Build a medium-hot fire in a charcoal grill, or heat a gas grill to high. Brush grill grate with oil. Grill to desired doneness, 5 to 7 minutes per side for medium-rare. Transfer to a work surface; let rest for 10 minutes. **DO AHEAD:** Can be made 1 day ahead. Let cool; cover and chill. Bring to room temperature before slicing.

SALAD

Mix onion and 1 Tbsp. vinegar in a large bowl. Let macerate for 10 minutes, tossing often. Add tomatoes, celery, and olives.

Whisk remaining 2 Tbsp. vinegar, olive brine, horseradish, Worcestershire sauce, Tabasco, and celery seeds in a medium bowl. Slowly whisk in oil. Add to bowl with tomato mixture; toss to coat. Season with salt and pepper. **DO AHEAD:** Can be made 4 hours ahead. Cover; chill.

Cut steak against the grain into ¼-inch-thick slices. Serve salad with steak.

IS IT DONE YET? How to Tell the Temperature of Steak

There are two methods for determining when it's time to take steak off the grill. You can figure it out by feel like the grillmasters do. Or you can use an instant-read thermometer. Here's how:

THE FINGER TEST

Things happen quickly when you're working with fire, and there's not always time for messing around with thermometers. Learn about doneness by pressing steaks firmly with your index finger when they're cooking. Is it soft? The steak is still rare. Poke it again two minutes later. Soft with a little resistance? Medium-rare. The muscle fibers continue tightening as the steak cooks through. The firmer it feels, the more well-cooked it is.

USING A THERMOMETER

If you want your steak medium-rare (which is our preferred doneness), remove meat from the grill when an instant-read thermometer inserted into the thickest part of the meat, away from the bone, registers 120°F (rare). You take it off the heat "early" because the internal temperature will rise a few degrees while the meat rests; the steak will be a perfect medium-rare by the time you slice it.

FLANK STEAK
with Chile and Watermelon Salad

<u>4 servings</u>

Both the steak and the salad pack some heat in this spicy dish. Sriracha, the wildly popular Asian chili sauce, goes into the marinade and the salad dressing, and the bell pepper and watermelon salad gets additional kick from red jalapeños.

STEAK

- 1½ Tbsp. fresh lime juice
- 1 Tbsp. grapeseed oil or extra-virgin olive oil
- 2 garlic cloves, minced
- 1 tsp. hot chili sauce (such as Sriracha)
- ½ tsp. grated peeled ginger
- ½ tsp. honey
- 1 1½-lb. flank steak

SALAD

- ¼ cup hot chili sauce (such as Sriracha)
- ¼ cup grapeseed oil or extra-virgin olive oil, plus more for brushing
- 3 Tbsp. seasoned rice vinegar
- 1¼ tsp. honey
  Kosher salt and freshly ground black pepper
- 4 large bell peppers, preferably assorted colors, cut into ½-inch squares
- 2 Tbsp. minced red jalapeños
- 2 cups ½-inch cubes seedless watermelon

STEAK

Whisk all ingredients except flank steak in a glass baking dish. Add steak; turn to coat. Cover and let marinate at room temperature, turning occasionally, for 2 hours. Alternatively, cover and chill, turning occasionally, for at least 4 hours and up to 1 day. Bring to room temperature before grilling.

SALAD

Whisk hot chili sauce, ¼ cup oil, vinegar, and honey in a small bowl; season dressing to taste with salt and pepper. Place peppers and chiles in a large bowl. Toss with 6 Tbsp. dressing. Let marinate at room temperature for 2 hours.

DO AHEAD: Can be made 8 hours ahead. Cover dressing and salad separately and chill. Bring to room temperature before serving.

Build a medium-hot fire in a charcoal grill, or heat a gas grill to high. Brush grill grate with oil. Grill steak with some marinade still clinging until cooked to desired doneness, about 4 minutes per side for rare. Transfer to a work surface; let rest for 10 minutes.

Slice steak thinly against the grain; transfer to a platter. Drizzle with some of remaining dressing from salad. Toss watermelon into pepper salad. Serve flank steak and salad with remaining dressing alongside.

Bonus Recipe
TAGLIATA

One of our favorite ways to prepare steak is also the simplest. *Tagliata*, which comes from the Italian *tagliare*, meaning "to slice or cut," takes just a few steps: Grill a steak, slice it, and place it on a bed of peppery arugula with some olive oil, shaved Parmesan, and lemon wedges. Done.

TENDERLOIN
with Roasted Garlic Sauce and Quinoa

4 servings

photo, right

SAUCE

2 large heads of garlic, top ⅓ trimmed to expose cloves

½ cup extra-virgin olive oil, more as needed

½ cup low-salt chicken broth, more as needed

 Kosher salt and freshly ground black pepper

BEEF

2 Tbsp. extra-virgin olive oil, plus more for brushing

1 1½-lb. piece beef tenderloin, trimmed

 Kosher salt and freshly ground black pepper

 Leek-Tomato Quinoa (recipe follows)

 Chopped fresh chives

Drizzle sliced beef tenderloin with a puréed garlic sauce made from two whole heads of garlic, and pair it with a warm quinoa salad with leeks and tomatoes.

SAUCE

Preheat oven to 350°F. Place garlic heads, cut side up, in a small ovenproof dish. Pour ½ cup oil over. Cover dish tightly with foil. Bake until garlic is soft, about 55 minutes. Remove garlic from oil; let cool. Pour oil from dish into a measuring cup; add more oil if necessary to measure ½ cup total. Squeeze out garlic from peel into a blender. Add broth and garlic oil; purée until smooth, thinning with more broth if desired. Season to taste with salt and pepper. **DO AHEAD:** Can be made 1 day ahead. Cover and chill. Rewarm sauce over medium-low heat and thin with more broth, if desired, before serving.

BEEF

Build a medium fire in a charcoal grill, or heat a gas grill to medium-high. Brush grill grate with oil. Rub beef all over with 2 Tbsp. oil. Season with salt and pepper. Grill beef, turning often, until an instant-read thermometer registers 120°F for rare (steak will carry over to 125°F, or medium-rare, as it rests), about 20 minutes. Transfer to a work surface and let stand for 10 minutes.

Slice beef against the grain into ⅓-inch-thick slices; arrange on a platter with Leek-Tomato Quinoa. Drizzle with sauce and sprinkle with chives.

Makes about 2¾ cups

Leek-Tomato Quinoa

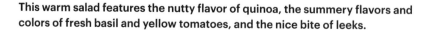

serve with tenderloin

1½ cups quinoa, well rinsed

½ tsp. kosher salt, more as needed

1 Tbsp. unsalted butter

2 cups finely chopped leeks, white and pale green parts only

¼ cup low-salt chicken broth

3 Tbsp. extra-virgin olive oil

2 medium-size yellow tomatoes, seeded, chopped

3 Tbsp. chopped scallions

3 Tbsp. chopped fresh basil

1 Tbsp. fresh lemon juice

 Freshly ground black pepper

This warm salad features the nutty flavor of quinoa, the summery flavors and colors of fresh basil and yellow tomatoes, and the nice bite of leeks.

Mix quinoa, ½ tsp. salt, and 2 cups water in a medium heavy saucepan. Bring to a boil. Reduce heat to medium-low, cover, and simmer until quinoa is just tender and almost all water is absorbed, about 20 minutes. Drain. Set aside.

Melt butter in a large nonstick skillet over medium heat. Add leeks; sauté until they begin to soften, about 5 minutes. Add broth. Cover and simmer until leeks are tender, about 5 minutes. Add quinoa and oil; stir until heated through, about 5 minutes. Stir in tomatoes, scallions, basil, and lemon juice. Season to taste with salt and pepper.

Rich tenderloin, buttery garlic, and nutty quinoa make for an **irresistible blend of textures and flavors**.

TENDERLOIN WITH ROASTED GARLIC SAUCE AND QUINOA

WHOLE TENDERLOIN
with Brown Sugar Spice Rub

SPICE RUB

2 Tbsp. (packed) dark brown sugar

1 Tbsp. smoked paprika

1 Tbsp. kosher salt

1½ tsp. ground chipotle chiles or ground ancho chiles

1 tsp. freshly ground black pepper

BEEF TENDERLOIN

1 3½-lb. beef tenderloin

2 Tbsp. extra-virgin olive oil, plus more for brushing

Large pieces of beef, like this whole tenderloin, benefit from coming to room temperature before grilling, which allows the meat to cook more evenly. Grill it over a 2-zone fire, searing over medium-hot coals and finishing over medium heat. Letting the beef rest after it comes off the grill gives the meat time to relax and the juices a chance to reabsorb.

SPICE RUB

Combine all ingredients in a small bowl. **DO AHEAD:** Can be made 2 days ahead. Store airtight at room temperature.

BEEF TENDERLOIN

Let beef stand at room temperature for 1 hour.

Build a 2-zone medium-hot/medium fire in a charcoal grill (see page 15), or heat a gas grill to high. Pat beef dry with paper towels; brush with 2 Tbsp. oil. Sprinkle all over with spice rub, using all of mixture (coating will be thick). Brush grill grate with oil. Place beef on grill (over medium-hot coals if using charcoal grill). Sear for 2 minutes on each side. Move beef to medium heat on charcoal grill, or reduce heat on gas grill to medium-high. Grill beef uncovered, moving beef to a cooler part of grill as needed to prevent burning, and turning occasionally, until an instant-read thermometer inserted into the thickest part of beef registers 120°F for rare (beef will carry over to 125°F, or medium-rare, as it rests), about 35 minutes. Transfer to a work surface; cover loosely with foil and let rest for 15 minutes. Slice beef thinly against the grain.

Kitchen Wisdom

THE MOST TENDER CUT Beef tenderloin is as tender as it gets, and for that reason it is one of the most expensive cuts. It can be grilled whole or sliced into individual filet mignon steaks; if you choose to cook it in one piece, look for a portion from the head end of the tenderloin for a more uniform size and shape. We like to **ramp up tenderloin's mild flavor**—try a smoky spice rub, a compound butter, or a zesty sauce.

SMOKED TRI-TIP
with Sicilian Herb Sauce

6 servings

3 Tbsp. fresh thyme leaves
2 garlic cloves
1½ tsp. dried oregano
1 tsp. kosher salt, more as needed
2 Tbsp. fresh lemon juice
½ cup extra-virgin olive oil, plus
    more for brushing
    Freshly ground black pepper
1 2½- to 2¾-lb. beef tri-tip roast

SPECIAL EQUIPMENT 3 cups oak, mesquite, or hickory wood chips, soaked in water for 1 hour and drained; a foil broiler pan (for wood chips if using gas grill)

This simple herb, lemon, and garlic sauce is called *salmoriglio* in Sicily. It's used as a sauce, not a marinade; you can mix it up in a minute and drizzle it over just about anything coming off your grill.

Blend thyme, garlic, oregano, and 1 tsp. salt in a food processor until garlic is finely chopped. With processor running, gradually add lemon juice, then ½ cup oil. Season herb sauce to taste with pepper and transfer to a bowl. **DO AHEAD:** Can be made 1 day ahead. Cover and chill. Bring to room temperature before using.

Season tri-tip generously on both sides with salt and pepper. Let stand at room temperature for at least 30 minutes and up to 2 hours.

Build a 2-zone medium-hot/medium fire in a charcoal grill (see page 15), or heat a gas grill to high. **If using a charcoal grill:** Sprinkle drained wood chips directly over coals. Replace grill grate and brush with oil. Place tri-tip on grate over medium-hot coals and sear for 7 minutes. Turn tri-tip over and move to medium heat. **If using a gas grill:** Place drained wood chips in foil broiler pan; place pan directly on gas flame. Replace grill grate and brush with oil. Place tri-tip on grate over foil pan and sear for 7 minutes (wood in pan will begin to smoke). Turn tri-tip over and reduce heat to medium-high.

Cover grill and cook until an instant-read thermometer inserted into the thickest part of tri-tip registers 120°F for rare (beef will carry over to 125°F, or medium-rare, as it rests), turning tri-tip occasionally, 12 to 13 minutes.

Transfer tri-tip to a work surface. Let stand for 10 minutes. Thinly slice roast against the grain. Serve, passing sauce separately.

SLOW-COOKED TRI-TIP
with Red Wine Barbecue Sauce

Slow cooking is the secret here: Rich, lean tri-tip (with a thin layer of fat left on to moisten the meat as it cooks) grills gently over low heat, basted with a smoky red wine barbecue sauce. Off the grill, the tri-tip is paired with slowly sautéed, deep golden brown caramelized onions.

CARAMELIZED RED ONIONS

2 Tbsp. (¼ stick) unsalted butter
2 Tbsp. extra-virgin olive oil
2½ lb. red onions (about 4 medium), halved, thinly sliced
2 tsp. balsamic vinegar
½ tsp. kosher salt
¼ tsp. freshly ground black pepper
¼ cup chopped fresh chives

TRI-TIP

1 tsp. garlic powder
1 tsp. kosher salt
½ tsp. freshly ground black pepper
2 1½- to 1¾-lb. beef loin tri-tip roasts, trimmed of all but ¼ inch of fat
2 Tbsp. extra-virgin olive oil, plus more for brushing
  Red Wine Barbecue Sauce (recipe follows)

CARAMELIZED RED ONIONS

Melt butter with oil in a large heavy nonstick skillet over medium heat. Add onions and cook, stirring frequently, until deep golden brown, about 30 minutes. Stir in vinegar, salt, and pepper. Remove from heat. **DO AHEAD:** Can be made 1 day ahead. Cover and refrigerate. Rewarm over medium heat before serving. Stir in chives just before using.

TRI-TIP

Build a 2-zone medium/low fire in a charcoal grill (see page 15), or heat a gas grill to medium-high. Mix garlic powder, salt, and pepper in a small bowl. Brush both sides of tri-tips with 2 Tbsp. oil and sprinkle with garlic powder mixture, pressing to adhere. Brush grill grate with oil. Grill tri-tips (over medium heat if using a charcoal grill) for 5 minutes per side. Move meat to low heat on charcoal grill, or reduce heat on gas grill to medium-low. Cover and grill tri-tips, brushing with barbecue sauce and turning every 10 minutes, until an instant-read thermometer inserted into the thickest part of meat registers 120°F for rare (tri-tip will carry over to 125°F, or medium-rare, as it rests), about 30 minutes longer.

Transfer tri-tips to a work surface; let rest for 10 minutes. Cut meat against the grain into very thin slices; arrange on a platter. Surround with caramelized onions and serve with remaining barbecue sauce.

Red Wine Barbecue Sauce

use with tri-tip

1 Tbsp. extra-virgin olive oil
1 large garlic clove, minced
¼ tsp. ground cumin
¼ tsp. ground chipotle, ancho, or guajillo chile
⅓ cup dry red wine
½ cup ketchup
1 Tbsp. apple cider vinegar
1 Tbsp. reduced-sodium soy sauce
⅛ tsp. liquid smoke

INGREDIENT INFO Look for ground chipotle chiles in the spice section of most supermarkets. Liquid smoke can be found at many supermarkets and at specialty foods stores.

Heat oil in a medium heavy saucepan over medium heat. Add garlic, cumin, and ground chile; stir for 1 minute. Add wine and simmer for 2 minutes. Stir in ketchup, vinegar, soy sauce, and liquid smoke; simmer for 2 minutes longer. **DO AHEAD:** Can be prepared 2 days ahead. Cover and chill.

TRI-TIP
with Chipotle Rub

4 to 6 servings

1 2- to 2½-lb. tri-tip steak (about 2 inches thick)
Kosher salt
⅓ cup Chipotle Rub (page 375)
Vegetable oil, for brushing

This flavorful steak gets even better when you season it with a bold chipotle rub, which gives the meat a deep, smoky flavor. Because this cut is so thick, it needs to rest longer than most other steaks. Slice it very thinly across the grain to help make it even more tender.

Sprinkle tri-tip with salt. Massage Chipotle Rub into meat. Let steak sit at room temperature for 1 hour or refrigerate uncovered overnight. Bring to room temperature before grilling.

Build a 2-zone medium-hot/medium fire in a charcoal grill (see page 15), or preheat a gas grill to high. Brush grill grate with oil. Cook tri-tip for 3 to 4 minutes per side (over medium-hot coals if using a charcoal grill), until nicely charred. Transfer to medium heat on charcoal grill, or reduce heat on gas grill to medium. Cook tri-tip for an additional 6 to 8 minutes per side or until an instant-read thermometer registers 120°F for rare (steak will carry over to 125°F, or medium-rare, as it rests). Transfer meat to a work surface; let rest for 10 minutes. Thinly slice against the grain.

Kitchen Wisdom

TRI-TIP, THE SECRET WEAPON This flavorful and relatively inexpensive cut is a local favorite in central California, where it's known as "Santa Maria steak." The cut is fairly lean and has a deep beefy flavor; it **benefits from strong marinades and stands up to bold spice rubs**. Brush it with extra-virgin olive oil just before grilling to help keep the meat moist, and be careful not to overcook it. Use an instant-read thermometer to check doneness; we recommend taking it off the grill when it hits 120°F.

On the grill, cross-cut Kalbi delivers the **deep, robust flavors of ribs**, but without a lengthy cooking time.

KALBI

SHORT RIBS
in Lettuce Leaves

6 servings

1 cup reduced-sodium soy sauce
½ cup (packed) dark brown sugar
4 garlic cloves, minced
1 Tbsp. toasted sesame oil
12 bone-in ⅓-inch-thick flanken-style short ribs
1½ cups short-grain rice (such as sushi rice)
1 tsp. salt
Vegetable oil, for brushing
Butter lettuce leaves
Red miso (fermented soybean paste)

INGREDIENT INFO Red miso, also called aka miso, is fermented soybean paste that adds a salty, roasted dimension to a dish. It's available in the refrigerated Asian foods section of some supermarkets and at natural foods stores and Japanese markets.

Korean barbecue is known for its salty-sweet-spicy balance and for the way it's served: Short ribs are grilled quickly, then wrapped in lettuce with sticky rice. The result is a great combination of flavors and textures. Ask your butcher for cross-cut beef short ribs (a.k.a. flanken style). They're different from other short ribs—cut thinly and across the bones, rather than between the bones. You can also find them at Korean markets.

Whisk soy sauce, sugar, garlic, and sesame oil in a large glass baking dish. **DO AHEAD:** Can be made 2 hours ahead. Let stand at room temperature.

Add ribs to marinade; turn to coat. Let marinate for 30 minutes at room temperature, turning occasionally.

Meanwhile, bring 3 cups water to a boil in a small saucepan. Stir in rice and salt; bring to a boil. Cover, reduce heat to low, and simmer until water is absorbed and rice is tender, about 17 minutes. Remove pan from heat.

Build a medium-hot fire in a charcoal grill, or heat a gas grill to high. Brush grill with vegetable oil. Grill ribs until cooked through, 2 to 3 minutes per side. Remove meat from bones and wrap in lettuce leaves with small amount of miso and sticky rice.

KALBI

4 to 6 servings

photo, left

½ cup reduced-sodium soy sauce
1½ Tbsp. raw sugar
1 Tbsp. minced garlic
1 tsp. toasted sesame oil
1 tsp. grated peeled ginger
½ tsp. freshly ground black pepper
½ cup chopped scallions, plus more, thinly sliced, for garnish
2 lb. bone-in ⅓-inch-thick flanken-style short ribs
Vegetable oil, for brushing

We fell in love with this bone-in cut—also known as Korean-style or cross-cut short ribs—at Korean barbecue joints. The sweet marinade may also be used to give any thin steak an Asian spin. Ask your butcher for cross-cut beef short ribs (a.k.a. flanken style) cut about ⅓ inch thick, or look for them at Korean markets.

Whisk soy sauce, sugar, garlic, sesame oil, ginger, pepper, and 2 Tbsp. water in a medium bowl. Stir in chopped scallions. **DO AHEAD:** Cover and chill marinade for up to 1 day.

Place short ribs in a resealable plastic bag; pour marinade over. Seal bag; turn to coat and chill for 3 hours. Let come to room temperature before grilling. Drain and pat dry with paper towels.

Build a medium fire in a charcoal grill, or heat a gas grill to medium-high. Brush grill grate with oil. Grill ribs for 2 to 3 minutes per side, or until just cooked through. Transfer to a platter and let rest for 5 to 10 minutes. Garnish with sliced scallions.

SMOKED BRISKET
with Ancho-Chile Sauce

4 tsp. kosher salt

1 Tbsp. (packed) light brown sugar

2 tsp. ground ancho chiles

1 tsp. paprika

1 tsp. ground cumin

1 tsp. granulated garlic

1 tsp. freshly ground black pepper

1 5- to 5½-lb. flat-cut brisket with ¼- to ½-inch layer of fat on one side

Ancho Chile Sauce (recipe follows) or store-bought barbecue sauce

SPECIAL EQUIPMENT 4 cups hickory or oak wood chips, soaked in water for 1 hour; a foil broiler pan (for wood chips if using gas grill); 2 foil baking pans (for brisket)

INGREDIENT INFO Look for ground ancho chiles in the spice section of many supermarkets and at Latin markets.

This is the real low-and-slow deal. Whether you're using charcoal or gas, maintaining a low temperature inside your grill is key to slowly cooking a brisket that's tender and oozing juices when sliced. Select a brisket with a good layer of fat on top, massage the sweet-spicy dry rub thoroughly into the meat, and set the meat on the grill with the fat side up to act as a natural moisturizer as the meat cooks. You can serve this with the Ancho Chile Sauce, or with your favorite store-bought barbecue sauce.

Mix first 7 ingredients in a small bowl. Rub spice blend over brisket. Wrap brisket in plastic; refrigerate for at least 2 hours and up to 24 hours. Bring to room temperature before grilling.

Prepare grill for smoking (see instructions on page 161). **If using a charcoal grill**: Build a low fire in a charcoal grill (you'll need to light more charcoal in chimney to replenish two or three times during grilling). Drain 2 cups wood chips; scatter directly over coals. Return top grate to grill. **If using a gas grill**: Heat grill to medium-low. Drain 2 cups wood chips. Place wood chips in foil broiler pan and place pan directly on gas flame. Return top grate to grill.

Unwrap brisket and arrange fat side up in foil baking pan; place pan on grate over unlit part of grill. Cover grill. Insert instant-read thermometer in top vent. Heat grill to 300°F. Cook brisket, adjusting vents and adding more charcoal or adjusting gas levels as needed to maintain temperature inside grill at 250°F, until an instant-read thermometer inserted into the center registers 160°F, about 3½ hours. Baste brisket occasionally with pan juices and add more drained wood chips as needed.

Remove pan with brisket. Wrap brisket tightly in 2 wide sheets of heavy-duty foil. Discard pan and juices. Place in clean foil baking pan. Return to grill over unlit side, maintaining internal grill temperature at 250°F, until an instant-read thermometer inserted into thickest part of center of brisket registers 190°F, about 1½ hours longer. Transfer brisket in pan to a rimmed baking sheet. Let rest for at least 1 hour and up to 2 hours.

Carefully unwrap brisket, saving any juices in foil. Transfer juices to a small pitcher. Place brisket on a work surface. Thinly slice brisket against the grain; transfer to a platter. Brush brisket with some juices. Serve with any remaining juices and Ancho Chile Sauce.

Ancho Chile Sauce

use with
smoked brisket

1 dried ancho chile, stemmed, seeded, coarsely torn
2 Tbsp. vegetable oil
1 cup chopped onion
1 Tbsp. tomato paste
3 garlic cloves, minced
½ cup dry red wine
½ cup ketchup
1 Tbsp. apple cider vinegar
1 Tbsp. (packed) dark brown sugar
2 tsp. Worcestershire sauce
¼ tsp. ground cumin
   Kosher salt and freshly ground black pepper

INGREDIENT INFO Dried ancho chiles are available at many supermarkets and at specialty foods stores and Latin markets.

Place chile in a medium bowl. Pour enough boiling water over to cover; let soak until soft, about 30 minutes. Drain, reserving soaking liquid.

Heat oil in a medium heavy saucepan over medium heat. Add onion and sauté until soft, stirring often, about 4 minutes. Add tomato paste; stir for 2 minutes. Add garlic and stir for 30 seconds. Add wine and softened chile; simmer for 2 minutes. Add 3 Tbsp. reserved chile soaking liquid, ketchup, and next 4 ingredients. Simmer for 3 minutes, stirring often. Season with salt and pepper. Remove from heat and let cool slightly. Purée sauce in a blender, adding more reserved soaking liquid by tablespoonfuls if too thick. **DO AHEAD:** Can be made 3 days ahead. Cover and chill. Rewarm before using.

Kitchen Wisdom

LOW AND SLOW: BRISKET AT HOME Wish you could make lusciously tender meat like the kind you get at hardcore barbecue joints in the middle of Texas? It takes commitment and patience, but it's definitely doable: Arm yourself with a **good rub** (for inspiration, check out the recipes starting on page 375)— and a **good amount of time**. Plan ahead so you have five to six hours for smoking and at least another hour in order to let it rest. Believe us, every second will be worth it.

BARBECUED BEEF RIBS
with Molasses-Bourbon Sauce

6 servings

MARINADE AND RIBS
- 1 12-oz. bottle pale ale
- ¼ cup mild-flavored (light) molasses
- 5 sprigs thyme
- 1 Tbsp. sugar
- 1 Tbsp. kosher salt
- 1 bay leaf
- ½ tsp. ground white pepper
- 16 short ribs or 8 whole ribs

SAUCE
- 1 Tbsp. vegetable oil, plus more for brushing
- 1 small onion, finely chopped
- 1 cup red wine vinegar
- 2 cups ketchup
- ½ cup mild-flavored (light) molasses
- ½ cup bourbon
- 1½ tsp. kosher salt
- ½ tsp. ground white pepper
  Leaves from 5 sprigs thyme

SPECIAL EQUIPMENT A foil baking pan (for drip pan)

Like spareribs, but beefier and meatier, beef short ribs are incredibly flavorful and well marbled. The meat is naturally tough, but a low temperature and long cooking time turn it into some of the most succulent meat you'll ever sink your teeth into.

MARINADE AND RIBS

Combine all ingredients except ribs with 1½ cups water in a medium heavy saucepan. Bring to a boil, stirring to dissolve sugar. Let marinade cool completely. Place ribs in a large heavy-duty resealable plastic bag; add marinade. Seal bag; turn to coat ribs. Refrigerate overnight, turning bag occasionally.

SAUCE

Heat 1 Tbsp. oil in a large heavy saucepan over medium-high heat. Add onion and sauté until golden brown, about 6 minutes. Add vinegar and boil until mixture is reduced to ¾ cup, about 5 minutes. Remove from heat. Add ketchup, molasses, bourbon, and ¼ cup water; stir to blend. Bring sauce to a simmer. Stir in salt and white pepper. Simmer for 10 minutes to blend flavors. Stir in thyme leaves.
DO AHEAD: Sauce can be prepared 1 day ahead. Cover and chill. Rewarm before using.

Prepare grill for smoking (see instructions on page 161). **If using a charcoal grill**: Build a medium fire in a charcoal grill, arranging coals on either side of lower grate. (You'll need to light more charcoal in chimney to replenish two or three times during grilling.) Fill drip pan halfway with water and place on lower grate between coals. **If using a gas grill**: Heat grill to medium-high. Fill drip pan halfway with water and place on unlit burner.

Return top grate to grill and brush with oil. Arrange ribs on top grate above water in pan. Cover grill. Insert instant-read thermometer in top vent. Adjust vents and add more charcoal or adjust gas levels as needed to maintain temperature inside grill between 250°F and 300°F. Cook ribs, turning ribs occasionally, and basting often with sauce during the last 10 minutes of cooking, until meat is very tender when pierced with knife, about 3 hours total. Open grill only when necessary to add fresh coals or turn or baste meat, and close lid quickly.

Transfer ribs to plates; brush with more sauce and serve, passing any remaining sauce separately.

— 136 —

HANGER-STEAK SALAD
with Tomato Vinaigrette

1 lb. hanger, skirt, or flank steak
1 tsp. kosher salt, more as needed
Freshly ground black pepper
1 medium tomato (about 6 oz.), halved
1 Tbsp. minced shallot
1 Tbsp. red wine vinegar
¼ cup plus 5 tsp. extra-virgin olive oil, divided; additional for brushing
4 spring onions or 6 scallions, bulbs halved, dark green parts discarded
5 ½-inch-thick slices rustic white bread, such as ciabatta
8 cups mixed summer lettuces (such as mizuna, baby mustard greens, and tatsoi)
¾ cup fresh basil leaves, torn into ½-inch strips

A good summer salad requires three things: fresh greens, a tart, seasonal dressing (here with grated tomato), and a light hand when tossing, so the lettuces stay perky.

Season steak with 1 tsp. salt and pepper; set aside. Grate cut sides of tomato on coarse holes of a box grater into a medium bowl down to the skin; discard skin. Add shallot and vinegar; whisk in ¼ cup oil. Season to taste with salt and pepper. Set aside. **DO AHEAD:** Tomato vinaigrette can be made 1 day ahead.

Build a medium-hot fire in a charcoal grill, or heat a gas grill to high. Brush grill grate with oil. Toss spring onions in a medium bowl with 1 tsp. oil and season with salt and pepper. Grill onions until just tender, 2 to 3 minutes per side. Cut into 2-inch pieces.

Grill steak until seared and cooked to desired doneness, 3 to 5 minutes per side for medium-rare, depending on steak's thickness. Transfer to a work surface. Let rest for about 10 minutes.

Meanwhile, make croutons: Brush both sides of bread slices with remaining 4 tsp. oil and season with salt and pepper. Grill bread until dark golden brown and nicely charred in spots, about 2 minutes per side. Set toast aside until cool enough to handle, then break toast into roughly 1-inch pieces.

Thinly slice steak against the grain. Toss lettuces, basil, spring onions, croutons, and some of the vinaigrette in a large bowl. Season to taste with salt and pepper.

Add steak and toss gently to coat. Serve with remaining vinaigrette alongside.

STRIP-STEAK SALAD
with Green Beans and Blue Cheese

3 8- to 9-oz. New York strip steaks
1 Tbsp. plus ½ cup extra-virgin olive oil, plus more for brushing
Kosher salt and freshly ground black pepper
1 lb. slender green beans, trimmed
6 cups arugula (about 5 oz.)
4 cups cherry tomatoes, halved
1¼ cups pitted Kalamata olives, halved
3 Tbsp. balsamic vinegar
1 cup crumbled blue cheese (about 4 oz.)

Steak salads are great for a few reasons—notably that the steak's juices meld deliciously with the vegetables and the dressing. And they're even (kind of) healthy. Here steak and blue cheese, a traditionally great pairing, team up with green beans.

Brush steaks with 1 Tbsp. oil; season with salt and pepper. Let stand at room temperature for 1 hour.

Cook green beans in a large pot of boiling salted water until crisp-tender, about 4 minutes. Drain. Transfer to a bowl of ice water and let cool. Drain.

Build a medium-hot fire in a charcoal grill, or heat a gas grill to high. Combine beans, arugula, tomatoes, and olives in a large bowl for salad. Whisk ½ cup oil and vinegar in a small bowl. Season dressing to taste with salt and pepper.

Brush grill grate with oil. Grill steaks until an instant-read thermometer registers 120°F for rare (steak will carry over to 125°F, or medium-rare, as it rests), about 4 minutes per side. Transfer to a work surface and let rest for 5 minutes. Cut steaks against the grain into strips.

Toss salad with enough dressing to coat. Season to taste with salt and pepper. Divide among 6 plates. Top with steak strips. Sprinkle cheese over.

THAI BEEF SALAD

photo, right

BEEF AND MARINADE

- 1 1-lb. beef tenderloin, cut into ½-inch-thick slices
- 9 garlic cloves, chopped
- ¼ cup hoisin sauce
- ¼ cup hot chili sauce (such as Sriracha) or hot chili paste (such as sambal oelek)
- ¼ cup mirin
- ¼ cup toasted sesame oil
- ¼ cup chopped peeled ginger
- ¼ cup chopped scallions
- 2 Tbsp. sesame seeds
- 1 Tbsp. fresh lime juice

DRESSING

- 3 Tbsp. fresh lime juice
- 2 Tbsp. reduced-sodium soy sauce
- 2 Tbsp. honey
- 1 Tbsp. rice vinegar
- 1½ tsp. mirin
- 1½ tsp. finely grated peeled ginger
- ½ tsp. toasted sesame oil
- ½ cup extra-virgin olive oil
- ¼ cup chopped fresh cilantro
  Kosher salt and freshly ground black pepper

SALAD

- 1 6-oz. package soba (Japanese-style noodles)
  Kosher salt
  Vegetable oil, for brushing
- 2 cups chopped scallions (about 1 large bunch)
- 1 cup matchstick-size strips peeled carrot (about 1 large)
- 1 cup matchstick-size strips daikon (Japanese white radish)
- 18 small fresh basil leaves
- 18 fresh cilantro leaves
- 18 fresh mint leaves

INGREDIENT INFO Hoisin sauce, hot chili sauce and paste, mirin, soba noodles, and daikon radishes can be found at supermarkets or Asian markets.

Both the beef tenderloin and the soba noodles cook quickly for this salad. The steak is naturally tender and is cut thin so it's best seared fast over hot embers to medium-rare. The soba noodles should be cooked like any pasta: al dente (if overcooked, they'll get mushy).

BEEF AND MARINADE

Place beef in a large resealable plastic bag. Whisk all remaining ingredients in a medium bowl to blend; pour over beef and seal bag. Turn bag to coat. Refrigerate overnight, turning bag occasionally. Bring to room temperature before grilling.

DRESSING

Combine first 7 ingredients in a blender. With blender running, gradually add olive oil. Add cilantro; blend until smooth. Season to taste with salt and pepper.

DO AHEAD: Dressing can be made 2 hours ahead. Cover and chill.

SALAD

Cook soba noodles in a large saucepan of boiling salted water, stirring occasionally, until tender but still firm to bite. Drain; rinse under cold water. Drain well. Transfer noodles to a large bowl; drizzle with 2 Tbsp. dressing. Let stand at room temperature.

Build a medium-hot fire in a charcoal grill, or heat a gas grill to high. Brush grill grate with oil. Remove beef from marinade; discard marinade. Grill beef with some marinade still clinging until cooked to desired doneness, about 2 minutes per side for medium-rare. Let stand at room temperature for 5 minutes. Cut beef against the grain into thin strips. Add to noodles.

Add scallions and all remaining ingredients to bowl with noodles and beef. Add remaining dressing and toss to coat.

Cutting beef tenderloin into ½-inch-thick slices before grilling helps it **soak up tons of flavor** from a tangy marinade.

THAI BEEF SALAD

CARNE ASADA TACOS

with Salsa Mexicana

6 to 8 servings

Vegetable oil, for brushing
8 poblano chiles
2 bunches scallions (about 12),
   dark green tops trimmed
2 lb. skirt steak, cut crosswise
   into 6-inch-wide pieces
4 garlic cloves, minced
   Kosher salt and freshly ground
   black pepper
   Corn or flour tortillas, for serving
2 avocados, peeled, pitted, sliced
   Lime wedges, for serving
   Salsa Mexicana (recipe follows)

INGREDIENT INFO Poblano chiles are available at some supermarkets and at specialty foods stores, farmers' markets, and Latin markets.

Arrachera **(skirt steak) is one of the most popular grilled meats in Mexico—served sizzling hot off the steel-drum grills of street vendors and at restaurants. This flavorful steak is seasoned with just garlic, salt, and pepper, and it makes for killer tacos when wrapped in a warm corn tortilla with roasted poblanos and scallions, avocado, lime, and a fresh salsa. This recipe calls for a generous amount of poblanos; use as many or as few as you like.**

Build a medium-hot fire in a charcoal grill, or heat a gas grill to high. Brush grill grate with oil. Grill chiles and scallions until charred all over, about 3 minutes for scallions and 5 minutes for chiles. Transfer scallions to a plate; tent with foil to keep warm. Transfer chiles to a large bowl; cover with plastic and let stand for 15 minutes. Peel and seed chiles; cut into 1-inch-wide strips. Transfer to a plate; tent with foil to keep warm.

Rub steak with garlic; season with salt and pepper. Grill until cooked to desired doneness, about 3 minutes per side for medium. Transfer to a work surface; let cool for 5 minutes. Grill tortillas until warm and slightly charred, about 10 seconds per side. Cut steak against the grain into strips.

Serve steak with tortillas, chiles, scallions, avocado slices, lime wedges, and Salsa Mexicana.

Salsa Mexicana

makes about 1½ cups

serve with
tacos

12 oz. tomatoes (about 2 medium),
   cut into ¼-inch cubes
1 medium white onion (about 7 oz.),
   cut into ¼-inch cubes
2 serrano or jalapeños, chopped,
   or up to 8 for more heat
¼ cup chopped fresh cilantro
3 Tbsp. fresh lime juice
   Kosher salt

Use as many serrano chiles or jalapeños as you like; if you're uncertain about the heat, start with two and add more to taste.

Combine first 5 ingredients in a medium bowl. Season to taste with salt.
DO AHEAD: Can be made 2 hours ahead. Let stand at room temperature.

STRIP STEAK SANDWICHES
on Garlic Baguette

6 servings

1½ tsp. extra-virgin olive oil, plus more for brushing

1½ tsp. herbes de Provence

2 1-lb. New York strip steaks (each ¾ to 1 inch thick), trimmed
Kosher salt and freshly ground black pepper

6 5- to 6-inch-long baguette sections, halved lengthwise

2 large garlic cloves, halved

3½ cups arugula (about 3 oz.)

2 large plum tomatoes, thinly sliced

INGREDIENT INFO Herbes de Provence is a dried herb mixture available in the spice section at some supermarkets and at specialty foods stores. If unavailable, substitute a combination of dried thyme, basil, savory, and fennel seeds.

Serve the steak warm or use it cold for picnic-perfect sandwiches. You could also put any leftover lean grilled steaks to use here.

Mix 1½ tsp. oil and herbes de Provence in a small bowl to blend. Rub oil mixture over both sides of steaks. Season with salt and pepper. Let stand at room temperature for 1 hour.

Build a medium-hot fire in a charcoal grill, or heat a gas grill to high. Brush grill grate with oil. Grill steaks to desired doneness, about 8 minutes per side for medium-rare. Transfer to a work surface and let rest for 10 minutes. Slice thinly and set aside. Alternatively, let cool completely, then wrap steaks tightly with plastic and chill. Cut cold steaks into ⅛-inch-thick slices before continuing.

Lightly brush cut sides of bread with oil. Grill, cut side down, until bread is golden, about 1 minute. Rub garlic halves over toasted sides of bread.

Place arugula over bottoms of bread. Top with meat, then with tomatoes. Season with salt and pepper. Cover with bread tops. Cut sandwiches in half. Serve warm or at room temperature, or wrap with foil and chill if packing for picnic. **DO AHEAD:** Can be made 2 hours ahead. Chill.

TRI-TIP SANDWICHES
with Marinated Watercress Salad

6 servings

½ cup extra-virgin olive oil, plus more for brushing

6 Tbsp. white balsamic vinegar

1¾ tsp. dry mustard, divided
Kosher salt and freshly ground black pepper

1 Tbsp. (packed) dark brown sugar

1 2-lb. tri-tip beef roast or flank steak

4 large plum tomatoes, very thinly sliced

1 bunch watercress, thick stems trimmed

½ white onion, very thinly sliced

6 5-inch pieces baguette, cut horizontally almost in half, opened flat

Marinating the salad at room temperature while the steaks cook gives the vegetables just enough time to exude juices that mix with the vinaigrette, resulting in a flavorful topping for these open-face steak sandwiches.

Whisk ½ cup oil, vinegar, and ¾ tsp. dry mustard in a large bowl. Season dressing to taste with salt and pepper. Transfer 2 Tbsp. dressing to a small bowl; whisk in sugar and remaining 1 tsp. dry mustard. Season beef all over with salt and pepper, then spread mixture from small bowl over. Let stand at room temperature for 1 hour.

Build a medium-hot fire in a charcoal grill, or heat a gas grill to high. Brush grill grate with oil. Grill beef, turning occasionally, until an instant-read thermometer inserted into the thickest part registers 120°F to 125°F for rare, turning occasionally, about 30 minutes. Transfer to a work surface; let rest for 10 minutes. Cut very thinly against the grain.

Meanwhile, add tomatoes, watercress, and onion to dressing in large bowl. Marinate while beef grills, tossing occasionally. Grill bread, cut side down, until just crusty, about 3 minutes; place on plates, grilled side up.

Arrange beef slices over bread. Using tongs and draining slightly, top with watercress salad.

LEMONY VEAL CHOPS
with Gremolata

6 servings

VEAL
- ½ cup extra-virgin olive oil
- 6 Tbsp. fresh lemon juice
- ⅓ cup chopped flat-leaf parsley
- 3 garlic cloves, crushed
- 1 Tbsp. minced fresh rosemary
- 6 8- to 10-oz. loin or rib veal chops (each about 1 inch thick)
  Kosher salt and freshly ground black pepper

TOPPING
- 3 Tbsp. chopped flat-leaf parsley
- 1 Tbsp. finely grated lemon zest
- 1½ tsp. minced fresh rosemary
- 1 tsp. minced garlic
  Vegetable oil, for brushing
  Kosher salt and freshly ground black pepper

A lemony parsley topping called gremolata is a simple Italian seasoning commonly used to top braised veal shanks, or osso buco. Traditionally it is made with just parsley, lemon, and garlic, but the addition of rosemary gives it a heartier flavor that stands up well to grilling.

VEAL
Whisk first 5 ingredients in a small bowl. Arrange veal chops in a 15x10x2-inch glass baking dish. Season chops on both sides with salt and pepper. Pour marinade over chops; turn to coat. Cover and refrigerate, turning occasionally, for at least 6 hours or overnight. Bring to room temperature before grilling.

TOPPING
Stir parsley, lemon zest, rosemary, and garlic in a small bowl to blend.

Build a medium-hot fire in a charcoal grill, or heat a gas grill to high. Brush grill grate with oil. Remove chops from marinade and season generously with salt and pepper. Grill chops until cooked to desired doneness, about 6 minutes per side for medium-rare. Transfer chops to a serving platter; sprinkle each with topping.

VEAL CHOPS
with Red Wine and Rosemary

6 servings

- 5 Tbsp. extra-virgin olive oil, plus more for brushing
- ¼ cup dry red wine
- 1½ Tbsp. chopped fresh rosemary
- 2 large garlic cloves, minced
- ½ tsp. kosher salt, more as needed
- ½ tsp. freshly ground black pepper, more as needed
- 6 8-oz. veal rib chops (each ¾ to 1 inch thick)
  Rosemary sprigs, for garnish

This red wine, rosemary, and garlic marinade is a classic Italian preparation for tender veal chops.

Whisk 5 Tbsp. oil, wine, rosemary, garlic, ½ tsp. salt, and ½ tsp. pepper to blend in a 13x9x2-inch glass baking dish. Add veal chops to dish and turn to coat with marinade. Let stand at room temperature for 1 hour or refrigerate up to 4 hours, turning veal occasionally. Bring to room temperature before grilling.

Build a medium-hot fire in a charcoal grill, or heat a gas grill to high. Brush grill grate with oil. Remove veal from marinade, shaking off excess. Season veal with salt and pepper. Grill veal to desired doneness, about 5 minutes per side for medium-rare. Transfer to a platter. Garnish with rosemary sprigs.

VEAL CHOPS
with Ancho-Chipotle Sauce

- 2 Tbsp. extra-virgin olive oil, plus more for brushing
- 1 red bell pepper, chopped
- 1 large dried ancho chile, stemmed, seeded, torn into small pieces
- 2 garlic cloves, chopped
- 1 shallot, chopped
- 1 cup apple cider
- 3½ cups low-salt chicken broth, divided
- 3 Tbsp. honey
- 2 Tbsp. coarsely ground coffee beans
- 1 cup beef broth
- 2 Tbsp. canned chipotle chiles in adobo
- ⅔ cup chopped fresh cilantro
- 8 ¾-inch-thick veal rib chops (about 8 oz. each)
  Kosher salt and freshly ground black pepper

INGREDIENT INFO Look for ancho chiles and for chipotle chiles in adobo at many supermarkets, and at specialty foods stores and Latin markets.

The rib chops here are equivalent to bone-in rib-eye steaks of beef—they're both superior cuts that are incredibly tender and have just the right amount of fat to add flavor and keep the chops and steaks juicy.

Heat 2 Tbsp. olive oil in a large heavy saucepan over medium heat. Add red bell pepper, ancho chile, garlic, and shallot and sauté until soft, about 8 minutes. Add apple cider and simmer for 5 minutes. Add 1 cup chicken broth and honey; simmer until reduced to 1½ cups, about 15 minutes. Add the remaining 2½ cups chicken broth, ground coffee beans, beef broth, and chipotle chiles. Boil until reduced to 2½ cups, stirring occasionally, about 15 minutes. Let cool slightly. Purée mixture in a blender. Strain through a fine-mesh sieve. Mix in cilantro. **DO AHEAD:** Sauce can be made 2 days ahead. Cover and refrigerate. Rewarm before continuing.

Build a medium fire in a charcoal grill, or heat a gas grill to medium-high. Brush grill grate with oil. Season veal with salt and pepper. Grill to desired doneness, about 5 minutes per side for medium. Brush with some of the chile sauce and grill for 1 minute longer. Serve with remaining chile sauce.

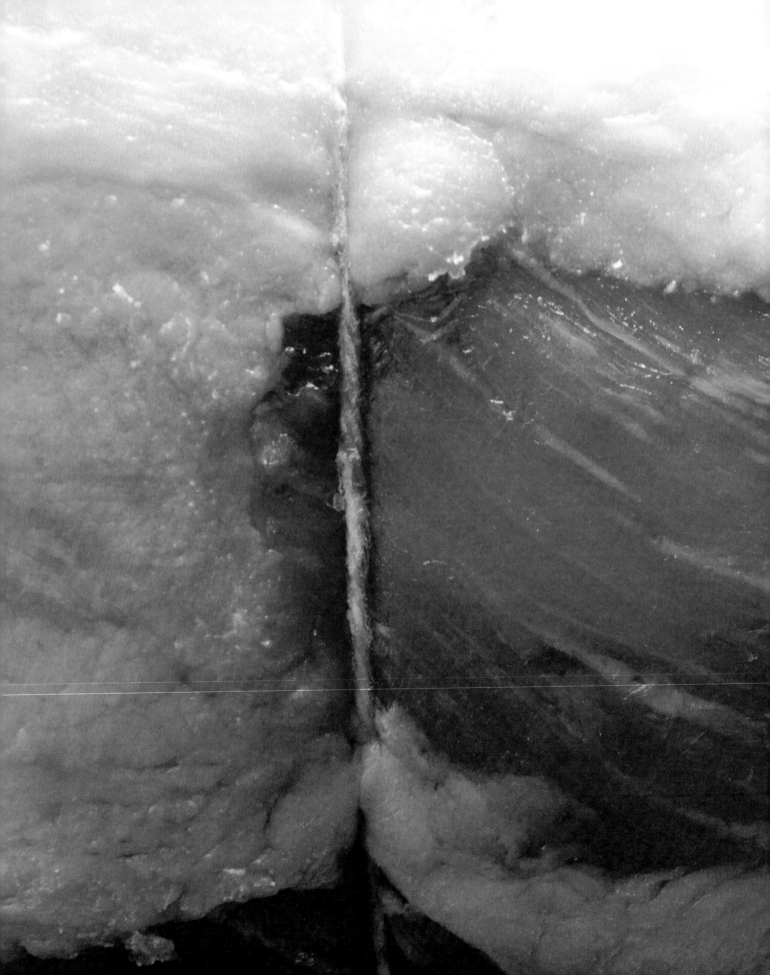

ch 5

PORK

PORK IS MORE THAN A FOOD. IT'S A MOVEMENT.

Celebrity chefs are flexing pig-tattooed forearms; we've got card-carrying bacon-of-the-month clubbers; and thanks to some enterprising farmers, heritage pork is garnering the kind of acclaim—and price tag—previously reserved for dry-aged steak.

Why all the hubbub? Well, to start with, this protein offers something for everyone. For people who like lean, buttery soft meat, there's pork tenderloin—liberally seasoned, quickly grilled, and sliced into rosy pink medallions. At the other end of the spectrum, there's the rich taste of slow-cooked spareribs—hopped-up on a dry rub, shellacked with a sweet sauce, and cooked for hours till the meat falls off the bone with just a tug.

In this chapter, you'll learn techniques to help you coax optimum flavor and tenderness from our favorite cuts, like chops and tenderloins (brining is always a smart move), and secrets for preparing ultra-tender grilled ribs. (Hint: The most important step happens *before* they hit the grill.) This comprehensive advice will help you feel confident when grilling any variety of pork. We're not saying you ought to run out and get a tattoo of a pig—but we are saying you ought to enjoy the whole hog.

PORK CHOPS
with Italian Relish

12 oz. plum tomatoes, seeded, chopped
¾ cup chopped red onion
¼ cup red wine vinegar
2 Tbsp. extra-virgin olive oil, plus more for brushing
1 Tbsp. chopped fresh basil or 1 tsp. dried
1 Tbsp. chopped fresh oregano or 1 tsp. dried
1 Tbsp. chopped garlic
Kosher salt and freshly ground black pepper
4 ¾- to 1-inch-thick center-cut pork chops

This dish is perfect for a weeknight dinner: First, make the simple relish, then drain off and use the liquid to marinate the chops while the grill heats up. Once they hit the grate, the pork chops will be done in less than 15 minutes.

Combine first 7 ingredients in a small bowl. Season with salt and pepper. Let stand for at least 15 minutes or up to 1 hour.

Build a medium fire in a charcoal grill, or heat a gas grill to medium-high. Arrange pork chops in an 8x8x2-inch glass baking dish. Drain liquid from relish; spoon liquid over pork. Let pork marinate for at least 15 minutes, turning occasionally. Brush grill grate with oil. Grill pork until an instant-read thermometer inserted into the center of pork chop reaches 145°F, about 6 minutes per side.

Transfer pork to plates. Spoon relish over and serve.

BRINED PORK CHOPS
with Molasses Barbecue Sauce

8 servings

1 cup (packed) dark brown sugar
1 small onion, thinly sliced
6 large garlic cloves, crushed
6 large thyme sprigs
1 Tbsp. kosher salt, more as needed
2 tsp. crushed red pepper flakes
8 8-oz. center-cut pork chops
Extra-virgin olive oil, for brushing
Freshly ground black pepper
Molasses Barbecue Sauce (page 162)

Don't worry that these chops will be too sweet—both the brine and the barbecue sauce feature dried crushed red pepper flakes and healthy quantities of garlic to balance out the intensity of the molasses.

Combine 4 cups water with first 6 ingredients in a large saucepan; bring to a boil. Remove from heat. Let cool completely.

Place pork in a large glass baking dish. Pour brine over. Cover; chill overnight.

Build a medium-hot fire in a charcoal grill, or heat a gas grill to high. Drain pork; pat dry. Brush pork with oil. Season with salt and pepper. Brush grill grate with oil. Grill pork until an instant-read thermometer inserted into the center of pork chop reaches 145°F, about 6 minutes per side for medium. Place on plates. Spoon Molasses Barbecue Sauce over.

PORK CHOPS
with Treviso and Balsamic Glaze

photo, right

3 Tbsp. kosher salt, more as needed
1½ Tbsp. sugar
4 ¾- to 1-inch-thick pork rib chops
1 head of Treviso radicchio
1 head of Belgian endive
 Extra-virgin olive oil, for brushing
 Freshly ground black pepper
¾ cup balsamic vinegar
1 Tbsp. butter
 Chopped flat-leaf parsley

INGREDIENT INFO If you can't find Treviso, use a small head of Chioggia (round) radicchio instead, and quarter it through the root end so that it stays intact on the grill.

A balsamic vinegar glaze lends these pork chops a rich, sweet flavor—one that is off-set by the charred, slightly bitter qualities of grilled endive and the torpedo-shaped radicchio called Treviso.

Build a medium-hot fire in a charcoal grill, or heat a gas grill to high. Mix 1½ cups water, 3 Tbsp. salt, and sugar in an 11x7x2-inch glass baking dish; stir until salt and sugar dissolve. Add pork chops; let brine for 20 minutes, turning occasionally.

Cut radicchio and endive lengthwise into quarters, keeping some core attached to each piece. Place on a rimmed baking sheet; brush with some oil. Season with salt and pepper. Boil vinegar in a small skillet until reduced to ¼ cup, about 5 minutes. Whisk in butter. Season glaze with salt and pepper.

Remove pork chops from brine; pat dry. Brush with oil; season with pepper. Brush grill grate with oil. Grill chops, radicchio, and endive until vegetables are softened and an instant-read thermometer inserted into the center of chops registers 145°F, 2 to 3 minutes per side for vegetables and 6 minutes per side for pork chops.

Transfer pork chops and vegetables to plates. Drizzle glaze over; sprinkle with chopped parsley.

Is It Done Yet?

STOP OVERCOOKING YOUR PORK For years, food safety experts said pork should be cooked to a moisture-zapping 160°F. But in recent years, the USDA has acknowledged that this is above the level necessary to kill pathogens, and lowered its guideline for whole cuts of pork to **145°F, which delivers juicier, rosier-hued meat** (think medium/medium-rare). To test for doneness, insert an instant-read thermometer through the side of the meat to the center (don't touch the bone).

+

A flavor-boosting quick brine (just 20 minutes, and you're done) **infuses maximum flavor** without lengthy prep time.

PORK CHOPS
WITH TREVISO AND BALSAMIC GLAZE

PORK CHOPS
with Tomatillo Salsa

———

12 tomatillos (about 1 lb.), husked, rinsed
4 garlic cloves
2 jalapeños
⅔ cup finely chopped white onion
⅔ cup (loosely packed) chopped fresh cilantro
   Kosher salt and freshly ground black pepper
6 1- to 1¼-inch-thick bone-in pork rib chops (each about 12 oz.)
   Extra-virgin olive oil, for brushing
1 garlic clove, halved
12 corn or flour tortillas

The tart, citrusy flavor of tomatillos is a nice counterpoint to the richness of pork. Charring tomatillos, garlic, and jalapeños is a Mexican cooking technique that softens their pungency and adds a deeper roasted flavor to salsa. Before using the tomatillos, remove their papery husks and rinse them under cold water to remove their sticky coating.

Preheat broiler. Place tomatillos, 4 garlic cloves, and jalapeños on a rimmed baking sheet. Broil, turning vegetables occasionally, until tender and slightly charred, about 7 minutes for garlic and 8 minutes for tomatillos and jalapeños. Transfer to a plate and let stand until cool enough to handle. Stem and seed jalapeños. Place tomatillos, garlic, jalapeños, onion, and cilantro in a food processor. Purée until almost smooth. Season tomatillo salsa with salt and pepper. **DO AHEAD:** Salsa can be made 1 day ahead. Cover and chill. Return salsa to room temperature before serving.

Build a medium-hot fire in a charcoal grill, or heat a gas grill to high. Brush grill grate with oil. Rub both sides of pork chops with halved garlic clove. Season with salt and pepper; brush with oil. Grill until an instant-read thermometer inserted into the center of pork registers 145°F, about 8 minutes per side. Transfer chops to a plate; let rest for 10 minutes. Grill tortillas until slightly charred, about 1 minute per side. Serve chops with tortillas and salsa.

SMOTHERED PORK CHOPS

———

2 large red bell peppers
2 Tbsp. vegetable oil, plus more for brushing
2 medium onions, thinly sliced
1 Tbsp. all-purpose flour
¼ cup dry white wine
2 Tbsp. apple cider vinegar
2 Tbsp. drained capers
1 cup low-salt chicken broth
1 Tbsp. chopped flat-leaf parsley
   Kosher salt and freshly ground black pepper
4 1- to 1¼-inch-thick bone-in pork rib chops (each about 12 oz.)

This comfort food favorite usually calls for the chops to be pan-fried, then simmered in a rich gravy until cooked through. But in our version, the extra-thick chops are grilled rather than fried, then smothered in a gravy with caramelized onions and roasted red bell peppers. Use bone-in chops to keep them juicy.

Char peppers over a gas flame, under broiler, or on a grill until charred on all sides. Enclose in a paper bag for 10 minutes. Peel and seed peppers; slice into thin strips.

Heat 2 Tbsp. oil in a large skillet over medium heat. Add onions and sauté until golden, about 15 minutes. Mix in flour; cook for 2 minutes. Add bell peppers, wine, vinegar, and capers; cook for 1 minute. Add broth. Increase heat; boil until sauce thickens enough to coat a spoon, about 4 minutes. Mix in parsley. Season with salt and pepper. **DO AHEAD:** Sauce can be made 1 day ahead. Cover and chill. Rewarm before using.

Build a medium-hot fire in a charcoal grill, or heat a gas grill to high. Brush grill grate with oil. Brush pork on all sides with oil. Season pork with salt and pepper. Grill until an instant-read thermometer inserted into the center of pork registers 145°F, about 8 minutes per side. Transfer chops to a platter. Spoon sauce over.

PORK CHOPS
with Cornbread-Bacon Dressing

Vegetable oil, for brushing
2 6-oz. bone-in pork rib chops
  Kosher salt and freshly ground
  black pepper
1 Tbsp. dried sage
3 bacon slices, chopped
1 medium onion, chopped
1½ cups cornbread stuffing mix
¾ cup low-salt chicken broth

This is such a simply prepared dish that you'll want to use the best quality pork chops you can buy; with just a generous sprinkle of kosher salt, freshly ground black pepper, and dried sage, the results will be spectacular. Add the super-quick cornbread dressing and you've got a holiday dinner in about half an hour.

Build a medium-hot fire in a charcoal grill, or heat a gas grill to high. Brush grill grate with oil. Sprinkle the pork chops with salt, pepper, and half of sage. Grill chops until an instant-read thermometer inserted into the center of the pork chop registers 145°F, about 4 minutes per side.

Meanwhile, sauté bacon in a heavy medium skillet over medium-high heat until crisp, about 5 minutes. Transfer bacon to paper towel–lined plate; drain. Add onion and remaining sage to skillet; sauté 4 minutes. Stir in stuffing mix and broth. Cover; simmer until dressing is heated through, about 4 minutes. Mix in bacon; season with pepper. Serve dressing with pork chops.

HERITAGE PORK: Why It's Worth It

In recent years, supermarket pork has gotten leaner—a lot leaner. In fact, some cuts actually have a fat content similar to that of skinless chicken. But who wants to eat pork that tastes like chicken? Without fat, pork has no flavor. Fortunately, there's a new—or very old—option.

THE HERITAGE STORY

It used to be that the majority of pork consumed in America came from **pasture-raised pigs of diverse breeds** who ate mainly what they foraged. And often, they were raised by independent farmers (rather than factory farms). The result? Flavorful meat that had plenty of fat. Thankfully, small farms throughout America have again started raising rare, heritage-breed pigs using environmentally sustainable methods that yield happy pigs and **rich, juicy meat**.

NAMES TO LOOK FOR

When you see pork that is identified as **Large Black**, **Red Wattle**, **Tamworth**, or **Berkshire**, you're on the right track. These heirloom varieties are the same moist, tender, well-marbled kinds of pork that your grandparents ate. We particularly like these purveyors: **Caw Caw Creek in South Carolina** and **Flying Pigs Farm in upstate New York**. Heritage pork doesn't come cheap, though. Expect to spend two to four times as much as for grocery-store varieties. Pricey? Yes. Worth it? Absolutely.

YUCATÁN-STYLE PORK CHOPS

3 Tbsp. kosher salt, more as needed
2 bay leaves
1 tsp. whole allspice
1 tsp. whole black peppercorns
4 large bone-in pork rib chops
Vegetable oil, for brushing
1 large white onion with skin, quartered through core with some core still attached to each
½ cup fresh lime juice
½ cup fresh orange juice
¼ cup coarsely chopped cilantro
½ small green cabbage, thinly sliced
1 avocado, halved, pitted, sliced
1 bunch red radishes, sliced

SPECIAL EQUIPMENT 2 cups wood chips, soaked in water for 1 hour; a foil baking pan (for drip pan); foil broiler pan (for wood chips, if using gas grill)

The inspiration for this recipe is *poc chuc*, a Mexican grilled pork dish flavored with citrus, topped with onions, and served with cabbage. The chops and vegetables are excellent served with warm corn tortillas.

Stir 2 cups water, 3 Tbsp. salt, bay leaves, allspice, and black peppercorns in a medium bowl until salt dissolves for brine. Arrange pork chops in a 13x9x2-inch baking dish. Pour brine over. Cover and refrigerate for 1 hour, turning occasionally.

Prepare grill for indirect heat with a drip pan (see page 16), building a medium-low fire in a charcoal grill, or heating a gas grill to medium. Drain wood chips. If using a charcoal grill, scatter wood chips evenly over coals. Alternatively, if using a gas grill, fill foil broiler pan with wood chips and place directly over flame. Brush grill grate with oil.

Grill onion quarters until browned (skin may burn), about 3 minutes per side. Let cool, then peel. Thinly slice and place in a bowl. Add lime juice and orange juice. Season onion mixture to taste with salt. Mix in cilantro.

Remove pork from brine; pat dry, then grill, covered, over drip pan until an instant-read thermometer inserted into the center of pork registers 145°F, 4 to 6 minutes per side. Transfer to a plate; let rest for 10 minutes.

Arrange cabbage on a platter. Top with pork, avocado, and radishes. Drain onions; scatter over pork and vegetables.

PORK TENDERLOIN
with Pipián Sauce

1 1- to 1¼-lb. pork tenderloin, cut into ½-inch-thick medallions
3 Tbsp. vegetable oil, divided, plus more for brushing
½ onion, coarsely chopped
¾ cup shelled pumpkin seeds (pepitas)
¼ cup peanuts (1½ oz.)
¼ cup sesame seeds (1½ oz.)
2 garlic cloves, minced
12 oz. tomatillos, husked
2 tsp. coarsely chopped seeded jalapeño
1½ cups fresh cilantro leaves
1½ cups torn romaine leaves
1¼ cups low-salt chicken broth
3 radishes, trimmed, chopped
Kosher salt and freshly ground black pepper

Pork tenderloin, pounded thin so that it grills quickly and evenly, gets an earthy, nutty accent from traditional Mexican *pipián* sauce. What's the secret to the sauce? Sauté the pumpkin seeds (pepitas) first to give them an even richer flavor.

Place pork between 2 sheets of waxed paper. Pound to ¼- to ½-inch thickness.
DO AHEAD: Can be made 4 hours ahead. Cover; chill.

Heat 2 Tbsp. oil in a large skillet over medium heat. Add next 5 ingredients. Sauté until seeds are lightly browned, about 4 minutes. Set aside.

Place 4 cups water, tomatillos, and jalapeño in a small saucepan. Simmer over medium heat until tomatillos are soft and an olive green color, about 15 minutes. Drain, reserving ¼ cup cooking liquid. Transfer tomatillos, jalapeño, reserved ¼ cup liquid, cilantro, romaine, broth, radishes, and seed mixture to blender. Blend sauce until smooth, stopping occasionally to push down ingredients.

Heat remaining 1 Tbsp. oil in a large skillet over medium heat. Add sauce; cook until thickened, about 4 minutes. Season to taste with salt and pepper.
DO AHEAD: Sauce can be made 2 hours ahead. Let stand at room temperature.

Build a medium-hot fire in a charcoal grill, or heat a gas grill to high. Brush grill grate with oil. Season pork with salt and pepper. Grill until just cooked through, about 2 minutes per side. Divide among 4 plates. Rewarm sauce over medium heat; spoon over pork.

SPICE-RUBBED TENDERLOIN
with Peach Barbecue Sauce

6 to 8 servings

3 1-lb. pork tenderloins,
    trimmed
    Extra-virgin olive oil, for brushing
4 tsp. coarsely ground black pepper
4 tsp. kosher salt
2½ tsp. garlic powder
    Peach Barbecue Sauce
    (page 163)

Fresh peaches and dried chiles give sweet heat to this grilled tenderloin. You can also use this simple method to prepare the tenderloin, and then pair it with any of the other sauces on pages 162–163.

Brush pork tenderloins with oil to coat. Arrange pork on a rimmed baking sheet. Mix black pepper, salt, and garlic powder in a small bowl to blend. Sprinkle seasoning mixture all over pork and let marinate for about 45 minutes. **DO AHEAD:** Tenderloins can be prepared 1 day ahead. Cover and refrigerate.

Build a medium-hot fire in a charcoal grill, or heat a gas grill to high. Brush grill grate with oil. Transfer ½ cup Peach Barbecue Sauce to a small bowl to use for basting. Grill pork, turning occasionally with tongs, until brown and an instant-read thermometer inserted into center registers 140°F, about 18 minutes. Brush pork all over with some basting sauce. Grill pork until glazed, turning and brushing with more basting sauce, about 3 minutes longer. Transfer pork to work surface; let rest for 10 minutes. Discard basting sauce.

Cut pork crosswise on slight diagonal into ½-inch-thick slices. Arrange pork slices on a platter. Drizzle pork with some warm sauce. Serve, passing remaining sauce separately.

PORK CUTLETS
with Mustard Crust

6 servings

    Vegetable oil, for brushing
½ cup Dijon mustard
¼ cup mayonnaise
1 Tbsp. chopped fresh tarragon
1 Tbsp. (packed) light brown sugar
2 lb. trimmed pork loin, cut
    crosswise into ½-inch-thick
    slices

Homemade "Dijonnaise"—a mixture of Dijon mustard and mayonnaise—coats the cutlets and gives them a flavorful crust. Because the cutlets are thin and naturally tender, they need just 2 to 3 minutes per side on the grill. Serve these with any of the slaws on pages 321–325.

Build a medium-hot fire in a charcoal grill, or heat a gas grill to high. Brush grill grate with oil. Whisk mustard, mayonnaise, tarragon, and brown sugar in a medium bowl. Brush mustard sauce generously on both sides of pork cutlets.

Grill pork until instant-read thermometer inserted into the center of pork registers 145°F, 2 to 3 minutes per side.

Sweet, sour, and piquant flavors blend together in this vibrant cherry salsa.

PORK TENDERLOIN
WITH CHERRY SALSA

PORK TENDERLOIN
with Cherry Salsa

6 servings

photo, left

1 cup coarsely chopped fresh cilantro, divided
½ cup minced shallots, divided
6 Tbsp. fresh lime juice, divided
¼ cup vegetable oil, plus more for brushing
2 pork tenderloins, about 2½ lb. total
8 oz. fresh cherries, stemmed, pitted, halved
1 fresh Fresno chile, red jalapeño, or Holland chile, thinly sliced crosswise
1 Tbsp. extra-virgin olive oil
Kosher salt and freshly ground black pepper

This is a great dish to make in the summertime, when ripe cherries are at their peak. For a quick weeknight meal, make the sauce and marinate the pork in the morning.

Build a medium-hot fire in a charcoal grill, or heat a gas grill to high. Combine ½ cup cilantro, ¼ cup shallots, 4 Tbsp. lime juice, and ¼ cup vegetable oil in a resealable plastic bag. Add pork; seal bag and turn to coat. Marinate pork at room temperature for 15 minutes, turning occasionally.

Meanwhile, combine remaining ½ cup cilantro, ¼ cup shallots, 2 Tbsp. lime juice, cherries, chile, and olive oil in a medium bowl. Season salsa lightly with salt and pepper and set aside to let flavors meld.

Remove tenderloins from marinade and season generously with salt and pepper.

Brush grill grate with vegetable oil. Grill tenderloins, turning frequently, until an instant-read thermometer inserted into the center of pork registers 145°F, about 15 minutes. Let rest for 10 minutes. Cut into thin slices and serve with salsa.

PORK TENDERLOIN
with Jamaican Spices

12 servings

9 Tbsp. extra-virgin olive oil, plus more for brushing
9 Tbsp. fresh lime juice
6 1-inch-long pieces peeled ginger
1½ Tbsp. kosher salt
1 Tbsp. ground allspice
1 Tbsp. ground coriander
1 Tbsp. freshly ground black pepper
3 1- to 1¼-lb. pork tenderloins
Purchased mango chutney

In this recipe, the tenderloins are cut nearly in half from one end to the other and opened up like a book. This serves two purposes: First, it gives a lot of room to brush on the flavor-packed Jamaican-style spice paste. Second, because the tenderloin is half as thick, it means that it cooks twice as fast.

Blend 9 Tbsp. oil and next 6 ingredients in a food processor until coarse paste forms.

Place tenderloins on a work surface. Cut each lengthwise almost in half, leaving about ¾ inch intact. Press each tenderloin open like a book. Spread seasoning paste all over each. Arrange on a rimmed baking sheet. Let tenderloins stand at room temperature for at least 1 hour, or cover and refrigerate for up to 1 day.

Build a medium-hot fire in a charcoal grill, or heat a gas grill to high. Brush grill grate with oil. Grill pork until an instant-read thermometer inserted into the thickest part registers 145°F, about 6 minutes per side. Transfer to a platter. Let pork rest for 15 minutes. Cut pork crosswise into ½-inch-thick slices and serve with chutney.

PORK RIB SATAY
with Peanut Sauce

5 large shallots, chopped
6 Tbsp. soy sauce
4½ Tbsp. distilled white vinegar
3 Tbsp. minced peeled ginger
1½ Tbsp. peanut oil
3 garlic cloves, minced
1½ tsp. ground coriander
1½ tsp. (packed) light brown sugar
¾ tsp. cayenne pepper
2 lb. baby back pork ribs, cut into
   4- or 5-rib sections
Vegetable oil, for brushing
Assorted sliced raw vegetables
   (such as carrots, cucumber,
   celery, and cauliflower florets)
Peanut Sauce (page 163)

These ribs feature the flavors of Southeast Asian satay, in which marinated strips or chunks of meat are traditionally threaded on skewers (think of the rib bones here as the "skewers"). The ribs are baked until they reach the point of fall-off-the-bone tender, then grilled to get a nice char just before serving. Cut them into individual ribs to serve as appetizers, or into 4- or 5-rib sections to serve as a main course with steamed jasmine rice.

Mix first 9 ingredients in a large resealable plastic bag. Add ribs. Seal bag; turn to coat ribs with marinade. Chill overnight.

Preheat oven to 325°F. Place each rack of ribs with marinade on a double layer of foil. Spoon some marinade over ribs. Wrap racks individually and divide between 2 baking sheets. Bake until ribs are tender, 1½ to 2 hours. Let ribs cool ribs slightly. **DO AHEAD:** Can be prepared 1 day ahead. Keep ribs enclosed in foil in pan and refrigerate.

Build a medium fire in a charcoal grill, or heat a gas grill to medium-high. Brush grill grate with oil. Grill ribs, turning frequently, until charred in places and heated through, 7 to 10 minutes. Transfer to a cutting board; cut between ribs to separate. Place ribs on platter. Arrange vegetables and Peanut Sauce alongside.

PORK RIBS: Three Cuts We Love

What's our favorite kind of rib for the grill? Basically, any kind that comes from a pig. Here's a breakdown of our three favorite rib cuts.

SPARERIBS

These meaty ribs are cut from the belly of a pig, right next to the bacon cut. This means they're **heftier and porkier** than the more dainty baby backs. A full rack usually consists of a slab of 11 to 14 ribs, weighs in around 3 pounds, and serves two or three people.

ST. LOUIS–STYLE RIBS

These are spareribs with the breastbone removed and the ends squared off for a neat presentation. **They cook evenly and fit better on the grill than full spareribs.** Figure a pound per person, so a 2-pound rack will feed two people.

BABY BACK RIBS

Baby backs are the shorter, tapered ribs from the animal's back. These **1- to 2½-pound racks are less fatty than spareribs** and cook in half the time. We love the quick-cooking, messy pleasure of baby backs. Individual ribs are ideal to serve as hors d'oeuvres.

BABY BACK RIBS
with Ginger-Honey Marinade

These quick-cooking ribs get powerful flavor from a marinade and sauce featuring seasonings indigenous to Cambodia—fresh ginger, fish sauce, and lime. Guests create their own dipping sauce by squeezing limes over salt and white pepper and mixing it all together.

RIBS AND MARINADE

- 2 2¼- to 2½-lb. baby back pork rib racks, cut into 6- or 7-rib sections
- ¼ cup chopped peeled ginger
- 6 garlic cloves, chopped
- 1 Tbsp. kosher salt
- 1 Tbsp. freshly ground black pepper
- 1 Tbsp. sugar
- 2 Tbsp. honey
- 2 Tbsp. fish sauce (such as nam pla or nuoc nam)
- 2 Tbsp. soy sauce

DIPPING SAUCE

- 6 tsp. ground white pepper, divided
- 6 tsp. kosher salt, divided
- 3 large limes, halved
  Vegetable oil, for brushing

RIBS AND MARINADE

Place ribs on a large rimmed baking sheet. Combine ginger, garlic, salt, black pepper, and sugar in a food processor and purée to blend well. Add honey, fish sauce, and soy sauce and process until blended. Spread spiced marinade on both sides of ribs (about 2 Tbsp. marinade per side for each rib section). Cover ribs with plastic wrap and refrigerate for at least 4 hours. **DO AHEAD:** Ribs and marinade can be made 1 day ahead; baste ribs occasionally with accumulated marinade on baking sheet. Keep chilled.

DIPPING SAUCE

Place each of 6 very small bowls on each of 6 small plates. Place 1 tsp. salt and 1 tsp. white pepper in neat mounds side by side in each bowl, then place 1 lime half on plate next to each bowl.

Build a medium fire in a charcoal grill, or heat a gas grill to medium-high. Brush grill grate with oil. Spoon any juices from baking sheet over ribs before grilling. Place rib racks, rounded (meaty) side down, on grill grate. Grill ribs, uncovered, 8 minutes per side, then cover grill and grill until ribs are cooked through, about 8 minutes longer per side.

Transfer ribs to a cutting board. Cut between bones into individual ribs. Transfer ribs to a platter. Before serving, allow each diner to squeeze juice from lime into bowl with salt and white pepper and stir until mixed, then dip ribs into sauce.

Bonus Recipe
LEMONGRASS RIBS

To give these ribs a Vietnamese spin, skip the dipping sauce and marinate the ribs for at least 2 hours in a mixture of: ½ cup chopped shallots; ¼ cup each of fish sauce, minced lemongrass, and water; 5 chopped garlic cloves; and 1 Tbsp. each sugar and chili-garlic sauce. Then grill as above.

BEST-EVER BARBECUED RIBS

photo, right

2½ Tbsp. kosher salt
1 Tbsp. dry mustard
1 Tbsp. paprika
½ tsp. cayenne pepper
½ tsp. freshly ground black pepper
8 lb. baby back ribs (8 racks) or spareribs (4 racks)
Vegetable oil, for brushing
Low-salt chicken broth (optional)
1½ cups store-bought or homemade barbecue sauce, plus more for serving

This go-to recipe for classic barbecued ribs embraces what we refer to as our "oven-cheat" method—a technique that'll get you ultra-tender meat without spending 12 hours manning a smoker. Choose your cut—baby backs or spareribs—and follow three simple steps: 1. Season. 2. Bake. 3. Grill. For sauce, whip up a batch of one of the sauces on pages 162–163 or use a store-bought variety.

Preheat oven to 325°F. Combine first 5 ingredients in a small bowl. Place each rack of ribs on a double layer of foil; sprinkle rub all over ribs. Wrap racks individually and divide between 2 baking sheets.

Bake ribs until very tender but not falling apart, about 2 hours for baby back ribs or 3 hours for spareribs. Carefully unwrap ribs; pour any juices from foil into a 4-cup heatproof measuring cup; reserve juices. Let ribs cool completely. **DO AHEAD:** Ribs can be baked up to 3 days ahead (the flavor will be more developed, and the cold ribs will hold together better on the grill as they heat through). Cover and chill juices. Rewrap ribs in foil and chill.

Build a medium-hot fire in a charcoal grill, or heat a gas grill to high. Brush grate with oil. Add broth or water to rib juices, if needed, to measure 1½ cups. Whisk in 1½ cups barbecue sauce to blend.

Grill ribs, basting with barbecue sauce mixture and turning frequently, until lacquered and charred in places and heated through, 7 to 10 minutes. Transfer to a cutting board; cut between ribs to separate. Transfer to a platter and serve with more barbecue sauce.

AMAZING RIBS: Three Steps to Perfection

Some of the tastiest ribs in this book—like our Best-Ever Barbecued Ribs—owe their tenderness not to a grill, but to the oven. Hear us out: Traditional ribs are smoked all day to slowly break down the tough connective tissue. This oven-cheat method takes only 2 to 3 hours, yet yields the same irresistible ribs.

SEASON

Preheat the oven to 325°F and **coat ribs with dry rub or marinade** (check out pages 375–383 for ideas). Bake ribs right away, or chill for a few hours for maximum flavor.

BAKE

Throw 'em in the oven. **Baby backs get 2 hours. Spare ribs go in for up to 3 hours** (see the recipes for specific timing). You can also bake ribs in advance and refrigerate overnight.

GRILL

Grill the ribs over **direct medium-high heat** until they're heated through (about 10 minutes), turning a few times and basting with sauce to get that shellacked coating.

BA's super simple **"oven-cheat" method** delivers jaw-dropping flavor with minimal planning and prep.

BEST-EVER BARBECUED RIBS

BABY BACK RIBS
with Bourbon Barbecue Sauce

6 racks of baby back ribs
1 cup bourbon
3 Tbsp. kosher salt
3 Tbsp. (packed) dark brown
   sugar
3 Tbsp. paprika
2 Tbsp. freshly ground black
   pepper
1 Tbsp. garlic powder
1 tsp. ground cumin
   Vegetable oil, for brushing
   Bourbon Barbecue Sauce
   (page 162)

SPECIAL EQUIPMENT 2 cups hickory chips soaked in 2 cups beer for 1 hour; a foil baking pan (for drip pan); small foil broiler pan (for wood chips, if using gas grill)

This is the real deal low-and-slow method for all of you backyard barbecue pitmasters: Ribs are slowly smoked until meltingly tender, all the while gaining authentic barbecue flavor. See the instructions at right for setting up your gas or charcoal grill as a smoker. Depending on the size of your grill, you may need to cut the rib racks into 4- or 5-rib portions to fit.

Arrange ribs in a large roasting pan. Pour bourbon over. Chill for 30 minutes, turning ribs often. Pour off and discard bourbon.

Whisk salt and next 5 ingredients in a medium bowl. Sprinkle spice mixture on both sides of ribs. Let stand for 1 hour.

Prepare grill for smoking (see next page); if using gas grill, heat to medium. Fill drip pan halfway with water and place on unlit portion of lower grate.

Remove 1 cup wood chips from beer and drain (keep remaining chips in beer). Scatter drained chips over coals in charcoal grill; alternatively, if using gas grill, spread drained wood chips in foil broiler pan and place directly on gas flame.

Replace upper grill grate and brush with oil. Arrange ribs on grate above drip pan. Cover grill with lid, positioning top vent directly over ribs. Place stem of instant-read thermometer through top vent, with gauge on outside and tip near ribs (thermometer should not touch meat or grill grate); leave in place during cooking. Check temperature after 5 minutes. Maintain temperature between 275° and 325°F by using top and bottom vents (leave any other vents closed).

After 1 hour, add more hot gray charcoal if using charcoal grill. Drain remaining 1 cup wood chips and sprinkle over charcoal in charcoal grill, or add to broiler pan on gas grill. Close grill lid.

Grill ribs until very tender and meat pulls away from bones, about 45 minutes longer, brushing with ¾ cup Bourbon Barbecue Sauce in the last 15 minutes.

Transfer ribs to a platter. Brush with ¾ cup more barbecue sauce. Serve, passing remaining sauce separately, if desired.

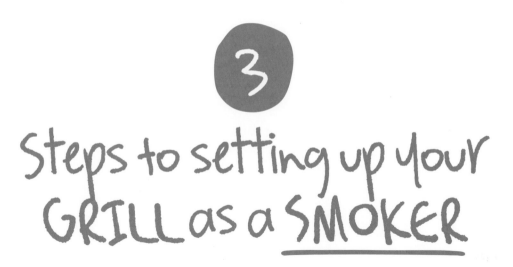

3
Steps to setting up your GRILL as a SMOKER

For true low-and-slow barbecuing (as opposed to grilling), you want to set things up so you can cook over indirect heat with the lid closed, and maintain a consistent temperature over several hours of cooking.

...on a CHARCOAL Grill

1

Let charcoal burn in charcoal chimney until gray; arrange on two sides of lower grate. (Add more gray coals about once an hour.)

2

Arrange foil baking pan (drip pan) in center; add water. If using wood chips, drain and scatter over coals.

3

Replace grill grate. Place meat over drip pan. Cover grill. Open or close vent to increase or lower temperature.

...on a GAS Grill

1

Heat grill according to instructions. Remove grill grate and place drip pan on unlit burner; add water as per recipe.

2

Drain wood chips; spread in foil broiler pan or wrap in heavy foil (leave packet open slightly). Place directly over flame.

3

Replace grill grate. Place meat over drip pan. Cover grill. Maintain temperature by adjusting burners or vents.

THE ARSENAL:
4 Sauces You Need in Your Repertoire

Use these sauces with their respective recipes (indicated to the right of each title name) or pair them with another cut of grilled pork—chops, ribs, or tenderloin. Mix it up, depending on what you're craving. But remember that sugars in sweet sauces can burn easily, so apply them at the *end* of the grilling time.

makes about 2½ cups

Bourbon Barbecue Sauce

use with
baby back ribs

2 cups ketchup
½ cup mild-flavored (light) molasses
⅓ cup bourbon
¼ cup Dijon mustard
3 Tbsp. hot pepper sauce
2 Tbsp. Worcestershire sauce
2 tsp. paprika
1 tsp. garlic powder
1 tsp. onion powder

This sauce is great on ribs, but it would also work well with chicken. Try it as an alternative sauce with the All-American Barbecued Chicken (page 41).

Combine all ingredients in a large heavy saucepan. Bring to a boil over medium heat, stirring occasionally. Reduce heat to medium-low; simmer uncovered, stirring frequently, until sauce thickens and flavors blend, about 15 minutes.
DO AHEAD: Sauce can be made 1 week ahead. Cover and chill.

makes 1½ cups

Molasses Barbecue Sauce

use with
brined pork chops

3 cups chicken stock or low-salt
  chicken broth
1 cup dry white wine
¼ cup apple cider vinegar
¼ cup chopped fresh tomato
¼ cup mild-flavored (light) molasses
3 Tbsp. minced shallots
2 Tbsp. chopped pitted dates
1 Tbsp. chopped garlic
½ tsp. crushed red pepper flakes
  Kosher salt and freshly ground
  black pepper

This sauce has a sweetness that we often crave when whipping up grilled ribs, and a little something else as well: a kick from crushed red pepper and garlic.

Combine the first 9 ingredients in a large heavy saucepan. Boil, stirring occasionally, until reduced to 1½ cups, about 20 minutes. Season to taste with salt and pepper.
DO AHEAD: Sauce can be prepared 1 day ahead. Cover and chill. Bring to a simmer before serving.

Peach Barbecue Sauce

4 oz. bacon slices, chopped

1 dried chile de árbol, broken in half

1 cup coarsely chopped onion

2 garlic cloves, chopped

1 Tbsp. Worcestershire sauce

1½ tsp. whole black peppercorns, crushed

2 small peaches (10 to 12 oz. total), halved, pitted, diced

1 cup ketchup

1 cup orange juice

1½ Tbsp. fresh lemon juice, more as needed

½ tsp. hot pepper sauce

Kosher salt and freshly ground black pepper

INGREDIENT INFO Look for chile de árbol at Latin American markets and at some specialty markets and supermarkets.

Start with ripe, juicy peaches for a luscious sweet-spicy sauce that pairs nicely with grilled pork tenderloin but would liven up any cut of pork. If you prefer, you can purée the sauce instead of straining it (remove the chile first if you want less heat).

Sauté bacon and chile de árbol in a large heavy saucepan over medium heat until bacon is crisp. Add onion and garlic; sauté until onion is translucent, about 5 minutes. Add Worcestershire and crushed peppercorns; stir for 1 minute. Add peaches and sauté until translucent, about 5 minutes. Add ketchup, orange juice, 1½ Tbsp. lemon juice, and hot pepper sauce. Simmer, stirring sauce often, until sauce thickens enough to coat spoon thickly, about 30 minutes.

Strain sauce into a medium bowl, pressing enough liquid and solids through strainer to yield 2 cups sauce; discard solids in strainer. Season sauce to taste with salt and more lemon juice, if desired. **DO AHEAD:** Sauce can be made 1 week ahead. Cover and chill. Rewarm before using.

Peanut Sauce

1 cup peanut oil

1 cup natural unsalted shelled peanuts

3 large shallots, thinly sliced

2 Tbsp. (packed) minced peeled fresh ginger

1 garlic clove, minced

3 anchovy fillets, packed in oil, drained, minced

1 Tbsp. (packed) light brown sugar

1½ tsp. hot chili paste (such as sambal oelek)

1 tsp. ground coriander

1 tsp. kosher salt, more as needed

½ tsp. ground cumin

2 Tbsp. fresh lemon juice

This sauce is traditionally served alongside the satays of Southeast Asia, but also makes a nice alternative to the sweet sauces that usually accompany grilled ribs. *Sambal oelek* gives it a great kick; you can find the hot chili paste at some supermarkets and at Asian markets.

Line a baking sheet with paper towels. Heat oil in a large skillet over medium heat. Add peanuts; fry until golden brown, watching closely to avoid burning, about 3 minutes. Using a slotted spoon, transfer peanuts to paper towels; let cool. Discard all but 1 Tbsp. oil in skillet. Finely grind peanuts in a food processor.

Heat oil in skillet over medium heat. Add shallots, ginger, and garlic; sauté until shallots are almost tender, 3 minutes. Add anchovies, sugar, chili paste, coriander, 1 tsp. salt, and cumin; stir for 1 minute. Add 2¾ cups water; simmer until shallots are tender, 5 minutes. Add peanuts; simmer until mixture thickens slightly, 5 minutes longer. Season to taste with salt. **DO AHEAD:** Sauce can be made 1 day ahead. Cover; chill. Before using, rewarm over low heat, stirring occasionally and adding more water to thin.

Stir lemon juice into sauce just before serving. Serve warm.

GRILLED BACON WITH STEAK SAUCE

GRILLED BACON
with Steak Sauce

photo, left

1 Tbsp. extra-virgin olive oil, plus
more for brushing
¼ cup minced onion
2 garlic cloves, minced
¼ cup (packed) light brown sugar
¼ cup red wine vinegar
2 Tbsp. Worcestershire sauce
1 tsp. kosher salt
1 tsp. freshly ground black pepper
1 cup canned tomato sauce
2 Tbsp. prepared horseradish
1 lb. ¼-inch-thick slices bacon

Yes, you can throw bacon on a grill, just like they do at the famed Peter Luger Steak House in Brooklyn. The key is to use slab bacon. Have your butcher cut ¼-inch-thick slices for you, or buy a hunk and slice it yourself. Then grill till crisp and serve it with sweet horseradish sauce. We've developed our own take on that condiment here, though you could also buy the real Luger version online (peterluger.com).

Heat 1 Tbsp. olive oil in a small saucepan over medium-low heat. Add onion and garlic and cook, stirring occasionally, until onion is soft and translucent, about 15 minutes. Stir in brown sugar, vinegar, Worcestershire, salt, and pepper. Bring to a simmer, then stir in tomato sauce. Simmer for 1 minute; remove from heat and let cool slightly. Stir in horseradish and let cool completely. **DO AHEAD:** Can be made 2 weeks ahead. Cover and chill.

Build a medium-low fire in a charcoal grill, or heat a gas grill to medium. Brush grate with oil. Grill bacon, turning often, until slightly rendered, crispy, and charred in spots, about 6 minutes. Serve bacon with steak sauce.

AGAVE-GLAZED PORK BELLY
with Grilled Pineapple

1 4-lb. boneless pork belly
4 tsp. kosher salt
2 tsp. freshly ground black pepper
6 poblano chiles, stemmed,
coarsely chopped
3 habanero chiles, stemmed, sliced
into ¼-inch rounds
3 serrano chiles, stemmed, chopped
1 cup agave syrup (nectar), divided
Vegetable oil, for brushing
1 pineapple (about 3½ lb.), peeled,
cored, cut into ½-inch rounds
¼ cup apple cider vinegar

INGREDIENT INFO All chiles are available at supermarkets, farmers' markets, or Latin markets. Agave syrup is available at supermarkets or natural foods stores.

Crispy, succulent, and with just a touch of sweetness, this dish showcases everything that is addictive about pork belly. Start a day before so pork can chill overnight.

Preheat oven to 250°F. Season pork belly all over with salt and pepper. Place chiles in a large roasting pan. Place pork belly, skin side down, on top of chiles; drizzle with ½ cup agave syrup. Pour remaining ½ cup agave syrup and 2 cups water into pan. Cover pan tightly with lid or 2 layers of foil.

Transfer to oven and cook pork for 3 hours, basting with pan juices every hour. Turn pork over. Cook until very tender, about 4 more hours.

Transfer pork to another roasting pan. Strain liquid from first roasting pan into a saucepan (there should be about 5½ cups); reserve chiles. Gently boil juices until reduced to about 1¼ cups, 45 to 50 minutes; add reserved chiles. Remove pan from heat. Let glaze cool; chill.

Meanwhile, cover pork with parchment or waxed paper. Top with a large plate. Place weights, such as large canned goods, on top. Chill overnight.

Reheat chile glaze. Build a medium-hot fire in a charcoal grill, or heat a gas grill to high. Brush grill grate with oil. Grill pineapple until nicely charred, 2 to 3 minutes per side.

Let grill cool to medium heat. Slice pork belly into 1-inch-thick pieces. Grill until warmed and crisp, about 3 minutes per side. Brush pork with some of the chile glaze. To serve, place 2 or 3 pineapple rounds on each plate; spoon chile glaze over, then top with pork belly. Drizzle with vinegar.

PIBIL-STYLE PORK
with Pickled Onions and Salsa

1 medium onion, quartered
    through core
4 garlic cloves
⅓ cup fresh lime juice
⅓ cup fresh orange juice
¼ cup achiote paste
1 Tbsp. red wine vinegar
2 tsp. kosher salt
1 tsp. freshly ground black pepper
1 tsp. ground cumin
½ tsp. dried oregano (preferably
    Mexican)
1 4½- to 5-lb. bone-in pork
    shoulder roast (Boston butt)
  Vegetable oil, for brushing
  Corn tortillas
  Yucatecán Pickled Onions
    (recipe follows)
  Habanero-Tomato Salsa
    (recipe follows)

INGREDIENT INFO Achiote paste is available at Latin markets.

SPECIAL EQUIPMENT A foil baking pan (for drip pan)

Some of the best Yucatecán barbecue, such as this achiote-scented *cochinita pibil*, comes not off the grill, but from an underground pit called a *pib*. Think of this as the Mexican version of a Carolina pulled pork sandwich, only the succulent shredded pork is served with corn tortillas and topped with pickled onion and a spicy salsa. The meat needs to marinate for 4 hours and then cook for about another 3½ hours, so plan ahead.

Heat a medium skillet over medium-high heat. Add onion and garlic to dry skillet and cook, turning occasionally, until browned in spots on all sides, about 8 minutes for onion and 4 minutes for garlic. Core and coarsely chop onion. Transfer onion and garlic to a blender. Add lime juice and next 7 ingredients to blender; purée until smooth. Transfer to a large resealable plastic bag; add pork. Seal bag, releasing excess air; turn to coat. Chill for at least 4 hours and up to 1 day, turning occasionally.

Prepare grill for smoking (see instructions on page 161). If using gas grill, heat to medium. Do not add water to drip pan.

Replace upper grill grate and brush with oil. Place pork, with some marinade still clinging, on grate above drip pan. Close lid; insert thermometer into hole in lid. Cook pork until an instant-read thermometer inserted into the center of roast registers 195°F, about 3½ hours, maintaining grill's internal temperature at around 350°F. If using charcoal grill, add more gray charcoal from a chimney after each hour of grilling.

Transfer pork to a cutting board and let rest for 10 minutes. Pull out and discard bone and any large lumps of fat. Using 2 forks or a large knife, shred the pork; transfer to a platter. Drizzle with a few spoonfuls of drippings from foil pan in grill, if desired.

Grill tortillas until slightly charred, about 10 seconds per side. Serve pork with tortillas, Yucatecán Pickled Onions, and Habanero-Tomato Salsa.

Yucatecán Pickled Onions

use with
pibil-style pork

1 large red onion, cut crosswise into ⅛-inch-thick slices, rings separated
2 garlic cloves, quartered
1 Tbsp. kosher salt
½ cup distilled white vinegar
½ tsp. dried oregano (preferably Mexican)
½ tsp. freshly ground black pepper
¼ tsp. ground cumin
3 whole allspice
1 bay leaf

These delicious onions can jazz up any kind of grilled meat or fish; they're also terrific in salads and sandwiches.

Combine 6 cups water, onion, garlic, and salt in a medium heavy saucepan. Bring to a boil, then boil for 1 minute. Drain. Return onion and garlic to same saucepan. Add vinegar and all remaining ingredients. Add enough water to saucepan just to cover. Bring to a boil over medium heat. Remove from heat, cover, and let cool. Transfer onion mixture to a bowl, cover, and chill overnight. **DO AHEAD:** Onions can be made 1 week ahead. Keep chilled.

Drain onions before serving.

Habanero-Tomato Salsa

use with
pibil-style pork

3 large tomatoes, cut into ¼-inch cubes
2 cups finely chopped white onion
½ cup finely chopped fresh cilantro
6 Tbsp. fresh lime juice
6 fresh habanero chiles or 8 serrano chiles, seeded, finely chopped
3 Tbsp. fresh orange juice
Kosher salt

This salsa packs some serious heat; use fewer habaneros if you prefer. And be sure to wear gloves when handling the chiles.

Mix first 6 ingredients in a large bowl. Season to taste with salt. **DO AHEAD:** Salsa can be made 2 hours ahead. Cover and let stand at room temperature.

TACOS AL PASTOR
with Smoky Two-Chile Salsa

photo, right

1 large white onion, halved
1 pineapple, peeled, cut crosswise into ½-inch-thick rounds
½ cup fresh orange juice
¼ cup distilled white vinegar
¼ cup guajillo chile powder
3 garlic cloves, halved
2 tsp. kosher salt
1 tsp. dried oregano
1 tsp. ground cumin
1 large or 2 small chipotle chiles and 1 to 2 tsp. adobo from canned chipotle chiles in adobo
1 2½- to 3-lb. boneless pork loin, cut into ½-inch-thick slices
Vegetable oil, for brushing
¼ cup chopped fresh cilantro
Corn tortillas
Smoky Two-Chile Salsa (recipe follows)
Lime wedges

INGREDIENT INFO Look for the chipotles at supermarkets or Latin markets.

This "shepherd's-style" taco features tender pork loin—infused with the flavors of a fruity pineapple-citrus marinade—and grilled pineapple rounds, chopped and served with corn tortillas.

Coarsely chop 1 onion half. Coarsely chop 2 pineapple rounds, discarding core; cover and chill remaining pineapple. Place chopped onion and chopped pineapple in a blender. Add orange juice and next 7 ingredients; purée marinade until smooth. Place pork in a large resealable plastic bag. Add marinade and seal bag, releasing excess air. Turn to coat. Chill for at least 4 hours and up to 1 day.

Build a medium-hot fire in a charcoal grill, or heat a gas grill to high. Brush grill grate with oil. Grill remaining pineapple rounds until warm and slightly charred, 4 to 6 minutes per side. Grill pork with some marinade still clinging until slightly charred and an instant-read thermometer inserted into center of pork reaches 145°F, 2 to 4 minutes per side. Transfer pineapple and pork to a work surface; chop pineapple into ½-inch cubes, discarding cores. Chop pork. Transfer to a platter; toss to combine.

Meanwhile, finely chop remaining onion half and place in a medium bowl. Add cilantro; toss to combine. Grill tortillas until warm and slightly charred, about 10 seconds per side.

Serve tortillas with pork-pineapple mixture, onion-cilantro relish, Smoky Two-Chile Salsa, and lime wedges.

Smoky Two-Chile Salsa

use with tacos al pastor

8 large dried guajillo chiles or New Mexico chiles, stemmed, seeded, coarsely torn
½ medium onion, halved lengthwise through core end
3 garlic cloves
1 or 2 chipotle chiles and 1 to 2 tsp. adobo from canned chipotle chiles in adobo
¼ cup chopped fresh cilantro
2 tsp. fresh lime juice
Kosher salt

INGREDIENT INFO Guajillo chiles are available at specialty foods stores and at Latin markets.

Here's a salsa with great depth of flavor from the combination of reconstituted dried guajillo chiles, canned chipotles, and adobo. This would also be excellent with grilled skirt steak, and even with omelets.

Place torn chiles in bowl. Add 2 cups hot water; soak for at least 2 hours or overnight. Drain chiles, reserving soaking liquid.

Heat a small nonstick skillet over medium heat. Add onion and garlic to dry skillet; cook until browned in spots, about 6 minutes for garlic and 10 minutes for onion. Trim core from onion. Place onion and garlic in a blender. Add drained chiles, 1 cup soaking liquid, 1 chipotle chile, 1 tsp. adobo, cilantro, and lime juice; purée until smooth. Add remaining chipotle and 1 tsp. adobo, if desired; purée. Transfer to bowl. Season to taste with salt. **DO AHEAD:** Salsa can be made 1 week ahead. Cover and chill.

Two kinds of dried chiles—chipotle and guajillo—equal an **earthy, unexpected departure** from the usual pico de gallo.

TACOS AL PASTOR

PULLED PORK SANDWICHES

with Carolina Red Sauce and Tangy Slaw photo, right

You know those pulled pork sandwiches of your dreams? The ones dripping with fat, juice, and vinegary barbecue sauce? That's what you're making here, smoking the pork slowly until it's fall-apart tender.

DRY RUB AND PORK

- 3 Tbsp. coarsely ground black pepper
- 3 Tbsp. (packed) dark brown sugar
- 3 Tbsp. paprika
- 2 Tbsp. kosher salt
- 1 tsp. cayenne pepper
- 2 untrimmed boneless pork shoulder halves (Boston butt; about 6 lb. total)

MOP

- 1 cup apple cider vinegar
- 2 Tbsp. Worcestershire sauce
- 1 Tbsp. coarsely ground black pepper
- 1 Tbsp. kosher salt
- 2 tsp. vegetable oil, plus more for brushing
- 12 soft hamburger buns, split
  Carolina Red Barbecue Sauce (recipe follows)
  Tangy Coleslaw (recipe follows)

SPECIAL EQUIPMENT 6 cups (about) oak or hickory chips, soaked in cold water for at least 30 minutes; foil baking pan (for drip pan); foil broiler pan (for wood chips, if using gas grill)

DRY RUB

Mix first 5 ingredients in a small bowl to blend.

Place pork, fat side up, on a work surface. Cut each piece lengthwise in half. Place on a large baking sheet. Sprinkle dry rub all over pork; massage into pork. Cover with plastic wrap; refrigerate for at least 2 hours. **DO AHEAD:** Can be made 1 day ahead. Keep chilled.

MOP

Mix first 4 ingredients plus 2 tsp. vegetable oil with ½ cup water in a medium bowl. Cover and refrigerate.

Prepare grill for smoking (see page 161). If using gas grill, heat to low. Drain 1 cup wood chips. If using charcoal grill, scatter wood chips over coals; if using gas grill, place in foil broiler pan and place directly on flame. Bring temperature of grill to 225° to 250°F. Replace upper grill grate and brush with oil. Place pork on grate over drip pan. Cover grill. Cook pork, turning and brushing with cold mop every 45 minutes, until meat thermometer inserted into center of pork registers 180°F, about 6 hours 45 minutes total. If using charcoal grill, add more gray charcoal from a chimney after each hour of cooking to maintain 225° to 250°F temperature. Add more drained wood chips (1 cup per hour) to maintain smoke level.

Transfer pork to a clean rimmed baking sheet. Let stand until cool enough to handle. Shred into bite-size pieces. Mound on a platter. Pour any juices from baking sheet over pork. **DO AHEAD:** Can be made 1 day ahead. Transfer pork and any juices to baking dish. Cover with foil; chill. Before continuing, rewarm pork, covered, in 350°F oven for about 30 minutes.

Divide pork among bottoms of buns. Drizzle lightly with Carolina Red Barbecue Sauce. Top with Tangy Coleslaw. Cover with tops of buns.

PULLED PORK SANDWICHES

Carolina Red Barbecue Sauce

makes about 2 cups

use with
pulled pork
sandwiches

1½ cups apple cider vinegar
½ cup ketchup
1 Tbsp. (packed) light brown sugar
1 tsp. kosher salt
½ tsp. crushed red pepper flakes

This is not a sweet barbecue sauce, but the true vinegary variety of North Carolina.

Stir all ingredients in a small bowl until sugar and salt dissolve. **DO AHEAD:** Can be prepared 3 days ahead. Cover and refrigerate.

Tangy Coleslaw

12 servings

use with
pulled pork
sandwiches

1 cup mayonnaise
½ cup Carolina Red Barbecue Sauce (see previous recipe)
1 2½-lb. green cabbage, quartered, cored, very thinly sliced
Kosher salt and freshly ground black pepper

Don't skip this—it adds fantastic flavor and crunch to the pulled pork sandwiches. It's also good enough to serve on its own.

Whisk mayonnaise and barbecue sauce in a large bowl to blend. Mix in cabbage. Season slaw to taste with salt and pepper. Refrigerate for 3 to 8 hours, tossing occasionally.

PORK GYROS

with Yogurt-Tomato Sauce, Onions, and Arugula

PORK

- ¼ cup extra-virgin olive oil
- ¼ cup dry red wine
- 3 garlic cloves, minced
- 1 small bay leaf, crumbled
- 1½ tsp. (packed) fresh oregano leaves
- ½ tsp. kosher salt
- ¼ tsp. freshly ground black pepper
- 2 1-lb. pork tenderloins

SAUCE

- 1½ cups plain Greek yogurt or whole-milk yogurt
- 2 Tbsp. chopped fresh dill
- 2 Tbsp. chopped seeded tomato
- 2 Tbsp. drained capers, chopped
- 2 garlic cloves, minced
- 1 Tbsp. red wine vinegar
- 1 Tbsp. tomato paste
   Kosher salt and freshly ground black pepper
   Vegetable oil, for brushing
- 6 7-inch diameter pita breads
- 1 red onion, halved, thinly sliced
- 24 large arugula leaves

The Greek gyro sandwich is traditionally made of thin strips of lamb that are sliced off of a rotating vertical spit-roaster. Here, juicy pork tenderloin replaces lamb, and you don't need a vertical spit—just your grill. Serve wrapped in a pita or on any kind of flatbread.

PORK

Combine first 7 ingredients in a large resealable plastic bag; shake to blend. Add pork to marinade; seal bag. Chill overnight, turning bag occasionally.

SAUCE

Stir first 7 ingredients in a medium bowl to blend. Season sauce to taste with salt and pepper. Cover and chill until ready to use, up to 1 day.

Build a medium fire in a charcoal grill, or heat a gas grill to medium-high. Brush grill grate with oil. Remove pork from bag. Grill until an instant-read thermometer inserted into the center of each tenderloin registers 145°F, about 18 minutes. Transfer to a work surface; let stand for 10 minutes (temperature will rise 5° to 10°F). Thinly slice into rounds.

Grill pitas until warmed through and softened, about 2 minutes per side. Cut pitas in half. Fill pita halves with pork, drizzle with sauce, then tuck in onion and arugula. Serve, passing remaining sauce separately.

LAMB

ROSY, TENDER MEAT. A CRISPY RIM OF FAT.

If it's been a while since you've had a lamb rib chop plucked from a fiery hot grate, you're missing out. Over the past few decades, the American grill has expanded to become a global grill. And no meat captures that broadened culinary outlook better than lamb. A quality lamb chop makes for one of the great pleasures of grilling; it's at once supremely simple and utterly indulgent.

For most of us, lamb is the *other* red meat, but the flavor of it packs a punch that steak can sometimes lack. And because of its bold character profile, it takes well to the assertive flavors of Middle Eastern, Indian, and Mediterranean cooking.

So although most of the recipes in this chapter might *start* with salt and pepper, they take you far beyond that, to a pomegranate-cumin glaze or an Asian five-spice butter. There's a world of flavor out there—savor it.

LAMB CHOPS
with Cilantro and Chile

4 servings

4 scallions, chopped
¼ cup (packed) fresh cilantro leaves with tender stems
¼ cup fresh lemon juice
2 Tbsp. extra-virgin olive oil, plus more for brushing
1 Tbsp. crushed red pepper flakes
Kosher salt
8 1- 1¼-inch-thick lamb loin chops or single rib chops
Freshly ground black pepper

A spicy paste made from cilantro and chile flakes is as simple as can be, and it gives the meat incredible flavor and a nice kick. Don't rush the marinating time; let the chops take on the flavors from the paste for a good hour.

Pulse scallions, cilantro, lemon juice, 2 Tbsp. oil, and red pepper flakes in a food processor until a smooth paste forms. Season chile paste with salt. Place lamb in an 8x8x2-inch glass baking dish. Season with salt and pepper. Coat lamb thinly on both sides with chile paste. Let stand at room temperature for 1 hour. **DO AHEAD:** Can be made 1 day ahead. Cover and chill. Let stand at room temperature for 1 hour before continuing.

Build a medium-hot fire in a charcoal grill, or heat a gas grill to high. Brush grill grate with oil. Grill lamb chops to desired doneness, 5 to 6 minutes per side for medium-rare.

LAMB CHOPS
with Minted Lemon Compote

4 servings

¾ cup dry white wine
½ cup sugar
¼ cup (packed) fresh mint leaves
2 lemons (preferably Meyer)
¼ tsp. kosher salt, more as needed
8 ¾-inch-thick lamb rib or lamb loin chops
Vegetable oil, for brushing
Freshly ground black pepper

The old-school lamb condiment, mint jelly, gets a fresh and delicious update with this compote, made by cooking down chopped lemons with a minty white wine syrup. We like Meyer lemons here because they are more aromatic than regular lemons and not quite as tart.

Bring wine, sugar, and mint to a boil in a small heavy saucepan, stirring until sugar dissolves. Remove from heat; let stand for 30 minutes. Strain syrup through a fine-mesh sieve into a medium saucepan; discard mint.

Using a vegetable peeler, remove peel (yellow part only) from lemons in strips. Place strips in a mini food processor. Following contour of fruit, cut away all white pith from lemons; discard pith. Working on a plate to catch juice, quarter lemons; discard seeds. Add lemons and accumulated juice to processor. Pulse lemon mixture until coarsely chopped; add to mint syrup in pan. Boil, stirring often, until compote is reduced to ⅔ cup, about 10 minutes. Stir in ¼ tsp. salt. Let cool.

Build a medium-hot fire in a charcoal grill, or heat a gas grill to high. Brush grill grate with oil. Season lamb with salt and pepper; brush with oil. Grill lamb, turning occasionally, to desired doneness, 8 to 10 minutes for medium-rare. Transfer lamb to plates and serve with compote alongside.

SPICED LAMB CHOPS
with Root Vegetables and Roasted Pepper Sauce

The lamb chops and the saffron-accented root vegetables get their flavor from spices used in Moroccan cooking. You can adjust the spice quantities in the yogurt marinade to your taste; just be sure to give the lamb enough time to marinate—the yogurt is tenderizing the meat at the same time that it's flavoring it.

LAMB

1½ cups plain whole-milk yogurt
6 Tbsp. fresh lemon juice
6 Tbsp. extra-virgin olive oil
1 Tbsp. ground cardamom
1 Tbsp. ground cumin
1½ tsp. cayenne pepper
4½ lb. lamb rib chops, excess fat trimmed, each cut between bones into individual chops

VEGETABLES

2 Tbsp. extra-virgin olive oil, plus more for brushing
2 Tbsp. (¼ stick) unsalted butter
4 large shallots, thinly sliced
2 large leeks (white and pale-green parts only), thinly sliced
¾ tsp. saffron threads
½ tsp. turmeric
2 large carrots, peeled, cut into 1-inch cubes
2 large rutabagas, peeled, cut into 1-inch cubes
2 large turnips, peeled, cut into 1-inch cubes
Kosher salt and freshly ground black pepper
Roasted Bell Pepper Sauce (recipe follows)

LAMB

Whisk yogurt, lemon juice, oil, cardamom, cumin, and cayenne in a medium bowl for marinade. Arrange chops in single layer on a large rimmed baking sheet. Pour marinade over; turn chops to coat. Cover and chill for at least 1 hour and up to 3 hours.

VEGETABLES

Heat 2 Tbsp. oil and butter in a large heavy skillet over medium heat. Add shallots, leeks, saffron, and turmeric; sauté for 5 minutes. Add carrots, rutabagas, turnips, and 1½ cups water. Cover and simmer, stirring occasionally, until vegetables are tender, about 25 minutes. Season to taste with salt and pepper.

Meanwhile, build a medium fire in a charcoal grill, or heat a gas grill to medium-high. Brush grill grate with oil. Remove lamb from marinade, allowing excess to drip off. Season lamb with salt and pepper. Grill to desired doneness, about 3 minutes per side for medium-rare.

Divide lamb chops among plates. Serve with vegetables and Roasted Bell Pepper Sauce alongside.

Roasted Bell Pepper Sauce

use with spiced lamb chops

1 7-oz. jar roasted red bell peppers
½ cup extra-virgin olive oil
Pinch of cayenne pepper
Kosher salt and freshly ground black pepper

Pulse bell peppers and their liquid, oil, and cayenne in a food processor or blender until a smooth purée forms. Transfer purée to a small heavy saucepan.
DO AHEAD: Can be made 2 days ahead. Cover and chill.

Cook sauce over medium heat, stirring occasionally, until warmed through, about 3 minutes. Season to taste with salt and black pepper. Transfer to a small bowl and serve.

LAMB SHOULDER CHOPS
with Za'atar Tomato Sauce

1 28-oz. can plum tomatoes in purée (preferably imported San Marzano)

¼ cup za'atar (about 1 oz.)

3 Tbsp. extra-virgin olive oil, divided, plus more for brushing

1 large garlic clove, minced
Kosher salt and freshly ground black pepper

4 ¾- to 1-inch-thick lamb shoulder blade chops

INGREDIENT INFO Look for za'atar at Middle Eastern markets and specialty foods stores, or make your own using the recipe on page 35.

For a Middle Eastern–meets–Mediterranean entrée that is fast, easy, and impressive for entertaining, try these chops, which are topped with a zesty tomato sauce spiked with za'atar, a spice blend that includes sumac, herbs, and sesame seeds.

Bring tomatoes with purée, za'atar, 2 Tbsp. oil, and garlic to a boil in a large saucepan over medium-high heat, stirring often. Stir, crushing tomatoes, until sauce thickens, about 10 minutes. Season sauce to taste with salt and pepper.

Build a medium fire in a charcoal grill, or heat a gas grill to medium-high. Brush grill grate with oil. Season lamb with salt and pepper. Brush with remaining 1 Tbsp. oil. Grill chops until cooked to desired doneness, 5 to 6 minutes per side for medium. Transfer chops to a platter and let rest for 5 minutes. Spoon warm sauce over lamb.

AT THE MARKET: How to Choose Your Chops

SPARERIBS

Once a throwaway cut, these riblets are cut from the breast and have become **a favorite among professional chefs**. Order from a butcher.

RACK OF LAMB

The **standing rib roast of lamb** may seem imposing, but it's smaller and easier to grill than beef. Each rack boasts 7 or 8 ribs. See page 182 for tips on how to handle it.

DOUBLE RIB CHOPS

For better control, make it a double. These **two-bone chops** are more forgiving than singles, and because you can grill them a bit longer, they'll take on a crispier sear.

SINGLE RIB CHOPS

Individual chops cook quickly, so sear them over very high heat for no more than 3 minutes per side. Allow at least two of these dainty ribs per person.

LOIN CHOPS

Don't overlook these **tender, mini T-bones**. One- to two-inch single- and double-cut loin chops take well to both simple seasonings as well as more complex marinades.

SHOULDER CHOPS

Including the blade and arm chops, these bone-in chops are the **thriftiest, most overlooked cuts**. Marinate them first, then sear over high heat. They can be grilled beyond medium.

CHAR SIU LAMB CHOPS

3 Tbsp. hoisin sauce

3 Tbsp. reduced-sodium soy sauce

2 Tbsp. Shaoxing wine (Chinese rice wine) or dry Sherry

1 Tbsp. sugar

1 tsp. Chinese five-spice powder

½ tsp. kosher salt

18 ½- to ¾-inch-thick lamb rib chops, excess fat trimmed
   Vegetable oil, for brushing

2 Tbsp. honey

INGREDIENT INFO Hoisin sauce is available in the Asian foods section of many supermarkets and at Asian markets. Chinese five-spice powder is a spice blend that usually contains ground fennel seeds, Sichuan pepper-corns, cinnamon, star anise, and cloves; it's available in the spice section of most supermarkets.

Char siu **is one of the most popular Chinese marinades, familiar to anyone who's ever ordered barbecued pork in a Chinese restaurant. Here it's used to give lamb chops a pleasant sweetness.**

Whisk hoisin sauce, soy sauce, wine, sugar, five-spice powder, and salt in a small bowl. Transfer to a large resealable plastic bag. Add lamb chops; seal bag and turn to coat. Chill, turning occasionally, for 4 hours. **DO AHEAD:** Can be made 1 day ahead. Keep chilled, turning occasionally.

Build a medium-hot fire in a charcoal grill, or heat a gas grill to high. Brush grill grate with oil. Remove lamb from marinade, with some marinade still clinging to surface, and grill until slightly charred and cooked to desired doneness, 2 to 3 minutes per side for medium-rare. Transfer lamb to a platter. Stir honey and 1 Tbsp. water in a small skillet over medium heat until warm. Brush over chops.

LAMB T-BONES
with Salsa Verde

photo, right

8 1- to 1¼-inch-thick lamb loin chops

¾ cup plus 2 Tbsp. extra-virgin olive oil, more as needed
   Kosher salt and freshly ground black pepper

½ cup fresh mint leaves, chopped

¼ cup chopped flat-leaf parsley

3 Tbsp. chopped tarragon leaves

1 Tbsp. brine-packed capers, drained, minced

½ tsp. crushed red pepper flakes

3 anchovy fillets, minced

1 garlic clove, minced
   Vegetable oil, for brushing

This pungent and minty all-purpose sauce complements the flavor of the char on thick-cut lamb T-bones (and on just about any grilled red meat).

Place lamb chops in a baking dish, drizzle with 2 Tbsp. olive oil, and season with salt and pepper. Let stand for 30 minutes.

Meanwhile, combine mint, parsley, tarragon, capers, red pepper flakes, anchovies, and garlic in a small bowl. Using a fork, whisk in ¾ cup olive oil. For a sauce with a looser consistency, whisk in more oil 1 Tbsp. at a time. Season sauce with salt and pepper.

Build a medium-hot fire in a charcoal grill, or heat a gas grill to high. Brush grill grate with vegetable oil. Grill lamb, turning occasionally, to desired doneness, 8 to 10 minutes for medium-rare. Transfer lamb to a serving board or platter. Spoon some of the sauce over top and serve remaining sauce alongside.

When prepping this minty sauce, **chop the herbs gently**—don't leave all the flavor on the cutting board.

LAMB T-BONES WITH SALSA VERDE

HERB–OLIVE OIL RACKS OF LAMB

photo, right

3 1½- to 1¾-lb. racks of lamb, excess fat trimmed
¾ cup extra-virgin olive oil, plus more for brushing
2 Tbsp. chopped flat-leaf parsley
2 Tbsp. chopped fresh rosemary
1½ tsp. crushed red pepper flakes (optional)
   Kosher salt and freshly ground black pepper

Marinate the lamb in the herbed olive oil for as long as possible—the longer, the better, but 1 to 6 hours is a good rule of thumb. If you only have an hour or so, let it stand at room temperature, turning occasionally; the marinade infuses faster this way than it does when being chilled.

Place lamb in a 15x10x2-inch glass baking dish. Whisk ¾ cup oil, parsley, rosemary, and red pepper flakes, if desired, in a small bowl. Pour marinade over lamb; turn to coat. Cover and chill, turning occasionally, for 6 hours. **DO AHEAD:** Can be made 1 day ahead. Keep chilled, turning occasionally.

Remove lamb from refrigerator and let come to room temperature. Build a medium-hot fire in a charcoal grill, or heat a gas grill to high. Brush grill grate with oil. Remove lamb from marinade and season all over with salt and pepper. Grill lamb racks, turning occasionally, until an instant-read thermometer inserted into the center registers 125°F for medium-rare, about 20 minutes (internal temperature will rise about 5°F as lamb rests).

Transfer lamb to a cutting board; let rest for 15 minutes. Cut lamb racks between bones into individual chops and serve.

4 Steps to RACK OF LAMB

A perfectly grilled rack of lamb is a showstopper, with a phenomenal crust and just the right contrast between a nice char and a juicy pink center. It's also less complicated than you think. Here's how to do it.

1 TRIM THE FAT

A rack of lamb comes with a thick white jacket of fat on the outside. Trim the fat a bit to **minimize flare-ups on the grill** caused by the fat dripping into the flames.

2 MAKE IT HOT

To get a good crust, you need heat. Use medium-high heat in a charcoal grill (or medium if the rub or marinade may burn), medium-high to high heat on a gas grill.

3 WORK THE TONGS

Sear the rack on three sides, turning it regularly with tongs, to ensure that it cooks evenly. The rack will need **20 to 25 minutes total.**

4 TAKE THE TEMPERATURE

For medium-rare, take it off the grill when an **instant-read thermometer hits 125°F.** The internal temperature will rise about 5 degrees while the lamb rests for 15 minutes.

When grilling a whole rack of lamb, you *will* get flare-ups. **Use tongs to turn the lamb frequently** and remove it from hot spots.

HERB–OLIVE OIL
RACK OF LAMB

RACK OF LAMB
with Chinese Five-Spice Sauce

⅓ cup chopped fresh cilantro
¼ cup honey
2 Tbsp. brandy
2 Tbsp. reduced-sodium soy sauce
3 garlic cloves, minced
2 1½-lb. racks of lamb, excess fat trimmed
  Vegetable oil, for brushing
  Kosher salt and freshly ground black pepper
1 cup low-salt chicken broth
5 Tbsp. oyster sauce
¼ cup fresh lemon juice
1 Tbsp. sugar
1 tsp. Chinese five-spice powder
2 scallions, thinly sliced
½ cup (1 stick) chilled unsalted butter, cut into small pieces

INGREDIENT INFO Look for oyster sauce at supermarkets or Asian markets.

The Asian-influenced sauce that accompanies this lamb gets additional richness from butter and brandy. The lamb is best when marinated overnight, so start preparing this the day before if possible. And for a polished presentation, ask your butcher to french the chops for you—this technique removes all the fat and membranes from the bones.

Whisk cilantro, honey, brandy, soy sauce, and garlic in a 15x10x2-inch glass baking dish. Add lamb; turn to coat. Cover and chill overnight, turning occasionally.

Build a medium fire in a charcoal grill, or heat a gas grill to medium-high. Brush grill grate with oil. Remove lamb racks from marinade, with some marinade still clinging to surface, and season with salt and pepper. Grill lamb, turning occasionally, until an instant-read thermometer inserted into the center registers 125°F for medium-rare, about 20 minutes (internal temperature will rise about 5°F as lamb rests).

Transfer lamb racks to a cutting board; let rest for 15 minutes.

Meanwhile, bring broth, oyster sauce, lemon juice, sugar, and five-spice powder to a boil, stirring occasionally, in small saucepan and cook until reduced to ¾ cup, about 12 minutes. Reduce heat to low. Add scallions and butter; stir until butter melts. Season sauce to taste with salt and pepper.

Cut lamb racks between bones into individual chops. Place chops on plates; spoon sauce over.

AT THE MARKET: The Origins of Lamb

Unlike most other kinds of meat, lamb typically comes clearly marked with a place of origin—such as Australia, New Zealand, or domestic. Here are a few of the most popular types:

DOMESTIC: COLORADO

Lamb from Colorado is **well marbled, with a beefy flavor**. These larger lambs are raised on mountainous pastureland, then finished on corn and grain. The bigger cuts, such as rib racks and legs, take particularly well to strong, assertive flavor pairings.

DOMESTIC: PASTURE-RAISED

These are smaller lambs that yield **lean, fine-grained, and mildly flavored meat** with little or no marbling. Pricier, but worth it. Go lighter on the seasonings and cooking times, so that the subtle flavors and delicate texture come through.

NEW ZEALAND

The "3 million people, 60 million sheep" jokes no longer apply, but New Zealand is still a big producer of lamb. Raised on pastureland for the entire course of its life, meat from this country is **prized for its tender, petite chops** and smaller legs.

AUSTRALIAN

This country is one of the largest producers of lamb in the world; this is the type you'll often find at the supermarket. It has a **mild, pleasantly gamy flavor**. Good for any kind of grilling, from ground shoulder for burgers to butterflied leg of lamb.

RACK OF LAMB
with Pine Nut Gremolata

Here's an excellent special-occasion dish that delivers when you want to wow your guests. The prep work is a bit involved, but much can be done in advance, and your efforts will be well rewarded. Gremolata, a blend of garlic, parsley, and lemon zest that usually accompanies osso buco, is enhanced here with slow-roasted grapes, pine nuts, and verjus—the result is a perfect combination of sweet and salty that makes a delicious foil for savory grilled lamb.

SAUCE

- 1 Tbsp. extra-virgin olive oil
- 1 small red onion, chopped
- 3 garlic cloves, minced
- 2 cups dry red wine
- ½ lb. stemmed seedless red grapes
- 2½ cups low-salt beef broth
- 2½ cups low-salt chicken broth
  Kosher salt and freshly ground black pepper

GREMOLATA AND LAMB

- ½ cup verjus, or ¼ cup apple cider vinegar and ¼ cup white grape juice
- ¼ cup sugar
- ½ lb. stemmed seedless red grapes
- ½ cup pine nuts, toasted
- 1½ Tbsp. chopped flat-leaf parsley
- 1½ Tbsp. thinly sliced fresh mint
- 1 tsp. finely grated lemon zest
- 1 tsp. extra-virgin olive oil, plus more for brushing
- 1 garlic clove, minced
  Kosher salt and freshly ground black pepper
- 2 1½- to 1¾-lb. racks of lamb, excess fat trimmed
  Curry powder, for seasoning

INGREDIENT INFO Verjus is a tart juice made from unripe fruit, usually wine grapes; it's available at specialty foods stores.

SAUCE

Heat oil in a large saucepan over medium heat. Add onion and garlic and sauté until onion is soft, about 5 minutes. Add wine and grapes. Simmer, stirring occasionally, until almost all liquid evaporates, about 20 minutes. Add both broths. Increase heat to medium-high and boil, stirring occasionally, until mixture is reduced to 2 scant cups, about 40 minutes. Strain into a large measuring cup, pressing on solids to extract as much liquid as possible; discard solids in strainer. Season sauce to taste with salt and pepper. **DO AHEAD:** Can be made 3 days ahead. Cover and chill.

GREMOLATA AND LAMB

Bring verjus and sugar to a boil in a small saucepan over medium-high heat, stirring until sugar dissolves. Boil until syrup is reduced to ¼ cup, about 5 minutes. Pour verjus syrup into a medium bowl and let cool.

Preheat oven to 250°F. Line a large rimmed baking sheet with foil. Scatter grapes on prepared sheet. Roast grapes until reduced in size by half, about 1½ hours. Let cool on sheet.

Stir grapes into verjus syrup. Add pine nuts, parsley, mint, lemon zest, oil, and garlic; toss to blend. Season gremolata to taste with salt and pepper. Let gremolata stand at room temperature for up to 1 hour.

Build a medium-hot fire in a charcoal grill, or heat a gas grill to high. Brush grill grate with oil. Season lamb all over with salt, pepper, and curry powder. Grill lamb, turning occasionally, until an instant-read thermometer inserted lengthwise into the center of lamb registers 125°F for medium-rare, about 20 minutes. Transfer to a cutting board; let rest for 15 minutes (internal temperature will rise about 5°F as lamb rests).

Slice lamb off the bones. Then slice crosswise into ½-inch-thick medallions. Separate bones for serving alongside. Divide lamb among plates; drizzle with sauce. Spoon gremolata over.

LEG OF LAMB
with Rosemary and Chile

photo, right

12 rosemary sprigs, halved

¾ cup extra-virgin olive oil, plus more for brushing

6 garlic cloves, coarsely chopped

2 Tbsp. finely grated lemon zest

4 tsp. crushed red pepper flakes, divided

1 6- to 8-lb. bone-in leg of lamb, aitch bone removed

Kosher salt and freshly ground black pepper

2 tsp. cumin seeds, coarsely ground

¼ cup fresh oregano leaves

1 Tbsp. red wine vinegar

A bone-in leg of lamb is cooked slowly over medium-low heat and basted often with a brush made of rosemary sprigs, which adds another layer of flavor. The tapered shape of the whole leg is perfect for a crowd: Thicker portions will yield rosy pink medium or medium-rare meat and thinner portions will yield medium-well meat. Ask your butcher to remove the aitch bone for easier carving.

Using kitchen twine, tie rosemary sprigs together in a tight bundle to make a brush. In a small bowl, stir together ¾ cup oil, garlic, lemon zest, and 3 tsp. pepper flakes. Set brush and basting sauce aside.

Season lamb generously with salt and pepper, then rub the remaining 1 tsp. pepper flakes and cumin all over; let stand at room temperature for 1 hour.

Build a medium-low fire in a charcoal grill, or heat a gas grill to medium. Brush grill grate with oil. Grill lamb, uncovered, turning and basting with the rosemary brush every 5 minutes, until a flavorful dark brown crust develops and an instant-read thermometer inserted into the thickest part of the leg registers 135°F for medium, about 1 hour. Transfer lamb to a large platter; let rest for 20 minutes.

Meanwhile, stir oregano leaves and vinegar into basting sauce and drizzle over lamb during final 10 minutes of resting. Transfer lamb to a carving board and carve. Serve on platter with basting sauce and juices accumulated during resting.

WHY WE LOVE: Leg of Lamb

Few cuts of meat are as versatile and tailor-made for the grill as leg of lamb. Legs range from 5 to 9 pounds, and since some parts are thicker than others, leg of lamb offers a range of pieces, from the medium-rare to medium-well spectrum, satisfying everyone. Any way you slice it, this is one dynamic cut.

INFINITE VARIETY

Leg of lamb is outstanding prepared myriad ways, either whole or broken down into its various parts:

- **Marinate a whole leg** and grill-roast it (see page 50 for the technique), or grill it slowly, uncovered, over low heat.
- **Select the top round** and grill it like a **small roast** for a few people, or cut it into cubes for **lamb kebabs**.
- **Butterfly it** and grill it over direct/indirect heat. Here's how ...

THE BUTTERFLY EFFECT

One of the greatest ways to prepare leg of lamb—and ideal for a crowd—is to **butterfly and marinate** it. Butterflying a leg of lamb means to open it up and remove the bone (we recommend asking a butcher to do this and to trim the excess fat). Once it's butterflied, the meat will lie flat; this increases surface area for easier marinating, reduces cooking time, and allows more of a crust to develop. Turn the page for some of our favorite recipes using this technique.

Lemon zest and chili flakes put a bright new spin on the classic combination of rosemary and lamb.

LEG OF LAMB WITH
ROSEMARY AND CHILE

LEG OF LAMB
with Guinness Sauce

1 5-lb. boneless leg of lamb, butterflied, excess fat trimmed (reserve bone and meat trimmings for sauce; about 6½ lb. with bone)
1 small onion, chopped
¾ cup chopped peeled carrots
1½ cups low-salt beef broth
½ cup Guinness Extra Stout
½ cup lager beer (we like Harp)
2 Tbsp. honey mustard
Vegetable oil, for brushing
⅓ cup balsamic vinegar
1 Tbsp. granulated garlic or garlic powder
3 Tbsp. lemon-pepper seasoning
2 Tbsp. (¼ stick) chilled unsalted butter, cut into 4 pieces
1 tsp. honey, more as needed
Kosher salt and freshly ground black pepper

SPECIAL EQUIPMENT A foil baking pan (for drip pan)

The classic British drink the Black and Tan—lager topped with stout—inspired the luscious sauce in this recipe. You can increase the amount of honey to balance out the bitterness of the stout. You'll need to order the leg of lamb ahead of time from your butcher. When you do, ask them to butterfly it and to reserve the bone and trimmings for you to use in the sauce.

Preheat oven to 350°F. Arrange reserved lamb bone and trimmings, onion, and carrots in a roasting pan. Roast, stirring occasionally, until browned, about 1 hour.

Discard lamb bone and pour off fat from roasting pan. Place pan over 2 burners; add broth and bring to a boil, scraping up any browned bits. Strain broth mixture through fine-mesh sieve into a medium saucepan; discard solids in strainer. Add stout, lager, and mustard to broth mixture. Boil sauce until reduced to ¾ cup, about 5 minutes. **DO AHEAD:** Can be made 1 day ahead. Cover and chill.

Prepare grill for indirect heat with a drip pan (see page 16), building a medium fire in a charcoal grill, or heating a gas grill to medium-high. Add water to drip pan to reach a depth of 1 inch. Brush grill grate with oil.

Open lamb like a book and place on a large rimmed baking sheet. Brush lamb all over with vinegar; sprinkle all over with granulated garlic, then lemon-pepper seasoning. Place lamb, boned side down, on grill grate directly over pan. Cover grill and cook lamb, turning occasionally and maintaining temperature of grill between 350° and 375°F, until an instant-read thermometer inserted into the thickest part of the leg registers 130°F for medium-rare (temperature of thinner parts of lamb will register between 135° and 145°F and will vary from medium to well-done), 1 to 1½ hours. (If using a charcoal grill, you may need to add additional charcoal from charcoal chimney to replenish halfway through grilling time.)

Transfer lamb to a cutting board; let rest for 15 minutes.

Rewarm sauce over medium-low heat. Whisk butter into sauce, 1 piece at a time, then whisk in 1 tsp. honey. Season sauce to taste with salt, pepper, and more honey, if desired. Thinly slice lamb against the grain; arrange on a platter and serve sauce alongside.

YOGURT-MARINATED LAMB
with Tabil Spice Blend

2 cups plain whole-milk yogurt, divided

1 tsp. plus 3½ Tbsp. Tabil Spice Blend (recipe follows)

5 large garlic cloves, minced, divided

1 tsp. kosher salt, more as needed

1 tsp. freshly ground black pepper, more as needed

¼ cup extra-virgin olive oil, plus more for brushing

2 Tbsp. fresh lemon juice

1 4- to 5-lb. boneless leg of lamb, butterflied, excess fat trimmed (about 6½ lb. with bone)

4 lemons, halved

Let the yogurt work its marinade magic overnight in this stunning main course. Not only does it tenderize the meat, but its tart creaminess also blends perfectly with the Mediterranean spice flavors that make up the Tabil Spice Blend.

Mix 1 cup yogurt, 1 tsp. Tabil Spice Blend, and 1 minced garlic clove in a small bowl. Season to taste with salt and pepper. Cover and chill. Whisk remaining 1 cup yogurt, remaining 3½ Tbsp. Tabil Spice Blend, remaining 4 minced garlic cloves, 1 tsp. salt, 1 tsp. pepper, ¼ cup oil, and lemon juice in a large bowl. Open lamb like a book and place in bowl; turn to coat. Cover and chill overnight, turning occasionally.

Build a medium-hot fire in a charcoal grill, or heat a gas grill to high. Brush grill grate with oil. Remove lamb from marinade, leaving some marinade still clinging to surface, and season with salt and pepper. Grill until an instant-read thermometer inserted into the thickest part of the leg registers 130°F for medium-rare, 10 to 15 minutes per side. Transfer lamb to a cutting board; let rest for 15 minutes.

Meanwhile, grill lemon halves, cut side down, until charred, about 5 minutes. Thinly slice lamb against the grain; arrange on a platter. Garnish with lemons and serve with reserved yogurt sauce alongside.

Tabil Spice Blend

use with yogurt-marinated lamb

3 Tbsp. coriander seeds

1½ Tbsp. cumin seeds

1 Tbsp. caraway seeds

1½ tsp. crushed red pepper flakes

SPECIAL EQUIPMENT A spice mill

This Tunisian spice blend would elevate virtually any grilled dish. We suggest making extra so that you can have some on hand all summer long to sprinkle on top of grilled lamb, fish, or flatbreads. A batch will keep for a month.

Finely grind all ingredients in spice mill. **DO AHEAD:** Can be made 1 month ahead. Store airtight at room temperature.

LEG OF LAMB WITH
TOMATO-FENNEL VINAIGRETTE

LEG OF LAMB
with Tomato-Fennel Vinaigrette

photo, left

Here's the perfect backyard dinner party entrée—it makes for a stunning presentation. You'll need to marinate the meat overnight so the flavors can meld together. And make the vinaigrette just before serving so the tomatoes don't turn to mush.

LAMB

9 garlic cloves, minced

2 Tbsp. chopped fresh rosemary

2 anchovy fillets packed in oil, drained, minced

2 tsp. fennel seeds

2 tsp. kosher salt

1½ tsp. coarsely cracked black peppercorns

¼ cup extra-virgin olive oil

1 4- to 5-lb. boneless leg of lamb, butterflied, excess fat trimmed (about 6½ lb. with bone)

VINAIGRETTE

1½ tsp. fennel seeds

1 lb. tomatoes, seeded, finely chopped (about 2 cups)

½ cup Kalamata or Niçoise olives, pitted, finely chopped

3 Tbsp. red wine vinegar

⅓ cup extra-virgin olive oil, plus more for brushing
Kosher salt and freshly ground black pepper

¼ cup thinly sliced fresh basil

INGREDIENT INFO Niçoise olives are small brine-cured black olives; they can be found at some supermarkets and at specialty foods stores and Italian markets.

LAMB

Combine garlic, rosemary, anchovies, fennel seeds, salt, and pepper in a small bowl or in a mortar. Using a sturdy wooden spoon or a pestle, mash mixture into a paste. Gradually mix in oil. Open lamb like a book and place in a 15x10x2-inch glass baking dish. Rub paste evenly over both sides of lamb. Cover with plastic wrap and chill overnight. Let lamb stand at room temperature for 1 hour before grilling.

VINAIGRETTE

Toast fennel seeds in a small dry skillet over medium heat, stirring often, until fragrant and slightly darker in color, 2 to 3 minutes. Transfer to a medium saucepan. Add tomatoes, olives, and vinegar; stir in ⅓ cup oil. Season vinaigrette to taste with salt and pepper.

Build a medium-hot fire in a charcoal grill, or heat a gas grill to high. Brush grill grate with oil. Place lamb on grill grate. Cover grill and open vents. Grill lamb, turning occasionally, until an instant-read thermometer inserted into the thickest part of the leg registers 130°F for medium-rare, about 25 minutes. Transfer lamb to a cutting board; let rest for 15 minutes. Place saucepan with vinaigrette on a slightly cooler part of barbecue and heat just until warm, about 5 minutes. Stir in basil.

Thinly slice lamb against the grain; arrange slices on a platter. Spoon vinaigrette over.

IS It Done Yet?

WELL, THAT DEPENDS ON THE CUT. To measure the doneness of thinner cuts like single chops, you can go by feel, but use an instant-read thermometer for larger pieces like a leg of lamb or whole racks. We recommend going with medium-rare (130°F) for leg of lamb, and for expensive (and therefore tender) cuts like loin and rib chops. Tougher, chewier cuts like blade chops and leg chops we cook to medium (140°F) or medium-well (150°F).

MUSTARD-SAGE
LEG OF LAMB

1 cup dry red wine

¾ cup chopped shallots (about 3 large)

½ cup whole grain Dijon mustard

⅓ cup plus 1 Tbsp. finely chopped fresh sage

¼ cup extra-virgin olive oil, plus more for brushing

3 garlic cloves, minced

1 cup low-salt beef broth

1 5¾-lb. boneless leg of lamb, butterflied, excess fat trimmed (about 7 lb. with bone)

Kosher salt and freshly ground black pepper

2 Tbsp. (¼ stick) chilled unsalted butter, cut into ½-inch cubes

SPECIAL EQUIPMENT A 2-gal. resealable plastic bag

Sage and mustard make a brilliant pairing with lamb; both are bold enough to match the flavor of the meat. Part of the marinade is reserved to make a rich reduction sauce. Zinfandel is a good choice for the red wine.

Whisk wine, shallots, mustard, ⅓ cup chopped sage, ¼ cup oil, and garlic in a medium bowl for marinade. Transfer ½ cup marinade to a small saucepan; add broth. Boil until sauce is reduced to ¾ cup, about 12 minutes. Place leg of lamb in a resealable bag. Pour remaining marinade into bag; seal. Turn bag to coat, arranging lamb in 1 flat piece. Place lamb in bag on a rimmed baking sheet and open lamb like a book. Cover and chill sauce and lamb separately, turning lamb occasionally, overnight.

Build a medium fire in a charcoal grill, or heat a gas grill to medium-high. Brush grill grate with oil. Remove lamb from marinade, with some marinade still clinging, and transfer to a large rimmed baking sheet. Open lamb like a book and season on both sides with salt and pepper. Transfer lamb to grill. Cover and grill lamb until charred outside and an instant-read thermometer inserted into the thickest part of the leg registers 130°F for medium-rare, 10 to 12 minutes per side (thicker pieces can be cut away from leg and grilled longer, if desired). Transfer lamb to a cutting board; let rest for 15 minutes.

Rewarm sauce. Whisk in butter and remaining 1 Tbsp. chopped sage and season to taste with salt and pepper. Thinly slice lamb against the grain. Arrange slices on a platter; spoon some sauce over. Serve, passing remaining sauce alongside.

LEG OF LAMB
with Ancho Chile Marinade

½ cup dry white wine

¼ cup extra-virgin olive oil, plus more for brushing

8 garlic cloves

4 Tbsp. fresh oregano leaves, divided

3 Tbsp. ancho chile powder

2 Tbsp. fresh lemon juice

2 scallions, 1 coarsely chopped, 1 finely chopped

1 Tbsp. (packed) dark brown sugar

2½ tsp. kosher salt

2½ tsp. freshly ground black pepper

1 4½-lb. boneless leg of lamb, butterflied, excess fat trimmed (about 5½ lb. with bone)

Ground ancho chiles (available at many supermarkets and at Latin markets) impart rich chile flavor but not excessive heat. Don't use regular chili powder instead; it will alter the flavor of the dish.

Purée wine, ¼ cup oil, garlic, 3 Tbsp. oregano, ancho chile powder, lemon juice, coarsely chopped scallion, sugar, salt, and pepper in a blender until smooth. Pour marinade into a 13x9x2-inch glass baking dish. Open lamb like a book; add to marinade and turn to coat evenly. Cover and chill overnight.

Build a medium fire in a charcoal grill, or heat a gas grill to medium-high. Brush grill grate with oil. Remove lamb from marinade, with some marinade still clinging to surface, and grill, turning once, until an instant-read thermometer inserted into the thickest part of the leg registers 130°F for medium-rare, 30 to 32 minutes. Transfer lamb to a cutting board; let rest for 15 minutes.

Meanwhile, combine remaining 1 Tbsp. oregano leaves and finely chopped scallion in a small bowl.

Thinly slice lamb against the grain; arrange slices on a platter. Pour any juices from cutting board over and sprinkle with oregano-scallion mixture.

LAMB KEBABS
with Golden Couscous

¾ cup extra-virgin olive oil, plus more for brushing
⅔ cup fresh lemon juice
6 large garlic cloves, minced
2 Tbsp. chopped fresh mint
4 tsp. finely grated lemon zest
4 tsp. kosher salt, more as needed
2 tsp. freshly ground black pepper, more as needed
2 tsp. ground coriander
1 tsp. ground cumin
1 4-lb. boneless leg of lamb, cut into 2-inch cubes
32 whole dried apricots, soaked in boiling water for 5 minutes
4 medium red onions, each cut into 8 chunks
Golden Couscous (recipe follows)

SPECIAL EQUIPMENT Sixteen metal skewers

In this recipe, lamb and apricots—both seasoned with aromatic spices—are cooked on separate skewers, as the apricots actually take longer to cook. Be sure to plump the apricots in boiling water before grilling so they won't burn.

Whisk ¾ cup oil, lemon juice, garlic, mint, lemon zest, salt, pepper, coriander, and cumin in a large bowl. Transfer ½ cup marinade to a small bowl; cover and chill. Add lamb to remaining marinade in large bowl; toss to coat. Let lamb marinate at room temperature for 2 hours. **DO AHEAD:** Can be made 1 day ahead. Cover and chill. Let stand at room temperature for 1 hour before continuing.

Build a medium-hot fire in a charcoal grill, or heat a gas grill to high. Brush grill grate with oil. Drain lamb; discard marinade. Thread lamb cubes onto 8 skewers, dividing equally. Thread apricots onto remaining 8 skewers alternately with onion chunks. Brush all skewers with some of reserved marinade. Season onion-apricot skewers with salt and pepper.

Arrange all skewers on barbecue. Grill lamb, turning occasionally, to desired doneness, about 8 minutes for medium-rare. Grill onion-apricot skewers, occasionally turning and basting with marinade and moving skewers to cooler part of barbecue if necessary to keep apricots from burning, until onions soften and begin to char, about 10 minutes.

Mound Golden Couscous on a large platter. Top with skewers.

Golden Couscous

use with lamb kebabs

6 cups low-salt chicken broth
6 Tbsp. (¾ stick) unsalted butter
3 cups chopped onions
2 tsp. turmeric
1 tsp. ground cumin
3 cups couscous (about 1 lb.)
Kosher salt and freshly ground black pepper
⅔ cup slivered almonds, toasted

This would also be a good accompaniment to grilled chicken, pork chops, or smoked pork shoulder.

Bring broth to a boil in a medium saucepan. Reduce heat to very low; cover to keep hot. Melt butter in a large heavy saucepan over medium heat. Add onions; sauté until tender and light golden, about 8 minutes. Add turmeric and cumin; stir for 1 minute. Add couscous; stir until coated with onion mixture. Mix in hot broth. Remove from heat. Cover and let stand until broth is absorbed and couscous is tender, about 12 minutes.

Fluff couscous with a fork. Season to taste with salt and pepper. Mound on a platter and sprinkle with almonds.

LAMB KEBABS
WITH POMEGRANATE-CUMIN GLAZE

LAMB KEBABS
with Pomegranate-Cumin Glaze

4 servings

photo, left

1 tsp. cumin seeds
½ cup extra-virgin olive oil, plus more for brushing
¼ cup pomegranate molasses
3 garlic cloves, minced
1 tsp. dried oregano
1 tsp. kosher salt, more as needed
½ tsp. freshly ground black pepper, more as needed
½ tsp. ground cinnamon
1 lb. boneless leg of lamb, excess fat trimmed, cut into ¾-inch cubes
1 large red bell pepper, cut into ¾-inch pieces

INGREDIENT INFO Pomegranate molasses is a thick pomegranate syrup that's available at some supermarkets, at Middle Eastern markets, and from kalustyans.com.

SPECIAL EQUIPMENT A 1-gal. resealable plastic bag; 8 metal skewers; a spice mill (optional)

The Middle Eastern–style glaze on these kebabs features pomegranate molasses and toasted cumin seeds. If you don't have a spice mill or mortar and pestle, you can grind the toasted seeds into a coarse powder by placing them in a resealable plastic bag and pounding them with a heavy rolling pin or the bottom of a cast-iron skillet.

Stir cumin seeds in a small skillet over medium heat until aromatic and lightly toasted, 2 to 3 minutes. Let cool and then finely grind cumin in a mortar with a pestle or in spice mill. Place ground cumin, ½ cup oil, pomegranate molasses, garlic, oregano, 1 tsp. salt, ½ tsp. pepper, and cinnamon in a resealable bag; close and shake to combine. Add lamb; turn to coat. Chill, turning occasionally, for at least 1 hour and up to 4 hours.

Remove lamb from marinade; discard marinade. Thread lamb and bell pepper onto each skewer, alternating as you go; place on a large rimmed baking sheet.
DO AHEAD: Can be made 2 hours ahead. Cover and chill.

Build a medium-hot fire in a charcoal grill, or heat a gas grill to high. Brush grill grate with oil. Season kebabs with salt and pepper. Grill kebabs, turning often, to desired doneness, about 4 minutes for medium-rare.

Kitchen Wisdom

THE BEST CUT FOR KEBABS Meat cut from the leg of the lamb is our choice for kebabs. You can use shoulder meat, but the leg's various muscles are more tender than the shoulder, and are easier to trim into manageable parts for skewering. Pricier tenderloin or chops would work, too, of course, but leg meat is a better value—it gets even more delicious with the marinades and bold seasonings associated with kebab recipes.

LAMB SKEWERS
with Sichuan Peppercorns

4 to 6 servings

1 cup (packed) fresh mint leaves, coarsely chopped
¾ cup fresh orange juice
½ cup (packed) light brown sugar
¼ cup apple cider vinegar
¼ cup dry Sherry
3 garlic cloves, chopped
1 Tbsp. chopped peeled ginger
1 Tbsp. finely grated orange zest
2 tsp. Sichuan peppercorns
1 tsp. pink peppercorns, crushed
1 tsp. reduced-sodium soy sauce
1 tsp. toasted sesame oil
1½ lb. boneless leg of lamb, excess fat trimmed, cut into 1-inch cubes
Vegetable oil, for brushing
Kosher salt and freshly ground black pepper

SPECIAL EQUIPMENT 4 to 6 metal skewers

A dynamic blend of Sichuan peppercorns, ginger, sesame oil, and soy sauce imparts an unexpected spin to the classic pairing of lamb and mint. The lamb tastes best if it marinates overnight, so if possible, begin preparing it a day ahead. Sichuan peppercorns (sometimes called wild pepper or sansho peppercorns) are not hard to find; look in Asian markets or at specialty foods stores.

Whisk first 12 ingredients in a medium bowl until brown sugar dissolves for marinade. Thread lamb onto metal skewers. Place kebabs in a 13x9x2-inch glass baking dish. Pour marinade over. Cover; chill overnight, turning occasionally.

Build a medium-hot fire in a charcoal grill, or heat a gas grill to high. Brush grill grate with vegetable oil. Transfer kebabs to a rimmed baking sheet; pour marinade into a small saucepan. Season kebabs with salt and pepper. Grill, turning occasionally, to desired doneness, about 8 minutes for medium-rare. Transfer kebabs to a platter. Boil marinade for 5 minutes. Strain through fine-mesh sieve into a small bowl; spoon over kebabs.

HERBED LAMB SKEWERS
with Baby Arugula and Lemon

8 servings

3 lb. boneless leg of lamb, excess fat trimmed, cut into 1- to 1½-inch cubes
¼ cup dry white wine
Kosher salt and freshly ground black pepper
6 Tbsp. extra-virgin olive oil, more as needed, divided; additional for brushing
2 large garlic cloves, minced
2 Tbsp. chopped fresh rosemary
1 Tbsp. chopped fresh mint
1 Tbsp. chopped fresh oregano
4 anchovy fillets packed in oil, drained, finely chopped (optional)
4 cups (packed) baby arugula
2 lemons, cut into wedges

SPECIAL EQUIPMENT 8 metal skewers

This quick, simple preparation delivers huge flavor with just a few ingredients: The lamb marinates in a mixture of fresh herbs, garlic, and finely chopped anchovies.

Place lamb in a large glass baking dish. Drizzle with wine and season lightly with salt and pepper. Mix 4 Tbsp. oil, garlic, all herbs, and anchovies in a small bowl. Add mixture to lamb; toss to coat. Cover; chill for 2 hours. **DO AHEAD:** Can be made 1 day ahead. Keep chilled, tossing occasionally.

Toss arugula and 2 Tbsp. oil in a large bowl to coat. Arrange on a large platter; season with salt and pepper.

Build a medium-hot fire in a charcoal grill, or heat a gas grill to high. Brush grill grate with oil. Thread lamb onto metal skewers and season with salt and pepper. Grill, turning occasionally, to desired doneness, about 10 minutes for medium-rare. Slide lamb from skewers onto arugula; serve with lemon wedges for squeezing over.

MEDITERRANEAN LAMB SALAD

¾ cup Dijon mustard

½ cup fresh lemon juice

3 2-oz. tins anchovy fillets packed in oil, drained, oil reserved, anchovies chopped

1⅓ cups extra-virgin olive oil, plus more for brushing

1½ cups (packed) chopped fresh basil, plus sprigs for garnish

1 cup chopped shallots
    Kosher salt and freshly ground black pepper

1 3½-lb. boneless leg of lamb, butterflied, excess fat trimmed (about 4 lb. with bone)

3 lb. small red-skinned potatoes, unpeeled, cut into ¾-inch cubes

2 lb. green beans or yellow wax beans, trimmed

1 lb. button or crimini (baby bella) mushrooms, sliced
    Fresh spinach or arugula leaves

The anchovies in this salad dressing add depth of flavor (without imparting a fishy taste), just as they do in Caesar salad dressing. Part of the dressing is used to marinate the lamb, and the rest coats the salad.

Whisk mustard, lemon juice, and reserved anchovy oil in a medium bowl. Gradually whisk in 1⅓ cups olive oil. Stir in anchovies, chopped basil, and shallots. Season dressing to taste with salt and pepper. Open lamb like a book and arrange in a large glass baking dish. Pour 1⅓ cups dressing over; turn to coat. Cover lamb and remaining dressing separately and chill for 6 hours. **DO AHEAD:** Can be made 1 day ahead. Keep chilled. Bring dressing to room temperature before continuing.

   Cook potatoes in a large pot of boiling salted water until tender, about 15 minutes. Drain well. Transfer to a large bowl. Add 1½ cups reserved dressing to warm potatoes and toss gently to coat. Cook beans in another large pot of boiling salted water until crisp-tender, 6 to 8 minutes. Drain and pat dry. Add beans and mushrooms to potatoes. Mix in ½ cup reserved dressing. Season salad to taste with salt and pepper.

   Build a medium-hot fire in a charcoal grill, or heat a gas grill to high. Brush grill grate with oil. Season lamb with salt and pepper. Remove lamb from marinade, with some marinade still clinging to surface. Grill lamb, occasionally brushing with some marinade from dish, until an instant-read thermometer inserted into the thickest part of the leg registers 130°F for medium-rare, about 12 minutes per side. Transfer to a cutting board and let rest for 15 minutes.

   Arrange vegetable salad on one platter and line another platter with spinach. Thinly slice lamb against the grain; arrange over spinach on a platter. Drizzle lamb with remaining dressing. Top with basil sprigs. Serve with vegetable salad alongside.

LAMB SANDWICHES
with Red Bell Pepper Aioli

makes 10

1 4½-lb. boneless leg of lamb, butterflied, excess fat trimmed (about 5¾ lb. with bone)
6 garlic cloves, thinly sliced
  Kosher salt and freshly ground black pepper
2 Tbsp. minced fresh thyme
1 Tbsp. dried savory
1 Tbsp. minced fresh rosemary
  Vegetable oil, for brushing
5 bunches scallions, trimmed
½ cup extra-virgin olive oil, divided
2 French baguettes, each cut crosswise into five 4- to 4½-inch-long pieces
  Red Bell Pepper Aioli (recipe follows)
1½ cups purchased tapenade

Slices of grilled leg of lamb, grilled scallions, and an easy roasted pepper aioli and tapenade create hearty and delicious sandwiches. Grilling the scallions gives a smoky flavor and subtle sweetness.

Open lamb like a book. Using a small sharp knife, make ½-inch-deep slits all over lamb. Insert garlic slices into slits. Season lamb with salt and pepper and sprinkle with thyme, savory, and rosemary, pressing herbs to adhere. Arrange in a large glass baking dish. **DO AHEAD:** Can be made 1 day ahead. Cover and chill.

Build a medium-hot fire in a charcoal grill, or heat a gas grill to high. Brush grill grate with vegetable oil. Place scallions in a large roasting pan. Drizzle ¼ cup olive oil over scallions; toss to coat. Season with salt and pepper. Cut baguette pieces in half horizontally. Brush cut sides of bread with remaining ¼ cup oil.

Grill lamb, turning occasionally, until an instant-read thermometer inserted into the thickest part of the leg registers 130°F for medium-rare, about 30 minutes. Transfer to a cutting board and let rest for 15 minutes.

Working in batches if necessary, arrange scallions in a single layer on grill. Cook until beginning to char, about 4 minutes per side. Transfer to a cutting board and chop coarsely. Place in a large bowl. Grill baguettes, cut side down, until golden brown, about 2 minutes; transfer to a plate.

Thinly slice lamb against the grain and arrange on a platter. Serve lamb with scallions, baguette pieces, Red Bell Pepper Aioli, and tapenade, allowing guests to assemble their own sandwiches.

Red Bell Pepper Aioli

makes about 2⅓ cups

use with lamb sandwiches

3 garlic cloves, peeled
3 Tbsp. extra-virgin olive oil
1 cup mayonnaise
1 15-oz. jar roasted red bell peppers, drained, patted dry
  Kosher salt and freshly ground black pepper

You can also serve this with grilled salmon, in chicken salad, or with bouillabaisse.

Finely chop garlic in a food processor. With machine running, gradually add oil to garlic. Add mayonnaise; blend well. Add bell peppers and pulse until finely chopped. Season aioli to taste with salt and pepper. **DO AHEAD:** Can be made 1 day ahead. Cover and chill.

LAMB BULGOGI

with Asian Pear and Sesame Dipping Sauce

LAMB

- 4 scallions, coarsely chopped
- 3 Tbsp. sugar
- 3 garlic cloves, coarsely chopped
- 1 2-inch piece ginger, peeled, cut into thin rounds
- ⅔ cup mirin
- ⅔ cup reduced-sodium soy sauce
- ⅓ cup toasted sesame oil
- 2 Tbsp. toasted sesame seeds
- 1 tsp. freshly ground black pepper
- 1 5½-lb. boneless leg of lamb, butterflied, excess fat trimmed (6½ to 7 lb. with bone)

DIPPING SAUCE AND GARNISHES

- 1 cup chopped cored peeled Asian pear (about ½ large)
- 10 scallions, 2 chopped, 8 trimmed
- ½ cup mirin
- ½ cup reduced-sodium soy sauce
- 3 Tbsp. sugar
- 3 Tbsp. toasted sesame oil
- 4 Tbsp. sesame seeds, toasted, divided
  Kosher salt and freshly ground black pepper
  Vegetable oil, for brushing
- 8 jalapeños, halved, seeded if desired
- 8 garlic cloves
- ½ cup Sriracha or gochujang (Korean red pepper paste)
- 1 large head of butter lettuce, leaves separated and left whole

INGREDIENT INFO Mirin is sold in some supermarkets and at Japanese markets. Gochujang is a spicy red pepper paste made with puréed fermented soybeans (miso) and hot chiles; it's available at Korean markets and online from koamart.com.

SPECIAL EQUIPMENT 3 metal skewers

Bulgogi, **which means "fire meat," is a traditional Korean dish that is usually made with marinated beef short ribs. This rendition calls for thin slices of leg of lamb instead and is a winner for backyard cookouts: Guests wrap grilled meat and other vegetables in lettuce leaves and doctor them with a slightly sweet dipping sauce and Sriracha or a red pepper paste called** *gochujang.*

LAMB

Pulse scallions, sugar, garlic, and ginger in a food processor, stopping occasionally to scrape down sides of bowl, until finely chopped. Transfer mixture to a medium bowl and add mirin, soy sauce, oil, sesame seeds, and pepper; whisk marinade to blend. Pour 1 cup marinade into a large glass baking dish. Open lamb like a book; add to baking dish. Pour remaining marinade over lamb, spreading to cover evenly. Cover dish and chill for 4 hours. **DO AHEAD:** Can be made 1 day ahead. Keep chilled, turning lamb occasionally.

DIPPING SAUCE AND GARNISHES

Purée pear and chopped scallions in a food processor until smooth. Add mirin, soy sauce, and sugar and process until sugar dissolves. Add sesame oil and 2 Tbsp. sesame seeds; process until oil is incorporated (most sesame seeds will remain intact). Transfer sauce to a 2-cup measuring cup. Season sauce to taste with salt and pepper. **DO AHEAD:** Can be made 1 day ahead. Cover and chill.

Build a medium fire in a charcoal grill, or heat a gas grill to medium-high. Brush grill grate with vegetable oil. Thread jalapeño halves onto 2 metal skewers, dividing equally. Thread garlic cloves onto third metal skewer, spacing cloves slightly apart. Place jalapeño and garlic skewers on a plate and set aside.

Remove lamb from marinade, with some marinade still clinging to surface; discard remaining marinade in dish. Grill lamb, turning once, until an instant-read thermometer inserted into the thickest part registers 130°F for medium-rare, 30 to 40 minutes (if lamb begins to burn, slide a large sheet of heavy-duty foil under lamb and continue to grill). Transfer lamb to a cutting board and let rest for 15 minutes.

Meanwhile, grill jalapeños, garlic, and remaining 8 trimmed scallions until slightly charred and tender, 3 to 4 minutes per side. Transfer to a work surface. Cut garlic cloves in half lengthwise. Cut scallions into 2-inch pieces.

Place Sriracha or gochujang in a small bowl. Stir dipping sauce to reblend and divide among 8 small dishes. Arrange lettuce leaves on a large serving platter to cover. Thinly slice lamb and arrange over lettuce leaves. Arrange jalapeños, garlic, and scallions around lamb. Sprinkle remaining 2 Tbsp. sesame seeds over. To serve, spread very small amounts of Sriracha or gochujang over lettuce leaf, fill lettuce with lamb and garnishes, fold ends of lettuce over filling, and dip in sauce.

ch 7

FISH

SALMON
203

WHOLE FISH
218

SWORDFISH & TUNA
209

PACKETS
225

WHITE FISH
213

SKEWERS
230

SANDWICHES &
SALADS
234

WHEN OUR CATCH IS FRESH

we like to cook it over a bed of hot coals. Fire and fish just go together.

In this chapter, you'll learn how to sear rich and meaty tuna and swordfish steaks, discover the ins and outs of grilling fatty salmon (which we consider the *real* chicken of the sea), and get tried-and-true tricks for managing delicate white fish, like halibut fillets and whole branzino stuffed with herbs and citrus. There's also an arsenal of salsas, sauces, and seasonings for elevating flavor.

Though you don't need a fishing rod to tackle this chapter, you will need a good relationship with a fishmonger who can help you pick out the freshest specimens of the sea. Beyond that, it's pretty simple, because the principles for cooking fish are the same no matter what kind you're grilling: Freshness is important; a hot fire reigns supreme; and maintaining a clean, well-oiled grill grate will simplify your life.

SOY-GLAZED SALMON

2 servings

3 Tbsp. (packed) dark brown sugar
4 tsp. prepared Chinese-style hot
   mustard or Dijon mustard
1 Tbsp. reduced-sodium soy sauce
1 tsp. unseasoned rice vinegar
2 7- to 8-oz. salmon steaks (about
   ¾ inch thick)
   Vegetable oil, for brushing

This quick, simple mix-and-grill recipe features a delicious sweet-hot glaze made with only four ingredients. These directions tell you how to grill the salmon steaks until they're cooked through. If you prefer your fillets medium or medium-rare, reduce the cooking time by 1 to 2 minutes per side.

Build a medium-hot fire in a charcoal grill, or heat a gas grill to high. Whisk brown sugar, mustard, and soy sauce in a medium bowl. Transfer 1 Tbsp. glaze to a small bowl; mix in vinegar and set aside.

   Brush one side of salmon steaks generously with half of glaze in medium bowl. Brush grill grate with oil. Grill salmon steaks, glazed side down, until glaze is slightly charred, about 4 minutes. Brush top side of salmon steaks with remaining glaze in medium bowl. Turn salmon over and grill until second side is slightly charred and salmon is just opaque in the center, about 5 minutes longer. Transfer salmon to plates. Drizzle reserved glaze from small bowl over salmon.

GREEN SHAWARMA SALMON

4 servings

1 cup chopped fresh cilantro
7 Tbsp. extra-virgin olive oil
¼ cup fresh lemon juice
2 garlic cloves, chopped
1 tsp. ground coriander
½ tsp. ground cardamom
½ tsp. ground cinnamon
½ tsp. ground ginger
   Kosher salt and freshly ground
   black pepper
4 6-oz. boneless salmon fillets

SPECIAL EQUIPMENT A fish grill basket
(optional)

The word *shawarma* comes from a Turkish word meaning "turn," and evokes spit-roasted meats on a vertical grill. This spiced fish shawarma turns that convention on its side and uses a fish basket to grill fillets with ease. You can use skin-on or skinless salmon, whichever you prefer.

Purée first 8 ingredients in a blender until smooth. Season marinade to taste with salt and pepper. **DO AHEAD:** Can be made 1 day ahead. Cover and chill.

   Place salmon fillets on a platter. Spoon marinade over fish and turn to coat. Cover; chill for at least 1 hour and up to 3 hours.

   Build a medium-hot fire in a charcoal grill, or heat a gas grill to high. Grill fish, using a grill basket if desired, until just cooked through, about 4 minutes per side.

SALMON FILLETS
with Ponzu Sauce and Vegetable Slaw

1 cup fresh orange juice
½ cup sake
¼ cup reduced-sodium soy sauce
¼ cup sugar
2 Tbsp. fresh lime juice
¼ tsp. crushed red pepper flakes
1½ tsp. cornstarch
   Vegetable oil, for brushing
6 7- to 8-oz. skin-on salmon fillets
   Vegetable Slaw (recipe follows)
1 Tbsp. black sesame seeds or
   toasted white sesame seeds
6 lemon wedges

INGREDIENT INFO Black sesame seeds are available at some supermarkets and at specialty foods stores and Asian and Indian markets.

Rich salmon fillets stand up well to the sweet-sour sauce used to glaze the fish on the grill. A slaw of crisp cucumber, jicama, carrot, and bell pepper adds contrast in flavor and texture to the succulent salmon.

Bring first 6 ingredients to a boil in a small heavy saucepan over medium-high heat, stirring ponzu sauce until sugar dissolves. Boil until reduced to 1⅓ cups, about 5 minutes. Stir cornstarch and 2 tsp. water in a small bowl until cornstarch dissolves. Add mixture to ponzu sauce and boil, stirring often, until sauce thickens and is clear, about 1 minute. **DO AHEAD:** Ponzu sauce can be made 1 day ahead. Cover and chill.

Build a medium-hot fire in a charcoal grill, or heat a gas grill to high. Brush grill grate with oil. Brush each salmon fillet with 1 Tbsp. ponzu sauce. Grill salmon, skin side up, for 3 minutes. Turn salmon fillets and brush each with another 1 Tbsp. ponzu sauce. Grill until salmon is just cooked through, about 5 minutes longer.

Transfer salmon fillets to plates. Top with Vegetable Slaw, dividing equally. Sprinkle with sesame seeds; serve with lemon wedges alongside for squeezing over.

Vegetable Slaw

use with salmon fillets

¼ cup honey
¼ cup yellow miso
1 Tbsp. fresh lemon juice
1 tsp. minced peeled ginger
1 tsp. reduced-sodium soy sauce
1 tsp. toasted sesame oil
½ cup plus 2 Tbsp. vegetable oil
   Kosher salt and freshly ground
   black pepper
1 cup matchstick-size strips
   peeled jicama
1 6-inch cucumber, peeled, seeded,
   cut into matchstick-size strips
1 red bell pepper, seeded, cut into
   matchstick-size strips
1 small carrot, peeled, cut into
   matchstick-size strips
¼ cup chopped fresh cilantro

This stand-out slaw showcases miso (fermented soybean paste). This flavor booster is one of our favorite secret weapons in the kitchen, because it delivers an umami kick with both sweet and salty notes. See page 325 for tips on creating perfect matchstick-size vegetables.

Purée first 6 ingredients and ¼ cup water in a blender until smooth. With machine running, gradually add vegetable oil; blend until smooth. Season miso dressing to taste with salt and pepper.

Combine jicama, cucumber, red bell pepper, carrot, and cilantro in a large bowl. Toss vegetables with miso dressing just to coat.

SMOKED SALMON FILLETS

6 servings

1 cup (packed) light brown sugar
1 cup granulated sugar
¼ cup salt
6 5- to 6-oz. skin-on salmon fillets

SPECIAL EQUIPMENT 3 cups (or more) wood chips, soaked in water for 30 minutes, drained; 2 foil broiler pans

Here's a straightforward way to give salmon incredible flavor. Brined salmon fillets are a revelation when cooked slowly over low heat and infused with smoky flavor from wood chips. We recommend cedar, alderwood, or any fruitwood like apple or cherry. Avoid using stronger woods such as hickory or mesquite—they'll overpower the natural flavor of the salmon. Start this recipe the day before; the salmon needs to brine overnight.

Stir brown sugar, granulated sugar, salt, and 4 quarts water in a large bowl until both sugars dissolve. Add salmon, skin side up, to brine, pressing to submerge. Cover and chill overnight.

Remove salmon from brine; discard brine. Rinse salmon under cold running water. Place salmon, skin side down, on a wire rack. Let stand until top is dry to the touch (do not pat dry), about 1 hour.

Build a medium-low fire in a charcoal grill, or heat a gas grill to medium. Place 3 cups drained wood chips in foil broiler pan. Set atop coals (if using a charcoal grill) or directly atop gas flame (if using a gas grill) for 5 minutes before grilling salmon. Position grill grate at least 6 inches above heat. Position vents on grill so that chips smoke and (if using a charcoal grill) charcoal burns but does not flame.

Using a skewer, pierce 6 holes evenly in bottom of second broiler pan. Arrange salmon, skin side down, in pan and place on grill. Cover grill; cook until salmon is firm to the touch and glaze forms over salmon, adding more wood chips to grill if needed, 30 minutes to 1 hour, depending on heat of grill.

Remove salmon from pan, leaving skin behind. Transfer salmon to a platter; serve warm or at room temperature. **DO AHEAD:** Can be made 1 day ahead. Cover; chill. Bring to room temperature before serving.

CEDAR PLANK SALMON

4 servings

photo, right

1 Tbsp. vegetable oil
Spice rub (optional)
4 8-oz. skinless, boneless salmon
   fillets
Kosher salt and freshly ground
   black pepper

SPECIAL EQUIPMENT 4 cedar planks

Cooking fish, meat, or chicken on a wood plank above an open fire keeps the protein moist and protected while infusing it with wonderful flavor. Master the technique, then add your own spin with your favorite dry rub, compound butter, or herb sauce.

Soak planks, weighting them down with a plate to keep them submerged, in warm water for at least 1 hour and up to 6 hours before you start grilling.

Build a 2-zone medium-hot/low fire in a charcoal grill (see page 15), or heat a gas grill to high, leaving one burner unlit. When coals have a light layer of gray ash on them, or when gas grill is hot, place planks over high heat for about 30 seconds per side to dry plank surface. Transfer planks to indirect heat (away from high heat) and brush with oil (or, if you are using a spice rub, sprinkle on planks as well as over salmon). Season salmon fillets with salt and pepper and arrange on planks; cover grill. Cook, checking every 5 minutes to make sure planks don't catch fire (some smoldering of underside is okay), until salmon is just cooked through, about 20 minutes. Serve on planks or transfer salmon to plates.

GETTING IT RIGHT: How to Grill on Cedar

Native American tribes from the Pacific Northwest originated the technique of grilling salmon on cedar planks. This method also works well with other kinds of fish and shellfish, especially fatty, rich varieties like trout, Arctic char, and shrimp.

SIZE MATTERS

We prefer grilling with planks that are ¾ **inch thick**. They're substantial enough to ensure that the wood won't go up in flames even on a higher heat. Planks thinner than that should stay on the cooler side of a 2-zone fire.

SOAK 'EM

Before you use them (*every* time you use them), **soak the planks in water**—at least 1 hour for ¾-inch-thick planks and at least 30 minutes for thinner ones. Put them on the grill wet (don't dry them off).

CLEANUP

If the planks are not too charred after you use them, **wash with warm soapy water**, let dry, and lightly oil with food-safe mineral oil before storing. Just be sure to soak them again before putting them back on the grill.

Grilling salmon on cedar planks imparts an incomparably **smoky, woodsy flavor and aroma** to the fish.

CEDAR PLANK SALMON

SIDE OF SALMON
with Lemon and Olive Oil

3 Tbsp. extra-virgin olive oil, plus more for brushing and drizzling
1 4-lb. whole side skin-on salmon fillet (preferably wild king), scaled, pin bones removed
Kosher salt and freshly ground black pepper
2 or 3 lemons, halved

SPECIAL EQUIPMENT A rimless baking sheet

This simple preparation—just olive oil, salt and pepper, lemons, and a whole side of salmon—allows the pure flavor of the fish to shine through, so use the best-quality salmon you can find. The richer flavor of wild salmon—like the mighty king (Chinook) or ruby-red sockeye—is well worth the splurge here. The key is achieving the right doneness. We recommend medium to medium-rare, so that the fish is still nice and moist. Wild salmon has a more delicate texture than farmed; the skin is supposed to stick to the grill when you remove the fish.

Build a medium-hot fire on one side of a charcoal grill, or preheat a gas grill to high (if using a 2-burner grill, light 1 burner on high; if using a 3-burner grill, leave center burner off and heat other 2 burners on high).

Brush a rimless baking sheet with some of the oil. Place fish, skin side down, on sheet. Rub the flesh side of salmon with 3 Tbsp. oil and season generously with salt and pepper.

Brush grill grate with oil. Slide the fish off the baking sheet and onto the grill grate over indirect heat. Cover; grill and cook until salmon is just cooked through and just opaque in the center, about 20 minutes.

Holding a spatula, slide it under the salmon between the flesh and skin, leaving the skin stuck to the grill. Use another spatula to gently push the fish off of the spatula onto a platter. Drizzle with more oil; season with salt and pepper. Serve with the lemon halves alongside for squeezing over.

Kitchen Wisdom

LEMON AID The next time you're grilling, reach for our secret weapon: lemons. Simply halve a couple of lemons, rub them with olive oil, and throw them on the grate a few minutes before your fish is done. The lemons will mellow and caramelize on the grill; when they're lightly charred, squeeze the juice over any fillet or whole fish (steak, too), or use it to make a fragrant vinaigrette.

SWORDFISH
with Fresh Tomato-Herb Salsa

4 servings

4 large fresh plum tomatoes
¼ cup chopped fresh basil
2 Tbsp. chopped fresh marjoram
  or oregano
1 shallot, minced
2 Tbsp. balsamic vinegar
1 Tbsp. extra-virgin olive oil, plus
  more for brushing
  Kosher salt and freshly ground
  black pepper
4 6-oz. swordfish steaks (¾ to
  1 inch thick)
  Freshly cracked black
  peppercorns

The Mediterranean-style salsa that accompanies this swordfish starts with a familiar tomato-basil pairing, then goes deeper with chopped fresh marjoram or oregano—both good matches for tomatoes.

Bring a medium saucepan of water to a boil. Score bottoms of tomatoes with 1-inch X. Add tomatoes to boiling water and blanch for 30 seconds. Drain. Transfer to a medium bowl. Cover with cold water; let cool. Peel tomatoes. Cut in half; squeeze out and discard juices. Chop tomatoes; transfer to a clean bowl. Add herbs, shallot, vinegar, and 1 Tbsp. oil. Season to taste with salt and pepper. **DO AHEAD:** Salsa can be made 1 hour ahead. Let stand at room temperature.

Build a medium-hot fire in a charcoal grill, or heat a gas grill to high. Brush fish and grill grate with oil. Season fish with salt and generous amount of cracked peppercorns. Grill fish, turning once, until just cooked through, about 4 minutes per side. Transfer fish to plates. Spoon tomato salsa over.

SWORDFISH
with North African Spice Rub

4 servings

photo, page 210

YOGURT SAUCE
½ cup plain nonfat yogurt
2 Tbsp. chopped fresh cilantro
1 large garlic clove, minced
  Kosher salt and freshly ground
  black pepper
SPICE RUB AND SWORDFISH
½ cup chopped onion
2 garlic cloves, chopped
2 tsp. caraway seeds
2 tsp. ground coriander
½ tsp. cayenne pepper
4 6-oz. swordfish steaks (¾ to
  1 thick)
  Vegetable oil, for brushing
  Lime wedges, for serving

The key to grilling swordfish steaks is to sear them over a hot fire and cook just until they're opaque and cooked through in the middle. This keeps them juicy, and—as with a steak—the internal temperature will rise a few degrees as the fish rests on the plate. Here a delicious paste-like spice rub envelops the fish, and the simple yogurt sauce is a cool complement.

YOGURT SAUCE
Whisk yogurt, cilantro, and garlic in a small bowl. Season sauce to taste with salt and pepper. **DO AHEAD:** Can be prepared 4 hours ahead. Cover and chill.
SPICE RUB AND SWORDFISH
Pulse onion, garlic, caraway seeds, coriander, and cayenne in a food processor until onion and garlic are very finely chopped and a paste forms. Spread spice rub on each side of swordfish steaks, dividing equally. **DO AHEAD:** Can be prepared 4 hours ahead. Cover and chill.

Build a medium-hot fire in a charcoal grill, or heat a gas grill to high. Brush grate with oil. Grill swordfish steaks until just cooked through, about 4 minutes per side. Transfer fish to plates. Let rest for 2 minutes. Top each with a dollop of yogurt sauce; serve with lime wedges for squeezing over.

Go for the bold with a **classic Tunisian spice blend** of caraway, coriander, and cayenne mixed with onion and garlic.

SWORDFISH WITH
NORTH AFRICAN SPICE RUB
(RECIPE ON PAGE 209)

TUNA STEAKS
with Cantaloupe Salsa

2 servings

¾ cup coarsely chopped cantaloupe
¼ cup chopped onion
2 Tbsp. chopped fresh cilantro
1 Tbsp. fresh lime juice
2 tsp. extra-virgin olive oil, plus more for brushing
1 tsp. minced seeded jalapeño
Kosher salt and freshly ground black pepper
2 5- to 6-oz. tuna steaks, such as yellowfin or bigeye (about ½ inch thick)

A simple swap of cantaloupe for tomatoes turns this salsa, similar to *pico de gallo*, into a refreshing summertime staple. The key here is to sear the tuna steaks quickly on a well-oiled grill grate over a medium-hot fire to give the tuna a crust without overcooking the center. This recipe can easily be doubled.

Build a medium-hot fire in a charcoal grill, or heat a gas grill to high. Mix cantaloupe, onion, cilantro, lime juice, 2 tsp. oil, and jalapeño in a small bowl. Season salsa to taste with salt and pepper. Let stand for 15 minutes.

Meanwhile, brush tuna steaks on both sides with oil and season with salt and pepper. Brush grill grate with oil. Grill tuna to desired doneness, about 3 minutes per side for medium.

Transfer tuna to plates and spoon salsa alongside.

THE STEAKS OF THE SEA: Swordfish and Tuna on the Grill

Swordfish and tuna are both meaty and firm, which makes them ideal for the grill. Here's what you need to know before firing them up:

SWORDFISH

Unlike milder fish, which can be overwhelmed by strong flavors, **swordfish steaks take well to bold marinades**. The optimal thickness for grilling is ½ to 1½ inches—and swordfish is also hefty enough to be cubed and skewered for kebabs. Cook swordfish until the pink or creamy white flesh just turns opaque. If a recipe calls for swordfish but your market doesn't have it, mahi-mahi or tuna will make a good substitute.

TUNA

Tuna has an outstanding texture, a medium flavor, and enough fat to keep it moist. It **tastes best when prepared rare or medium-rare** over a hot fire to develop a savory crust before the center over-cooks. Ask for steaks to be cut at least ½ inch thick, then encrust them with spices such as cracked peppercorns. Avoid endangered bluefin tuna. Troll- or pole-and-line-caught yellowfin, albacore, bigeye, and skipjack tuna are more sustainable alternatives. See page 234 for more information.

FENNEL-CRUSTED TUNA

with Lemon Aioli and Couscous

2 tsp. fennel seeds

1 tsp. coriander seeds

1 tsp. whole black peppercorns, plus freshly ground black pepper

1½ tsp. kosher salt, divided

⅓ cup mayonnaise

3 Tbsp. chopped fresh chives

2 Tbsp. fresh lemon juice

4 garlic cloves, minced, divided

8 Tbsp. extra-virgin olive oil, divided, plus more for brushing

1 carrot, peeled, coarsely chopped

¼ cup chopped red onion

2 tsp. chopped fresh thyme

½ lb. sugar snap peas, stringed

2 cups couscous

2 Tbsp. chopped fresh dill

2½ lb. tuna steaks, such as yellowfin (about 1¼ inches thick)

SPECIAL EQUIPMENT A spice mill

A nutty blend of toasted fennel, coriander seeds, and black peppercorns adds a nice crust to tuna and enhances its flavor. When you do your toasting, always let the spices cool off before grinding—they become more brittle when cool, making them easier to crush. The tart lemon aioli and couscous are ideal counterpoints to the tuna.

Toast fennel seeds, coriander seeds, and peppercorns in a small heavy skillet over medium heat, shaking skillet occasionally, until fragrant, about 3 minutes. Let cool completely. Grind spice mixture in spice mill. Transfer to a small bowl; mix in 1 tsp. salt. **DO AHEAD:** Can be made 2 days ahead. Store spice mixture airtight at room temperature.

Whisk mayonnaise, chives, lemon juice, and half of garlic in a small bowl. **DO AHEAD:** Lemon aioli can be made 2 days ahead. Cover and chill.

Heat 2 Tbsp. oil in a large heavy skillet over medium-high heat. Add carrot and onion and sauté until crisp-tender, about 3 minutes. Add thyme and remaining garlic and sauté for 1 minute. Add remaining ½ tsp. salt and 2¼ cups water; bring to a boil. Add snap peas and cook until crisp-tender, about 1 minute. Using a slotted spoon, transfer peas to a plate. Immediately add couscous to water in skillet and stir to combine. Cover and remove from heat. Let stand for 5 minutes. Fluff couscous with a fork. Transfer to a bowl and let cool completely. Mix in peas and dill. Season to taste with pepper. **DO AHEAD:** Couscous can be made 2 hours ahead. Let stand at room temperature.

Build a medium-hot fire in a charcoal grill, or heat a gas grill to high. Coat tuna with remaining 6 Tbsp. oil. Sprinkle with spice mixture. Brush grill grate with oil. Grill tuna until seared outside and rare in the center, about 4 minutes per side. Chill uncovered for 1 hour; cut into ½-inch-thick slices.

Spoon couscous onto plates. Top with tuna and drizzle with lemon aioli.

SEARED TUNA STEAKS
with Wasabi-Scallion Mayonnaise

4 servings

½ cup mayonnaise
2 Tbsp. minced scallions (white and pale green parts only)
1 tsp. wasabi paste (Japanese horseradish paste), more as needed
2 Tbsp. teriyaki sauce
1 Tbsp. reduced-sodium soy sauce
1 Tbsp. unseasoned rice vinegar
4 8-oz. tuna steaks, such as yellowfin (about 1 inch thick)
Vegetable oil, for brushing

INGREDIENT INFO Wasabi paste is available at Japanese markets and in the Asian foods section of some supermarkets.

Yellowfin tuna, which is also known as ahi, is an excellent base for Asian flavors. In this recipe, tartar sauce gets an Asian spin with scallions in place of sweet pickle, and wasabi instead of hot pepper sauce.

Whisk mayonnaise, scallions, and 1 tsp. wasabi paste in a small bowl, adding more wasabi paste if desired. Cover wasabi-scallion mayonnaise and chill.

Whisk teriyaki sauce, soy sauce, and vinegar in another small bowl. Place tuna steaks in a resealable plastic bag. Add teriyaki mixture; seal bag. Turn bag to coat tuna. Let stand at room temperature, turning bag occasionally, for 30 minutes.

Build a medium-hot fire in a charcoal grill, or heat a gas grill to high. Brush grill grate with oil. Drain tuna steaks. Grill tuna to desired doneness, about 4 minutes per side for medium. Transfer tuna steaks to plates. Top each tuna steak with about 2 Tbsp. wasabi-scallion mayonnaise.

HALIBUT
with Basil-Shallot Butter

6 servings

1½ cups (loosely packed) fresh basil leaves
1 large shallot, coarsely chopped
½ cup (1 stick) unsalted butter, room temperature
1 tsp. grated lemon zest
Kosher salt
Extra-virgin olive oil, for brushing
6 6-oz. halibut fillets

Using compound butters, like this basil-shallot butter, is a simple and decadent way to add flavor and succulence to grilled fish. If you end up with any leftover butter, toss it with pasta, spread it over grilled bread, or melt and drizzle it over grilled vegetables. See page 396 for more flavor combinations.

Finely chop basil and shallot in a mini food processor. Add butter, 2 Tbsp. at a time, and process, stopping occasionally to scrape down sides, until blended. Transfer to a small bowl; stir in lemon zest and season with salt.

Build a medium fire in a charcoal grill, or heat a gas grill to medium-high. Brush grill grate with oil. Brush fish fillets on both sides with oil. Grill until fillets are just opaque in the center, about 4 minutes per side. Transfer fish to plates. Immediately spread some basil-shallot butter over fish. Pass additional basil-shallot butter at the table.

SPICED HALIBUT
with Red Pepper Harissa

1 red jalapeño
1 garlic clove, peeled
4 5- to 6-oz. halibut or mahi-mahi
   fillets
2 large red bell peppers, quartered
   lengthwise, seeded
¼ cup extra-virgin olive oil, plus
   more for brushing
   Kosher salt and freshly ground
   black pepper
2 tsp. ground coriander, divided
2 tsp. ground cumin, divided
1 lemon, halved

SPECIAL EQUIPMENT A thin metal skewer

Harissa **is a complex, piquant North African sauce that's often used in soups and stews, as a flavoring for couscous, as a spread for sandwiches, and as a rub for meat. This versatility makes it one of the rock stars of sauces. And here, we take it one step further—grilling the ingredients to infuse an even smokier flavor.**

Build a medium-hot fire in a charcoal grill, or heat a gas grill to high. Thread jalapeño and garlic clove onto metal skewer. Brush jalapeño, garlic, fish, and bell peppers with oil; season with salt and pepper. Sprinkle fish with ½ tsp. coriander and ½ tsp. cumin. Brush grill grate with oil. Grill fish, bell peppers, jalapeño, and garlic until vegetables are tender and charred and fish is just cooked through, about 4 minutes per side for fish and 8 minutes per side for vegetables. Grill lemon, cut side down, until charred, about 3 minutes. Transfer fish to a platter and tent with foil to keep warm.

Peel charred parts of skin from bell peppers and cut stem from jalapeño; discard skin and stem, and transfer jalapeño and bell peppers to a blender. Add garlic clove and remaining 1½ tsp. coriander, 1½ tsp. cumin, and ¼ cup oil to blender. Process until coarse purée forms. Season sauce generously to taste with salt and pepper.

Place fish fillets on plates. Squeeze grilled lemon over and spoon sauce over fish.

IS It Done Yet?

HALIBUT: DON'T OVERDO IT Halibut is lean, so it can easily overcook. Remove it from the grill when it's just opaque in the center and let the carryover heat finish cooking it to perfection.

HALIBUT
with Zucchini Salsa Verde

10 oz. zucchini (about 2 medium), trimmed, chopped
½ cup chopped fresh cilantro, plus leaves for garnish
⅓ cup chopped white onion
5 Tbsp. fresh lime juice
2½ Tbsp. chopped seeded jalapeño
1¼ tsp. finely grated lime zest
2¼ tsp. kosher salt, divided
1¼ tsp. freshly ground black pepper
1¼ tsp. ground coriander
6 6-oz. skinless halibut fillets (or cod, mahi-mahi, or hake)
Vegetable oil, for brushing

This recipe is a great way to put to use all the zucchini that's available in the middle of summer. Here it makes a fresh stand-in for tomatillos in a Mexican *salsa verde*, resulting in a versatile sauce that's delicious with halibut or any meaty white fish like cod, mahi-mahi, or hake.

Combine zucchini, ½ cup cilantro, and next 4 ingredients in a blender. Add 1¼ tsp. salt. Purée until salsa is smooth. **DO AHEAD:** Can be made 2 hours ahead. Transfer to a small bowl; cover and chill.

Build a medium-hot fire in a charcoal grill, or heat a gas grill to high. Stir remaining 1 tsp. salt, pepper, and coriander in a small bowl. Pat fish dry. Sprinkle fish on all sides with coriander mixture. Brush grill grate with oil. Grill fish until just opaque in the center, 3 to 4 minutes per side, depending on thickness.

Transfer fish to plates. Spoon some salsa over. Garnish with cilantro leaves. Serve with remaining salsa alongside.

TROUT
with Almonds and Lemon Butter

½ cup (1 stick) unsalted butter
¼ cup fresh lemon juice
2 Tbsp. chopped fresh mint
2 tsp. grated lemon zest
1 garlic clove, minced
Vegetable oil, for brushing
4 6-oz. skin-on trout fillets
Kosher salt and freshly ground black pepper
⅔ cup sliced almonds, toasted

Look for thick, moist trout fillets with the skin on, and be sure the scales have been removed. Also, ask the fishmonger to remove the pin bones that run in a line down the center of each fillet. Trout is delicate, so if you're tentative about turning it over on the grill, use a fish grill basket.

Whisk butter, lemon juice, mint, lemon zest, and garlic in a small saucepan over medium-low heat until butter melts and mixture is blended.

Build a medium fire in a charcoal grill, or heat a gas grill to medium-high. Brush grill grate with oil. Brush flesh side of trout with some of lemon butter. Season with salt and pepper. Grill trout, flesh side down, until beginning to brown, about 1½ minutes. Using a large metal spatula, turn trout over and grill, brushing with more lemon butter, until cooked through, about 2 minutes longer. Transfer trout to plates, placing skin side down. Bring remaining lemon butter to a boil and drizzle over trout. Sprinkle trout with almonds.

MAHI-MAHI
with Thai Coconut Sauce

4 servings

1 cup canned unsweetened coconut milk
1 8-oz. bottle clam juice
2 Tbsp. fresh lime juice
4 tsp. minced peeled ginger
2 garlic cloves, minced
1 tsp. fish sauce (such as nam pla or nuoc nam)
1 to 2 tsp. minced seeded serrano chile
4 Tbsp. chopped fresh cilantro, divided
4 Tbsp. minced scallions, divided
  Kosher salt and freshly ground black pepper
4 6-oz. mahi-mahi fillets
  Vegetable oil, for brushing

The rich, aromatic flavors of classic Thai coconut soup (tom kha gai)—lime, ginger, chile, cilantro, and fish sauce—enliven this sauce. You won't need an entire can of coconut milk to make this sauce, so we recommend using the extra milk to make rice for serving alongside this dish.

Build a medium-hot fire in a charcoal grill, or heat a gas grill to high. Combine first 6 ingredients in a medium skillet. Add 1 to 2 tsp. minced chile, depending on level of heat desired; boil until sauce thickens slightly and is reduced to generous ¾ cup, 8 to 9 minutes. Remove from heat; stir in 2 Tbsp. cilantro and 2 Tbsp. scallions. Season coconut sauce to taste with salt and pepper.

Brush fish all over with ¼ cup coconut sauce; season with salt and pepper. Brush grill grate with oil. Grill fish until opaque in the center and grill marks appear, 5 to 7 minutes per side, depending on thickness. Divide remaining coconut sauce among plates; top with fish. Sprinkle with remaining cilantro and scallions.

BLACK COD
with Fried Garlic and Chiles

6 servings

6 Tbsp. extra-virgin olive oil, preferably Spanish, plus more for brushing
6 7- to 8-oz. black cod fillets (about 1 inch thick)
  Kosher salt and freshly ground black pepper
4 garlic cloves, thinly sliced
1 dried guindilla chile, crumbled, or ½ tsp. crushed red pepper flakes
3 Tbsp. chopped flat-leaf parsley

This Basque-style dish calls for seasonings as simple as a sprinkle of sea salt, a splash of olive oil, and a generous dose of garlic and chile. We recommend using Alaskan black cod (which is also called sablefish), not only because it's the most sustainable option, but also because its moist, white flesh has a velvety, rich flavor and firm, flaky texture.

Build a medium-hot fire in a charcoal grill, or heat a gas grill to high. Brush grill grate with oil. Season fish on both sides with salt and pepper. Place fish in grill basket or directly on grill grate, skin side down. Grill fish until opaque in the center, 4 to 5 minutes per side. Transfer to a platter; cover to keep warm.

Heat 6 Tbsp. oil in a small skillet over high heat. Add garlic and sauté until fragrant and light golden, about 1 minute. Add crumbled chile; stir for 15 seconds. Immediately pour garlic-chile oil over fish. Sprinkle with parsley.

SEA BASS
with Miso-Mustard Sauce

4 servings

1 tsp. prepared Chinese-style hot mustard or Dijon mustard

⅓ cup white miso (fermented soybean paste)

3 Tbsp. rice vinegar

2 Tbsp. mirin

4 tsp. sugar

1 tsp. reduced-sodium soy sauce
   Extra-virgin olive oil, for brushing

4 5- to 6-oz. sea bass fillets

8 scallions, trimmed
   Kosher salt and freshly ground
   black pepper
   Toasted sesame seeds, for garnish

INGREDIENT INFO Miso comes in various shades, ranging from white to brown. The lighter varieties are less salty and mellower in flavor than the darker ones. The white miso called for here is aged for just a few months. White miso, also known as *shiro miso*, and mirin are available at Japanese markets and natural foods stores and in the Asian foods section of some supermarkets.

This Japanese preparation lends sea bass a savory-sweet flavor, thanks to mustard, mirin, and miso (a fermented soybean paste with a bold and salty flavor). Miso is important here for two reasons: The pungent paste imparts a unique savoriness to meaty sea bass and also encourages browning on the grill, thanks to its natural sugar content.

Whisk mustard and 2 tsp. water in a small bowl until smooth. Combine miso, vinegar, mirin, sugar, and soy sauce in a small saucepan over medium heat. Stir until smooth, about 3 minutes. Whisk in mustard mixture. **DO AHEAD:** Miso-mustard sauce can be made 1 day ahead. Rewarm over low heat before using.

Build a medium-hot fire in a charcoal grill, or heat a gas grill to high. Brush grill grate with oil. Brush fish and scallions with oil. Season both with salt and pepper. Grill fish until opaque in the center, about 4 minutes per side. Grill scallions until beginning to brown, about 3 minutes per side. Divide fish and scallions among plates. Spread sauce atop fish. Sprinkle sesame seeds over sauce.

Steps to Grilling WHOLE FISH

Grilling a whole small fish—like branzino, rainbow trout, or black bass—is one of the great treats of the grill. The skin protects the flesh, the bones keep the meat moist, and you can stuff the cavity with citrus, herbs, and spices. The following method works best for a fish in the 1- to 3-lb. range.

❶ PREP AND SCORE

Ask your fishmonger to gut and scale the fish for you. As for the head, we leave it on because there's extra meat in those fish cheeks, but you can have it removed, if you prefer.

When you're ready to grill, **score the fish** by slicing into the flesh at an angle down to the bone, making parallel slashes every 1 inch down the side of the fish. Repeat on the other side.

❷ ADD SEASONING

Sprinkle the flesh, inside the slashes, and the cavity of fish with kosher salt and freshly ground black pepper.

To add more layers of flavor, stuff the cavity with **whole sprigs of fresh herbs** like thyme, marjoram, or parsley and thinly sliced half-moons of **lemon, lime, or tangerines**.

❸ OIL THE FISH AND THE GRILL

Coat the fish with about **1 Tbsp. extra-virgin olive oil**. Just as important, clean the grill well and brush it with oil just before cooking (after you've built the fire or heated the gas grill).

Fish has a tendency to stick to the grill, so doubling up on the oil gives you a better shot at removing the grilled fish from the grate in one piece.

❹ LAY IT ON AN ANGLE

Place fish **diagonally on the grate**. With more surface area over the hot grate, the skin takes a better sear.

Now: Don't touch it! If you prod the fish too soon, you'll tear the skin. Let it cook for about 4 minutes; this allows the skin to crisp and stop sticking to the grill. Then slide a lightly oiled fish spatula underneath and gently turn it. Grill the fish for about 4 minutes more.

Once you lay a whole fish down on the grate, **don't touch it!** Let it sit for a few minutes and *then* turn it over.

A scored and seasoned whole fish comes off the grill with **crispy, crunchy skin** and moist, tender flesh.

WHOLE FISH WITH
TANGERINE AND MARJORAM

WHOLE FISH
with Tangerine and Marjoram

photo, left

Vegetable oil, for brushing
2 1- to 1¼-lb. whole bone-in porgy,
   gray snapper, or branzino,
   cleaned
   Kosher salt and freshly ground
   black pepper
8 sprigs marjoram, plus 1 Tbsp.
   fresh marjoram leaves
2 tangerines or small oranges,
   peeled, separated into
   segments, seeded, divided
2 Tbsp. extra-virgin olive oil

Here's a testament to the simple deliciousness of a grilled whole fish stuffed with citrus and herbs. The grilling should be simple, too: Place the fish on the hot grill and leave it alone for about 4 minutes. Once it gets a good sear, it will lift easily from the grill so you can turn it over. See "4 Steps to Grilling Whole Fish" on page 218 for more.

Prepare a medium-hot fire in a charcoal grill, or heat a gas grill to high. Brush grill grate with vegetable oil. Make 3 deep diagonal slices spaced about 1½ inches apart on each side of fish. Season skin and cavity with salt and pepper. Stuff each fish with 4 marjoram sprigs and segments from ½ tangerine. Rub each fish with 1 Tbsp. oil. Grill fish until skin no longer sticks, 3 to 4 minutes. Using a metal spatula, carefully turn fish and grill until cooked through, 3 to 4 more minutes.

   Transfer to platters and garnish with remaining tangerine segments and marjoram leaves.

SARDINES
with Lemon and Herbs

18 whole fresh sardines or large
    anchovies, gutted, cleaned,
    scaled, patted dry
 1 tsp. kosher salt
 3 Tbsp. coarsely chopped
    flat-leaf parsley
 3 Tbsp. coarsely chopped fresh
    cilantro
 2 tsp. finely grated lemon zest
 ⅓ cup coarsely chopped pitted
    brine-cured green olives
 3 Tbsp. finely chopped red onion
    Extra-virgin olive oil, for brushing
    Freshly ground black pepper
    Lemon wedges

Fresh sardines—which bear no resemblance to the canned variety—taste fantastic when grilled. When buying the sardines, ask your fishmonger to gut, clean, and scale them for you.

Place sardines in an 11x7x2-inch glass baking dish. Season fish with salt. Cover and chill for 30 minutes.

   Meanwhile, build a medium-hot fire in a charcoal grill, or heat a gas grill to high. Combine parsley, cilantro, and lemon zest in a small bowl. Mix olives and onion in another small bowl. Brush sardines lightly with oil. Sprinkle half of herb mixture over sardines; turn to coat. Brush grill grate with oil. Grill sardines until just opaque in the center, 1 to 2 minutes per side, depending on size.

   Arrange sardines on a platter. Sprinkle with olive mixture, then remaining herb mixture. Season with pepper. Serve with lemon wedges for squeezing over.

BUTTERFLIED TROUT
with White Beans and Caper Vinaigrette

2 servings

photo, right

¼ cup (½ stick) unsalted butter
1 Tbsp. extra-virgin olive oil, plus more for brushing
¼ cup minced shallots
2 Tbsp. white balsamic vinegar or white wine vinegar
1 Tbsp. drained capers
1 tsp. chopped fresh rosemary
Kosher salt and freshly ground black pepper
1 15-oz. can white beans, rinsed, drained
1 tsp. finely grated lemon zest
2 whole trout, cleaned, boned, butterflied (about 10 oz. each)
1 cup coarsely sliced arugula

A warm, buttery vinaigrette—made with white balsamic vinegar, shallots, capers, and rosemary—brings together crisp grilled trout with a quick salad of warm beans and arugula. Ask your fishmonger to remove the backbone from the fish so that you can butterfly it for cooking on the grill.

Build a medium-hot fire in a charcoal grill, or heat a gas grill to high. Cook butter in a small skillet over medium heat, stirring often, until brown, about 4 minutes. Remove from heat. Whisk in 1 Tbsp. oil, then shallots, vinegar, capers, and rosemary. Season vinaigrette to taste with salt and pepper.

Mix beans, lemon zest, and 2 Tbsp. vinaigrette in a medium heavy skillet. Season to taste with salt and pepper.

Brush a little vinaigrette over flesh side of trout; season with salt and pepper. Place skillet with beans on edge of grill to let warm through. Brush grill grate with oil. Grill trout, flesh side down, until brown, about 2 minutes. Turn trout over; grill until cooked through, about 2 minutes longer. Transfer trout to plates. Mix arugula into warm beans; spoon over trout. Rewarm remaining vinaigrette; spoon over trout and beans.

WHOLE BRANZINO
with Ladolemono

2 to 4 servings

2 whole bone-in branzino or black sea bass (about 1½ lb. each), cleaned
Extra-virgin olive oil, for brushing
Kosher salt and freshly ground black pepper
½ cup Ladolemono (page 390)
1 Tbsp. dried oregano, preferably Greek

Ladolemono, with its one-to-one acid-to-oil ratio (in contrast to the usual one-to-three), is a classic Greek vinaigrette, and it gives bright flavor to grilled octopus, shrimp, squid, or the smoky, crispy skin of a whole branzino.

Build a medium-hot fire in a charcoal grill, or heat a gas grill to high. Brush grill grate with oil. Brush fish with oil and season skin and cavity with salt and pepper. Grill fish, turning once, until cooked through, about 10 minutes.

Transfer to a platter. Drizzle with Ladolemono and crumble oregano over.

A butterflied whole trout **cooks quickly on the grill**—and creates a tasty foundation for the warm salad and vinaigrette.

BUTTERFLIED TROUT WITH
WHITE BEANS AND CAPER VINAIGRETTE

WHOLE BASS
with Lemon and Fennel

4 servings

¼ cup extra-virgin olive oil
2 Tbsp. fresh lemon juice
2 garlic cloves, crushed
   Kosher salt and freshly ground
   black pepper
2 1½-lb. whole striped or black bass
   or branzino, cleaned
½ cup (packed) coarsely chopped
   fresh fennel fronds, divided
5 ⅛-inch-thick lemon slices

SPECIAL EQUIPMENT A fish grill basket

The flavors of fennel fronds and lemon slices infuse the fish while it cooks. This recipe uses only the fronds, but you can also cut the bulb into wedges, toss them with salt, pepper, and olive oil, and grill them alongside the fish. For best results, use a fish grill basket for this recipe. It should be large enough to hold a whole fish yet snug enough to keep it and the lemon slices from moving around.

Build a medium-hot fire in a charcoal grill, or heat a gas grill to high. Whisk first 3 ingredients in a medium bowl. Season garlic oil with salt and pepper.

Make three ½-inch-deep diagonal slits in skin on sides of fish. Brush fish generously inside and out with garlic oil. Season fish inside and out with salt. Stuff slits with ¼ cup fennel fronds. Place remaining ¼ cup fennel fronds inside fish, dividing equally. Place fish in grilling basket and top fish with lemon slices, overlapping slightly. Close grilling basket (fish and lemon slices should be secured by basket). Grill fish until cooked through, about 10 minutes per side.

Remove fish with lemon slices from basket and carefully transfer to a platter.

WHOLE BASS
with Orange-Saffron Butter

6 servings

½ cup (1 stick) unsalted butter,
   room temperature
3 Tbsp. frozen orange juice
   concentrate, thawed
½ tsp. Champagne vinegar or white
   wine vinegar
   Large pinch of saffron threads
6 whole striped bass, branzino, or
   trout (about 1 lb. each), cleaned
2 large oranges (1 juiced; 1 halved
   lengthwise, then thinly sliced)
   Kosher salt or coarse sea salt and
   freshly ground pepper
   Vegetable oil, for brushing

Whole grilled fish gets a citrusy kick from fresh orange juice, orange slices, and a saffron-seasoned butter with orange juice concentrate; the warmth of the melted butter brings out the flavor of the saffron threads. The slits along the sides of the fish not only provide the perfect opening to check doneness, but also allow the seasonings to penetrate the fish for more flavor.

Combine butter, orange juice concentrate, vinegar, and saffron in a small saucepan. Set aside.

Using a small sharp knife, cut diagonal slits on both sides of fish at 1-inch intervals. Arrange fish on a rimmed baking sheet. Drizzle fresh orange juice into slits and cavities of fish and season with salt and pepper. Fill cavities with orange slices (about 3 per fish). Cover loosely and let stand at room temperature for at least 30 minutes and up to 1 hour.

Build a medium-hot fire in a charcoal grill, or heat a gas grill to high. Brush grill grate and fish with oil. Place saucepan with orange-saffron butter at edge of grill to let warm through, stirring occasionally. Season orange-saffron butter to taste with salt and pepper. Grill fish until just opaque in the center, about 5 minutes per side. Transfer to plates. Serve with warm orange-saffron butter alongside.

FLOUNDER IN PACKETS
with Corn and Tasso Maque Choux

4 ¼-inch-thick shallot slices, divided
4 Tbsp. (½ stick) unsalted butter, divided
4 small garlic cloves, sliced, divided
8 thin lime slices, divided
4 thin orange slices, divided
4 6-oz. flounder or John Dory fillets, preferably skin-on
   Kosher salt
   Cayenne pepper
8 sprigs thyme, divided
8 Tbsp. dark beer, divided
4 Tbsp. dry white wine, divided
   Corn and Tasso Maque Choux (recipe follows)

We love cooking fish alongside flavorful aromatics in foil packages (which is referred to as _en papillote_ when parchment packets are used in place of foil), because it's an eye-catching, no-frills way to lock in juices and steam the fish. See page 226 for tips on preparing the packets.

Fold a 24x12-inch piece of heavy-duty foil in half crosswise; open foil and place on a work surface. Separate rings of 1 shallot slice; scatter over one side of foil. Top with 1 Tbsp. butter, a sliced garlic clove, 2 lime slices, and 1 orange slice. Season 1 fillet on both sides with salt and cayenne. Arrange fillet, skin side down, atop seasonings on foil. Top fillet with 2 thyme sprigs. Spoon 2 Tbsp. beer and 1 Tbsp. wine around fillet. Fold foil over fish, pressing onto fillet, and crimp edges to form tight seal (see page 226). Repeat with remaining foil, seasonings, and fillets.

Build a medium-hot fire in a charcoal grill, or heat a gas grill to high. Arrange packets on grill grate. Grill fish until just cooked through (a toothpick poked through the foil will slide through fish easily), about 10 minutes. Carefully open packets (steam will escape); transfer to plates. Serve with Corn and Tasso Maque Choux alongside.

Corn and Tasso Maque Choux

use with flounder

   Extra-virgin olive oil, for brushing
4 ears of corn, preferably bicolored, shucked, divided
   Kosher salt and freshly ground black pepper
   Cayenne pepper
3 Tbsp. unsalted butter, divided
¼ cup (1 oz.) matchstick-size strips tasso or Black Forest ham
½ cup sliced shallot
¼ cup chopped celery
¼ cup diced seeded poblano chile
1 Tbsp. chopped fresh thyme
1 large garlic clove, thinly sliced
3 cups diced seeded red tomatoes
3 scallions, thinly sliced

Maque choux is a traditional Louisiana corn-based side dish that tastes like jazzed-up succotash; here it is prepared with Cajun _tasso_ ham. Grate the corncobs to extract milky juices and impart extra corn flavor to the dish.

Build a medium-hot fire in a charcoal grill, or heat a gas grill to high. Brush grill grate with oil. Brush 1 ear of corn with oil, then season with salt, black pepper, and cayenne. Grill corn, turning occasionally, until cooked through and slightly charred, about 14 minutes. Set grilled corn aside.

Cut kernels off remaining 3 ears of corn. Place kernels in a large bowl.

Using the coarse side of a box grater, grate any milky juices from cobs into a medium bowl. Coarsely grate ear of grilled corn, then any milky juices from cob, into same bowl.

Melt 1 Tbsp. butter in a large heavy saucepan over medium heat. Add tasso and sauté until almost crisp, 4 to 5 minutes. Add shallots, celery, chile, thyme, and garlic. Sauté until celery is translucent, about 4 minutes. Add corn kernels; sauté for 3 minutes. Add tomatoes with juices and grilled corn with juices. Cover, reduce heat to low, and simmer for 8 minutes. Mix in remaining 2 Tbsp. butter. Season with salt and pepper. Sprinkle with scallions.

FISH FILLET PACKETS
with Cherry Tomatoes, Squash, and Basil

photo, right

2 cups very thinly sliced assorted summer squash (such as zucchini, yellow crookneck, and pattypan)

¼ cup thinly sliced shallot

¼ cup thinly sliced fresh basil, plus ¼ cup basil leaves

20 cherry tomatoes, halved

4 Tbsp. dry white wine

4 Tbsp. extra-virgin olive oil, divided

Kosher salt and freshly ground black pepper

4 6-oz. skinless white flaky fish fillets (such as Atlantic cod or halibut)

Three superstars of summer—summer squash, basil, and ripe tomatoes—shine in this simple, fresh recipe. As for the fish, go with whatever flaky white fish looks freshest, such as cod or halibut.

Fold four 24x12-inch pieces of heavy-duty foil in half crosswise; open foil and place on a work surface. Divide squash among pieces of foil, arranging in layers on one half of each piece of foil. Sprinkle shallots and sliced basil over, dividing equally. Scatter tomato halves around squash. Drizzle each with 1 Tbsp. wine and ½ Tbsp. oil; add ½ Tbsp. water to each packet. Season with salt and pepper. Place a fish fillet atop each portion of vegetables. Season with salt and pepper and drizzle ½ Tbsp. oil over each fillet.

Fold and crimp edges of foil to seal packages. **DO AHEAD:** Can be made 4 hours ahead. Chill. Let stand at room temperature for 15 minutes before continuing.

Build a medium fire in a charcoal grill, or heat a gas grill to medium-high. Place packets on grill grate. Grill until fish is just cooked through (a toothpick poked through the foil will slide through fish easily), about 10 minutes. Carefully cut open packets (steam will escape). Garnish with basil leaves.

GETTING IT RIGHT: How to Grill Fish in Packets

Gently braising and steaming fish with aromatics and vegetables in sealed packets is, hands down, one of the most impressive and crowd-pleasing ways to serve delightfully moist, flavorful fish. (Bonus: There's zero cleanup involved.) Use heavy-duty aluminum foil that won't burn on the grill.

① **Arrange fish, herbs, and vegetables** on one half of a 24x12-inch piece of heavy-duty foil. Drizzle with wine or broth and olive oil.

② Season fish and vegetables with salt and pepper. **Fold foil over** to enclose ingredients.

③ Starting along one short side, **tightly crimp the edges** of the foil. Continue crimping to form a tight seal. Put packets on the grill.

④ Cook until **fish is cooked through** (a toothpick poked through the foil will slide easily through the flesh).

Grilling fish with vegetables in foil packets keeps the fish moist and **creates a delectable sauce.**

FISH FILLET PACKETS WITH
CHERRY TOMATOES, SQUASH, AND BASIL

HALIBUT PACKETS
with Tomato and Fennel

6 ¾-inch-thick halibut fillets
12 tsp. extra-virgin olive oil
Kosher salt and freshly ground
black pepper
12 tsp. purchased olive tapenade
3 medium heirloom tomatoes, each
cut into 8 wedges
1 medium fennel bulb, halved, cored,
thinly sliced (about 2 cups)
6 tsp. chopped fresh tarragon
6 tsp. grated lemon zest
12 tsp. dry vermouth

These simple and delicious packets are ideal for entertaining: You can prepare them ahead of time, then just throw them on the grill when you're ready to eat. And guests will love opening the packets and getting a whiff of the tarragon and lemon.

Cut six 24x12-inch pieces of foil and place on a work surface; fold each piece in half crosswise. Open foil and place a fish fillet on one side of each piece of foil. Drizzle each fillet with 2 tsp. oil; turn fish to coat. Season with salt and pepper. Spread each with 2 tsp. tapenade and top with 4 tomato wedges, ⅓ cup fennel, 1 tsp. tarragon, 1 tsp. lemon zest, and 2 tsp. vermouth. Season with salt and pepper. Fold and crimp edges of foil to seal packages. Transfer packets to a baking sheet.

Build a medium-hot fire in a charcoal grill, or heat a gas grill to high. Place packets on grill grate; cover grill with lid. Cook until fish is just cooked through (a toothpick poked through the foil will slide through fish easily), about 8 minutes. Carefully open packets (steam will escape), place contents on plates, and serve.

MAHI-MAHI PACKETS
with Pickled Onions and Habanero-Tomato Salsa

4 6- to 8-oz. mahi-mahi fillets
¼ cup achiote paste
2 Tbsp. distilled white vinegar
2 Tbsp. fresh lime juice
2 Tbsp. fresh orange juice
2 garlic cloves, minced
1 tsp. dried oregano
½ tsp. kosher salt or sea salt
½ tsp. freshly ground black pepper
¼ cup dry white wine
4 bay leaves
4 sprigs epazote or flat-leaf parsley
2 plum tomatoes, thinly sliced
2 limes, thinly sliced
Yucatecán Pickled Onions
(optional; recipe follows)
Habanero-Tomato Salsa (optional;
recipe follows)

INGREDIENT INFO Achiote paste, made from achiote seeds, and epazote are available at Latin markets.

Grilled fish dishes, like this mahi-mahi preparation, are ubiquitous throughout Mexico's Yucatán Peninsula. The fish is infused with the earthy, exotic flavors of a vibrant red *recado rojo* marinade. To cook it, wrap the fillets up in foil (which is a more accessible option than the traditional Yucatecán banana leaves); see our step-by-step guide to folding foil packets on page 226.

Place fish in a 13x9x2-inch glass baking dish. Whisk achiote paste and next 7 ingredients in a medium bowl. Pour achiote mixture over fish; turn fish to coat. Cover and chill for 1 hour.

Fold two 36x12-inch pieces of heavy-duty foil in half; open foil and place on a work surface. Remove 2 fillets from marinade, with some marinade still clinging, and place crosswise on one side of one piece of foil, spacing 2 inches apart. Repeat with remaining 2 fillets on second sheet of foil. Drizzle wine around fish. Top each fillet with 1 bay leaf and 1 epazote sprig. Fold foil over fish and crimp edges to form a tight seal.

Build a medium-hot fire in a charcoal grill, or heat a gas grill to high. Arrange packets on grill grate. Cover and grill until fish is just cooked through (a toothpick poked through the foil will slide through fish easily), about 10 minutes.

Carefully open packets (steam will escape). Transfer fish to plates. Garnish with tomato and lime slices. Serve with Yucatecán Pickled Onions and Habanero-Tomato Salsa, if desired.

Yucatecán Pickled Onions

use with mahi-mahi

makes about 1½ cups

1 large red onion, cut crosswise into ⅛-inch-thick slices, rings separated
2 garlic cloves, quartered
1 Tbsp. kosher salt
½ cup distilled white vinegar
3 whole allspice
1 bay leaf
½ tsp. dried oregano, preferably Mexican
½ tsp. freshly ground black pepper
¼ tsp. ground cumin

These pickled onions deliver a tart, cool counterpoint to the smoky char of a variety of grilled foods. They're an outstanding accompaniment to the mahi-mahi and other grilled fish, but we also encourage you to try them with grilled chicken, pork, and beef, in other Latin bites such as tacos and *tortas*, and on your favorite burger.

Bring onion, garlic, salt, and 6 cups water to a boil in a medium heavy saucepan. Boil for 1 minute. Drain. Return onion and garlic to same saucepan. Add vinegar and all remaining ingredients. Add water to just cover onion. Bring to a boil over medium heat. Remove from heat; cover and let cool. Transfer onion mixture to a bowl, cover, and chill overnight. **DO AHEAD:** Can be made 1 week ahead. Keep chilled. Drain onion rings and serve.

Habanero-Tomato Salsa

use with mahi-mahi

makes about 3 cups

3 large tomatoes, cut into ¼-inch cubes
2 cups finely chopped white onion
½ cup finely chopped fresh cilantro
6 Tbsp. fresh lime juice
6 habanero chiles or 8 serrano chiles, seeded, finely chopped
3 Tbsp. fresh orange juice
Kosher salt

INGREDIENT INFO Habanero chiles are available at some supermarkets and at Latin markets.

This is a basic *salsa fresca*, but with a spicier, more citrus-driven flavor. Even when seeded, habaneros provide a scorching heat to this salsa. If you want a milder version, try Fresno chiles or jalapeños. Always wear gloves when working with hot chiles.

Mix first 6 ingredients in a large bowl. Season to taste with salt. **DO AHEAD:** Can be made 2 hours ahead. Cover and let stand at room temperature.

FISH BROCHETTES PROVENÇALE

1½ Tbsp. minced fresh basil
2 tsp. minced fresh marjoram
2 tsp. minced fresh thyme
1 tsp. minced fresh rosemary
1 tsp. minced fresh sage
½ tsp. chopped fennel seeds
¼ tsp. finely chopped dried lavender blossoms
1 1½-inch-diameter zucchini, cut into eight ½-inch-thick rounds
1 slender eggplant, unpeeled, trimmed, halved lengthwise, cut into eight 1- to 1¼-inch pieces
8 mini plum tomatoes or large cherry tomatoes
16 mini bell peppers in assorted colors (from one 5-oz. package), or 1 bell pepper cut into 1-inch squares
1 small red onion, cut into 4 wedges, each wedge halved crosswise, layers kept intact
5 Tbsp. extra-virgin olive oil, divided, plus more for brushing
   Kosher salt and freshly ground black pepper
1½ lb. halibut, cut into 1½-inch cubes
5 Tbsp. fresh lemon juice, divided
2 garlic cloves, minced
⅓ cup dry white wine

SPECIAL EQUIPMENT 12 metal skewers

INGREDIENT INFO Dried lavender blossoms, also called culinary lavender buds, are available at some supermarkets and farmers' markets, at many natural foods stores, and from deandeluca.com.

The array of herbs that make up the classic *herbes de Provence* mixture is used here in fresh form. The pairing with halibut is ideal, but the marinade could also be used as a seasoning for grilled chicken. Vegetables should go on a different skewer because they'll take longer to cook than the halibut.

Mix first 7 ingredients in a small bowl. Place zucchini, eggplant, tomatoes, bell peppers, and onion in a large bowl. Add 1 Tbsp. herb mixture and 1 Tbsp. oil to vegetables. Season to taste with salt and pepper; toss to coat. Thread 1 mini pepper, 1 zucchini round, 1 eggplant piece, 1 tomato, 1 onion piece, and 1 more mini pepper onto each of 8 skewers. **DO AHEAD:** Herb mixture and vegetables can be made 4 hours ahead. Cover separately and chill.

Place fish in a medium bowl; sprinkle 2 Tbsp. herb mixture over. Add 3 Tbsp. oil, 3 Tbsp. lemon juice, and garlic; season with salt and pepper and toss to coat. Cover and chill, tossing occasionally, for at least 1 hour and up to 2 hours.

Simmer wine, remaining 2 Tbsp. lemon juice, and remaining 1 Tbsp. oil in a small saucepan until reduced to ⅓ cup, about 3 minutes. Stir in remaining herb mixture. Season sauce to taste with salt and pepper. Set aside.

Build a medium-hot fire in a charcoal grill, or heat a gas grill to high. Brush grill grate with oil. Divide fish cubes among remaining 4 skewers. Grill vegetable skewers, turning occasionally, until vegetables are slightly charred and tender, 10 to 12 minutes. Grill fish skewers, turning occasionally, until fish is cooked through, 8 to 10 minutes.

Place 1 fish skewer and 2 vegetable skewers on each plate. Drizzle sauce over.

TUNA AND
RED ONION SPIEDINI

6 Tbsp. garlic-flavored olive oil
2 Tbsp. fresh lemon juice
4 tsp. chopped fresh rosemary
   Kosher salt and freshly ground
   black pepper
1 11- to 12-oz. tuna steak, cut into
   1-inch pieces
12 1x1x¼-inch red onion pieces
8 lemon slices, halved
   Vegetable oil, for brushing
4 cups mixed baby greens
   (about 2 oz.)

SPECIAL EQUIPMENT 4 metal skewers

These tuna brochettes are flavored with simple ingredients characteristic of Italian grilling—garlic, lemon, rosemary—and served over baby greens tossed with the same dressing that goes on the fish.

Build a medium-hot fire in a charcoal grill, or heat a gas grill to high. Whisk oil, lemon juice, and rosemary in a small bowl. Season dressing with salt and pepper. Pour half of dressing into a medium bowl for salad.

   Thread tuna, onion, and lemon slices alternately onto skewers. Brush with dressing from small bowl; season with salt and pepper. Brush grill grate with vegetable oil. Grill, turning and brushing often with dressing, until tuna is just opaque in the center and onion is slightly charred and tender, about 8 minutes.

   Toss greens with reserved dressing in medium bowl. Mound salad on plates; top with skewers.

GETTING IT RIGHT: How to Grill Fish on Skewers

Brochettes, kebabs, *spiedini*, *kushiyaki*: Whatever you call it, food cooked on skewers is delicious and great for entertaining. Cooking fish on skewers is simple—just keep a few things in mind.

THINK BIG

Use meaty, steak-like fish such as tuna, swordfish, or halibut. You want fish with some heft that can be cut easily into cubes and that won't fall apart on the skewer.

KEEP IT UNIFORM

Cut fish into **uniform cubes, between 1 and 1½ inches**, to ensure even cooking. If you're grilling vegetable pieces alongside, make them the same size as the fish.

PACK 'EM RIGHT

Arrange pieces loosely on the skewers so they don't touch. **(If too close, they'll take too long to cook.)** And always leave 1 inch clear at either end of skewers for easy handling.

MAKE IT HOT

Working over a medium-hot fire in a charcoal grill or high heat on a gas grill, **give the fish a good sear** and cook it quickly. If the heat's too low, the fish will dry out before it finishes cooking.

GINGER-WASABI HALIBUT BROCHETTES

2 servings

1½ Tbsp. Dijon mustard
¾ tsp. wasabi powder, or
   1½ Tbsp. prepared white
   horseradish
3 Tbsp. chopped fresh chives
1½ Tbsp. dry Sherry
1 Tbsp. minced peeled ginger
12 oz. halibut steak, cut into
   1-inch pieces
   Vegetable oil, for brushing
1 red bell pepper, cut into
   1-inch squares
   Kosher salt and freshly ground
   black pepper

SPECIAL EQUIPMENT 4 metal skewers

INGREDIENT INFO Wasabi powder is available at Japanese markets and some supermarkets.

Try these brochettes on a weeknight when you're looking for deep flavors with minimal effort. The marinade's combination of fragrant ginger and fiery wasabi (Japanese horseradish powder) provides a spicy, sweet kick. Make sure the halibut fillets are at least 1 inch thick so that it's easy to create large pieces for skewering.

Build a medium-hot fire in a charcoal grill, or heat a gas grill to high. Stir Dijon mustard and wasabi in a medium bowl to blend. Mix in chives, Sherry, and ginger. Add fish; stir gently to coat. Let stand at room temperature for 15 minutes.

Brush grill grate with oil. Thread fish on skewers alternately with bell pepper squares. Season with salt and pepper. Grill, turning occasionally, until fish is just opaque in the center and bell peppers are slightly charred, turning occasionally, about 8 minutes.

TUNA KEBABS
with Ginger-Chile Marinade

4 servings

3 Tbsp. unseasoned rice vinegar
2 Tbsp. finely grated peeled ginger
2 Tbsp. peanut oil
2 Tbsp. honey
2 Tbsp. reduced-sodium soy sauce
2 Tbsp. toasted sesame oil
1 serrano chile, seeded, minced
1 Tbsp. chopped fresh cilantro, plus
   more for garnish
   Freshly ground white pepper
1½ lb. 1¼-inch-thick ahi tuna, cut into
   1¼-inch cubes
   Vegetable oil, for brushing
1 large red bell pepper, cut into
   1-inch squares
1 large sweet onion (such as Maui or
   Vidalia), cut into 1-inch squares

SPECIAL EQUIPMENT 6 metal skewers

Large pieces of ahi—or yellowfin—tuna stand up heartily to the strong Asian flavors in this marinade. Cut tuna into cubes before marinating so seasonings can fully penetrate. You can also use the marinade when serving whole seared tuna fillets. See page 231 for more information on skewering fish.

Whisk first 7 ingredients and 1 Tbsp. cilantro in a medium bowl to blend; season to taste with white pepper. Transfer 3 Tbsp. marinade to a small bowl and set aside. Add tuna to remaining marinade in medium bowl and toss to coat. Chill for at least 30 minutes and up to 45 minutes.

Build a medium-hot fire in a charcoal grill, or heat a gas grill to high. Brush grill grate with oil. Alternate tuna cubes, bell pepper squares, and onion squares on each of 6 metal skewers. Grill, turning frequently, to desired doneness, about 4 minutes total for medium-rare. Transfer to a platter. Drizzle reserved marinade over; sprinkle with cilantro.

SARDINE TARTINES
with Onion and Arugula

12 whole sardines, butterflied, or six
   6-inch-long skin-on trout or
   mackerel fillets
2 Tbsp. extra-virgin olive oil, plus
   more for brushing
1 Tbsp. chopped flat-leaf parsley
1 Tbsp. chopped fresh thyme
2 tsp. finely grated lemon zest
1 tsp. piment d'Espelette, or ½ tsp.
   crushed red pepper flakes
6 ⅓-inch-thick slices sweet onion
   (such as Maui or Vidalia)
   Kosher salt and freshly ground
   black pepper
6 6-inch-long baguette slices, cut
   ½ inch thick on a sharp diagonal
3 Tbsp. unsalted butter, room
   temperature
   Fleur de sel
   Arugula leaves
1 Tbsp. extra-virgin olive oil
½ tsp. fresh lemon juice
6 lemon wedges

INGREDIENT INFO Fleur de sel is available
at some supermarkets and at specialty
foods stores.

The French term *tartine* **can refer to a buttered slice of bread that's topped with a spread or to an open-face sandwich, such as this one, which showcases the flavors of the Mediterranean: Fresh sardines are enhanced with herbs, lemon, and a sprinkle of the delicately flavored sea salt** *fleur de sel.* **If you can't find fresh sardines, try fillets of trout or mackerel instead.**

Place fish, skin side down, in a 13x9x2-inch glass baking dish. Whisk 2 Tbsp. olive oil and next 4 ingredients in a small bowl. Spread herb mixture over fish. Cover and chill for at least 2 hours and up to 8 hours.

Build a medium fire in a charcoal grill, or heat a gas grill to medium-high. Brush grill grate with olive oil. Brush onion slices with olive oil; season with kosher salt and pepper. Grill onion until just tender and slightly charred, about 2 minutes per side. Grill bread slices until slightly charred, about 1 minute per side. Spread 1 side of each bread slice with butter. Season fish with fleur de sel and pepper. Grill fish until just opaque in the center, about 3 minutes per side. Remove bones from fish.

Place arugula in a medium bowl. Drizzle with extra-virgin olive oil and lemon juice and toss; season to taste with fleur de sel and pepper. Arrange some arugula leaves atop each bread slice; top with grilled onion. Top onion on each bread slice with 2 sardines or 1 trout or branzino fillet, trimming fish to fit. Garnish with lemon wedges.

Kitchen Wisdom

DARK MEAT OF THE SEA Ask hard-core fish lovers what they cook in the summer and chances are they'll say **fresh mackerel or bluefish.** These beautiful fish with rich, oily flesh are terrific on the grill: They remain juicy while their strong flavors take well to a char. Buy fresh pieces and cook them the same day. Score and grill whole fish, or grill fillets skin side down. Pair with bold flavors: lemon juice or rice vinegar cut with fish sauce and sugar, plus chiles, garlic, or *sambal oelek.* Use high heat to sear them.

SALMON CLUB SANDWICH

6 Tbsp. mayonnaise

5 Tbsp. minced fresh basil, divided

1 tsp. grated lemon zest

3 Tbsp. extra-virgin olive oil, plus
more for brushing

1 Tbsp. fresh lemon juice

4 5- to 6-oz. skinless salmon fillets
(each about ¾ inch thick)

8 slices bacon

1 small red onion, sliced

8 ½-inch-thick sourdough or
country-style white bread slices
(each about 5x3 inches)

8 tomato slices

8 lettuce leaves

The classic club sandwich gets a twist with fresh-off-the-grill salmon fillets and sautéed onions on grilled slices of sourdough spread with homemade lemon-basil mayo. A traditional club calls for three slices of bread, but here you'll just use two, in order to let the other flavors take center stage.

Mix mayonnaise, 2 Tbsp. basil, and lemon zest in a small bowl to blend. **DO AHEAD:** Can be made 1 day ahead. Cover and chill.

Mix remaining 3 Tbsp. basil, 3 Tbsp. oil, and lemon juice in a large glass baking dish. Add salmon; turn to coat. Cover; chill for at least 1 hour and up to 4 hours.

Cook bacon in a large heavy skillet over medium-high heat until crisp. Using tongs, transfer bacon to paper towels to drain. Add onion to drippings in skillet. Sauté until onion is tender and beginning to brown, about 5 minutes.

Build a medium-hot fire in a charcoal grill, or heat a gas grill to high. Brush grill grate with oil. Grill fish until just opaque in center, about 3 minutes per side. Grill bread until just golden, about 2 minutes per side.

Spread mayonnaise mixture over 1 side of bread slices. Top each of 4 bread slices with 2 bacon slices, 2 tomato slices, ¼ of onion, 1 salmon fillet, and 2 lettuce leaves. Cover with remaining bread slices.

AT THE MARKET: The Case for Choosing Sustainable Fish

At *Bon Appétit,* we think of seafood as a natural resource and we treat it with respect. That's why we recommend that you try to buy from fisheries that catch or farm using sustainable fishing practices. Here's a quick guide to making smart fish choices when you're at the market.

WILD VS. FARMED SALMON

There's a variety of choices when it comes to purchasing salmon. But at *Bon Appétit,* we have a clear favorite, and that's **wild salmon**. For sustainability and optimum flavor, it can't be beat. If farmed fish is the only option available to you, try to make sure it's raised using sustainable farming methods. Ask your fishmonger for information on the sourcing of their seafood.

MORE FISH IN THE SEA

A growing number of fisheries practice sustainable methods, helping turn the tide, so to speak, on widespread problems such as overfishing, habitat damage, and bycatch—the unintended catching and waste of other species. To learn more, see the **Monterey Bay Aquarium's Seafood Watch list**, an authoritative guide to the best fish choices; visit **montereybayaquarium.org** or download the mobile app to refer to when you're at the store.

MAHI-MAHI TACOS

PICO DE GALLO

- 5 plum tomatoes, seeded, chopped
- ½ small yellow onion, finely chopped
- 4 scallions, thinly sliced (white and pale green parts only)
- ½ cup chopped fresh cilantro
- 1 tsp. chopped fresh oregano
- 1 tsp. fresh lemon juice
- 1 jalapeño, seeded, minced
  Kosher salt and freshly ground black pepper

CREMA MEXICANA

- ¼ cup heavy cream
- 2 Tbsp. sour cream
  Kosher salt and freshly ground black pepper
  Hot pepper sauce

TACOS

- 1 Tbsp. paprika
- 1 tsp. dried oregano, preferably Mexican
- 1 tsp. dried thyme
- 1 tsp. garlic powder
- 1 tsp. kosher salt
- 1 tsp. onion powder
- ½ tsp. freshly ground black pepper
- ¼ tsp. cayenne pepper
- 1 1-lb. mahi-mahi fillet
  Vegetable oil, for brushing
- 8 6-inch corn tortillas, warmed
- 1 cup finely shredded cabbage
- 1 lime, cut into wedges

What's better than fresh grilled fish topped with a tart and herby *pico de gallo*, cool *crema*, and a big squeeze of lime juice? In San Diego, the classic fish taco is deep-fried, but for this version we rely on high-quality fish that gets a boost from a spicy dry rub. Substitute the Mexican variety of oregano if you can for a more authentic and floral flavor.

PICO DE GALLO

Combine first 7 ingredients in a medium bowl. Season to taste with salt and pepper.

CREMA MEXICANA

Whisk cream and sour cream in a small bowl to blend. Season to taste with salt, pepper, and hot pepper sauce.

TACOS

Build a medium-hot fire in a charcoal grill, or heat a gas grill to high. Combine first 8 ingredients in a small bowl. Sprinkle over fish. Brush grill grate with oil. Grill fish until cooked through, about 5 minutes per side. Transfer to a bowl; using a fork, coarsely shred fish.

Fill tortillas with fish, cabbage, and pico de gallo. Drizzle with crema. Squeeze lime wedges over tacos.

TUNA STEAKS
with Olive Salad

A salad of briny olives in a citrusy vinaigrette, with a good dose of garlic and fresh herbs, tops smoky grilled tuna. You can also try the olive salad in a cold-cut sandwich or with grilled lamb or chicken.

SALAD

- ⅔ cup brine-cured black olives (such as Kalamata; about 4 oz.), pitted, coarsely chopped
- ⅔ cup cracked green olives (about 4 oz.), pitted, coarsely chopped
- ⅔ cup Niçoise olives (about 4 oz.), pitted, coarsely chopped
- ⅓ cup finely chopped red onion
- ¼ cup chopped fresh basil
- ¼ cup finely chopped red bell pepper
- 3 Tbsp. fresh lemon juice
- 2 Tbsp. chopped fresh mint
- 1 Tbsp. finely chopped garlic
- 1 Tbsp. finely grated lemon zest
- 1 Tbsp. extra-virgin olive oil
  Kosher salt and freshly ground black pepper

TUNA

- 6 Tbsp. extra-virgin olive oil, plus more for brushing
- ¼ cup fresh lemon juice
- 3 Tbsp. finely chopped garlic
- 2 tsp. dried oregano
  Kosher salt and freshly ground black pepper
- 6 7-oz. tuna steaks (¾ inch thick)

SALAD

Combine all ingredients except salt and pepper in a medium bowl. Season to taste with salt and pepper. Let stand for 20 minutes. **DO AHEAD:** Can be prepared 1 day ahead. Cover and chill.

TUNA

Whisk 6 Tbsp. oil, lemon juice, garlic, and oregano in a 13x9x2-inch glass baking dish. Season to taste with salt and pepper. Add tuna and turn to coat. Cover with plastic and chill, turning occasionally, for at least 30 minutes and up to 4 hours.

Build a medium-hot fire in a charcoal grill, or heat a gas grill to high. Brush grill grate with oil. Grill tuna until just opaque in the center, about 4 minutes per side. Transfer tuna to plates. Spoon salad atop tuna.

SEA BASS SALAD
with Mango, Grapefruit, and Avocado

FISH

- 2 Tbsp. minced garlic
- 2 Tbsp. paprika
- 1 Tbsp. chili powder
- 1 Tbsp. extra-virgin olive oil
- 2 tsp. dried oregano
- 1½ tsp. ground allspice
- ¼ cup fresh pink grapefruit juice
  Kosher salt and freshly ground
  black pepper
- 6 4- to 5-oz. sea bass fillets

SALAD

- 5 Tbsp. fresh pink grapefruit juice
- ¼ cup extra-virgin olive oil, plus
  more for brushing
- 2 Tbsp. Sherry vinegar
- 1½ Tbsp. chopped fresh mint
- 1 Tbsp. chopped peeled ginger
  Kosher salt and freshly ground
  black pepper
- 1 5-oz. package mixed baby greens
  (about 10 cups)
- 3 pink grapefruits, peel and pith
  cut away, segments cut from
  between membranes
- 2 large mangoes, peeled, pitted,
  thinly sliced
- 1 avocado, peeled, pitted, thinly
  sliced

Freshly squeezed grapefruit juice is a nice counterpoint to grilled sea bass and the rich tastes of mango and avocado. With this recipe, it's best to use pink grapefruits, which are a little sweeter than white ones.

FISH

Line a rimmed baking sheet with waxed paper. Pulse first 6 ingredients in a food processor until almost smooth. Add grapefruit juice and blend well. Season spice mixture with salt and pepper. Season fish with salt and pepper. Rub 2 tsp. spice mixture over each fillet; place on prepared baking sheet. Refrigerate for 2 hours.

SALAD

Whisk grapefruit juice, ¼ cup oil, vinegar, mint, and ginger in a small bowl. Season dressing to taste with salt and pepper. **DO AHEAD:** Dressing can be made 2 hours ahead. Let stand at room temperature.

Build a medium-hot fire in a charcoal grill, or heat a gas grill to high. Brush grill grate with oil. Brush fish with oil. Grill until just opaque in the center, about 3 minutes per side. Transfer fish to a platter.

Toss greens and some dressing in a large bowl just to coat; divide among plates. Arrange grapefruit segments and mangoes atop greens; drizzle with some dressing. Place 1 fish fillet alongside each salad. Top fish with avocado. Pass any remaining dressing at the table.

SHELL FISH

WE THANK THE FIRST ANGLER

who was bold—and hungry—enough to look past all the protective armor, scoop shellfish out of the ocean, and cook it over an open fire. If you've ever cracked open a just-grilled lobster to dunk into butter and sprinkle with sea salt, you know what we're talking about. Simple fact: When you cook shellfish over hot coals, they take on the incomparable sweet and salty flavors of sea and smoke.

In this chapter, we celebrate grilled shellfish in all their glory and explain how to handle them with ease. That means wild-caught U.S. shrimp, the most bountiful and egalitarian of all shellfish, in straightforward recipes for weeknight dinners or lazy weekends at the beach. You'll also find meaty, quick-cooking scallops; grill-roasted clams; and, of course, delectable and luxurious lobsters, natural partners for the grill.

So, light a fire and embrace two simple shellfish principles: Grill them hot, and grill them fast. Prepare your side dishes ahead of time, open the wine, and seat your friends at the table. Once the shellfish hits the grill grate, dinner will be ready in minutes.

BUTTERFLIED SHRIMP
with Chive Butter

6 servings

¼ cup Dijon mustard
¼ cup fresh lemon juice
1 cup (2 sticks) unsalted butter, melted
6 Tbsp. chopped fresh chives, plus whole fresh chives
 Freshly ground black pepper
36 jumbo shrimp, peeled, deveined, butterflied
 Kosher salt
 Vegetable oil, for brushing

As these butterflied shrimp cook over the hot grate, they'll open up, creating more surface area for the chive-butter sauce. To butterfly the shrimp, first peel and devein them (see detailed instructions on page 244), then use a paring knife to cut through the outer curve, from top to bottom, without slicing through the shrimp.

Build a medium-hot fire in a charcoal grill, or heat a gas grill to high. Place mustard in a medium bowl; whisk in lemon juice, then butter. Mix in chopped chives. Season to taste with pepper. Transfer ½ cup chive butter to small bowl for brushing shrimp; set aside remaining sauce separately.

 Arrange shrimp, cut side up, on a rimmed baking sheet. Brush shrimp with chive butter from small bowl. Season with salt and pepper. Brush grill grate with oil. Grill shrimp just until opaque in center, about 3 minutes per side. Arrange on plates and brush with reserved chive butter. Garnish with whole chives.

NEW ORLEANS–STYLE GRILLED SHRIMP

4 servings

24 shell-on large shrimp, preferably wild American
1 small onion, sliced
1 lemon, thinly sliced
8 bay leaves
2 Tbsp. fresh oregano leaves
2 Tbsp. Worcestershire sauce
1 Tbsp. Old Bay seasoning
2 tsp. hot chili paste (such as sambal oelek)
2 tsp. kosher salt
¼ tsp. freshly ground black pepper
8 Tbsp. (1 stick) unsalted butter, cut into cubes
 Warm crusty bread

INGREDIENT INFO Hot chili paste is available in the Asian foods section of many supermarkets and at Asian markets.

Roll up your sleeves. These shrimp are steamed in foil packets and served with the shells on to seal in juices, leaving the peeling to your guests.

Using small scissors, cut shrimp shells along their curved backs. Remove vein, keeping shell intact. Combine shrimp and next 9 ingredients in a large bowl; toss to coat.

 Place four 16x12-inch sheets of heavy-duty foil on a work surface. Divide shrimp mixture among sheets. Gather edges of foil to the center but do not crimp. Add 2 Tbsp. butter and ¼ cup water to each portion. Fold foil into packets, crimping edges to seal. **DO AHEAD:** Can be made 4 hours ahead. Chill. Let stand at room temperature for 15 minutes before continuing.

 Build a medium fire in a charcoal grill, or heat a gas grill to medium-high. Grill packets until shrimp are just opaque in the center, about 30 minutes. Carefully cut open packets (steam will escape). Transfer shrimp mixture to bowls and serve with bread alongside.

Steps to PERFECT SHRIMP

Shrimp is America's favorite shellfish. It's sweet, meaty, simple to cook, and plentiful. And it even tastes better when enhanced with a nice char from a hot grill. There's no great mystery to grilling shrimp, but there are steps you can take—starting at the market—to make it outstanding.

❶ THINK DOMESTIC

When buying shrimp, it pays to **go all-American**. Why? Because the majority of shrimp sold in the U.S. is imported, often from areas where farming practices leave a lot to be desired.

There are incredible varieties of wild shrimp right off our own coasts. See **"At the Market: American Shrimp" on page 246** for a guide to our favorites and when to use them.

❷ SIZE THEM UP

Figure out how big (or small) you want to go. To do this, consider your recipe:

Is shrimp the star of the show? Buy "colossal." These are sold with the cryptic code U/10 or U/15: "U" means "under," so there are fewer than 10 or 15 shrimp per pound. In other words, they're huge.

Jumbo to large shrimp are especially versatile. Look for codes "16/20" to "31/35" indicating the number of shrimp per pound.

Making a salad or sandwich? Get medium-size shrimp (36/40 or 41/50), and use a grilling basket to cook them.

❸ TO PEEL OR NOT TO PEEL?

Grilling shrimp with or without their shells gives two deliciously different results.

UNPEELED: Shells **seal in flavor and juices and protect meat** from the heat of the grill. This is best for delicacies like Royal Reds and spot prawns. They are messier to eat since you have to peel them with your hands.

PEELED: Without the shell, the **flesh chars and caramelizes,** and takes on the flavor of a marinade. This is great for sandwiches, pasta, or salads. Buy shrimp already peeled, or see page 244 for tips on how to peel and devein them.

❹ SKEWER 'EM RIGHT

Want to know what's annoying? A bunch of shrimp twirling around on skewers when you're trying to turn them on the grill. To avoid that:

Use flat metal skewers. The shape minimizes twirling, and the metal won't burn on the grill like bamboo skewers can. (If you *do* use bamboo, soak them in water for 1 hour beforehand so they don't burn.)

Thread the shrimp tightly. This keeps them from spinning *and* increases the cooking time, giving them an extra minute to develop a char.

❺ GO HIGH AND HOT

Once they're on the grill, use **medium-high to high heat**, for 2 to 3 minutes per side. This way they get a nice char (if they're unpeeled) but stay moist and juicy.

You can also grill shrimp **on a cedar plank** (see recipe on page 247), which is quick and infuses them with even more smoky flavor.

Or steam them **in foil packets** (see page 226) for especially moist, juicy results.

BUTTERFLIED SHRIMP
with Garlic-Herb Sauce

6 servings

BRINE
- ⅓ cup kosher salt
- ⅓ cup (packed) light brown sugar
- 1½ lb. shell-on large shrimp

MARINADE
- ¼ cup extra-virgin olive oil, plus more for brushing
- 2 Tbsp. dry white wine
- 2 garlic cloves, minced
- 1 Tbsp. chopped flat-leaf parsley
- ¼ tsp. crushed red pepper flakes
  Roasted Garlic-Herb Sauce (recipe follows)

In this recipe, shrimp are quick-brined and marinated, and then grilled inside their shells to help retain natural juices and give added flavor. Keep in mind, shrimp cook pretty quickly, so have your pesto-like sauce ready to serve before placing the shrimp on the grill.

BRINE
Stir salt, brown sugar, and 4 cups water in a medium bowl until sugar dissolves. Add shrimp. Chill for at least 1 hour. **DO AHEAD:** Can be made 3 hours ahead. Keep chilled. Drain and rinse shrimp.

MARINADE
Using kitchen shears or a sharp knife, cut shrimp in their shells along full length of back (do not cut all the way through; leave shells on). Remove veins. Open shrimp flat like a book.

Whisk ¼ cup oil, wine, garlic, parsley, and red pepper flakes in a medium bowl to blend. Add shrimp and toss to coat; let stand for 30 minutes.

Build a medium-hot fire in a charcoal grill, or heat a gas grill to high. Brush grill grate with oil. Place shrimp, flesh side down, on grill. Grill shrimp until just opaque in the center, about 2 minutes per side. Transfer shrimp to a platter. Serve with Roasted Garlic-Herb Sauce.

Roasted Garlic-Herb Sauce

makes about 1 cup

serve with butterflied shrimp

- 2 heads of garlic, top ¼ inch of each cut off and discarded
- 1 tsp. plus ⅔ cup extra-virgin olive oil
- 1 cup chopped flat-leaf parsley
- 4 anchovy fillets packed in oil, drained, rinsed
- 2 Tbsp. chopped fresh basil
- 2 Tbsp. drained capers
- 1 Tbsp. finely grated lemon zest
  Kosher salt and freshly ground black pepper

This pesto-like sauce would be great with any grilled seafood.

Preheat oven to 400°F. Place garlic on a large sheet of foil. Drizzle 1 tsp. oil over and wrap tightly in foil. Roast until garlic is soft, about 1 hour. Let cool slightly. Squeeze garlic from papery skin into a small bowl and mash with the back of a fork.

Combine mashed garlic, parsley, anchovies, basil, capers, and lemon zest in a food processor. With machine running, slowly blend in remaining ⅔ cup oil. Season sauce to taste with salt and pepper. **DO AHEAD:** Can be made 1 day ahead. Cover and chill. Bring to room temperature before using.

SWEET-AND-SPICY SHRIMP
with Mint Sauce

photo, right

¼ cup (packed) light brown sugar or dark brown sugar

3½ Tbsp. fresh lemon juice, divided

2 Tbsp. plus ½ cup vegetable oil, divided, plus more for brushing

2 tsp. cayenne pepper

2 tsp. finely grated lemon zest

½ tsp. salt, plus more as needed

2 lb. large shrimp, peeled, deveined

2 cups (packed) fresh mint leaves

SPECIAL EQUIPMENT 6 or more metal skewers

Brown sugar brings out the natural sweetness of the shrimp, and cayenne delivers the heat. If you like a mild molasses flavor, use light brown sugar; for a stronger molasses flavor, use dark brown sugar.

Mix brown sugar, 2 Tbsp. lemon juice, 2 Tbsp. oil, cayenne, lemon zest, and ½ tsp. salt in a medium bowl. Add shrimp and toss to coat. Let marinate for at least 30 minutes or up to 1 hour.

Meanwhile, place mint, remaining 1½ Tbsp. lemon juice, and remaining ½ cup oil in a food processor. Pulse, scraping down sides occasionally, until mint is finely chopped and mixture is smooth. Season mint sauce to taste with salt.

Build a medium-hot fire in a charcoal grill, or heat a gas grill to high. Brush grill grate with oil. Thread shrimp onto skewers. Grill shrimp until just opaque in the center, 2 to 3 minutes per side. Serve with mint sauce.

HOW TO: Peel and Devein Shrimp

You can buy shrimp that have already been peeled and deveined (that's what "P&D" on the package means), but it will cost you more. To do it yourself—and save some money—use this technique.

1 **Hold shrimp between thumb and forefingers** with the legs facing you. Starting from both corners near the shrimp's head end, begin pulling back the shell.

2 **Continue working toward the tail** down the underside of the shrimp, pulling the shell from the body on both sides as you go. (It's easier to remove if it's in one piece.)

3 Flip shrimp and gently **pinch the tail to remove the peel and tail** in one piece. You can save the shells (freeze them for up to two months in resealable plastic bags) and use them to make stock.

4 **Use a paring knife** to make a ⅛-inch-deep cut down the back of the shrimp. Use the tip of the knife to remove the vein; discard. Put shrimp in bowl set over a bowl of ice; repeat with remaining shrimp.

Peeled shrimp soak up a sweet-spicy **marinade with brown sugar and cayenne** and take on a perfect char on a fiery hot grill.

SWEET-AND-SPICY SHRIMP
WITH MINT SAUCE

CHILE-GLAZED SHRIMP
with Tomatillo-Cilantro Sauce

1 lb. tomatillos, husked, rinsed

1 medium onion, coarsely chopped

1 Tbsp. minced seeded jalapeño

1 garlic clove, crushed

3 Tbsp. extra-virgin olive oil, divided, plus more for brushing

2 Tbsp. chopped fresh cilantro
Kosher salt and freshly ground black pepper

24 jumbo shrimp, peeled, deveined, tails left intact

2 Tbsp. ground mild chile (such as ancho or New Mexico)

1 tsp. onion powder

½ tsp. garlic powder
Queso fresco or feta cheese, for topping

INGREDIENT INFO Ground New Mexico chiles and *queso fresco* are available at some supermarkets, at specialty foods stores, and at Latin markets.

The shrimp get fantastic flavor, but not an overdose of heat, from the ground chile and the onion and garlic powders; the tomatillo-cilantro sauce adds a nice piquant contrast. Frying the tomatillo sauce in a little oil is a classic technique of Mexican cuisine that blends and concentrates all the flavors of the salsa.

Cook tomatillos in a large pot of boiling salted water until tender and olive green in color, about 5 minutes. Drain; transfer to a food processor. Add onion, jalapeño, and garlic and process until tomatillo sauce is almost smooth.

Heat 1 Tbsp. oil in a medium skillet over medium heat. Add tomatillo sauce (mixture may splatter) and bring to a boil. Reduce heat and simmer, stirring occasionally, until slightly thickened, about 5 minutes. Let cool completely, then stir in cilantro and season to taste with salt and pepper. **DO AHEAD:** Can be made 1 day ahead. Cover and chill. Bring to room temperature before using.

Build a medium-hot fire in a charcoal grill, or heat a gas grill to high. Brush grill grate with oil. Toss shrimp with remaining 2 Tbsp. oil in a large bowl. Add ground chile, onion powder, and garlic powder; toss to combine. Season shrimp with salt and pepper and grill until just opaque in the center, 2 to 3 minutes per side.

Spoon about 3 Tbsp. tomatillo sauce into middle of each plate. Arrange shrimp atop sauce and sprinkle with queso fresco.

AT THE MARKET: American Shrimp

These days, a lot of the shrimp we eat in the United States comes from Asia—but there are superb wild shrimp here in our own waters. Here are some of our favorites, all of which are great for grilling.

BROWN

Abundant in Gulf waters, brown shrimp account for more than half of our domestic catch. Their **earthy crawfish flavor** makes them a good match for intensely flavored marinades.

PACIFIC WHITE

We love these, with their **nutty taste and firm texture**. They work in virtually any recipe.

PINK

From Florida's west coast, with **classic shrimp flavor**. Plump and perfect for the grill.

ROYAL RED

These come from the deeper, cold waters of the Gulf and off the coast of New England. There's a little extra fat on them, so they have the **luxurious taste of mini-lobsters**. If you find them (late summer through fall), buy them.

SPOT PRAWNS

Chefs' favorites, these have **candy-sweet buttery flesh** and are wonderful grilled head-on in the shell to trap the sweet juices. Found along the Pacific Coast from Alaska to Santa Barbara, they're a bit pricey but delicious.

CEDAR-PLANKED SHRIMP
with Pumpkin Seed Salsa

4 servings

2 large red bell peppers
⅓ cup shelled natural unsalted pumpkin seeds (pepitas)
2 garlic cloves
1 whole canned chipotle chile in adobo
1 Tbsp. Sherry vinegar
1 tsp. dried oregano
½ cup extra-virgin olive oil, plus more for brushing
Kosher salt and freshly ground black pepper
24 large shrimp, peeled, deveined

SPECIAL EQUIPMENT 2 untreated red cedar planks (each about 15x7x¾ inches), soaked in water for 1 hour, drained

INGREDIENT INFO Canned chipotle chiles are dried, smoked jalapeños in a spicy tomato sauce called adobo. They are available at many supermarkets and at specialty foods stores and Latin markets.

Grilling shrimp on a cedar plank gives them a wonderful smoky flavor that pairs nicely with the garlicky sauce enriched with pumpkin seeds. Look for cedar planks at cookware stores, or order them online from fireandflavor.com or natures-cuisine.com. Choose planks that are about ¾ inch thick (see page 206 for info on grilling with planks).

Build a medium-hot fire in a charcoal grill, or heat a gas grill to high. Brush grill grate with oil. Place bell peppers on grill grate. Cover and grill, turning frequently, until bell peppers are blistered and blackened on all sides, about 15 minutes. (Or char bell peppers over gas flame or in broiler until blackened on all sides.) Enclose bell peppers in a paper bag and let stand for 10 minutes. Peel, seed, and coarsely chop bell peppers.

Sauté pumpkin seeds in a small dry skillet over medium heat until lightly toasted, about 5 minutes. Let cool in skillet.

With food processor running, add garlic, bell peppers, pumpkin seeds, chipotle, vinegar, and oregano and process until finely chopped. With machine running, gradually add ½ cup oil and process until mixture is almost smooth. Season salsa to taste with salt and pepper. Transfer to a bowl. **DO AHEAD:** Can be made 3 days ahead. Cover and chill. Bring to room temperature before using, and prepare grill as above.

Place soaked, drained cedar planks on hot grill grate and heat until cedar begins to smoke, 10 to 20 minutes, depending on thickness of cedar. Season shrimp with salt and pepper. Arrange 12 shrimp on each plank. Cover grill and cook shrimp without turning, until just opaque on bottom (the underside cooks last when cooking on planks), about 5 minutes. Transfer planks with shrimp to a heatproof platter. Divide shrimp among plates and spoon salsa alongside.

SHRIMP AND APRICOTS
with Peanut Sauce and Bok Choy

9 Tbsp. canned apricot nectar, divided

6 Tbsp. smooth natural peanut butter, stirred to combine

⅓ cup (packed) dark brown sugar

3 Tbsp. seasoned rice vinegar

2 Tbsp. reduced-sodium soy sauce

2 tsp. hot chili paste (such as sambal oelek), more as needed

Freshly ground black pepper

16 large shrimp, peeled, deveined

6 heads of baby bok choy, halved lengthwise

6 apricots, halved lengthwise and pitted

Kosher salt

Vegetable oil, for brushing

INGREDIENT INFO Hot chili paste is available in the Asian foods section of many supermarkets and at Asian markets.

Sweet and savory combine in this Indonesian-style dish, where a traditional peanut sauce is amped up with sweet apricot nectar, and the shrimp are grilled alongside bok choy and fresh apricots. Serve with jasmine or basmati rice.

Build a medium-hot fire in a charcoal grill, or heat a gas grill to high. Whisk 5 Tbsp. apricot nectar, peanut butter, brown sugar, vinegar, soy sauce, and 2 tsp. chili paste in a medium bowl until smooth; season sauce to taste with pepper and more chili paste. Transfer ¼ cup sauce to a small bowl.

Arrange shrimp, bok choy, and apricot halves on a rimmed baking sheet. Brush with remaining 4 Tbsp. apricot nectar; then brush with ¼ cup sauce from small bowl. Season with salt and pepper. Brush grill grate with oil. Grill until shrimp are just opaque in the center, bok choy halves are just tender, and apricots are slightly charred, about 2 minutes per side for apricots and 2 to 3 minutes per side for shrimp and bok choy. Mound shrimp, bok choy, and apricots on a platter. Drizzle with some sauce. Serve with remaining sauce alongside.

SHRIMP SKEWERS
with Tzatziki, Spinach, and Feta

4 servings

1 cup plain nonfat Greek yogurt
1 cup ¼-inch cubes English
   hothouse cucumber
3 Tbsp. chopped fresh dill
2 Tbsp. fresh lemon juice,
   plus more for drizzling
2 Tbsp. chopped shallots
1¼ tsp. finely crushed aniseed,
   divided
   Kosher salt and freshly ground
   black pepper
   Extra-virgin olive oil, for brushing
   and drizzling
1 lb. large shrimp, peeled, deveined,
   tails left intact
8 cups baby spinach leaves
¾ cup crumbled feta

SPECIAL EQUIPMENT 4 metal skewers

Tzatziki **is a popular Greek sauce made from yogurt, cucumbers, dill, and garlic (although here we use shallots). Serve any leftover** *tzatziki* **with pita chips, as a substitute for mayo on grilled chicken sandwiches, or as a sauce for grilled lamb.**

Mix yogurt, cucumber, dill, 2 Tbsp. lemon juice, shallots, and ¾ tsp. aniseed in a small bowl; season tzatziki generously with salt and pepper. Cover and chill.
DO AHEAD: Can be prepared 6 hours ahead and chilled. Stir before serving.
   Build a medium-hot fire in a charcoal grill, or heat a gas grill to high. Brush grill grate with oil. Thread shrimp onto skewers, dividing evenly. Brush shrimp all over with oil; season with salt and pepper and sprinkle with remaining ½ tsp. aniseed. Grill until shrimp are just opaque in the center, 2 to 3 minutes per side.
   Divide spinach among 4 plates; drizzle lightly with lemon juice and oil. Top each with 1 shrimp skewer. Spoon tzatziki over shrimp and sprinkle with feta.

SKEWERED SHRIMP
with Rosemary

6 servings

36 large shrimp, peeled, deveined
2 Tbsp. extra-virgin olive oil, plus
   more for brushing
5 tsp. chopped fresh rosemary, plus
   several whole sprigs for garnish
   Kosher salt and freshly ground
   black pepper

SPECIAL EQUIPMENT 12 metal skewers

This easy, elegant dish serves six for dinner but would also make an excellent appetizer for a crowd. Keep things simple with a side of lemony orzo or couscous.

Combine shrimp, 2 Tbsp. oil, and chopped rosemary in a large bowl; toss to coat.
DO AHEAD: Can be made 1 day ahead. Cover and chill.
   Build a medium-hot fire in a charcoal grill, or heat a gas grill to high. Brush grill grate with oil. Line a platter with rosemary sprigs as a bed for shrimp. Thread 3 shrimp onto each skewer. Season with salt and pepper. Grill until shrimp are just opaque in the center, 2 to 3 minutes per side. Arrange skewers atop rosemary on platter.

SHRIMP AND SAUSAGE SKEWERS
with Paprika Glaze

6 servings

¾ cup extra-virgin olive oil, plus more for brushing

4 large garlic cloves, minced

2 Tbsp. chopped fresh thyme

5 tsp. smoked paprika

4 tsp. Sherry vinegar

¾ tsp. kosher salt

½ tsp. freshly ground black pepper

½ tsp. crushed red pepper flakes

12 extra-large shrimp (13 to 15 per lb.), peeled, deveined

1 lb. cooked smoked sausage, such as andouille or linguiça, cut into 1-inch-long pieces

12 cherry tomatoes

12 2-layer sections red onion wedges

SPECIAL EQUIPMENT 6 metal skewers

The skewers stacked with plump sausage and juicy shrimp aren't on the grill long enough for fresh sausages to cook through, so this recipe uses fully cooked smoked sausages instead, such as Louisiana's andouille or linguiça, the Portuguese smoked pork sausage; or use your own favorite.

Whisk ¾ cup oil, garlic, thyme, paprika, vinegar, salt, black pepper, and red pepper flakes in a medium bowl for glaze. Transfer half of glaze to a small bowl and reserve for serving.

Thread shrimp, sausage pieces, cherry tomatoes, and onion sections alternately onto skewers, dividing evenly. Arrange skewers on a large rimmed baking sheet. **DO AHEAD:** Can be made 6 hours ahead. Cover and chill skewers and bowls of glaze separately.

Build a medium-hot fire in a charcoal grill, or heat a gas grill to high. Brush grill grate with oil. Brush skewers on both sides with glaze from medium bowl. Grill, turning and brushing occasionally with more glaze, until shrimp are just opaque in the center, 6 to 8 minutes.

Arrange skewers on plates. Serve with reserved bowl of glaze alongside.

PERNOD-FENNEL SPOT PRAWNS

4 servings

2 lb. head- and tail-on Santa Barbara spot prawns or jumbo shrimp

5 Tbsp. extra-virgin olive oil, divided, plus more for brushing

2 garlic cloves, minced

½ tsp. crushed red pepper flakes

3 Tbsp. Pernod or ouzo (unsweetened anise liqueur)

2 Tbsp. chopped fennel fronds, divided, plus 1 fennel bulb, very thinly sliced crosswise

Kosher salt and freshly ground black pepper

6 cups (loosely packed) baby arugula (about 5 oz.)

2 Tbsp. fresh lemon juice

Pernod and fennel lend a subtle licorice note to Santa Barbara spot prawns, a West Coast delicacy. Simple preparations like this let the buttery flavor and langoustine-like texture of the prawns shine. But feel free to use any jumbo American shrimp.

Using a small knife or kitchen shears, butterfly prawns from tail to base of head, leaving peel and head on; devein.

Heat 3 Tbsp. oil in a small saucepan over medium heat. Add garlic and red pepper flakes; sauté until aromatic, about 30 seconds. Transfer to a medium bowl; stir in Pernod and 1 Tbsp. fennel fronds. Season marinade with salt and pepper. Add prawns; toss to coat. Let marinate at room temperature, tossing occasionally, for 30 minutes.

Build a medium-hot fire in a charcoal grill, or heat a gas grill to high. Brush grill grate with oil. Grill prawns, brushing with marinade from bowl, until bright pink and just opaque in the center, about 2 minutes per side. Transfer to a plate. Mix sliced fennel bulb and arugula in a large bowl. Drizzle lemon juice and remaining 2 Tbsp. oil over; toss to coat. Season to taste with salt and pepper.

Arrange salad on a platter. Top with prawns, and garnish with remaining 1 Tbsp. fennel fronds.

SPICY SHRIMP
with Lemongrass Sambal

This recipe for a spicy paste, or sambal, is a great example of complex Balinese cuisine. The shrimp are grilled in their shells, making them incredibly succulent.

SAMBAL

6 Thai chiles or 2 serrano chiles or jalapeños, preferably red, plus more as needed, seeded, coarsely chopped

1½ cups coarsely chopped shallots (about 8 oz.)

¼ cup chopped peeled ginger

3 Tbsp. chopped lemongrass (from bottom 4 inches of 2 large stalks)

6 macadamia nuts

4 garlic cloves, coarsely chopped

2 tsp. (packed) light brown sugar

2 tsp. turmeric

1½ tsp. salt

1 tsp. ground coriander

1 tsp. paprika

1 bay leaf, crumbled

½ tsp. freshly ground black pepper

2 Tbsp. vegetable oil, more as needed

MARINADE AND SHRIMP

3 Tbsp. vegetable oil, plus more for brushing

2 Tbsp. fresh lime juice

3 lb. shell-on large shrimp, or 2½ lb. peeled large shrimp, deveined, tails left intact

INGREDIENT INFO Lemongrass is sold in the produce section of some supermarkets and at Asian markets.

SAMBAL

Pulse 6 Thai chiles (or 2 serrano chiles or jalapeños) and next 12 ingredients in a food processor until finely chopped and paste forms. Add more chopped chiles to taste, if desired, and pulse until paste forms. Transfer sambal to a small bowl. Heat 2 Tbsp. oil in a large heavy saucepan over medium-high heat. Add sambal and cook, stirring constantly and adding more oil by tablespoonfuls if mixture is dry, until fragrant and lightly browned, about 7 minutes. Stir in 1 cup water; reduce heat to medium and simmer, stirring often, until most of water is absorbed but mixture is still creamy, stirring often, about 4 minutes. Transfer to a small bowl and let cool. **DO AHEAD:** Can be made 1 day ahead and chilled.

MARINADE AND SHRIMP

Whisk 3 Tbsp. oil, lime juice, and 2 Tbsp. sambal in a small bowl. **DO AHEAD:** Can be made 1 day ahead. Cover and chill. Rewhisk marinade before using, adding more oil by teaspoonfuls if marinade is too thick.

If using shell-on shrimp, use kitchen scissors to cut shrimp shell along rounded back of tail; scrape out vein with tip of small knife. Place shrimp in a large glass baking dish. Brush shrimp all over with marinade. Let shrimp marinate at room temperature for at least 15 minutes and up to 30 minutes.

Meanwhile, build a medium-hot fire in a charcoal grill, or heat a gas grill to high. Brush grill grate with oil. Grill shrimp until just opaque in the center, 2 to 3 minutes per side. Divide shrimp among plates. Rewarm remaining sambal and spoon atop shrimp.

Even better than steamed lobsters, grilled lobsters deliver the **bonus of carmelized char, plus crispy bits** for added texture.

CHINESE STYLE LOBSTER WITH GINGER, GARLIC, AND SOY SAUCE

CHINESE-STYLE LOBSTER

photo, left

6 servings

with Ginger, Garlic, and Soy Sauce

1½ cups extra-virgin olive oil, plus more for brushing
9 Tbsp. reduced-sodium soy sauce
6 Tbsp. minced peeled ginger
6 garlic cloves, minced
6 2-lb. live lobsters
   Kosher salt and freshly ground black pepper
6 Tbsp. chopped scallions

This minimalist, Asian-influenced dish is best with freshly boiled and grilled lobster; don't try to substitute frozen lobster tails. See page 254 for tips on working with live lobsters. The natural contour of the lobster shells will lock in the sauce and keep the meat juicy.

Combine 1½ cups oil, soy sauce, ginger, and garlic in a medium saucepan. Cook over low heat, stirring occasionally, until garlic and ginger begin to brown, about 8 minutes. Set aside. **DO AHEAD:** Sauce can be made 1 day ahead. Cover and chill. Rewarm before using.

Build a medium-hot fire in a charcoal grill, or heat a gas grill to high. Bring a large pot of water to a boil. Drop 1 lobster headfirst into pot. Cover and cook for 2 to 3 minutes (lobster will not be fully cooked). Using tongs, transfer lobster to baking sheet. Return water to boil. Repeat with remaining lobsters.

Transfer 1 lobster, shell side down, to work surface. Using a large heavy knife or cleaver, cut lobster lengthwise in half from center to end of head (knife might not cut through shell; if necessary, use poultry shears), then cut in half from center to end of tail. Scoop out and discard gray vein, gills, and sand sac from head. Leave any red roe or green tomalley intact, if desired. Repeat with remaining lobsters.

Brush grill grate with oil. Place lobster halves, cut side up, on grill. Brush cut side of lobsters with some sauce; season with salt and pepper. Cover grill; grill lobsters until just opaque in the thickest portion of the tail, about 9 minutes. Using tongs, transfer lobsters to a platter. Brush with more sauce and season with scallions. Serve with remaining sauce alongside.

LEMON-TARRAGON LOBSTER

2 servings

¼ cup (½ stick) unsalted butter
2 Tbsp. fresh lemon juice
1½ tsp. finely grated lemon zest
2 Tbsp. chopped fresh chives
1 Tbsp. chopped fresh tarragon
  Kosher salt and freshly ground
  black pepper
2 1½-lb. live lobsters
  Vegetable oil, for brushing

The classic lobster accompaniment—melted butter—gets a fresh spin with lemon juice, lemon zest, and the anise-like flavor of tarragon.

Build a medium-hot fire in a charcoal grill, or heat a gas grill to high. Stir butter, lemon juice, and lemon zest in a small saucepan over low heat until butter melts. Mix in chives and tarragon; season to taste with salt and pepper. Set pan at edge of grill to keep sauce warm.

Meanwhile, bring a large pot of water to a boil. Drop lobsters headfirst into water. Cover and cook for 2 to 3 minutes (lobsters will not be fully cooked). Using tongs, transfer lobsters to a work surface. Using a large heavy knife or cleaver, cut lobster lengthwise in half from center to end of head (knife might not cut through shell; if necessary, use poultry shears), then cut in half from center to end of tail. Scoop out and discard gray vein, gills, and sand sac from head. Leave any red roe or green tomalley intact, if desired. Crack claws. Brush cut side of lobsters with 1 Tbsp. butter sauce.

Brush grill grate with oil. Grill lobsters, cut side down, for 4 minutes. Turn and grill 4 minutes longer. Turn again so that cut side is down and grill until lobster meat is opaque but still juicy, about 2 minutes longer. Using tongs, transfer lobsters to plates. Brush with sauce. Serve, passing any remaining sauce separately.

HOW TO: Prepare Lobster for the Grill

For the most delicious grilled lobster, you have to start with a live lobster. This requires that the lobster be killed and partially cooked just before it hits the grate. There are a few different ways to do it, but this method is the most simple and straightforward.

Bring water to boil in large pot. Add lobster headfirst. Cover pot tightly. Boil lobsters 2 to 3 minutes. **Using tongs, remove lobster** (now red) from pot.

Place lobster belly side up on work surface. Put tip of large knife in center; **cut from center to end of head**, then from center to end of tail.

Discard the **gray vein, gills, and sand sac** from head. Keep the red roe and green tomalley intact, if desired.

LOBSTER PAELLA

½ cup extra-virgin olive oil

¾ lb. smoked Spanish chorizo, sliced into ½-inch-thick rounds

6 green garlic stalks, thinly sliced, or 2 leeks, white and pale green parts only, finely chopped

1 Tbsp. smoked paprika

2½ cups short-grain rice (such as calasparra, Valencia, or bomba)

¼ tsp. saffron threads

7 cups hot seafood or chicken stock, plus more as needed
Kosher salt

3 1¼-lb. lobsters, parcooked and halved lengthwise (see instructions on page 254), claws cracked

2 cups fresh shelled or thawed frozen peas

½ cup finely chopped flat-leaf parsley

3 lemons, halved

SPECIAL EQUIPMENT A 16- to 18-inch paella pan, available at amazon.com or tienda.com, or use a heavy skillet at least 16 inches in diameter

INGREDIENT INFO Spanish chorizo and calasparra, Valencia, and bomba rice can be ordered from tienda.com.

Paella, the classic Spanish one-pot meal, is perfect for a crowd. This recipe for six is designed for cooking over charcoal—though a gas grill on high heat works in a pinch. The only thing you need is a large paella pan or extra-large skillet at least 16 inches in diameter. Buy live lobsters, then parcook and split them following the instructions on page 254.

Prepare a hot fire in a charcoal grill. Let burn down to red-hot coals; rake to edge of grill. (For backup, start a second round of coals in a charcoal chimney, on pavement nearby.) Put paella pan on grill grate; heat oil. Add chorizo and garlic; cook until golden, 3 to 4 minutes.

Add paprika and rice; cook, stirring often, until rice is coated, 2 minutes. Add saffron to hot stock. Add stock to rice mixture and season to taste with salt; stir to distribute ingredients. Let cook, undisturbed and rotating pan every 2 to 3 minutes, until stock simmers and rice begins to absorb liquid, about 10 minutes.

Arrange lobster halves over rice. Continue cooking, rotating pan often and adding more coals from charcoal chimney to maintain even heat under the pan, until rice is almost tender and lobster is cooked through, about 10 minutes.

Scatter peas on top. (If the liquid evaporates before the rice is tender, add more hot stock.) Cook without stirring, allowing rice to absorb all the liquid, so that a crust (the socarrat) develops on the bottom and the edges begin to dry out and get crusty, 5 to 10 minutes longer, for a total cooking time of about 40 minutes.

Remove pan from grill. Cover with large clean kitchen towels and let rest for 5 minutes. Garnish with parsley and serve with lemons, making sure to scrape some socarrat from the bottom of the pan onto each plate.

ROSEMARY-SKEWERED SCALLOPS

photo, right

12 large diver scallops, side muscle removed

4 6-inch sprigs rosemary

2 Tbsp. extra-virgin olive oil, plus more for brushing

Kosher salt and freshly ground black pepper

1 large lemon, halved crosswise

In this rustic dish, sturdy fresh rosemary sprigs serve as the skewers. First, trim the sprigs to roughly 6-inch lengths, then use a small knife to carefully whittle the thicker ends to a point. Thread the scallops onto the rosemary skewers. It's easier than it sounds, and it will give you loads of flavor with only six ingredients.

Thread 3 scallops onto each rosemary sprig. Drizzle with 2 Tbsp. oil and season with salt and pepper.

Build a medium-hot fire in a charcoal grill, or heat a gas grill to high. Brush grill grate with oil. Place lemon halves, cut side down, on grill. Grill scallops until golden brown and just opaque in center, 3 to 4 minutes per side. Transfer to plates and serve caramelized lemon halves on the side for squeezing over.

GREEK-STYLE SEA SCALLOPS

2 Tbsp. extra-virgin olive oil, plus more for brushing

2 large garlic cloves, minced

1½ Tbsp. chopped fresh oregano or 1½ tsp. dried

Kosher salt and freshly ground black pepper

12 large sea scallops, side muscle removed

1 large lemon, halved lengthwise, each half cut crosswise into 6 slices to create half-moons

8 bay leaves or fresh bay leaves

SPECIAL EQUIPMENT 4 metal skewers

The garlic, oregano, lemon, and olive oil that season the scallops are hallmarks of Greek cooking. The seasoned oil works well with peeled large shrimp, too.

Whisk 2 Tbsp. oil, garlic, and oregano in a medium bowl. Season to taste with salt and pepper. Add sea scallops and toss to coat.

Build a medium-hot fire in a charcoal grill, or heat a gas grill to high. Brush grill grate with oil. Thread 3 scallops, 3 lemon slices, and 2 bay leaves alternately onto each skewer. Grill scallops until golden brown and just opaque in the center, 3 to 4 minutes per side.

For best results with this simple dish, **use hardy rosemary.** The more delicate variety won't work here.

ROSEMARY-SKEWERED SCALLOPS

SCALLOPS AND NECTARINES
with Corn and Tomato Salad

DRESSING

- 3 Tbsp. fresh lime juice
- 1½ tsp. finely grated lime zest
- ⅛ tsp. (heaping) piment d'Espelette or chili powder
- 3 Tbsp. extra-virgin olive oil
  Kosher salt and freshly ground black pepper

BASIL PURÉE

- ¾ cup (loosely packed) fresh basil leaves
- ¼ cup extra-virgin olive oil
  Kosher salt

SALAD

- Extra-virgin olive oil, for brushing
- 3 firm but ripe nectarines (white or yellow), each cut into 6 wedges
- 24 large sea scallops, side muscle removed
  Kosher salt and freshly ground black pepper
- 1½ cups fresh corn kernels (about 2 large ears of corn)
- 24 grape tomatoes or cherry tomatoes, halved
- ⅓ cup thinly sliced fresh basil leaves
  Kosher salt

INGREDIENT INFO Piment d'Espelette is the ground powder of a small, dried, hot red chile grown in Espelette, France. It is available at specialty foods stores and from zingermans.com.

This main-course salad features beautiful summer ingredients, including sweet, crisp corn and fresh basil. Blanching the basil leaves before you purée them helps them retain their bright green color.

DRESSING

Whisk lime juice, lime zest, and piment d'Espelette in a small bowl. Gradually whisk in oil. Season dressing to taste with salt and pepper. **DO AHEAD:** Can be made 1 day ahead. Cover and chill. Bring to room temperature and rewhisk before using.

BASIL PURÉE

Blanch basil in a small pot of boiling salted water for 30 seconds; drain. Squeeze to remove as much water as possible, then coarsely chop. Purée basil and oil in a blender until smooth. Transfer to a small bowl. Season to taste with salt. **DO AHEAD:** Can be made 1 day ahead. Cover and chill. Bring to room temperature before using.

SALAD

Build a medium-hot fire in a charcoal grill, or heat a gas grill to high. Brush grill grate with oil. Brush nectarines, then scallops with oil; season with salt and pepper. Grill scallops until golden brown and just opaque in the center, 3 to 4 minutes per side. Grill nectarines until slightly charred, 1 to 2 minutes per side. Transfer scallops and nectarines to a platter.

Arrange 4 scallops on each plate. Toss corn and 2 Tbsp. dressing in a medium bowl. Toss tomatoes with 1 Tbsp. dressing in another medium bowl; season to taste with salt and pepper. Spoon corn around scallops. Scatter tomatoes over corn. Arrange nectarine wedges decoratively on plates. Drizzle some dressing over scallops, then spoon some basil purée over. Sprinkle sliced basil leaves and salt over salad and serve.

MANILA CLAMS
with Lemon-Ginger Butter and Grilled Baguette

4 to 6 first-course servings

6 Tbsp. (¾ stick) unsalted butter, room temperature
2 Tbsp. minced shallot
1½ Tbsp. fresh lemon juice
1½ Tbsp. minced flat-leaf parsley
¾ tsp. finely grated lemon zest
¾ tsp. minced peeled ginger
Kosher salt and freshly ground black pepper
6 ½-inch-thick diagonal-cut baguette slices
3 lb. Manila clams or small littleneck clams, scrubbed

SPECIAL EQUIPMENT A foil baking pan

These small Manila clams are grill-roasted—placed in a foil pan and cooked in a closed grill. This way all their juices, instead of being lost to the grill, are saved in the pan and then blended with the luscious lemon-ginger butter.

Build a medium-hot fire in a charcoal grill, or heat a gas grill to high. Using a rubber spatula, blend butter, shallot, lemon juice, parsley, lemon zest, and ginger in a small bowl; season to taste with salt and pepper. Thinly spread lemon-ginger butter on 1 side of each bread slice.

Arrange clams in single layer in foil pan. Place pan on grill grate, cover grill, and cook just until clams open, 8 to 10 minutes (discard any clams that do not open).

Using a slotted spoon, transfer grilled clams to shallow bowls, dividing evenly. Grill bread until slightly charred, 1 to 2 minutes per side. Add remaining lemon-ginger butter to juices in pan; stir on grill until melted. Pour juices from pan over clams. Serve with bread.

GRILL-ROASTED CLAM LINGUINE

4 servings

¼ cup extra-virgin olive oil
4 garlic cloves, chopped
1½ tsp. finely grated lemon zest, divided
¾ tsp. crushed red pepper flakes
1⅓ cups Sauvignon Blanc or other non-oaky white wine
2½ Tbsp. fresh lemon juice
3 anchovy fillets packed in oil, drained, minced (optional)
2 Tbsp. chopped flat-leaf parsley, divided
Kosher salt
4 dozen small littleneck clams, scrubbed
12 oz. linguine
Lemon wedges, for serving

The classic Italian pasta dish is even better when the clams are grilled and tossed with a garlic-lemon-wine sauce. Clams cooked on the grill pop open when done, just as they do when steamed. Uncover the grill during the last 5 minutes to keep an eye on the clams and watch them open up.

Heat oil in a small deep saucepan over medium-low heat. Add garlic, ¾ tsp. lemon zest, and red pepper flakes. Sauté until garlic is soft, about 3 minutes. Add wine, increase heat, and boil until mixture is reduced to 1 cup, about 6 minutes. Remove sauce from heat; mix in lemon juice, anchovies, 1 Tbsp. parsley, and remaining ¾ tsp. lemon zest. Season to taste with salt. **DO AHEAD:** Can be made 2 hours ahead. Let stand at room temperature. Rewarm before using.

Build a medium-hot fire in a charcoal grill, or heat a gas grill to high. Arrange clams on grill grate. Cover grill. Cook clams for 5 minutes. Uncover and cook without turning until clams open, transferring clams, retaining juices in shells, to a rimmed baking sheet as they open, about 5 minutes longer (discard any clams that do not open).

Meanwhile, cook pasta, stirring occasionally, in a large pot of boiling salted water until just tender but still firm to the bite. Drain pasta and transfer to a large bowl. Add sauce and remaining 1 Tbsp. parsley and toss vigorously to combine. Gently stir in clams and divide among bowls. Serve with lemon wedges.

SALT-GRILLED OYSTERS
with Bacon and Cayenne Butter

photo, right

3 slices hickory-smoked or applewood-smoked bacon, cut crosswise into ½-inch-wide strips

1 cup (2 sticks) unsalted butter, cut into ½-inch cubes

4 garlic cloves

1½ Tbsp. chopped flat-leaf parsley

1½ Tbsp. chopped fresh cilantro

½ tsp. cayenne pepper

½ tsp. kosher salt

½ tsp. freshly ground black pepper

2½ Tbsp. dry white wine

2 Tbsp. fresh lemon juice
   Rock salt

24 freshly shucked oysters (such as Malpeque or bluepoint), on the half shell

Talk about decadent: Oysters are grilled on a bed of rock salt while a pat of bacon-cayenne butter melts over them. When making the butter, add the wine and lemon juice slowly while the food processor is running; this will ensure that the mixture is emulsified—which simply means that the butter is uniformly dispersed in the liquid to create a creamy consistency. If you wrap it tightly, the butter will keep for a month in the freezer.

Cook bacon in a medium heavy skillet over medium heat, stirring occasionally, until crisp. Using a slotted spoon, transfer bacon to a food processor. Add butter, garlic, parsley, cilantro, cayenne, kosher salt, and black pepper and pulse, occasionally scraping down sides of bowl, until smooth. With machine running, gradually add wine, then lemon juice; continue to process until blended.

Transfer butter mixture to a sheet of parchment paper, waxed paper, or plastic wrap, placing on edge closest to you. Fold paper over and roll butter mixture into a 2-inch-diameter log, using paper as aid. Twist ends tightly. Chill butter until firm, at least 2 hours. **DO AHEAD:** Can be made 2 days ahead. Keep chilled.

Build a medium-hot fire in a charcoal grill, or heat a gas grill to high. Spread ½-inch-thick layer of rock salt on a large rimmed baking sheet. Place baking sheet on grill grate and heat for 20 minutes.

Cut twenty-four ⅛-inch-thick rounds from cayenne-butter log. Transfer hot baking sheet from grill to a heatproof surface. Nestle oysters in hot rock salt. Top each oyster with a slice of cayenne butter.

Return baking sheet with oysters to grill grate. Close grill and cook until butter melts and starts to brown, 6 to 8 minutes. Spoon a shallow layer of additional rock salt onto each plate. Nestle 4 grilled oysters in salt on each plate and serve.

If you end up with a little bit of extra seasoned butter, **spread it onto grilled bread** or melt a pat on top of a grilled steak.

SALT-GRILLED OYSTERS
WITH BACON AND CAYENNE BUTTER

WHOLE CALAMARI
with White Bean Salad

1 lb. fresh or thawed frozen cleaned calamari (whole bodies only; reserve tentacles for another use)

1 cup extra-virgin olive oil, divided, plus more for brushing

1 Tbsp. chopped fresh oregano

1 Tbsp. chopped fresh thyme

3 garlic cloves, minced

2 Tbsp. (packed) chopped fresh chives

2 Tbsp. (packed) fresh basil leaves

1 Tbsp. fresh lemon juice
   Kosher salt and freshly ground black pepper

2 15-oz. cans small white beans, rinsed, drained

2 8-oz. bottles clam juice

1 small onion, quartered through root end

2 bay leaves

2 Tbsp. finely chopped flat-leaf parsley

1 5-oz. package mixed baby greens

Instead of the more common rings used for fried calamari, this recipe uses whole grilled calamari bodies; save the tentacles to make fried calamari another time. And yes, calamari really does take just minutes to cook—any longer and it gets tough and rubbery.

Mix calamari, ½ cup oil, oregano, thyme, and garlic in a medium bowl. Let marinate at room temperature for 1 hour.

Purée ¼ cup oil, chives, and basil in a blender until only small pieces of herbs remain. Strain herb oil through a fine-mesh sieve into a small bowl, pressing on solids to release as much oil as possible; discard solids in sieve.

Whisk ¼ cup oil and lemon juice in another small bowl. Season lemon vinaigrette to taste with salt and pepper. **DO AHEAD:** Calamari, herb oil, and lemon vinaigrette can be prepared 1 day ahead. Cover separately and chill. Bring herb oil and vinaigrette to room temperature and rewhisk before using.

Bring beans, clam juice, onion, and bay leaves to a boil in a medium saucepan. Reduce heat to medium-low and simmer until onion softens and flavors blend, about 15 minutes. **DO AHEAD:** Can be made 2 hours ahead. Let stand at room temperature.

Build a medium-hot fire in a charcoal grill, or heat a gas grill to high. Brush grill grate with oil. Remove calamari from marinade, with some marinade still clinging, and place on a grill grate. Season with salt and pepper. Grill calamari until slightly charred and beginning to puff up, 1 to 2 minutes per side. Transfer calamari to a plate; tent with foil to keep warm.

Rewarm beans. Drain; discard onion and bay leaves. Stir parsley into beans. Place greens in a large bowl. Drizzle lemon vinaigrette over; toss to coat. Season salad to taste with salt and pepper; divide among plates. Spoon white beans onto each plate alongside salad, dividing equally. Top white beans with calamari. Drizzle herb oil over calamari and serve.

SHRIMP SPINACH SALAD

with Fennel and Bacon-Balsamic Vinaigrette

6 servings

- 6 Tbsp. extra-virgin olive oil, plus more for brushing
- 1 Tbsp. fennel seeds, crushed
- 1 tsp. crushed red pepper flakes
- 1¾ lb. large shrimp, peeled, deveined
- Kosher salt and freshly ground black pepper
- 2 fennel bulbs (about 12 oz. total), fronds chopped, bulbs cut into ⅓-inch-thick wedges with some core still attached to each wedge
- 12 oz. baby spinach leaves
- 2 cups chopped seeded peeled tomatoes
- Bacon-Balsamic Vinaigrette (recipe follows)

SPECIAL EQUIPMENT 12 metal skewers

Classic spinach salad with warm bacon dressing is easily adapted for the grill and updated with the addition of shrimp and a double hit of fennel: both fresh grilled fennel bulbs and crushed fennel seeds in the marinade.

Mix 6 Tbsp. oil, fennel seeds, and red pepper flakes in a small bowl. Thread shrimp onto skewers, dividing evenly. Place on a rimmed baking sheet. Pour oil mixture over; turn to coat. Season with salt and pepper. Cover and chill for 30 minutes.

Build a medium-hot fire in a charcoal grill, or heat a gas grill to high. Brush fennel wedges with oil. Season with salt and pepper. Brush grill grate with oil. Grill fennel until golden and beginning to soften, about 3 minutes per side. Transfer to a large bowl. Grill shrimp until just opaque in the center, 2 to 3 minutes per side. Transfer shrimp to a plate; tent with foil.

Add spinach and tomatoes to fennel. Toss with enough warm Bacon-Balsamic Vinaigrette to coat. Divide salad among plates. Sprinkle with bacon reserved from vinaigrette. Remove shrimp from skewers and arrange around salad. Garnish with fennel fronds.

Bacon-Balsamic Vinaigrette

makes about 1 cup

use with shrimp spinach salad

- 5 slices thick-cut bacon, cut crosswise into ½-inch pieces
- 5 Tbsp. extra-virgin olive oil
- ¼ cup balsamic vinegar
- 3 Tbsp. minced shallot
- 3 garlic cloves, minced
- 1 Tbsp. (packed) light brown sugar
- Kosher salt and freshly ground black pepper

Instead of heating up the kitchen, you can also cook this dressing in an ovenproof skillet right on the grill.

Cook bacon in a large heavy skillet over medium heat, stirring occasionally, until crisp. Using a slotted spoon, transfer bacon to paper towels to drain (reserve as garnish for Shrimp Spinach Salad). Pour off all but 3 Tbsp. drippings from skillet; whisk oil into drippings in skillet.

Whisk vinegar, shallot, garlic, and brown sugar in a small bowl. Add to drippings and oil in skillet. Stir over medium-low heat just until warm. Season to taste with salt and pepper. Use vinaigrette warm.

GAZPACHO SALAD
WITH SHRIMP

6 servings

2 medium heads of garlic, separated into cloves (about 24), peeled

12 Tbsp. extra-virgin olive oil, divided, plus more for brushing

1½ lb. shell-on large shrimp, deveined
Kosher salt and freshly ground black pepper

8 firm plum tomatoes, halved lengthwise

2 bunches scallions, root ends trimmed

1 1-lb. sweet onion (such as Vidalia or Maui), cut into ½-inch-thick slices

1 red bell pepper, quartered, cored

1 yellow bell pepper, quartered, cored

1½ large cucumbers, preferably English hothouse, peeled, halved lengthwise

2 6x3x1-inch slices country-style bread

2 cups grape tomatoes (about 1 pint), halved

¼ cup red wine vinegar

1 tsp. hot pepper sauce

½ cup thinly sliced fresh basil
Lime wedges, for serving

Gazpacho is transformed into an Italian *panzanella* (bread salad): The vegetables are grilled and then tossed with cubes of garlicky grilled bread and a red wine vinaigrette. Adding grilled shrimp creates a delicious main-course salad. A large rimmed baking sheet comes in handy to hold the grilled vegetables.

Build a medium-hot fire in a charcoal grill, or heat a gas grill to high. Set aside 2 garlic cloves for bread slices. Place remaining garlic on a double layer of heavy-duty foil; drizzle 3 Tbsp. oil over. Fold up foil around garlic and seal packet. Place directly on grill grate and cook until garlic is very tender and golden, about 30 minutes. Open packet; let garlic cool.

Toss shrimp and 1 Tbsp. oil in a medium bowl to coat; season with salt and pepper. Combine plum tomatoes, scallions, sweet onion, bell peppers, and 2 Tbsp. oil in a large bowl; toss to coat. Arrange cucumber halves and bread slices on a baking sheet; brush with 2 Tbsp. oil. Season all vegetables with salt and pepper.

Brush grill grate with oil. Grill shrimp until just opaque in the center, 2 to 3 minutes per side; transfer to another medium bowl and let cool. Grill vegetables, turning frequently, until crisp-tender, about 3 minutes for plum tomatoes and scallions, 5 minutes for cucumbers, and 10 minutes for sweet onion and bell peppers. Transfer vegetables to a large rimmed baking sheet. Grill bread slices until just beginning to crisp and grill marks appear, about 2½ minutes per side. Rub bread with reserved garlic cloves, then discard garlic cloves.

Peel shrimp; transfer to a large bowl. Cut all vegetables and bread into ½- to ¾-inch pieces; add to shrimp along with any accumulated juices. Stir in grilled garlic cloves and grape tomatoes. Whisk remaining 4 Tbsp. oil, vinegar, and hot pepper sauce in a small bowl; pour over salad and toss to coat. **DO AHEAD:** Can be made 1 hour ahead. Let stand at room temperature.

Stir basil into salad. Season to taste with salt and pepper. Serve with lime wedges for squeezing over.

SHRIMP SALAD
with Corn and Avocado

VINAIGRETTE

- 1½ tsp. finely grated orange zest
- 6 Tbsp. fresh orange juice
- 3½ Tbsp. white wine vinegar
- 2 Tbsp. chopped fresh chives
- ¼ cup extra-virgin olive oil
  Kosher salt and freshly ground
  black pepper

SALAD

- 1 10-oz. bag red pearl onions
- 2 lb. large shrimp, peeled, deveined
- 3 large ears of corn, husked
- 1 ciabatta or pain rustique, cut
  crosswise into 1-inch-thick slices
  Extra-virgin olive oil, for brushing
  Kosher salt and freshly ground
  black pepper
- 2 tsp. hot smoked Spanish paprika
- 12 cups mâche (about 7 oz.)
- 2 avocados, halved, pitted, peeled,
  cut into ¾-inch cubes

INGREDIENT INFO Hot smoked Spanish paprika is sometimes labeled Pimentón Picante or Pimentón de La Vera Picante. It is available at specialty foods stores and from latienda.com.

SPECIAL EQUIPMENT 12 metal skewers

Almost all the ingredients in this fresh summer salad are grilled: the shrimp, pearl onions, corn, and bread slices. Then they're tossed with avocados and mâche, a tender lettuce with small leaves and a mild flavor. Because it is so delicate, keep the mâche well chilled and add it to the salad just before serving so it doesn't become limp. If you can't find mâche, use butter lettuce instead and tear it into bite-size pieces.

VINAIGRETTE

Whisk orange zest, orange juice, vinegar, and chives in a small bowl. Slowly whisk in oil. Season vinaigrette to taste with salt and pepper. **DO AHEAD:** Can be made 4 hours ahead. Cover and chill. Bring to room temperature and rewhisk before using.

SALAD

Bring a small saucepan of water to a boil. Add pearl onions and boil for 3 minutes. Drain; let onions cool slightly. Peel onions, leaving root ends intact. **DO AHEAD:** Can be made 4 hours ahead. Cover and let stand at room temperature.

Build a medium fire in a charcoal grill, or heat a gas grill to medium-high. Thread pearl onions onto skewers; thread shrimp onto separate skewers. Place onion skewers, shrimp skewers, corn, and bread slices on 2 large rimmed baking sheets. Brush onions, shrimp, corn, and bread with oil; season with salt and pepper. Sprinkle shrimp on both sides with paprika. Brush grill grate with oil. Grill onions and corn until tender, about 5 minutes per side. Grill bread slices until browned. Grill shrimp until just opaque in center, 2 to 3 minutes per side.

Transfer vegetables, shrimp, and bread to a work surface. Cut corn kernels off cobs; place corn kernels in a very large bowl. Remove shrimp and onions from skewers and add to bowl. Add mâche and avocados. Drizzle salad with dressing to coat and toss. Season to taste with salt and pepper. Transfer salad to a large rimmed platter and serve with bread.

VEGETABLES

WHAT'S THE SECRET

to preparing beautifully grilled vegetables that are tender on the inside and touched with a caramelized char on the outside? Well, start by buying fresh, ripe vegetables that are in season. Choose what you think looks beautiful—from height-of-summer sweet corn and shiny aubergine eggplant to fingerling potatoes or even grocery-store red onions. Whatever you choose, the heat of a grill will extract the natural sugars within them, and a drizzle of balsamic vinegar, a pat of butter, or a splash of *salsa verde* will supply the finishing touches.

Whether your main course is a whole grilled fish, a rack of dry-rubbed ribs, or a platter of plump and juicy burgers, it deserves satisfying, beautiful accompaniments. And the grilled vegetables on the following pages are exactly what you want.

NEW POTATOES
with Parmesan and Herbs

3 lb. unpeeled medium
   red-skinned potatoes
   Kosher salt
4 Tbsp. extra-virgin olive oil,
   divided, plus more for brushing
   Freshly ground black pepper
1 cup thinly sliced scallions
3 Tbsp. chopped flat-leaf parsley
3 Tbsp. freshly grated
   Parmesan
3 garlic cloves, finely chopped
2 tsp. chopped fresh oregano

Fresh oregano and parsley, along with a hearty handful of grated Parmesan, enliven grilled new potatoes. It's important to boil the potatoes before grilling to achieve the ideal crisp-on-the-outside, creamy-in-the-center balance.

Cook potatoes in a large pot of boiling salted water until tender, about 15 minutes. Drain potatoes; let cool.

Build a medium fire in a charcoal grill, or heat a gas grill to medium-high. Cut potatoes in half; transfer to a large bowl. Add 2 Tbsp. oil; toss to coat. Season with salt and pepper and toss again. Brush grill grate with oil. Grill potatoes until golden, turning occasionally, about 5 minutes. Transfer to a shallow bowl. Drizzle remaining 2 Tbsp. oil over. Add all remaining ingredients; toss to coat. Season to taste with salt and pepper. Serve warm.

FINGERLING POTATOES
with Niçoise Olives and Scallions

1½ lb. fingerling potatoes
2 Tbsp. extra-virgin olive oil
   Kosher salt and freshly ground
   black pepper
¼ cup Niçoise olives, pitted, halved
4 scallions, thinly sliced diagonally

INGREDIENT INFO Niçoise olives are small, brine-cured black olives sold at some supermarkets and at specialty foods stores and Italian markets.

Here's an ideal way to put a grill basket to work. If the basket's holes are small enough, you can even throw the olives and scallions in with the potatoes toward the end of the cooking time.

Build a medium fire in a charcoal grill, or heat a gas grill to medium-high. Cut in half lengthwise any potatoes that are larger than your thumb. Toss potatoes with oil in a large bowl. Season with salt and pepper. Transfer to a grill basket.

Grill, shaking basket frequently, until potatoes are golden brown on all sides and tender, about 15 minutes. Transfer potatoes to a large bowl. Immediately add olives and scallions to hot potatoes and toss to coat.

CAMPFIRE POTATOES

photo, right

16 medium Yukon Gold potatoes (about 2 inches in diameter), halved
3 Tbsp. kosher salt
2 Tbsp. extra-virgin olive oil
6 unpeeled large garlic cloves, smashed
1 tsp. chopped fresh thyme
½ tsp. finely chopped fresh rosemary

This camping-friendly method will reward you with the irresistible aroma of garlic and herbs—just be careful when you unwrap the foil after the potatoes are done cooking, as there will be a release of very hot steam.

Place potatoes in a large saucepan. Add salt and enough water to cover by 1 inch. Bring to a boil, then reduce heat to medium-low, and simmer potatoes until tender, about 10 minutes. Drain. Return to same saucepan. Add all remaining ingredients to potatoes; toss to coat. Let cool.

Arrange six 12-inch squares of foil on a work surface. Divide potato mixture among foil squares, placing 1 garlic clove atop potatoes on each square. Crimp foil to seal packets. **DO AHEAD:** Can be made 2 hours ahead. Let stand at room temperature.

Build a medium-hot fire in a charcoal grill, or heat a gas grill to high. Place potato packets on grill and cook, turning occasionally, until heated through and sizzling, about 15 minutes. Transfer packets to plates. Pierce foil with a fork to release steam. Open packets carefully (hot steam will escape).

BALSAMIC RADICCHIO
with Pecorino

⅓ cup extra-virgin olive oil, plus more for brushing
¼ cup balsamic vinegar
6 garlic cloves, chopped
1 Tbsp. chopped fresh rosemary
1 tsp. finely grated orange zest
½ tsp. crushed red pepper flakes
  Kosher salt and freshly ground black pepper
4 large heads of radicchio, each quartered through core end
3 oz. Pecorino, shaved with a vegetable peeler

A dunk in a balsamic marinade and a quick turn on the grill mellows and sweetens radicchio's bite. Use tongs when handling the radicchio to keep the wedges intact. Pair with grilled pork chops or chicken.

Build a medium fire in a charcoal grill, or heat a gas grill to medium-high. Whisk ⅓ cup oil and next 5 ingredients in a large bowl to blend. Season marinade to taste with salt and pepper. Mix in radicchio; marinate for 15 minutes.

Brush grill grate with oil. Using tongs, arrange radicchio on grill; season with salt and pepper. Grill, turning occasionally, until edges are slightly charred, about 6 minutes. Transfer radicchio to a platter. Drizzle with remaining marinade and sprinkle with shaved cheese.

+ This recipe calls for Yukon Golds, but **fingerlings, baby reds, and creamer potatoes** are also terrific for packets on the grill.

CAMPFIRE POTATOES

10
Great VEGETABLES for GRILLING

The colors and textures of grilled vegetables are a delicious addition to any meal. When you're dealing with smaller vegetables that might fall through the grate, thread them onto skewers or throw them into a cast-iron skillet or a grill basket.

ASPARAGUS

Snap the fibrous ends off of thin asparagus, or peel fat asparagus. **Grill whole**, spreading them in a single layer perpendicular to the grill grate. Drizzle with extra-virgin olive oil and sprinkle with sea salt.

ONIONS

Cut **½-inch-thick slices** and skewer them (one skewer down the left, one down the right). For **wedges**, cut onion in half, keeping part of core attached. Season with extra-virgin olive oil, salt, and balsamic vinegar. Once grilled, cover with foil until you're ready to serve, and let them steam.

EGGPLANT

Cut larger eggplant **crosswise into ½-inch rounds**. Long, thin Asian eggplant varieties can be **halved lengthwise**. Small, colorful heirloom varieties are also popping up—you can **grill them whole**, thread them onto skewers, or toss them into a grill basket.

FENNEL

Trim stalks and fronds. **Cut the bulb into slices or wedges**, keeping some core attached to help the layers stay intact. Brush with oil before putting it on the grill.

SWEET POTATOES

Peel the potatoes and **slice lengthwise** into ½-inch pieces. Brush with extra-virgin olive oil, sprinkle with sea salt, then grill them over medium heat. Once they're cooked, serve with a vinaigrette of olive oil and lime juice, and a handful of herbs.

GRILLED PEPPERS

Grill **halved and seeded** peppers, then chop into smaller pieces for serving. Consider using different colors for a colorful plate. You can also **char whole peppers** on the grill, then peel and cut into strips.

GREENS & LEAFY VEGETABLES

Greens, endive, and radicchio are great when grilled. Cut **smaller heads in half** lengthwise. Quarter **larger greens lengthwise** (leave core attached so they hold together). Top with a vinaigrette and Parmesan cheese.

TOMATOES

Use firm, ripe fruit to prevent them from falling through the grate. **Cut larger tomatoes in half**; the skin helps them hold together. Leave smaller cherry and grape varieties whole, and grill them **using skewers or a basket**. Spike with lemon juice and chopped fresh herbs.

ZUCCHINI

Cut large zucchini lengthwise **into ½-inch-wide strips** or on a sharp diagonal into ½-inch-wide slices. Smaller squash can be **halved lengthwise**. If you find the really small baby varieties, they can be **grilled whole**.

MUSHROOMS

Large mushrooms, such as portobello or bigger shiitakes, can be **grilled whole, torn into pieces, or sliced**. For smaller varieties, such as button mushrooms, **skewer them or cook in a cast-iron skillet**. Remove the tough stems from shiitake mushrooms, if using. Garnish with torn basil.

VEGETABLE MEDLEY
with Lemon, Thyme, and Mustard Basting Sauce

BASTING SAUCE
- ½ cup (1 stick) unsalted butter, diced
- ⅓ cup chopped shallots
- ¼ cup extra-virgin olive oil
- 3 Tbsp. Dijon mustard
- 2 Tbsp. fresh lemon juice
- 2 Tbsp. chopped fresh thyme
- 1 Tbsp. grated lemon zest
  Kosher salt and freshly ground black pepper

VEGETABLES
- 2 large ears of corn, husked, each cut crosswise into 4 pieces
- 1 1-lb. eggplant, trimmed, cut into ½-inch-thick rounds
- 1 large red onion, peeled, cut through root end into ¾-inch thick wedges with some core attached to each
- 1 large red bell pepper, seeded, cut lengthwise into 6 strips
- 1 large yellow or green bell pepper, seeded, sliced into 6 strips
- 1 zucchini, quartered lengthwise
- 8 asparagus spears, trimmed
- 1 large carrot, peeled, cut on a deep diagonal into ¼-inch slices
  Vegetable oil, for brushing
  Kosher salt and freshly ground black pepper
  Lemon wedges, for serving

Make sure your vegetables are cut into pieces small enough to cook through in just a few minutes (this is a great use for a grill basket). A soft, wide pastry brush is the best tool for applying an even coating of the basting sauce. Any combination of the vegetables listed here will do.

BASTING SAUCE
Combine first 7 ingredients in a medium heavy saucepan. Whisk over medium heat until butter melts and sauce is well blended. Season to taste with salt and pepper. **DO AHEAD:** Can be made 3 hours ahead. Cover and chill. Whisk over low heat to rewarm before using.

VEGETABLES
Arrange corn pieces, eggplant rounds, and onion wedges in a single layer on a large rimmed baking sheet. Arrange bell pepper strips, zucchini spears, asparagus spears, and carrot slices in a single layer on another large rimmed baking sheet. Transfer ½ cup sauce to a small saucepan and reserve for dipping. Brush both sides of vegetables lightly with some of remaining basting sauce.

Build a medium-hot fire in a charcoal grill, or heat a gas grill to high. Brush grill grate with oil. Grill corn, eggplant, and onion, brushing occasionally with basting sauce and turning with tongs, until tender and lightly charred, 6 to 8 minutes. Transfer to a large platter as vegetables finish grilling. Tent loosely with foil to keep warm.

Grill bell peppers, zucchini, asparagus, and carrot, brushing occasionally with basting sauce and turning with tongs, until tender and lightly charred, about 6 minutes. Transfer to same platter, arranging alongside other vegetables. Season all vegetables with salt and pepper. Garnish platter with lemon wedges.

Place saucepan with reserved ½ cup sauce at edge of grill and whisk until warmed through. Transfer to a small bowl. Serve vegetables, passing warm dipping sauce separately.

+

Colorful baby squash and juicy tomatoes shine in **this simple preparation:** just olive oil, salt and pepper, and fresh basil.

BLISTERED BABY SQUASH
WITH GRILLED TOMATOES

GAZPACHO
with Tomatillos and Pepitas

Vegetable oil, for brushing

½ cup (generous) unsalted shelled pumpkin seeds (pepitas, about 2½ oz.)

2 lb. tomatillos, husked, rinsed

1 fresh poblano chile

1 garlic clove, pressed

1 cup vegetable broth

Kosher salt and freshly ground black pepper

⅓ cup chopped scallions

¼ cup chopped fresh cilantro

¼ cup extra-virgin olive oil

1 small diced unpeeled cucumber (preferably English hothouse)

1 avocado, pitted, peeled, diced

1 12-oz. container cherry tomatoes, halved or quartered if large

This bright Mexican take on gazpacho is an awesome showcase for tomatillos. Their tartness is tamed with grilling—and paired with a bit of crunch, thanks to *pepitas* (pumpkin seeds). Charred poblano adds a smoky note; look for it at a supermarket or Latin market. The soup needs to chill for a few hours before serving.

Build a medium-hot fire in a charcoal grill, or heat a gas grill to high. Brush grill grate with vegetable oil. Finely grind pepitas in a food processor; leave in processor. Grill tomatillos and poblano chile, turning occasionally, until tomatillos are slightly charred and soft and chile is charred all over, 12 to 15 minutes. Add tomatillos to processor. Peel, seed, and coarsely chop chile; add to processor. Add garlic; process to a coarse purée. Transfer to a large bowl. Stir in vegetable broth. Season soup to taste with salt and pepper. Cover; chill until cold, about 3 hours.

   Mix in scallions and all remaining ingredients. Divide soup among bowls.

BLISTERED BABY SQUASH
with Grilled Tomatoes

photo, left

Extra-virgin live oil, for brushing

2 cups yellow and green baby pattypan squash (9 to 10 oz.)

6 baby zucchini

6 medium tomatoes, each halved through core

Kosher salt and freshly ground black pepper

Chopped fresh basil or oregano, for garnish

Any small vegetable can be prepared with the simple grilling technique used here. Experiment with new potatoes, baby artichokes, or whatever else is in season.

Build a medium-hot fire in a charcoal grill, or heat a gas grill to high. Brush grill grate with oil. Brush pattypan squash, zucchini, and tomatoes with oil; season vegetables generously with salt and pepper. Grill vegetables, turning occasionally and repositioning for even grilling, until blistered and slightly charred, about 8 minutes for squash and zucchini and about 6 minutes for tomatoes. Transfer vegetables to a platter; sprinkle with basil.

SESAME EGGPLANT
with Scallions

photo, right

½ cup extra-virgin olive oil, plus more for brushing

5 large scallions, 4 coarsely chopped, 1 thinly sliced for garnish

2 Tbsp. reduced-sodium soy sauce

2 tsp. toasted sesame oil

2 tsp. sesame seeds
  Freshly ground black pepper

2 large eggplants (about 2½ lb. total), cut crosswise into ½-inch thick slices

Eggplant is sensational charred and tenderized on the grill. This preparation with a soy-sesame sauce pairs especially well with grilled black cod or other white fish, or with pork tenderloin. Serve it warm or at room temperature.

Purée ½ cup olive oil, chopped scallions, soy sauce, and sesame oil in a blender. Transfer mixture to a small bowl. Stir in sesame seeds; season mixture with pepper. **DO AHEAD:** Can be made 1 day ahead. Cover and chill.

  Build a medium-hot fire in a charcoal grill, or heat a gas grill to high. Brush grill grate with oil. Generously brush 1 side of each eggplant slice with scallion mixture. Place eggplant slices, seasoned side down, on grill. Brush tops of eggplant slices with scallion mixture. Grill until tender and charred in spots, about 4 minutes per side. Transfer to a platter. Garnish with thinly sliced scallions. Serve eggplant warm or at room temperature. **DO AHEAD:** Can be made 2 hours ahead. Let stand at room temperature.

QUICK-GRILLED JAPANESE EGGPLANT

3 Japanese eggplants, trimmed, halved lengthwise
  Kosher salt and freshly ground black pepper

⅓ cup extra-virgin olive oil, plus more for brushing

1 Tbsp. chopped fresh mint

2 garlic cloves, pressed

½ tsp. crushed red pepper flakes

½ tsp. ground cumin

¼ tsp. ground cinnamon

No need for a long soak: Slender and tender Japanese eggplant needs just a quick coat of garlicky marinade before grilling. Drizzle any leftover marinade over grilled chicken.

Build a medium-hot fire in a charcoal grill, or heat a gas grill to high. Arrange eggplant, cut sides up, on a large rimmed baking sheet; season with salt and pepper. Whisk ⅓ cup oil, mint, garlic, crushed red pepper flakes, cumin, and cinnamon in a small bowl to blend. Season oil mixture to taste with salt and pepper. Brush oil mixture generously over cut sides of eggplant. Let stand for 10 minutes.

  Brush grill grate with oil. Arrange eggplant on grill, cut sides down. Grill until beginning to brown and grill marks appear, 3 to 4 minutes. Turn eggplant over. Grill until tender, 4 to 5 minutes longer. Transfer to a platter; brush with any remaining oil mixture.

+

Long, slender Japanese eggplant would also work well with the **Asian-inspired flavors** of this scallion-sesame sauce.

SESAME EGGPLANT WITH SCALLIONS

CORN
with Honey–Ancho Chile Butter

8 servings

8   Tbsp. (1 stick) unsalted
       butter, room temperature,
       divided
1   Tbsp. ground ancho chiles
1   tsp. ground cumin
1   Tbsp. honey
½   tsp. dried oregano
½   tsp. kosher salt
¼   tsp. granulated garlic or
       garlic powder
¼   tsp. onion powder
       Vegetable oil, for brushing
8   ears of corn, husked

INGREDIENT INFO Ground ancho
chiles are available in the spice
section of many supermarkets
and at Latin markets.

This side dish pairs sweet grilled corn with ground ancho chile and a drizzle of honey. Briefly warming the spices in melted butter releases their aromatic oils. Pair any leftover chile butter with roasted sweet potatoes or cornbread.

Melt 2 Tbsp. butter in a small skillet over medium-low heat. Add ground chiles and cumin; stir for 10 seconds. Transfer to a medium bowl; whisk in honey and let cool for 10 minutes. Add remaining 6 Tbsp. butter, oregano, salt, granulated garlic, and onion powder to skillet. Whisk until seasoned butter is smooth.
DO AHEAD: Can be made 2 days ahead. Cover; chill. Bring to room temperature before using.

Build a medium-hot fire in a charcoal grill, or heat a gas grill to high. Brush grill grate with oil. Grill corn, turning often, until just tender and charred in spots, 10 to 12 minutes. Serve with honey–ancho chile butter.

EMBER-ROASTED CORN

6 servings

6   ears of corn, in husks
       Melted unsalted butter
       Kosher salt

This is campfire-inspired cooking at its best—you'll need a charcoal grill or a fire pit (if you're planning a clambake on the beach, so much the better). You're going to cook the corn directly in the coals, to impart a particularly smoky flavor. Soak the ears before burying them in the coals so the kernels don't dry out, and keep the husks on for protection during cooking.

Gently pull husks away from corn (do not detach from cob); remove silk. Pull husks back up over corn to evenly cover kernels. Secure husks tightly with string or a small strip of foil. Soak corn in a large pot of water for at least 15 minutes and up to 1 hour (this will prevent them from drying out during roasting).

Meanwhile, build a hot fire in a charcoal grill. Allow fire to burn down until coals are completely covered with ashes (or use ash-covered coals remaining from grilling a main course). Move most of coals to one side of the bottom of the grill and arrange half of corn in a single layer; cover corn with coals and repeat on the other side with remaining coals and corn, spreading coals evenly over corn. Roast corn until most of the kernels are deep golden brown, about 10 minutes (some kernels will be flecked with a deeper char). Remove husks, brushing off any ashes with a pastry brush. Serve corn with butter for brushing over and salt for seasoning.

CORN SALAD
with Manchego and Lime

Vegetable oil, for brushing
6 ears of sweet yellow corn, husked
2 Tbsp. (¼ stick) unsalted
   butter, melted
   Kosher salt and freshly ground
   black pepper
1 jalapeño, seeded, finely diced
½ tsp. crushed red pepper
   flakes
1 lime, cut into 4 wedges
1 cup finely grated Manchego
   cheese
¼ cup thinly sliced fresh chives
2 tsp. finely grated lime zest

INGREDIENT INFO Manchego cheese, a Spanish cheese made from sheep's milk, is sold at some supermarkets and at specialty foods stores.

Vibrant lime zest and nutty Manchego cheese punch up a summery corn salad. Use a sharp knife to slice the grilled corn kernels off the cob. For maximum impact, add the zest to the dish just before serving.

Build a medium-hot fire in a charcoal grill, or heat a gas grill to high. Brush grill grate with oil. Grill corn, turning often, until just tender and charred in spots, 10 to 12 minutes. Let cool. Cut kernels from cobs. Place kernels in a large bowl. Add butter; stir. Season to taste with salt and pepper.

Transfer corn to a large wide bowl or deep platter; sprinkle jalapeño and crushed red pepper flakes over. Squeeze lime wedges over; sprinkle with cheese, chives, and lime zest.

GRILLED CORN: To Husk or Not to Husk?

What's better than sweet summer corn on the cob? *Grilled* corn on the cob. The only question is, which way will you cook it? Both are delicious—it just depends on your preference.

THE CASE FOR LEAVING THE HUSK ON: TENDER & JUICY

If you keep the husk on, it holds in the juices, steams the kernels, and renders sweet, tender corn. For best results, **soak ears in water for at least 15 minutes**, then peel back husks all the way (keep them attached to the cob) and remove silk. Spread regular butter or a compound butter (see page 396) over the corn, pull husks back up, secure with a strip of foil, and throw on the grill.

THE CASE FOR HUSKING: CARAMELY AND CHEWY

This method delivers a luscious char and chewy texture. To do it, **remove husks and silk, brush corn with oil**, and **throw ears onto grill over medium-hot to high heat**. Serve on the cob, or cut off the kernels and add to salads or salsas. (For the record, we feel that the most mouthwatering way to prepare husked corn on the grill is to make *elote,* the Mexican grilled corn on page 281.)

A splash of lime juice balances the richness of **Cotija cheese and mayonnaise** in this Mexican-style preparation.

ELOTE (MEXICAN GRILLED CORN)

ELOTE
(Mexican Grilled Corn)

8 servings

photo, left

Vegetable oil, for brushing
1 tsp. chili powder
½ tsp. cayenne pepper
8 ears of corn, husked
¼ cup mayonnaise or unsalted butter
½ cup crumbled Cotija cheese, Parmesan, or ricotta salata (salted dry ricotta cheese)
1 lime, cut into 8 wedges

SPECIAL EQUIPMENT A pastry brush

In recent years, this addictive way of preparing corn—brushing charred kernels with mayonnaise and a tangy, spicy combination of chili, lime, and Cotija cheese—has become incredibly popular. It's also great for serving family-style: Put all of the ingredients out separately and let your guests top the corn however they wish.

Build a medium-hot fire in a charcoal grill or heat a gas grill to high. Brush grill grate with oil. Combine chili powder and cayenne in a small bowl.

Grill corn, turning occasionally with tongs, until cooked through and lightly charred, about 10 minutes. Remove from grill and immediately brush each ear with 1½ tsp. mayonnaise. Sprinkle each with 1 Tbsp. cheese and a pinch of chili powder mixture. Squeeze 1 lime wedge over each ear and serve.

ONION STEAKS
with Honey-Mustard Sauce

4 to 6 servings

¼ cup extra-virgin olive oil, plus more for brushing
2 Tbsp. (¼ stick) unsalted butter, melted
¼ cup Dijon mustard
¼ cup honey
1 Tbsp. chopped fresh summer savory or thyme
1½ tsp. Worcestershire sauce
2 large sweet onions (such as Walla Walla, Vidalia, or Maui), peeled, cut horizontally into ½-inch-thick rounds
Kosher salt and freshly ground black pepper

SPECIAL EQUIPMENT 10 metal skewers

Forget about fried onion rings. These grilled, caramelized onion slices are a burger's best friend. Cut the onion slices ½ inch thick so that you can run two thin skewers horizontally through each slice; this keeps the rings intact on the grill.

Build a medium-hot fire in a charcoal grill, or heat a gas grill to high. Whisk ¼ cup oil and butter in a small bowl to blend. Whisk Dijon mustard and next 3 ingredients in another small bowl to blend for glaze.

To keep slices intact, run 2 thin metal skewers horizontally through each onion round, parallel to each other and spaced 1 to 1½ inches apart. Brush both sides of onion rounds with oil mixture. Season onion rounds with salt and pepper. Brush grill grate with oil. Grill onions, turning and brushing often with oil mixture, until beginning to char, about 11 minutes.

Brush top side of onions with mustard glaze. Grill until glaze begins to bubble, about 2 minutes. Turn onions; brush with mustard glaze and grill until beginning to caramelize, about 1 minute longer. Transfer onions to a platter. Brush again with mustard glaze.

CORN
with Hoisin-Orange Butter

¼ cup (½ stick) unsalted butter, room temperature
1 Tbsp. hoisin sauce
2½ tsp. finely grated orange zest
¾ tsp. chili-garlic sauce
Kosher salt and freshly ground black pepper
Vegetable oil, for brushing
6 ears of white corn, husked
Chopped fresh cilantro

INGREDIENT INFO Hoisin sauce and chili-garlic sauce are available in the Asian foods section of many supermarkets and at Asian markets.

Baste husked corn with sweet-and-spicy hoisin butter to yield richly caramelized kernels. See "To Husk or Not to Husk?" on page 279 for more information about grilling corn in or out of the husk.

Build a medium-hot fire in a charcoal grill, or heat a gas grill to high. Mix first 4 ingredients in a small bowl to blend. Season to taste with salt and pepper. Brush grill grate with oil. Grill corn, turning occasionally, until beginning to soften, 8 to 10 minutes. Brush all over with hoisin butter; continue to grill, brushing occasionally with more hoisin butter, until corn is tender and charred in spots, about 5 minutes longer. Transfer to a platter; brush with more hoisin butter. Sprinkle with cilantro.

GETTING IT RIGHT: How to Master the Timing Game

That classic cook's challenge—how to get everything on the table at the same time—
takes on a new twist when you're grilling. Here's how to make sure the veggies are done when you want them.

VEGGIES FIRST

If you're making something that will only spend a few minutes on the grill, such as boneless chicken breasts or slices of pork tenderloin, grill the vegetables first so they're taken care of. It's okay if they're not piping hot—most vegetables taste great warm or at room temperature.

VEGGIES AFTER

If you're grilling larger pieces of meat that need to rest after grilling, such as steaks or a rack of lamb, grill the meat first. Then, while the meat is resting on the cutting board, clean the grate with a wire brush and throw the veggies on the grill.

ALL TOGETHER

If your grill is big enough to accommodate everything at once, start with longer-cooking vegetables (such as potatoes or corn) on one side, then add quicker-cooking proteins on the other side. For food safety, use separate utensils for the raw protein and the veggies.

ARTICHOKES
with Sesame Dipping Sauce

DIPPING SAUCE
- ½ cup mayonnaise
- 3 Tbsp. Worcestershire sauce
- 2 Tbsp. extra-virgin olive oil
- 2 Tbsp. toasted sesame oil
- 1½ Tbsp. honey
- 1 Tbsp. fresh lemon juice
- ¾ tsp. seasoned salt
  Freshly ground black pepper

ARTICHOKES
- 2 Tbsp. fresh lemon juice
- 4 large artichokes
- ⅓ cup extra-virgin olive oil, plus more for brushing
- 1 garlic clove, minced
  Kosher salt and freshly ground black pepper

SPECIAL EQUIPMENT A grill basket (optional)

Artichokes are great on the grill, and this creamy dipping sauce offers a welcome departure from melted butter. You can prepare the sauce and parcook the artichokes the day before—which makes this an easy, party-friendly appetizer.

DIPPING SAUCE

Whisk mayonnaise, Worcestershire sauce, olive oil, sesame oil, honey, lemon juice, and seasoned salt in a small bowl to blend. Season to taste with pepper. **DO AHEAD:** Can be made 1 day ahead. Cover and chill.

ARTICHOKES

Fill a large bowl with cold water; add lemon juice. Cut off stem and the top quarter of 1 artichoke. Snap off outer 2 rows of leaves. Cut artichoke lengthwise into 6 wedges. Using a small knife, cut out choke and prickly leaves from the center of artichoke wedges. Place artichoke in lemon water. Repeat with remaining artichokes.

Place a metal steamer rack on bottom of a large pot. Add just enough water to touch bottom of rack; bring to a boil. Place artichokes on rack in pot. Reduce heat to medium, cover, and steam artichokes, adding more water if necessary, until tender, about 15 minutes. Let cool. **DO AHEAD:** Can be made 1 day ahead. Wrap and chill.

Build a medium-hot fire in a charcoal grill, or heat a gas grill to high. Stir ⅓ cup olive oil and minced garlic in a small bowl to blend. Brush garlic oil over artichokes; season with salt and pepper. Brush grill grate with oil or place artichoke wedges in grill basket. Grill artichokes, turning occasionally, until slightly charred, about 8 minutes. Serve with dipping sauce.

Kitchen Wisdom

NO, USING A GRILL BASKET ISN'T CHEATING. Actually, these handy metal baskets (see page 18) are an ideal way to turn small, unwieldy ingredients into **bites of charred deliciousness**. You can fill your basket with countless options: pearl onions, mushrooms, green beans, and all those baby vegetables, like the mini pattypan squash on page 275.

GRILLED HALLOUMI
with Watermelon and Basil-Mint Oil

photo, right

½ cup coarsely chopped fresh basil

3 Tbsp. coarsely chopped fresh mint, plus thinly sliced mint for garnish

1 garlic clove, coarsely chopped

½ cup extra-virgin olive oil, plus more for brushing

Kosher salt and freshly ground black pepper

12 oz. cherry tomatoes on the vine

1 8- to 9-oz. package Halloumi cheese, cut crosswise into 8 slices

6 small triangles thinly sliced watermelon, rind removed

INGREDIENT INFO Halloumi is available at some supermarkets and at specialty foods stores, and natural foods stores.

Halloumi is our favorite cheese for grilling, and it makes the perfect accompaniment to a refreshing watermelon salad. Both are topped with a distinctive green herb oil that takes just seconds to make and adds intense summery zing.

Build a medium-hot fire in a charcoal grill, or heat a gas grill to high. Purée basil, chopped mint, and garlic in a blender. With machine running, add ½ cup oil. Set a strainer over a small bowl; strain, pressing on solids. Season to taste with salt and pepper.

Brush grill grate with oil. Drizzle 2 Tbsp. basil-mint oil over tomatoes and cheese; season with salt and pepper. Grill tomatoes, turning occasionally, until charred and bursting, about 4 minutes. Grill cheese until nicely charred in spots and beginning to melt, about 45 seconds per side.

Arrange watermelon on a platter. Top with cheese and tomatoes. Drizzle remaining herb oil over; garnish with sliced mint.

ZUCCHINI
with Garlic Butter Baste

8 medium zucchini, trimmed, halved lengthwise

½ cup (1 stick) unsalted butter

2 Tbsp. fresh lemon juice

1 Tbsp. chopped fresh rosemary

2 garlic cloves, minced

1 tsp. lemon-pepper seasoning

¼ tsp. curry powder

Kosher salt and freshly ground black pepper

Vegetable oil, for brushing

¼ cup freshly grated Parmesan (optional)

The herbed butter baste on zucchini literally melts into the vegetables while it grills. The secret ingredient? A touch of curry powder, which adds a subtle, smoky note. Finish things off with a sprinkling of Parmesan.

Build a medium fire in a charcoal grill, or heat a gas grill to medium-high. Score cut side of zucchini halves with diagonal cuts about ¼ inch deep and spaced at 1-inch intervals. Combine butter, lemon juice, rosemary, garlic, lemon-pepper seasoning, and curry powder in a small heavy saucepan. Stir over low heat until butter melts and flavors blend. Season to taste with salt and pepper. Brush seasoned butter over cut side of zucchini. Brush grill grate with oil. Grill zucchini until charred on all sides and just beginning to soften, about 12 minutes. If desired, turn zucchini, cut side up, and sprinkle with cheese; close grill and cook until cheese just softens, about 1 minute.

GRILLED HALLOUMI WITH WATERMELON AND BASIL-MINT OIL

Does it get any better than onions **basted slowly in a butter-Worcestershire sauce** on the grill?

GRILL-ROASTED VIDALIA ONIONS

GRILL-ROASTED VIDALIA ONIONS

photo, left

12 3- to 4-inch-diameter Vidalia
    onions, peeled
    Kosher salt and freshly ground
    black pepper
12 Tbsp. Worcestershire sauce
12 Tbsp. (1½ sticks) unsalted
    butter

This minimalist side dish takes seconds to prep: Everything goes inside foil packets, where the onions slowly become tender in the savory butter sauce. The onions cook for an hour, so throw the packets on the grill while you tackle the main course.

Build a medium-hot fire in a charcoal grill, or heat a gas grill to high. Cut both ends off each onion. Cut a ¼-inch-deep X in root end of each. Place each onion on a 12-inch square of foil, X side up. Season with salt and pepper. Top each with 1 Tbsp. Worcestershire sauce and 1 Tbsp. butter. Seal onions in foil.

    Grill foil-wrapped onions until very tender, moving packets around for even cooking (but not turning over), about 1 hour. Open onion packets carefully to reserve juices. Transfer onions to a platter and spoon juices over.

Bonus Recipe
VEGETABLE PACKETS

Grilling in foil is a snap because you can prepare packets ahead of time (and clean-up is a breeze). To do it, **place chopped vegetables on a large sheet of heavy-duty foil**. Drizzle with oil or place a pat of butter on top. Season with salt, pepper, herbs, lemon zest, and even a splash of wine if you like. Seal packets (see page 226). Grill until tender, 15 to 30 minutes.

SWEET POTATOES, ONIONS, AND BELL PEPPER

6 servings

½ cup extra-virgin olive oil, plus more for brushing

1½ Tbsp. chopped fresh thyme

2 lb. red-skinned sweet potatoes, peeled, cut into ½-inch-thick rounds

1 onion, cut through root end into ½-inch-thick wedges with some core attached to each

1 red bell pepper, cut into thin strips
    Kosher salt and freshly ground black pepper

2 Tbsp. apple cider vinegar

A splash of cider vinegar brings out sweetness in this colorful autumnal mix of grilled vegetables. Serve with grilled chicken or pork.

Build a medium fire in a charcoal grill, or heat a gas grill to medium-high. Whisk ½ cup oil and thyme in a small bowl to blend. Place sweet potatoes, onion, and bell pepper in a large bowl. Drizzle with ¼ cup oil mixture and toss to coat. Season vegetables generously with salt and pepper. Brush grill grate with oil. Grill vegetables, turning often, until tender and slightly charred, about 15 minutes for pepper and about 20 minutes for sweet potatoes and onion. Transfer vegetables to a platter.

Whisk vinegar into remaining oil mixture. Season vinaigrette to taste with salt and pepper; drizzle over vegetables. Serve warm or at room temperature.

EGGPLANT AND TOMATO GRILLED CHEESE

2 servings

3 Tbsp. extra-virgin olive oil, plus more for brushing

2 large garlic cloves, minced

1 12-inch-long piece of baguette, halved horizontally

1 1-lb. eggplant, trimmed, cut lengthwise into 6½-inch-thick slices

3 medium firm tomatoes, thickly sliced (about 10 slices total)
    Kosher salt and freshly ground black pepper

3 oz. soft fresh goat cheese

12 fresh basil leaves

Open-face sandwiches of grilled eggplant, tomatoes, and basil showcase summer produce at its best. Goat cheese is a creamy foil for the charred vegetables.

Build a medium-hot fire in a charcoal grill, or heat a gas grill to high. Combine 3 Tbsp. oil and garlic in a small bowl; stir to blend. Let stand for 15 minutes so flavors develop.

Brush cut sides of baguette and both sides of eggplant slices and tomato slices with garlic oil. Brush grill grate with oil. Grill cut sides of baguette until toasted, about 2 minutes. Transfer baguette, cut side up, to plate. Season eggplant and tomatoes with salt and pepper. Grill eggplant until cooked through, about 6 minutes per side; transfer to a plate. Grill tomatoes until warmed through, about 1 minute per side; transfer to a plate.

Spread goat cheese on cut sides of bread, dividing equally. Overlap eggplant slices, then tomato slices, atop cheese, covering bread completely. Garnish with basil leaves. Cut each sandwich into 4 sections and arrange on 2 plates.

POLENTA SQUARES

with Corn, Red Onion, and Cucumber Salad

1 tsp. kosher salt, more as needed

1 cup polenta or instant polenta

¼ cup freshly grated Parmesan

3 Tbsp. fresh lime juice

2 Tbsp. extra-virgin olive oil

1 garlic clove, minced

Salt and freshly ground black pepper

Vegetable oil, for brushing

4 ears of corn, husked

1 large red onion, cut into ½-inch-thick slices

2½ cups chopped seeded tomatoes

1¼ cups chopped unpeeled cucumber (preferably English hothouse)

⅓ cup chopped fresh mint

Make this dish with cooled leftover polenta, or start the recipe 6 hours ahead to give the polenta time to set. This would be excellent with grilled steaks or leg of lamb.

Bring 4 cups water and 1 tsp. salt to a boil in a large heavy saucepan. Gradually add polenta, whisking until mixture is boiling and smooth. Reduce heat to low. Cook, whisking often, until very thick, about 25 minutes. (Alternatively, cook instant polenta according to package instructions.) Whisk in cheese. Spread polenta evenly in an 8x8x2-inch glass baking dish. Let cool slightly. Cover; chill for at least 6 hours.

Whisk lime juice, olive oil, and garlic in a large bowl to blend; season dressing to taste with salt and pepper.

Build a medium fire in a charcoal grill, or heat a gas grill to medium-high. Brush grill grate with vegetable oil. Brush corn and onion slices with vegetable oil; season with salt and pepper. Grill corn and onion, turning often, until tender and lightly charred, 10 to 12 minutes for corn and 15 minutes for onion. Transfer to a rimmed baking sheet and let cool. Cut corn kernels from cobs. Coarsely chop onion. Add corn, onion, tomatoes, cucumber, and mint to dressing in large bowl; toss to coat. Season to taste with salt and pepper.

Cut polenta into 4 squares. Cut each square diagonally into 2 triangles. Brush polenta with oil. Grill until heated through and grill marks appear, about 5 minutes per side. Divide salad among 4 plates. Place 2 polenta triangles alongside each salad.

EGGPLANT CAPRESE
with Tomato and Basil Vinaigrette

1 1-lb. eggplant, trimmed, cut crosswise into ½-inch-thick rounds

¼ cup extra-virgin olive oil, plus more for brushing

Kosher salt and freshly ground black pepper

1 large plum tomato (about 4 oz.)

⅓ cup chopped fresh basil, plus sprigs for garnish

1 Tbsp. white wine vinegar

2 7- to 8-oz. balls fresh mozzarella, drained, thinly sliced

2 lb. heirloom tomatoes (about 4 large; preferably assorted colors), thinly sliced

This is *caprese* salad like you've never had it before: fresh mozzarella layered with tender slices of grilled eggplant and drizzled with a charred tomato dressing. Use imported buffalo mozzarella if you can find it.

Build a medium fire in a charcoal grill, or heat a gas grill to medium-high. Arrange eggplant rounds on a rimmed baking sheet. Brush both sides of eggplant with oil and season with salt and pepper. Brush grill grate with oil. Grill eggplant, turning occasionally and moving to cook evenly, until slightly charred and tender, about 5 minutes. Transfer to a foil-lined rimmed baking sheet. Brush plum tomato with oil; grill, turning often, until skin is charred and split, about 5 minutes. Transfer to sheet with eggplant and let cool.

Core plum tomato; place in a blender. Add chopped basil, vinegar, and ¼ cup oil. Blend until smooth. Season vinaigrette to taste with salt and pepper. Transfer to a small bowl. **DO AHEAD:** Eggplant and vinaigrette can be made 2 hours ahead. Let stand at room temperature.

Overlap eggplant rounds, cheese slices, and heirloom tomato slices on individual plates or a large platter. Season with salt and pepper; drizzle with vinaigrette and garnish with basil sprigs.

Kitchen Wisdom

PUT THAT CAST-IRON SKILLET TO WORK. Think about it: Your grill is actually one big burner. That means you can **move a lot of cooking outside** in the summer. Just put a cast-iron skillet on the grill and add olive oil, peak-season vegetables (like the stunning carrots at right), and seasonings. No worries about overcooking the steak while you're in the kitchen sautéing the sides.

For the simplest side dish known to man, slap a **well-seasoned cast-iron skillet** down on the grill and add vegetables and seasonings.

FLATBREADS & PIZZA

WHETHER YOU CALL IT PIZZA OR FLATBREAD,

there's something irresistible about fresh dough grilled over an open fire. It's charred, it's bubbly, it's chewy, it's crispy. It can serve as a canvas for all manner of toppings, from simple to ambitious. Or it can be cut into wedges and dredged through dips or slathered with spreads. Wrap it around grilled meats just as you would a pita. Or simply top it with olive oil and sea salt and devour it.

Whether you end up making your own yeast-risen dough or you just stop by your local pizzeria or market to pick up a few balls of dough (trust us, there's no shame in *not* doing everything from scratch), making pizza at home is as fun as it is delicious. Or how about trying something even simpler than pizza? Slice up fresh bread, toast it on the grill, and create inventive crostini or bruschetta.

The recipes in this chapter are a versatile bunch—they can serve as starters, sides, or main courses. And they're a clever way to surprise guests who might be expecting the usual steak or burgers.

makes about 10

CORIANDER AND CUMIN FLATBREAD

1 tsp. cumin seeds
1 tsp. coriander seeds
3 lb. Homemade Flatbread dough (page 298) or store-bought fresh pizza dough, room temperature
Extra-virgin olive oil, for brushing
1 Tbsp. chopped flat-leaf parsley

SPECIAL EQUIPMENT A spice mill (optional)

These fragrant flatbreads are a great accompaniment to Mediterranean or Middle Eastern dishes. To extract the most flavor and aroma from the spices, toast and crush the coriander and cumin seeds yourself.

Combine cumin seeds and coriander seeds in a small dry skillet. Stir over medium heat until aromatic and lightly toasted, about 2 minutes. Transfer to a mortar or spice mill and crush seeds coarsely.

Line 2 baking sheets with parchment paper. Turn out dough onto a floured work surface. Divide dough into 10 equal pieces. Roll each piece into a ball. Cover with plastic wrap and let rest on floured surface for 15 minutes.

Using your fingers, dimple each ball, then press and stretch each into a 3½- to 4-inch round. Place dough rounds on prepared baking sheets, spacing apart. Brush each round lightly with olive oil. Sprinkle cumin-coriander mixture and parsley over each; press lightly to adhere. Cover with plastic wrap and let rise for 30 minutes.

Build a medium fire in a charcoal grill, or heat a gas grill to medium-high. Brush grill grate with oil. Using a metal spatula, transfer flatbreads, plain side down, to grill and cook until lightly browned in spots and cooked through, 3 to 4 minutes per side. Transfer to a platter and scatter parsley over.

Steps to Tasty FLATBREADS

Our master dough recipe (see page 298) is yeasty, tangy, and easy to work with. But even if you don't have time to make your own, no worries. Just purchase a ball of dough from your local pizzeria or a specialty market, and then follow these steps:

①   **②**   **③**   **④**

SHAPE THE DOUGH

Right before you're ready to grill, flour whatever surface you're working on, grab your dough, and **move quickly**. Press each flatbread or pizza with your hands (or use a rolling pin) into a shape of ¼-inch thickness. And it doesn't have to be perfectly round!

GET IT TO THE GRILL

To transport your dough to the grill, start by lightly dusting a rimless baking sheet or pizza peel with flour. **Transfer your rolled-out dough to the sheet.**

If you're grilling a lot of flatbreads or pizzas, keep rolled-out dough in the refrigerator between batches so it doesn't puff up.

GET IT ON THE GRILL

Tilt the baking sheet and use your fingers to carefully invert the dough onto the grill grate.

Make sure the grate is clean, smooth, and well-oiled. Trust us—if you don't oil that grate, you *will* end up with flatbread dough stuck to it, and it *will* be a pain in the neck to clean up.

LET IT TAKE A CHAR

Let the magic happen. After about 1 minute, gently lift an edge and peek underneath. You're looking for a light char around the edge. Keep checking until the dough is charred but not burnt, then flip it with tongs and grill the reverse side until the flatbread is just cooked through.

Next up, toppings. See page 306 for creative ideas. Or eat it absolutely plain. It's that good.

+ A North African–inspired sauce, chile oil, and crumbled cheese are added here **after the flatbread comes off the grill.**

HOMEMADE FLATBREAD WITH CHARMOULA AND ANCHO CHILE OIL
(RECIPE ON PAGE 298)

HOMEMADE FLATBREAD

with Charmoula and Ancho Chile Oil

photo, page 297

2½ tsp. active dry yeast
4¾ cups all-purpose flour, plus more
   for dusting
2¼ cups whole wheat flour
2 Tbsp. kosher salt
½ cup sour cream
   Vegetable oil, for brushing
   Green Charmoula (recipe follows)
   Ancho Chile Oil (recipe follows)
   Grated Cotija or Parmesan
     cheese, for topping

INGREDIENT INFO Dried ancho chiles are available at Latin markets, specialty foods stores, and many supermarkets.

Here is a master recipe for tender, chewy flatbreads—just right for slathering with a punchy North African–inspired charmoula sauce and drizzling with lively ancho chile oil. Or top the flatbread with cheese and vegetables, wrap it around grilled meat, or eat it straight off the grill. When making flatbreads, always work on a clean and well-oiled grill. And make sure to leave the dough on the grill long enough for it to take on a nice char (just like a steak). For more flatbread instructions, see page 296.

Dissolve yeast in 3 cups warm water in a large bowl. Add both flours; mix with your fingertips until a shaggy dough forms. Cover bowl with plastic wrap and let rest at room temperature for 20 minutes.

Sprinkle salt over dough, then add sour cream; knead until well incorporated and dough pulls away from sides of bowl and holds together in a loose, wet ball, about 5 minutes (dough will be very soft; lightly moisten your hands to prevent sticking if needed). Cover bowl with plastic wrap and let dough rise at room temperature for 30 minutes.

Knead dough an additional 4 or 5 times to deflate. **DO AHEAD:** Cover and chill for up to 2 days. (Dough will develop in flavor and continue to rise slowly in refrigerator.) Alternatively, let dough stand at room temperature until doubled in volume, 3 to 4 hours (the warmer and more humid your kitchen is, the faster it will rise). Chill for 1 hour before grilling to make it easier to handle.

Build a medium-hot fire in a charcoal grill, or heat a gas grill to high. Divide dough into 8 equal portions. Generously flour a work surface. Working with 1 or 2 portions at a time (depending on how many flatbreads will fit on your grill), roll out dough or press with your hands into a ¼-inch-thick shape.

Brush grill grate with oil. Grill flatbreads until lightly charred on one side and no longer sticking to grill, 2 to 3 minutes. Using a metal spatula, turn flatbreads and grill until cooked through, 1 to 2 minutes longer.

Top with Green Charmoula, Ancho Chile Oil, and cheese (or other desired toppings) and serve immediately.

Green Charmoula

serve with flatbread

1 jalapeño, stemmed, seeded, coarsely chopped
1 cup extra-virgin olive oil
½ cup flat-leaf parsley leaves
½ cup (loosely packed) fresh cilantro leaves
½ cup (loosely packed) fresh mint leaves
½ tsp. chopped peeled ginger
Kosher salt and freshly ground black pepper

This zippy chile-herb sauce is also great drizzled over grilled seafood.

Pulse first 6 ingredients in a blender or food processor until a coarse purée forms. Season to taste with salt and pepper. **DO AHEAD:** Sauce can be made 1 day ahead. Cover and chill. Let come to room temperature before using.

Ancho Chile Oil

serve with flatbread

2 oz. dried ancho chiles, stemmed, seeded, torn into pieces
2 garlic cloves, smashed
1 red Fresno chile or red jalapeño, stemmed, seeded
1 cup vegetable oil
2 Tbsp. red wine vinegar
1 tsp. ground coriander
1 tsp. ground cumin
Kosher salt

There are myriad uses for this oil—keep it in your fridge and use it on salads or on anything grilled, including fish, steak, and vegetables.

Heat first 7 ingredients in a small saucepan over medium heat until fragrant and just beginning to bubble. Remove from heat. Let steep for 1 hour.
    Purée mixture in a blender until smooth. Strain through a fine-mesh sieve into a small bowl; discard solids in sieve. Season oil to taste with salt. **DO AHEAD:** Can be made 1 week ahead. Cover and chill.

FLATBREADS
with Tunisian Vegetable Salsa

makes 8

4 lb. Homemade Flatbread dough (see page 298) or store-bought fresh pizza dough, room temperature

Extra-virgin olive oil, for brushing

1 Tbsp. (about) Tabil Spice Blend (page 189)

Kosher salt and freshly ground black pepper

Tunisian Vegetable Salsa (recipe follows)

Feel free to use store-bought fresh dough, or make your own (using the Homemade Flatbread recipe on page 298). Brush the spice blend onto flatbreads before grilling.

Turn dough out onto a floured work surface. Divide into 8 equal pieces. Roll into balls; space 2 inches apart. Cover with a kitchen towel; let rest for 15 minutes.

Build a medium-hot fire in a charcoal grill, or heat a gas grill to high. Lightly brush 4 rimless baking sheets with oil. Working with 1 dough ball at a time on floured work surface, roll out into a 9-inch round. Place 2 dough rounds on each prepared sheet. Brush one side of each round lightly with oil; season with Tabil Spice Blend, salt, and pepper.

Brush grill grate with oil. Working in batches, invert flatbreads onto grate (spice side down). Brush top with oil, season with salt and pepper, and turn over and grill until lightly charred in spots and cooked through, 1 to 1½ minutes per side. Serve with Tunisian Vegetable Salsa.

---

makes about 4 cups

Tunisian Vegetable Salsa

use with flatbreads

¼ cup extra-virgin olive oil, plus more for brushing

4 large unpeeled garlic cloves

4 plum tomatoes (about 12 oz. total)

2 small whole unpeeled onions (8 oz. total)

2 large red bell peppers

1 large poblano chile

1 Japanese eggplant (about 5 oz.)

Fresh lemon juice

Kosher salt and freshly ground black pepper

SPECIAL EQUIPMENT 1 metal skewer

INGREDIENT INFO Poblano chiles are available at some supermarkets and at specialty foods stores, farmers' markets, and Latin markets.

Skewered and grilled whole garlic cloves give this vibrant sauce a smoky sweetness. Make the salsa as chunky or as smooth as you like.

Build a medium-hot fire in a charcoal grill, or heat a gas grill to high. Brush grill grate with oil. Thread garlic cloves onto metal skewer. Put garlic skewer, tomatoes, onions, peppers, chile, and eggplant on grill grate. Grill, turning occasionally, until tender and lightly charred all over, 6 to 7 minutes for garlic and tomatoes; 10 minutes for eggplant; 15 minutes for peppers and chile; 20 minutes for onions. Place peppers and chile in a large bowl; cover with plastic wrap and let stand for 15 minutes.

Peel, seed, and coarsely chop peppers and chile. Coarsely chop tomatoes and eggplant. Peel and coarsely chop onions. Pulse all vegetables in a food processor, along with ¼ cup oil, until puréed to desired consistency. Transfer to a large bowl. Season to taste with lemon juice, salt, and pepper.

+

Work quickly when
handling dough—and
make sure your **work
surface is well-floured**.

PIZZA BIANCA
with Rosemary and Sea Salt

1 lb. store-bought fresh pizza
   dough, room temperature
   Extra-virgin olive oil, for brushing
1 tsp. minced fresh rosemary,
   divided
   Sea salt and freshly ground black
   pepper

Topped with only olive oil, fresh rosemary, and coarse sea salt, *pizza bianca* is a Roman dish that more closely resembles seasoned flatbread than it does typical pizza. Serve the bread alongside *salumi* (like prosciutto and hard salami) and cheese on an antipasto platter, or with soup or salad for a light meal.

Build a medium-hot fire in a charcoal grill, or heat a gas grill to high. On a floured work surface, roll out dough to a 15-inch round. Brush 1 side of dough round with oil, then sprinkle with ½ tsp. rosemary, sea salt, and pepper. Slide onto floured rimless baking sheet. Brush grill grate with oil. Invert dough onto grill, seasoned side down. Brush top with oil, then sprinkle with remaining ½ tsp. rosemary, sea salt, and pepper. Turn over and grill until just golden, about 4 minutes per side.

GETTING IT RIGHT: How to Grill Pizza

What's the difference between pizza and flatbread? Not much. Basically, grilled pizza is a dolled-up grilled flatbread. The difference comes in when you add toppings. Here's how to master grilled pizza.

CHOOSE THE DOUGH

For all the pizzas in this chapter, there are two options: The first, of course, is **store-bought**; we like the fresh pizza dough from Whole Foods. But you can also make your own—it's easier than it sounds—using the **Homemade Flatbread** recipe on page 298.

TWICE OVER THE FIRE

In an oven, you always start a pizza with the toppings in place. But **with grilling, you have to cook the dough on its own first,** to get it sturdy enough to hold the cheese, vegetables, and meat so they won't fall through the grate. Add your toppings, then put it back on the grill for one more quick round over the fire.

USE YOUR TOOLS

A **rimless baking sheet** and a **metal spatula** will help you maneuver the pizza to and from the grill. You'll need **tongs** to lift dough while it's cooking, so you can check how things are coming along. And oiling the grate is essential. Reapply it generously with a **brush** or **crumpled foil** if you grill more than one pizza (and you *will* want more than one).

GRILLED PIZZA
PROVENÇALE

1½ cups chopped seeded
    plum tomatoes (about 3 large)
2 large bunches arugula, chopped
12 Kalamata olives or other brine-
    cured black olives, pitted, halved
1 Tbsp. extra-virgin olive oil, plus
    more for brushing
2 tsp. chopped garlic
    Kosher salt and freshly ground
    black pepper
    All-purpose flour (for dusting)
1 lb. store-bought fresh
    pizza dough, room temperature
1 cup crumbled soft fresh goat
    cheese (about 5 oz.)

Fresh goat cheese and a garlicky salad of arugula, tomatoes, and olives transport this pizza to the south of France. Grill the dough on its own first before adding the toppings and giving the pizza a final blast of heat.

Build a medium-hot/medium-low 2-zone fire in a charcoal grill (see page 15), or heat a gas grill to high. Stir tomatoes, arugula, olives, 1 Tbsp. olive oil, and garlic in a medium bowl to combine; season topping with salt and pepper.

Sprinkle rimless baking sheet with flour. Roll out pizza dough on floured work surface to a 15-inch round. Transfer to prepared sheet. Brush grill grate with oil. Place dough round on hotter side of grill and cook until lightly charred on one side and no longer sticking, 2 to 3 minutes. Using tongs, turn dough over and grill until cooked through, 1 to 2 minutes longer. Transfer grilled pizza dough, darker side up, to rimless baking sheet. If using gas grill, reduce heat to medium.

Spread topping over crust. Sprinkle with goat cheese.

Slide pizza from baking sheet to cooler side of grill. Cover grill and cook pizza until bottom is crisp, about 5 minutes.

Use a vegetable peeler to make the thin slices of zucchini and eggplant for this fresh-flavored pizza.

ZUCCHINI AND EGGPLANT PIZZA WITH
TAPENADE AND FONTINA (LEFT)

ZUCCHINI AND EGGPLANT PIZZA
with Tapenade and Fontina

photo, left

2 medium zucchini (about 12 oz. total), trimmed, cut lengthwise into ¼-inch-thick slices

2 Japanese eggplants (about 10 oz. total), cut lengthwise into ¼-inch-thick slices

Extra-virgin olive oil, for brushing and drizzling

Kosher salt and freshly ground black pepper

All-purpose flour, for dusting

2 lb. store-bought fresh pizza dough, room temperature

½ cup store-bought black olive tapenade (about 5½ oz.)

2 Tbsp. minced fresh marjoram or fresh oregano

½ tsp. crushed red pepper flakes

1 cup (packed) coarsely grated Fontina cheese

⅔ cup freshly grated Pecorino

½ cup chopped flat-leaf parsley

There isn't any meat in this vegetarian-friendly pizza, but you won't miss it: Ultra-creamy Fontina cheese and a slick of black olive tapenade provide plenty of flavor. You'll want to start the pizzas on the hot side of the grill until the bottoms are firm and the dough is set, then transfer the pizzas to the cool zone after adding the toppings.

Build a medium-hot/medium-low 2-zone fire in a charcoal grill (see page 15), or heat a gas grill to high. Arrange zucchini and eggplant slices on 2 large baking sheets. Brush vegetables with oil; season with salt and pepper. Brush grill grate with oil. Transfer vegetables to grate and grill on the hotter side of the grill until tender and golden brown, about 4 minutes per side. Transfer to a platter.

Sprinkle 2 rimless baking sheets with flour. Divide dough into 2 equal pieces; roll out each piece on a floured work surface to a 15-inch round. Transfer to prepared baking sheets. Brush grill grate with oil. Place one dough round on hotter side of grill and cook until lightly charred and no longer sticking, 2 to 3 minutes. Using tongs, turn dough over and grill until cooked through, 1 to 2 minutes longer. Transfer grilled pizza dough, darker side up, to rimless baking sheet. Repeat with second dough round. If using gas grill, reduce heat to medium.

Spread ¼ cup tapenade over each pizza; arrange grilled zucchini and eggplant slices over. Sprinkle each with 1 Tbsp. marjoram and ¼ tsp. crushed red pepper flakes. Drizzle lightly with oil. Sprinkle each with ½ cup Fontina and ⅓ cup Pecorino.

Slide one pizza from baking sheet to cooler side of grill. Cover grill and cook pizza until cheese melts and bottom is crisp, about 5 minutes. Repeat with second pizza. Sprinkle pizzas with parsley.

PIZZA

with Pears, Pecorino, and Walnuts

photo, right

All-purpose flour, for dusting
2 lb. store-bought fresh pizza dough, room temperature
Vegetable oil, for brushing
12 oz. aged Manchego, Parmesan, or Pecorino
2 pears (about), halved, cored, very thinly sliced
⅔ cup walnut pieces, coarsely broken
Freshly cracked black pepper
Extra-virgin olive oil, for drizzling

This sweet-and-savory pizza mines the flavors of a classic Italian cheese plate: slices of ripe pear, a wedge of Pecorino, and a handful of cracked walnuts.

Build a medium-hot/medium-low 2-zone fire in a charcoal grill (see page 15), or heat a gas grill to high. Sprinkle 2 rimless baking sheets with flour. Divide dough into 2 equal pieces; roll out each piece on a floured work surface to a 15-inch round. Transfer to prepared baking sheets. Brush grill grate with oil. Place one dough round on grate on hotter side of grill and cook until lightly charred and no longer sticking, 2 to 3 minutes. Using tongs, turn dough over and grill until cooked through, 1 to 2 minutes longer. Using a spatula, transfer crust to rimless baking sheet. Repeat with second dough round. If using a gas grill, reduce heat to medium.

Thinly slice cheese; arrange atop crusts, leaving a ½-inch plain border. Cover cheese with a single layer of pear slices (there may be some pear left over), then scatter walnuts over.

Working one at a time, slide pizzas from baking sheets onto cooler part of grill. Cover grill and cook pizzas until cheese softens and bottoms are crisp, 4 to 5 minutes. Transfer pizzas to work surface. Season with pepper; drizzle with oil.

GRILLED PIZZA: Take your Toppings over the Top

One of the greatest things about making pizza at home is that you don't even need a recipe—just start with a drizzle of olive oil, end with salt and pepper, and get creative in between.

TOMATOES

Crush canned Italian plum tomatoes with your hands, or purée them in a blender. Spread almost to the edges of the pie.

THE CHEESE

We also like to use another soft variety in addition to mozzarella, such as ricotta or Robiola. For contrast, use one grated hard cheese, like Parmesan.

CARAMELIZED ONIONS

They improve just about everything (see recipe on page 81). Since they are sweet, pair them with something salty, like prosciutto.

LARDONS

Cut strips of bacon crosswise into ½-inch pieces. Render them on a baking sheet in a 400°F oven until almost crisp (they'll cook further on the pizza).

BRUSSELS SPROUTS

Shave or shred them thinly with a knife or mandoline.

FRESH OREGANO

Sprinkle some of this traditional pizza herb just before serving.

ARUGULA

For a fresh hit of peppery flavor, scatter some over the pie when it comes off the grill.

Surprise your guests with **toppings you won't find at the pizzeria** down the street.

PIZZA WITH PEARS, PECORINO, AND WALNUTS

+

Dough **cooks very quickly** on the grill; keep an eye on it to **ensure that it doesn't burn**.

SAUSAGE AND FIG PIZZA
WITH GOAT CHEESE

PIZZA
with Mozzarella, Clams, and Tomatoes

makes one
15-inch pizza

2 Tbsp. extra-virgin olive oil, plus
  more for brushing
2 garlic cloves, minced
¼ tsp. crushed red pepper flakes
1 cup (packed) grated mozzarella
  (about 4 oz.)
3 Tbsp. chopped flat-leaf parsley
2 Tbsp. freshly grated Parmesan
1 Tbsp. chopped fresh thyme or
  1 tsp. dried
1 lb. store-bought fresh pizza
  dough, room temperature
2 large plum tomatoes, thinly sliced
1 6½-oz. can chopped clams,
  drained

In the mecca of pizza—a.k.a. New Haven, Connecticut—the ultimate pie is topped with little more than olive oil, garlic, and clams. We think our spin, with thin slices of summer-ripe tomatoes, delivers a welcome note of sweetness. Though canned chopped clams will work here, freshly shucked littlenecks will make it otherworldly.

Build a medium-hot/medium-low 2-zone fire in a charcoal grill (see page 15), or heat a gas grill to high. Mix 2 Tbsp. oil, garlic, and crushed red pepper flakes in a small bowl. Let stand for 10 minutes.

Combine mozzarella, parsley, Parmesan, and thyme in a medium bowl. Brush a large rimless baking sheet with oil. Roll out dough on baking sheet to a 15-inch round.

Brush grill grate with oil. Place dough on hotter side of grill and cook until lightly charred and no longer sticking, 2 to 3 minutes. Turn dough over and grill until cooked through, 1 to 2 minutes longer. Using a spatula, transfer grilled crust, darker side up, to rimless baking sheet. If using a gas grill, reduce heat to medium.

Brush top of crust with oil mixture. Cover with tomato slices and sprinkle with clams and cheese mixture.

Slide pizza from baking sheet onto grate over cooler part of grill. Cover grill and cook pizza until cheeses melt and bottom of pizza is crisp, about 3 minutes.

SAUSAGE AND FIG PIZZA
with Goat Cheese

makes one
15-inch pizza

Extra-virgin olive oil, for brushing
  and drizzling
1 lb. store-bought fresh pizza
  dough, room temperature
1 cup coarsely grated Fontina
  cheese (about 4 oz.)
  Fresh arugula, for topping
2 grilled sausages, sliced ⅓ inch
  thick
6 fresh figs, quartered
2 thin red onion slices, rings
  separated
1 cup crumbled soft fresh goat
  cheese (about 4 oz.)

Merguez (lamb) sausages would pair especially well with the figs on this Middle Eastern–inflected pizza, but you may use any kind of sausage you like.

Build a medium-hot/medium-low 2-zone fire in a charcoal grill (see page 15), or heat a gas grill to high. Brush grill grate with oil. On a floured work surface, roll out pizza dough to a 15-inch round. Brush top with oil.

Place dough, oiled side down, on hotter side of grill and cook until golden on bottom, about 4 minutes. Turn dough over and grill until cooked through, 1 to 2 minutes longer. Using a spatula, transfer grilled crust, darker side up, to rimless baking sheet. If using a gas grill, reduce heat to medium.

Top with Fontina, arugula, sausages, figs, and onions. Drizzle with more oil.

Slide pizza from baking sheet onto cooler part of grill. Cover grill and cook pizza until Fontina melts and pizza is cooked through, about 4 minutes. Top with goat cheese. Grill until goat cheese softens, about 1 minute.

CROSTINI
with Peach, Prosciutto, and Ricotta

makes 12

12 slices rustic white bread, such as ciabatta
1 large ripe peach (or 2 medium)
¾ cup (about) fresh ricotta, preferably sheep's milk
  Freshly ground black pepper
4 thin slices prosciutto
  Honey, for drizzling

This sweet-and-salty starter was inspired by the classic Italian pairing of prosciutto and melon, but it has a Georgia accent. The key to success with this dish is using peaches that are as ripe and juicy as possible. (See more crostini tips below.)

Grill bread (see below).

Halve, pit, and thinly slice peach into 24 slices. Spoon about 1 Tbsp. fresh ricotta onto each toast slice and season with pepper. Tear prosciutto into feathery pieces and drape a few pieces over ricotta on each toast slice. Drizzle with honey and top with 2 peach slices each.

GETTING IT RIGHT: How to Make Crostini

When the clock is ticking and you need to feed a crowd, the simplest, most delicious solution for a starter comes in the form of crostini. Brush slices of good bread with olive oil and grill until the edges are crisp and the crumbs are golden. Then doctor up the slices. Here's how to make crostini like a pro:

THE BREAD

Buy a good-quality, sturdy **artisanal loaf**. We always go for rustic whites or healthy whole grain breads with hearty character that will stand up to a little char around the edges.

THE GRILL

Slice bread about ½ inch thick, **brush both sides with olive oil**, and grill slices on a medium-hot grill for **1 to 2 minutes per side**, until grill marks are almost black and the bread is toasted.

THE GARLIC

After the bread comes off the grill, while it's still hot, **rub one side with a halved garlic clove**. This step is essential: It lays a flavor foundation that will enhance whatever other ingredients you choose to put on top.

THE TOPPINGS

Simplicity is key. Avoid precarious mounds of vegetables. Instead, use slices of **peak-season tomatoes** or **ripe avocado**, sprinkled with (yep, you guessed it) **salt** and **pepper** and drizzled with good **extra-virgin olive oil**. (See more topping ideas on page 314.)

TOMATO CROSTINI
with Mozzarella and Thai Basil

makes 12

12 slices artisanal seven-grain or sesame bread
½ garlic clove
2 cups halved cherry or grape tomatoes (about 10 oz.)
1 minced small shallot
1 Tbsp. toasted sesame oil
1 Tbsp. unseasoned rice vinegar
 Sea salt and freshly ground black pepper
12 slices fresh mozzarella
 Thai basil leaves, for garnish

Sesame oil and rice vinegar spin the *caprese* eastward. The vinaigrette in this Asian-inflected appetizer would taste delicious on the more expected cucumber or daikon radish, but when tossed with sweet cherry tomatoes and paired with mozzarella, the resulting flavors transcend global boundaries.

Grill bread (see page 310) and rub cut side of garlic on one side of each bread slice.

In a bowl, combine tomatoes, shallot, oil, and vinegar. Season to taste with salt and pepper; let sit for 15 minutes.

Put mozzarella slices on toasts. Spoon tomato mixture over mozzarella and garnish with Thai basil leaves. Season to taste with salt and pepper.

GRILLED CORN CROSTINI
with Crema Mexicana and Cilantro

makes 12

 Vegetable oil, for brushing
2 ears of corn, husked
 Kosher salt and freshly ground black pepper
12 slices ciabatta
½ garlic clove
¼ cup crema mexicana or sour cream
3 Tbsp. crumbled feta
12 lime wedges
 Fresh cilantro leaves, for garnish
 Chili powder, for sprinkling

INGREDIENT INFO Crema mexicana is a cultured Mexican cream with a slightly nutty flavor and the consistency of thin sour cream; it's available at some supermarkets and at Latin markets.

Our favorite Mexican street food—*elote*—gets the crostini treatment in this simple starter. The success of this recipe hinges on great bread and perfectly ripe corn—the combination of the sweet grilled kernels and tangy *crema mexicana* is marvelous.

Build a medium-hot fire in a charcoal grill or heat a gas grill to high. Brush grill grate with oil. Brush corn with oil. Season corn with salt and pepper; grill until slightly charred and tender. Slice corn off the cob in wide strips.

Grill bread (see page 310) and rub cut side of garlic on one side of each bread slice.

Mix crema mexicana with feta. Smear toasts with crema mixture. Top crema with grilled corn. Squeeze a lime wedge over each. Garnish with cilantro leaves and sprinkle with chili powder.

Don't be afraid of the char: Almost-burnt toast is a great base for countless toppings.

SMOKED TROUT CROSTINI
with Crème Fraîche and Pickled Onion

makes 12

¼ cup thinly sliced red onion
¼ cup red wine vinegar
1 Tbsp. sugar
½ tsp. kosher salt
12 slices artisanal pumpernickel
    bread
½ cup crème fraîche
1 tsp. lemon zest
¼ tsp. freshly ground black pepper
12 oz. smoked trout
    Chopped chervil or dill

Dense, dark pumpernickel forms the crisp base of our version of the classic Scandinavian-style *smørrebrød*. Quick-pickled onions take half an hour to make and will keep in the refrigerator for 2 weeks. Use them as a topping for burgers, fish tacos, or sandwiches.

Combine onion, vinegar, sugar, and salt with ¼ cup hot water in a bowl; let onions pickle for 30 minutes.

Grill bread (see page 310).

Combine crème fraîche, lemon zest, and pepper in a bowl. Spoon crème fraîche mixture onto toasts. Top each with about 1 oz. smoked trout and a few slices drained pickled onions. Garnish with chervil.

CRAB CROSTINI
with Chile and Mint

makes 12

12 slices artisanal Pullman or
    sourdough bread
8 oz. cooked jumbo lump crabmeat
3 Tbsp. aioli or mayonnaise
2 Tbsp. fresh lime juice
1 Tbsp. finely chopped fresh mint,
    plus thinly sliced mint leaves
    for garnish
1 stemmed, seeded, and minced
    Fresno chile or red jalapeño
    Kosher salt and freshly ground
    black pepper

Briny-sweet crab and piquant chiles shine when married with mayo and fresh lime juice. For the best results, use the freshest, highest-quality crab available and adjust the amount of chiles to bring the heat level to your liking.

Grill bread (see page 310).

In a medium bowl, gently combine crabmeat with aioli, lime juice, chopped mint, and chile. Season to taste with salt and pepper. Spoon about 1 Tbsp. crab mixture onto each toast and garnish with sliced mint leaves.

PEA CROSTINI
with Mint and Parmesan

12 slices artisanal baguette
½ garlic clove
1 cup fresh (or frozen, thawed) peas
  Kosher salt
2 Tbsp. extra-virgin olive oil
  Shaved Parmesan, for garnish
  Torn mint leaves, for garnish
  Balsamic vinegar, for garnish

No need to pull out your food processor to make this. Instead, you can simply mash blanched peas and a couple of tablespoons of olive oil with the back of a fork. To maximize the bright flavors, finish the dish with a drizzle of syrupy, aged balsamic vinegar.

Grill bread (see page 310) and rub with cut side of garlic clove on one side of each bread slice.

Blanch peas in a large saucepan of boiling salted water until just tender, about 2 minutes for fresh peas or 1 minute for frozen. Drain peas; transfer to a bowl. Season with salt. Add oil and mash with the back of a fork.

Spread about 1 Tbsp. pea mixture over each toast. Garnish with shaved Parmesan, mint, and a few drops of balsamic vinegar.

RECIPE IDEAS: Crostini, 6 ways

What *doesn't* taste good on a crunchy slice of grilled bread? Here are some of our favorite add-ons:

AVOCADO

1 Spread slices of **soft, ripe avocado** over bread and sprinkle with sea salt. Drizzle some **lime juice** or olive oil over; sprinkle with crushed **red pepper flakes**.

PAN CON TOMATE

2 Rub or grate the cut side of a **fat, juicy tomato** over bread for classic Spanish *pan con tomate*. On top of that? A little sea salt never hurts.

RICOTTA WITH LEMON ZEST

3 Spread toast with **ricotta** (preferably **sheep's milk**). Add a drizzle of **olive oil**, a sprinkle of **sea salt**, and finally, **lemon zest** for added zing.

BURRATA

Top with olive oil, salt, and soft, fresh **imported** or **domestic Italian cheeses**, such as buffalo mozzarella or *burrata* (distefanocheese.com).

TAPENADE

Flavor-rich purées such as **tapenade**, **pesto**, **harissa**, and **hummus** add another vibrant layer.

PEA SMASH

Create a purée of **smashed cooked peas**, **fava beans**, **edamame**, or other **legumes** mixed with olive oil, lemon juice, and salt.

CROSTINI: THE TOPPINGS

PICKLED FIG CROSTINI
with Robiola and Pistachio Oil

makes 12

½ cup red wine vinegar

2 Tbsp. sugar

6 dried figs

2 Tbsp. toasted shelled pistachios

¼ cup extra-virgin olive oil

12 slices rustic white bread, such as ciabatta

6 oz. (about) Robiola cheese, room temperature

INGREDIENT INFO Robiola, a cow's-milk and sheep's-milk blend, is a mild-flavored soft cheese with a creamy consistency. It's available at Italian markets or murrayscheese.com.

Quick-pickled figs add a sweet-tart note to this variation of our favorite party appetizer. The recipe may be made with fresh figs if in season, but dried figs (available year-round) will plump up and soften in the brine. Toast the shelled pistachios in a dry, heavy frying pan over medium heat for 5 to 6 minutes, stirring often and watching closely to prevent the nuts from burning.

Combine vinegar, sugar, and figs with ¼ cup water in a saucepan; bring to a simmer. Remove from heat and let sit until figs soften, about 30 minutes. Halve figs lengthwise.

Finely crush pistachios and combine with oil. Grill bread (see page 310).

Smear Robiola cheese onto warm toasts. Top with halved figs. Drizzle with pistachios in oil.

GARLIC BREAD
with Rosemary and Parmesan

makes 8

photo, right

2 Tbsp. (¼ stick) unsalted butter, room temperature

2 Tbsp. chopped fresh rosemary

6 Tbsp. extra-virgin olive oil

1¼ cups grated Parmesan (about 3½ oz.)

5 large garlic cloves, minced

1 baguette, halved lengthwise, then crosswise (4 pieces total), each piece diagonally scored ¾ inch deep at 1½-inch intervals

This is garlic bread like you've never seen before. A ramped-up version of the pizza-joint staple is slathered with a garlicky blend of butter and olive oil and seasoned with fresh rosemary and nutty Parmesan cheese.

Blend butter and rosemary in a food processor. Gradually add oil and process until incorporated. Mix in Parmesan. **DO AHEAD:** Can be made 1 day ahead. Cover and refrigerate. Bring to room temperature and mix in garlic before continuing.

Build a medium-hot fire in a charcoal grill, or heat a gas grill to high. Spread cheese mixture over cut sides of bread. Wrap each piece of bread loosely in foil. Grill in foil until bread is crusty and golden, about 8 minutes.

Score each slice of bread before grilling to **let the seasoned butter work** its magic.

GARLIC BREAD WITH
ROSEMARY AND PARMESAN

SIDES & SALADS

WHEN DOES A GRILLED STEAK BECOME A MEAL?

When you flank it with an array of salads, slaws, and sides.

Side dishes can be as simple as tossing perfectly ripe tomatoes with extra-virgin olive oil, sea salt, and fresh basil. Or taking just-shucked corn kernels and spiking them with lime juice, chiles, cilantro, extra-virgin olive oil, and sea salt (when in doubt, add good olive oil and salt). Or you can go for a heartier salad of, say, couscous or quinoa with fresh herbs, ripe vegetables, and a bracing vinaigrette.

And then there's slaw. Have you ever made your own? The difference between homemade and store-bought is remarkable. Same with potato salad. The ones in this chapter taste so much better than the overly sweet, gloppy stuff that's available at the deli counter.

No matter which recipe you're trying out, remember: When it comes to sourcing ingredients, fresher is always better. Buy produce at the peak of ripeness. Look for the juiciest fruits, and fragrant, just-picked herbs. Those are the flavors and textures that go best with that beautifully grilled steak or fish.

CLASSIC COLESLAW

8 to 10 servings

⅔ cup mayonnaise
¼ cup minced onion
3 Tbsp. minced dill pickle, plus
    2 Tbsp. pickle juice from jar
2 Tbsp. distilled white vinegar
1 Tbsp. prepared horseradish
1 Tbsp. sugar
1 tsp. kosher salt
½ tsp. celery seeds
½ tsp. freshly ground black pepper
8 to 9 cups shredded cabbage,
    carrots, and fennel

Here's the home-run picnic coleslaw you've been looking for. The dressing recipe makes enough for 8 to 9 cups of shredded cabbage, carrots and fennel. As with all the salads in this chapter, feel free to mix up the amount and type of vegetables according to what's in season and what you're in the mood for. To ensure maximum crunch, add dressing right before serving rather than way in advance.

Whisk first 9 ingredients in a large bowl to blend. **DO AHEAD:** Can be made 1 day ahead. Keep chilled.

  Add shredded vegetables and toss to coat.

CARROT SLAW
with Cilantro and Chile

4 to 6 servings

photo, page 323 (1)

12 oz. carrots, preferably assorted
    colors, peeled, julienned
    (about 4 cups)
2 Tbsp. vegetable oil or grapeseed
    oil
1 Tbsp. fresh lime juice
1½ tsp. sugar
½ tsp. kosher salt, more as needed
2 jalapeños, seeded, minced
½ cup (loosely packed) fresh
    cilantro leaves
¾ tsp. ground coriander
    Freshly ground black pepper

Using a combination of red, white, yellow, and/or purple carrots makes this dish over-the-top gorgeous. The dressing of cilantro, lime, and jalapeño makes for a great slaw that can also double as an unexpected topping for fish tacos or a crunchy filling for sandwiches.

Toss carrots, oil, lime juice, sugar, salt, and jalapeños in a large bowl. Let marinate, tossing occasionally, for 15 minutes.

  Add cilantro and coriander; toss to evenly incorporate. Season to taste with salt and pepper.

Kitchen Wisdom

RAW TALENT A slaw—or coleslaw—is a mixture of shredded or julienned vegetables and fruit, tossed in a tangy dressing. The **pairing of crisp textures with the bright acidity of a dressing** makes slaws an ideal complement to the char and richness of grilled meats and fish. Think beyond traditional cabbage: Really, any hardy, shreddable vegetable will work.

CANDY-STRIPE BEET AND CARROT SLAW

4 to 6 servings

photo, right (2)

¼ cup plain Greek yogurt
1 tsp. finely grated orange zest
3 Tbsp. fresh orange juice
1 Tbsp. fresh lemon juice
1 Tbsp. finely chopped fresh dill
5 2-inch-diameter candy-stripe (Chioggia) beets, peeled, julienned
1 medium carrot, peeled, julienned
Kosher salt and freshly ground black pepper

Candy-stripe beets, also known as Chioggia beets, look just like they sound—with eye-catching red and white stripes. Their colors stay intact in this yogurt-based dressing (as opposed to bleeding the way that red beets would), which makes for a lovely presentation. If you can't find Chioggias, use golden or red beets—the presentation won't be as dazzling, but they'll still be delicious.

Whisk yogurt, orange zest, orange juice, lemon juice, and dill in a medium bowl. Add beets and carrot and toss to combine. Season to taste with salt and pepper.

CELERY, APPLE, AND FENNEL SLAW

4 to 6 servings

photo, right (3)

3 Tbsp. extra-virgin olive oil
2½ Tbsp. apple cider vinegar
1½ Tbsp. coarsely chopped fresh tarragon
2 tsp. fresh lemon juice
¼ tsp. sugar
3 celery stalks, thinly sliced on a diagonal, plus ¼ cup (loosely packed) celery leaves
2 small fennel bulbs, thinly sliced crosswise, plus 1 Tbsp. chopped fennel fronds
1 firm, crisp apple (such as Pink Lady, Gala, or Granny Smith), julienned
Kosher salt and freshly ground black pepper

The original, traditional Waldorf salad consists of a mix of apples, celery, and walnuts with a creamy dressing. Delicious, absolutely—but we find that version has almost *too* much crunch. So we skip the walnuts and use tarragon in place of parsley. (If you can't live without walnuts, toast them in a dry pan over medium heat before adding to the salad.) Serve with grilled fish or pork.

Whisk first 5 ingredients in a medium bowl. Add celery and celery leaves, fennel bulbs and fennel fronds, and apple; toss to coat. Season to taste with salt and pepper.

2

3

4

+

If you love coleslaw, **invest in a mandoline.** It's the ultimate tool for making airy julienne and paper-thin vegetable slices.

1

FAST, EASY, FRESH:
FOUR OF OUR FAVORITE SLAWS

TUSCAN KALE CAESAR SLAW

photo, page 323 (4)

¼ cup fresh lemon juice

8 anchovy fillets packed in oil, drained

1 garlic clove

1 tsp. Dijon mustard

¾ cup extra-virgin olive oil

½ cup finely grated Parmesan, divided

Kosher salt and freshly ground black pepper

1 large hard-boiled egg, peeled

14 oz. Tuscan kale or other kale, center stalks removed, thinly sliced crosswise (about 8 cups)

INGREDIENT INFO Tuscan kale, also called cavolo nero, Lacinato, black kale, or dinosaur kale, is available at most supermarkets and at farmers' markets.

The crisp-tender texture and robust flavor of Tuscan kale stands up to the tart, Caesar-like dressing (which includes mustard and anchovy fillets). In addition to serving this hearty slaw as a side dish, it would also be impressive as a main-course salad served alongside grilled chicken, beef, or lamb. If you can't find Tuscan kale, it's fine to use another variety.

Purée first 4 ingredients in a blender until smooth. With machine running, slowly add oil, drop by drop, until creamy dressing forms. Transfer dressing to a bowl and stir in ¼ cup Parmesan. Season to taste with salt and pepper. Cover and chill. **DO AHEAD:** Dressing can be made 2 days ahead. Keep chilled.

Separate egg white from yolk. Using the back of a spoon, press egg white through a coarse-mesh strainer set over a small bowl. Repeat with egg yolk, using a clean strainer and bowl. **DO AHEAD:** Can be made 6 hours ahead. Cover bowls separately and chill.

Toss kale and dressing in a large bowl to coat. Season to taste with salt and pepper. Sprinkle with remaining ¼ cup Parmesan and sieved eggs.

Kitchen Wisdom

HOW TO DRESS THE SLAW You know that 3:1 rule that everyone goes by when making a classic vinaigrette? Forget it. With slaws you want something closer to a **1:1 ratio of fat (olive oil or mayo) to acid (vinegar or citrus juice)**. Why? Because slaw is best when it's bright and tangy, not oily. Once you've got the 1:1 base, add a little honey or sugar to bring out the ingredients' natural sweetness. **Dress the slaw right before serving** to maintain the crunch.

STONE-FRUIT SLAW

1 Tbsp. grated peeled ginger
1 Tbsp. unseasoned rice vinegar
1 Tbsp. vegetable oil
2 tsp. (packed) light brown sugar
¼ tsp. curry powder
⅛ tsp. crushed red pepper flakes
1½ lb. assorted firm stone fruit (about 5; such as plums, nectarines, peaches, or apricots), julienned
2 scallions, thinly sliced on a diagonal
Kosher salt and freshly ground black pepper

A blend of fresh ginger, rice vinegar, and curry powder infuses this slaw with a chutney-like flavor and helps draw out juices from peak-season stone fruit. Serve it as a side or condiment for grilled tandoori chicken or pork. Select stone fruit that are slightly underripe. They are firmer and easier to julienne than soft, juicy ones.

Whisk first 6 ingredients in a medium bowl. Add fruit and scallions; toss gently to coat. Season to taste with salt and pepper.

GETTING IT RIGHT: How to Julienne Vegetables for Slaw

The main difference between a slaw and a salad is the size of ingredients: Many slaws call for a perfect julienne. Food processors are great (use a shredding disk for cabbages and a julienne disk for carrots and other hard vegetables). But if you want to go manual, use a mandoline and/or a chef's knife. Here's how:

Some mandolines have a julienne attachment. If so, use it. If not, use a **mandoline with a straight blade** to produce thin slices. Slice carrots on the long bias, beets into large rounds. Then ...

Stack the fruit or vegetable slices into manageable piles 3 or 4 slices high and **run an 8-inch chef's knife through the stack,** making julienne cuts that are as wide as the slices are thick (about ⅛ inch).

OLD-FASHIONED POTATO SALAD

8 to 10 servings

photo, right

2¾ lb. medium red-skinned potatoes, peeled (about 8)
1¼ tsp. kosher salt, more as needed
½ cup mayonnaise
¼ cup sweet pickle juice from jar
1½ Tbsp. Dijon mustard
1 tsp. sugar
¼ tsp. freshly ground black pepper, more as needed
5 large hard-boiled egg yolks
2 Tbsp. chopped red onion
2 Tbsp. chopped flat-leaf parsley
Paprika, for sprinkling
8 to 10 sweet pickle chips

This spin on Southern-style potato salad gets a kick from sweet pickle juice and mashed eggs. When scooping portions for guests, don't forget the most crucial step: a slice or two of pickle on top of each serving.

Place potatoes in a large pot. Add water to cover by 2 inches, season with salt, and bring to a boil. Reduce heat to medium and cook until potatoes are tender when pierced with a knife, 20 to 30 minutes. Drain. Place potatoes in a large bowl and let cool slightly.

Meanwhile, whisk mayonnaise, pickle juice, mustard, sugar, ¼ tsp. pepper, and 1¼ tsp. salt in a small bowl for dressing.

Using a large wooden spoon, coarsely smash potatoes, leaving some larger pieces mixed with some well-mashed pieces. Add dressing and egg yolks to potatoes and toss to coat, coarsely mashing egg yolks. Add onion and parsley; gently toss to evenly incorporate. Season to taste with more salt and pepper, if desired. **DO AHEAD:** Can be made 1 day ahead. Cover and chill.

Divide potato salad among bowls; dust with paprika. Top each serving with a pickle chip.

POTATO SALAD
with Radishes and Herb Vinaigrette

8 to 10 servings

3 lb. medium Yukon Gold potatoes (about 8), peeled
Kosher salt and freshly ground black pepper
1 celery stalk, finely chopped
½ cup extra-virgin olive oil
½ cup fresh lemon juice
½ cup minced shallot
½ cup thinly sliced scallion
1 Tbsp. Dijon mustard
1 tsp. grated garlic
1 tsp. sugar
8 radishes (6 oz.), thinly sliced
2 Tbsp. chopped flat-leaf parsley
2 Tbsp. chopped fresh tarragon

Radishes add terrific crunch and color to this salad, while a tarragon-and-parsley-spiked vinaigrette keeps things light and fresh. Bonus: Like many slaws, this salad tastes as delicious when served cold as it does when served at room temperature.

Cook potatoes in lightly salted water until just tender in center but not falling apart, about 20 minutes. Drain, then transfer to a baking sheet; cool for 5 minutes. Slice potatoes into ¼-inch-thick rounds and spread out on baking sheet; season to taste with salt and pepper and cool for 5 minutes more.

Meanwhile, combine celery, oil, lemon juice, shallot, scallion, mustard, garlic, and sugar in a large bowl; whisk until well combined. Season to taste with salt and pepper. **DO AHEAD:** Dressing can be made 2 days ahead and chilled.

Add radishes, parsley, tarragon, and potatoes to bowl and toss gently to evenly coat. Season to taste with salt and pepper.

This tangy, eggy potato salad—which gets revved up with a **splash of pickle juice**—is a classic for summer barbecues.

OLD-FASHIONED POTATO SALAD

PICKLED-BEAN POTATO SALAD

2 shallots, halved lengthwise, very
  thinly sliced (about 1 cup)
6 Tbsp. red wine vinegar, more as
  needed
  Kosher salt
3 lb. baby Yukon Gold potatoes
  Freshly ground black pepper
1 cup mayonnaise, more as needed
  Large pinch of smoked paprika
3 cups coarsely chopped trimmed
  watercress, purslane, or wild
  arugula
1 cup 2-inch pieces store-bought
  pickled green beans
2 to 3 large hard-boiled eggs,
  peeled, quartered
¾ cup chopped flat-leaf parsley
  or celery leaves

Pickled green beans add a snappy tang to this potato salad. Make the salad as tart or as creamy as you like by adjusting the amount of vinegar or mayonnaise.

Place shallots in a small bowl. Stir in 6 Tbsp. red wine vinegar and a large pinch of salt; set aside.

Cook potatoes in a large saucepan of boiling salted water until just tender, about 30 minutes. Drain potatoes; transfer to a large bowl. Lightly crush potatoes with the back of a large spoon. Add shallot-vinegar mixture to hot potatoes and toss to coat. Season with salt and pepper.

Whisk 1 cup mayonnaise and paprika in a small bowl; add to potatoes and toss to coat. Fold in watercress, beans, and eggs and season to taste with salt, pepper, and more vinegar, if desired. Add more mayonnaise, if a creamier consistency is desired. **DO AHEAD:** Can be made 1 day ahead. Cover and chill. Return to room temperature before serving. Stir in additional mayonnaise if mixture is dry.

Garnish with parsley.

Kitchen Wisdom

TWO SECRETS OF POTATO SALAD 1. Always **drain potatoes** as soon as they are tender to prevent them from falling apart. 2. **Dress potatoes** while they're still warm. This way the dressing can soak into them instead of just coating the outside.

POTATO SALAD
with Lemon–Olive Oil Dressing

2 lb. red-skinned potatoes, peeled, cut into 1-inch pieces
¼ cup extra-virgin olive oil
½ cup finely chopped red bell pepper
½ cup finely chopped red onion
¼ cup fresh lemon juice
3 Tbsp. chopped fresh oregano
2 Tbsp. chopped fresh mint
2 tsp. kosher salt
¾ tsp. freshly ground black pepper

A few simple moves elevate this salad from ordinary to standout. Start by peeling red-skinned potatoes—this allows them to soak up maximum flavor from the bright, tangy dressing. Once the skins are off, you'll steam (rather than boil) the potatoes. This gentler method keeps their shape intact and prevents them from getting waterlogged.

Place potatoes in a steamer basket set over a large pot of boiling water. Steam just until tender, about 10 minutes. Transfer potatoes to a large bowl. Add oil to potatoes and toss to coat. Mix in bell pepper, onion, lemon juice, oregano, mint, salt, and pepper. **DO AHEAD:** Can be made 4 hours ahead. Cover and chill. Let stand at room temperature for 1 hour before serving.

BASMATI RICE SALAD
with Summer Vegetables

1 small shallot, chopped
2 Tbsp. chopped fresh flat-leaf parsley
2 Tbsp. red wine vinegar
2 tsp. fresh thyme leaves
   Kosher salt and freshly ground black pepper
⅓ cup extra-virgin olive oil
2 cups cooked basmati rice, cooled
2 cups bite-size pieces assorted vegetables (such as radishes, tomatoes, peas, summer squash, or shredded carrots)
¾ cup torn mixed greens, sprouts, and herbs
⅓ cup chopped red, yellow, or white onion or scallions
2 Tbsp. toasted pine nuts (optional)

Create endless riffs on this salad by using the vibrant herb dressing with your favorite grains. This recipe calls for long-grain basmati rice, which is a shining star in pilafs and salads because it doesn't clump. But it would also taste excellent made with farro or quinoa.

Pulse first 4 ingredients in a blender until combined; season to taste with salt and pepper. With blender running, slowly drizzle in oil. Process dressing until well blended.

Place remaining ingredients in a large bowl; drizzle with 3 Tbsp. dressing and toss to coat. Pass remaining dressing alongside for drizzling over.

BLACK BARLEY SALAD
with Fennel and Radishes

photo, right

2 cups black or pearl barley, rinsed
 Kosher salt
1 large fennel bulb (about 10 oz.),
  bulb cut lengthwise into ¼-inch
  slices, 2 Tbsp. fronds set aside
2 Tbsp. plus ½ cup extra-virgin
  olive oil
 Freshly ground black pepper
⅓ cup fresh orange juice
¼ cup fresh lime juice
1 small shallot, minced
2 Tbsp. chopped fresh dill, plus
  ½ cup dill sprigs, divided
1 tsp. finely grated orange zest
4 large radishes, thinly sliced,
  divided
¼ cup oil-cured olives, pitted,
  halved lengthwise

Black barley is hearty and slightly chewy. It creates great texture contrasts when paired with raw and cooked vegetables. If you can't find it, substitute pearl barley.

Preheat oven to 425°F. Place barley in a medium pot and add water to cover by 1½ inches. Season with salt. Bring to a boil; reduce heat and simmer uncovered until barley is tender and water is absorbed, 40 to 45 minutes. Spread out barley on a large rimmed baking sheet; let cool.

While barley is cooking, toss fennel slices and 2 Tbsp. oil in a medium bowl to coat. Season with salt and pepper. Spread fennel slices out in a single layer on another rimmed baking sheet. Roast until fennel is crisp-tender and beginning to brown in spots, about 18 minutes. Let fennel cool on baking sheet. **DO AHEAD:** Barley and fennel can be prepared 1 day ahead. Cover separately and refrigerate.

Whisk both juices, shallot, chopped dill, and zest in a medium bowl. Gradually whisk in remaining ½ cup oil; season vinaigrette to taste with salt and pepper.

Transfer barley to a large bowl; add roasted fennel, along with any accumulated juices on baking sheet. Add half of radishes, all the olives, and ¼ cup dill sprigs. Drizzle ½ cup orange vinaigrette over and toss to coat; season with salt and pepper. Arrange salad on a large platter.

Scatter remaining radishes, reserved fennel fronds, and remaining ¼ cup dill sprigs over salad. Pass remaining orange vinaigrette alongside for drizzling over.

5 Steps to GREAT GRAINS

Full-flavored grain salads are easy to free-style. The goal is to create a tempting mix of flavors, colors, and textures. Here's a cheat sheet to building your own.

1 COOK YOUR GRAINS

There's a world of grains out there, from **quinoa to barley and beyond**. Two cups of raw grains will serve about six people as a main course or eight as a side.

2 ADD TEXTURE

Go for a mix of **raw, chopped vegetables plus roasted and caramelized** ones. Shave some thinly, grate others, and coarsely chop the rest. Add toasted nuts for crunch.

3 GET DRESSED

The dressing should be **simple and tart**, to complement the grains, not overpower them. Blend citrus juice or vinegar with enough olive oil to coat the grains.

4 COLORIZE

Add **color as well as flavor** with a variety of extras. Chopped herbs are a must (our go-tos are parsley and chives), and chiles, tart fruit, and toasted spices are always good choices.

5 SEASON

Add half a cup of dressing to the grains; season with salt and pepper. Mix in the remaining ingredients and dressing. **Taste, season, and repeat** until you get an irresistible bite.

+

Whole grains don't just pack a **nutritional punch**—they also give backbone to toss-together salads.

BLACK BARLEY SALAD WITH FENNEL AND RADISHES

BLACK RICE
with Mango and Peanuts

2 oranges
¼ cup fresh lime juice, more as needed
2 Tbsp. vegetable oil
1 Tbsp. fish sauce (such as nam pla or nuoc nam; optional)
2 cups black rice (preferably Lotus Foods Forbidden Rice)
  Kosher salt
2 just-ripe mangoes, peeled, pitted, cut into ½-inch dice
1 cup finely chopped red onion (about ½ large onion)
1 cup fresh cilantro leaves
½ cup unsalted, dry-roasted peanuts
6 scallions, thinly sliced
2 jalapeños, seeded, minced

INGREDIENT INFO Black rice, a Chinese heirloom grain, has a delicious toasty flavor that enlivens sweet and savory dishes alike. Look for it at some supermarkets, Whole Foods markets, or at lotusfoods.com.

Fruit adds vibrant color and sweetness to savory grain salads. Here, mangoes and oranges mix well against the deep purple hue of black rice. We like it best served alongside grilled fish.

Remove peel and white pith from oranges. Working over a medium bowl to catch juices and using a small sharp knife, cut between membranes to release orange segments into bowl. Squeeze membranes over bowl to release any juices. Strain juices through a fine-mesh sieve into a small bowl; reserve orange segments.

Add ¼ cup lime juice, oil, and fish sauce, if using, to bowl with orange juice; whisk to blend. Set dressing aside.

Bring rice and 2¾ cups water to a boil in a large saucepan. Season lightly with salt. Cover, reduce heat to low, and simmer until all liquid is absorbed and rice is tender, about 25 minutes. Remove pan from heat and let stand for 15 minutes. Spread out rice on a rimmed baking sheet, drizzle with dressing, and season lightly with salt; let cool.

Place mangoes and all remaining ingredients in a large bowl. Add rice and toss gently to combine. Season lightly with salt and more lime juice, if desired.

QUINOA TABBOULEH

1 cup quinoa, rinsed well
½ tsp. kosher salt, more as needed
2 Tbsp. fresh lemon juice
1 garlic clove, minced
½ cup extra-virgin olive oil
  Freshly ground black pepper
1 large English hothouse cucumber
  or 2 Persian cucumbers, cut into
  ¼-inch pieces
1 pint cherry tomatoes, halved
⅔ cup chopped flat-leaf parsley
½ cup chopped fresh mint
2 scallions, thinly sliced

The refreshing Middle Eastern salad gets an of-the-moment upgrade with quinoa. The tiny nutritional powerhouse—which replaces bulgur here—is loaded with protein, which makes this dish both a delicious vegetarian main course and a summer-suitable side. Go ahead and play with the proportions of parsley and mint based on your tastes.

Bring quinoa, salt, and 1¼ cups water to a boil in a medium saucepan over high heat. Reduce heat to medium-low, cover, and simmer until quinoa is tender, about 10 minutes. Remove from heat and let stand, covered, for 5 minutes. Fluff with a fork.

Meanwhile, whisk lemon juice and garlic in a small bowl. Gradually whisk in olive oil. Season dressing to taste with salt and pepper.

Spread out quinoa on a large rimmed baking sheet; let cool. Transfer to a large bowl; mix in ¼ cup dressing. **DO AHEAD:** Can be made 1 day ahead. Cover remaining dressing and quinoa separately; chill.

Add cucumber, tomatoes, parsley, mint, and scallions to bowl with quinoa; toss to coat. Season to taste with salt and pepper. Drizzle remaining dressing over.

CURRIED SPELT SALAD

2 cups spelt, semi-pearled farro, or
  whole wheat berries, rinsed
1 tsp. kosher salt, more as needed
2 Tbsp. vegetable oil
2½ tsp. curry powder
2 tsp. yellow mustard seeds
¾ tsp. ground cardamom
¾ tsp. ground coriander
6 small carrots, peeled, cut into
  ¼-inch dice
  Freshly ground black pepper
¼ cup apple cider vinegar
1 cup thinly sliced red onion (about
  ½ large onion)
½ lemon cut lengthwise, ends
  removed, finely chopped with
  peel (about ½ cup)
3 cups chopped grilled chicken
  (optional)
2 cups baby or wild arugula
2 cups (packed) cilantro sprigs with
  tender stems
2 Tbsp. extra-virgin olive oil

Spelt is a type of wheat that has a toothsome texture and a slightly sweet, nutty flavor. Paired with grilled chicken (to add protein), it makes for a lively, aromatic dish—though it's just as satisfying on its own as a vegetarian side. If you can't find spelt, semi-pearled farro or whole wheat berries will also do the trick.

Place spelt and 1 tsp. salt in a medium pot. Add water to cover by 1½ inches. Bring to a boil; reduce heat to medium-low and simmer, uncovered, until spelt is tender and water is mostly absorbed, about 1 hour (or 12 to 15 minutes if using semi-pearled farro). Drain; place in a large bowl.

Meanwhile, heat vegetable oil in a medium saucepan over medium heat. Add curry, mustard seeds, cardamom, and coriander; cook, stirring often, until spices are fragrant and mustard seeds begin to pop, 2 to 3 minutes. Stir in carrots and season with salt and pepper. Cook, stirring often, until carrots are crisp-tender, 5 to 6 minutes.

Add cider vinegar and stir until evaporated, 1 to 2 minutes. Stir in onion and lemon. Remove pan from heat and stir until onion is wilted, 1 to 2 minutes. Add vegetable mixture to bowl with spelt. Season to taste with salt and pepper. Let cool. **DO AHEAD:** Can be made 1 day ahead. Cover and chill.

Add chicken, if using, arugula, cilantro, and olive oil to spelt mixture; toss to combine. Transfer salad to a large platter.

GRILLED GREEN BEANS
with Lemon and Thyme

8 servings

2 lb. green beans, trimmed
2 Tbsp. (¼ stick) unsalted butter
2 tsp. chopped fresh thyme
1 tsp. finely grated lemon zest
  Kosher salt and freshly ground
    black pepper

SPECIAL EQUIPMENT A grill basket

When fresh, tender green beans are all over the markets, you'll find yourself going back to this easy-to-prepare side again and again. If you're serving it either at room temperature or chilled from the refrigerator, replace the butter with olive oil, which won't harden when cold.

Build a medium-hot fire in a charcoal grill, or heat a gas grill to high. Place green beans in a grill basket and grill until beans are crisp-tender, 5 to 6 minutes.

Melt butter in a large skillet over medium-high heat. Add beans, thyme, and lemon zest; season to taste with salt and pepper. Toss until heated, about 5 minutes.

BONUS RECIPES: Corn off the Cob, 4 Ways

Corn on the cob is an iconic summer side dish, whether grilled in or out of the husk (see page 279). But don't stop there. Cut the grilled kernels from the cob and include them in refreshing summer salads or sides—or mix into salsas as toppings for grilled chicken, skirt steaks, or pork chops.

ZESTY SIDE DISH

Mix corn kernels with chopped fresh cilantro and jalapeños. Season with salt. Toss with a vinaigrette of lime juice and olive oil seasoned with kosher salt and freshly ground pepper.

SIMPLE SALSA

Stir corn together with cucumbers and chopped red onion; season salsa with red wine vinegar, olive oil, and chopped fresh oregano or basil.

MAIN COURSE

Gently combine grilled corn kernels with grilled shrimp, avocado, halved cherry tomatoes, sliced scallions, and arugula. Toss with vinaigrette.

SWEET AND SAVORY

Mix corn with chopped cooked bacon, slices of sweet onion, and chopped fresh cilantro. Toss it all together with a Sherry vinaigrette.

SUMMER CORN SAUTÉ
with Tons of Herbs

6 servings

¼ cup (½ stick) unsalted butter
1 large shallot, chopped
1 tsp. cumin seeds
6 cups fresh corn kernels (cut from about 9 large ears)
1 tsp. kosher salt, more as needed
¾ tsp. freshly ground black pepper
1 cup chopped assorted fresh herbs (such as basil, cilantro, chives, and flat-leaf parsley)
¼ cup chopped fresh dill
¼ cup chopped fresh tarragon

We all love corn on the cob with butter and salt. But if you're in the mood for a twist, add a new dimension by slicing raw or grilled kernels off the cob and quickly sautéing them with herbs and aromatic cumin seeds.

Melt butter in a large heavy skillet over medium heat. Add shallot and cumin seeds. Sauté until shallot is golden brown, about 4 minutes. Add corn kernels, 1 tsp. salt, and pepper. Sauté until corn is tender, about 5 minutes. Remove from heat and mix in all herbs. Season to taste with salt. Transfer corn to a serving bowl.

SUCCOTASH

makes 6 cups

3 ears sweet corn
6 Tbsp. (¾ stick) unsalted butter
¾ cup chopped red bell pepper
¾ cup chopped onion
2 cups chopped tomatoes
Kosher salt and freshly ground black pepper
2 cups fresh or thawed frozen lima beans
1 sprig thyme

Why do Southerners love this classic summertime medley of corn, lima beans, and tomatoes? Because it's uncomplicated to prepare yet delivers a variety of color, texture, and flavor.

Cut corn kernels from cobs and scrape cobs with back of knife to release juices. Reserve kernels and juices; discard cobs.

Melt butter in a large saucepan over medium heat. Add bell pepper and onion and cook, stirring occasionally, until onion is soft and translucent, about 15 minutes. Add tomatoes and season with salt and pepper. Simmer until tomatoes release juices and thicken slightly, about 10 minutes. Stir in lima beans and ½ cup water and simmer until beans are tender, about 10 minutes. Fold in corn with juices and thyme sprig and simmer until corn is just tender, about 3 minutes. Remove and discard thyme sprigs. **DO AHEAD:** Succotash may be made 3 days ahead. Cover and chill.

ROOT BEER BAKED BEANS

photo, right

4 slices applewood-smoked
   bacon, cut crosswise into
   1-inch pieces
3½ cups chopped onions
2 garlic cloves, minced
4 15-oz. cans cannellini beans
   (white kidney beans),
   rinsed, drained
1½ cups root beer, preferably
   artisanal
3 Tbsp. apple cider vinegar
3 Tbsp. mild-flavored (light)
   molasses
2 Tbsp. Dijon mustard
2 Tbsp. tomato paste
1½ tsp. chili powder
1 tsp. kosher salt
1 tsp. freshly ground black pepper

Sweet, salty, and robust, these are the baked beans you grew up polishing off at backyard barbecues. You'll never reach for a can again. To get the most delicious flavor, we highly recommend using artisanal root beer made with cane sugar (not corn syrup). Our favorites are Faygo and Fitz's.

Preheat oven to 400°F. Cook bacon in a large ovenproof pot over medium heat, stirring occasionally, until crisp. Using a slotted spoon, transfer bacon to paper towels. Add onions to drippings in pot; cook, stirring occasionally, until beginning to brown, about 8 minutes. Add garlic; stir for 1 minute. Add beans, root beer, vinegar, molasses, mustard, tomato paste, chili powder, salt, and pepper; mix well. Stir in bacon; bring to a boil. Transfer to oven; bake uncovered until liquid thickens, about 30 minutes.

HEIRLOOM TOMATOES
with Shell Beans Vinaigrette

1 Tbsp. extra-virgin olive oil
1 cup chopped sweet onion
   (such as Vidalia or Maui)
4 garlic cloves, minced
1 bay leaf
½ tsp. plus 1 Tbsp. chopped fresh
   thyme
4 cups shelled fresh or frozen
   black-eyed peas (about 20 oz.)
2 cups low-salt chicken broth
¼ cup balsamic vinegar
¼ cup extra-virgin olive oil
   Kosher salt and freshly ground
   black pepper
4 fresh medium basil leaves,
   thinly sliced
4 medium heirloom tomatoes
   (different varieties, if possible),
   sliced

The term *shell bean* generally refers to any bean that has to be removed from the pod before eating. Black-eyed peas, fava beans, and cranberry beans all fall into this category. Look for them at farmers' markets during the summer when they're at their peak. You could also substitute thawed frozen fava beans out of their pods, edamame, or peas. The precise cooking time may vary depending on the mix you end up with, but the results will be delicious no matter what.

Heat olive oil in a medium saucepan over medium-high heat. Add onion; sauté for 4 to 5 minutes. Add garlic, bay leaf, and ½ tsp. thyme; stir for 1 minute. Add peas and broth; bring to a boil. Cover with lid slightly ajar; reduce heat to medium-low. Simmer, stirring occasionally, until peas are soft, about 25 minutes. Drain. Transfer to a large microwave-safe bowl.

Whisk vinegar and extra-virgin olive oil in a small bowl. Season to taste with salt and pepper. Pour over warm peas; toss to coat. **DO AHEAD:** Can be made 2 days ahead. Cover and chill. Bring to room temperature before continuing.

Stir basil and remaining 1 Tbsp. thyme into peas. Discard bay leaf. Season to taste with salt and pepper. Arrange tomato slices on a platter. Season with salt and pepper. Spoon warm or room-temperature peas over tomatoes.

A bottle of root beer serves as a **short-cut to extra flavor** in our spin on a campfire favorite.

ROOT BEER BAKED BEANS

BLACK BEANS
with Chorizo and Chipotle Cream

BEANS

1½ cups dried black beans

2 onions, 1 halved, 1 chopped
(about 2 cups chopped)

1 bay leaf

1 tsp. dried oregano

2 Tbsp. extra-virgin olive oil

2 links fresh chorizo sausage (6 to
7 oz. total), casings removed

2 Tbsp. finely chopped fresh
cilantro

2 garlic cloves, minced

2 tsp. minced seeded jalapeño

½ tsp. ground cumin

Kosher salt and freshly ground
black pepper

CHIPOTLE CREAM

½ cup sour cream

1¼ tsp. chipotle hot pepper sauce

1 tsp. fresh lime juice

Kosher salt

Finely chopped fresh cilantro,
for garnish

The chorizo used in this recipe is the Mexican variety—a sausage of uncooked ground pork or beef that's loaded with spices and imparts a lot of flavor. If you can't find chipotle hot sauce, use adobo sauce from canned chipotles.

BEANS

Place beans in a large saucepan. Add water to cover by 2 inches; soak overnight.

Drain beans. Return to saucepan. Add onion halves, bay leaf, and oregano. Add cold water to cover by 2 inches. Bring to a boil, reduce heat to low, and simmer, stirring occasionally, until beans are very tender, 1½ to 2 hours. Drain beans, reserving cooking liquid. Discard onion halves and bay leaf.

Heat oil in a large heavy deep nonstick skillet over medium heat. Add chorizo and cook, breaking up with the back of a spoon, until brown, 4 to 5 minutes. Using a slotted spoon, transfer chorizo to a small bowl. Add chopped onion to drippings in skillet. Cook, stirring often, until soft and golden brown, about 10 minutes. Add cilantro, garlic, jalapeño, and cumin; stir for 1 minute. Add beans, ¾ cup reserved cooking liquid, and chorizo to onion mixture. Stir to distribute evenly. Simmer over medium-low heat until heated through and flavors are blended, 3 to 4 minutes. Season to taste with salt and pepper. **DO AHEAD:** Can be made 1 day ahead. Chill uncovered until cool, then cover and keep chilled. Rewarm over medium heat before serving.

CHIPOTLE CREAM

Whisk first 3 ingredients in a small bowl to blend. Season to taste with salt.
DO AHEAD: Can be made 1 day ahead. Cover and chill. Rewhisk before serving.

Transfer beans to a large bowl. Garnish with chipotle cream and chopped cilantro.

GRILLED PANZANELLA

1½ cups small to medium fresh
   basil leaves, divided
⅔ cup plus 2 Tbsp. extra-virgin
   olive oil, divided
1 large shallot, thinly sliced
1 small Fresno chile or red
   jalapeño, seeded, finely
   chopped
2 Tbsp. fresh lemon juice
2 tsp. finely grated lemon zest
   Kosher salt and freshly ground
   black pepper
3 lb. ripe tomatoes, assorted
   colors and sizes
1 12-oz. loaf rustic or sourdough
   bread, cut into ½-inch-thick
   slices
1 garlic clove, halved

The rustic ingredients in this Italian tomato-and-bread salad would be the perfect showcase for homegrown tomatoes, preferably still warm from the sun. They're adorned with a delicious lemony basil dressing and share the bowl with smoky grilled bread. A quick rub of garlic over the grilled bread is essential; it adds just the right amount of pungency.

Set a fine-mesh sieve over a large bowl. Purée ¾ cup basil leaves and ⅓ cup plus 2 Tbsp. oil in a blender until smooth and only tiny flecks of basil remain. Strain mixture into bowl, pressing on solids to extract as much oil as possible; discard solids. Whisk shallot, chile, lemon juice, and lemon zest into basil oil. Season to taste with salt and pepper. **DO AHEAD:** Dressing can be made 1 day ahead. Cover and chill. Return to room temperature and rewhisk before using.

Slice tomatoes into assorted wedges, rounds, and cubes; add to bowl with dressing. Toss to coat; let marinate at room temperature for 30 minutes.

Meanwhile, build a medium-hot fire in a charcoal grill, or heat a gas grill to high. Brush bread with remaining ⅓ cup olive oil. Season with salt and pepper. Grill bread until charred in spots, about 2 minutes per side. Rub grilled bread with cut sides of garlic clove. Tear bread into 1- to 2-inch pieces.

Add remaining ¾ cup basil leaves and bread to bowl with tomato mixture; toss to coat. Season panzanella to taste with salt and pepper.

LITTLE GEM SALAD
with Feta and Cumin

2¼ cups crumbled feta (about 10 oz.;
   preferably Bulgarian), divided
1 cup plus 3 Tbsp. plain whole-milk
   yogurt
1 tsp. ground cumin
1 tsp. finely grated lemon zest
1 small garlic clove, chopped
   Kosher salt and freshly ground
   black pepper
1 tsp. cumin seeds
1½ lb. Little Gem lettuce or hearts of
   romaine, stemmed, leaves torn
2 Tbsp. fresh oregano leaves

This salad and its creamy-tangy dressing is a new staple in our salad arsenal. If you can't find Little Gem—a cross between baby romaine and butter lettuce that has crisp texture and a gentle flavor—use romaine hearts. This would be terrific paired with grilled lamb or chicken or with Green Shawarma Salmon (page 203).

Purée 1¾ cups feta, yogurt, ground cumin, lemon zest, and garlic in a food processor until smooth. Transfer to a medium bowl. Season dressing to taste with salt and pepper.

Toast cumin seeds in a small skillet over medium heat, stirring, until seeds are aromatic and slightly darker in color, 3 to 4 minutes. Let cool.

Toss lettuce in a large bowl with dressing just to coat. Season salad to taste with salt and pepper. Garnish with remaining ½ cup feta, cumin seeds, and oregano.

A **kaleidoscope of bright colors and flavors** meld beautifully in this ultra-fresh corn salad. It's summer in a bowl.

CHARRED CORN SALAD
WITH BASIL AND TOMATOES

CHARRED CORN SALAD
with Basil and Tomatoes

8 servings photo, left

Vegetable oil, for brushing
12 ears of corn, husked
6 Tbsp. extra-virgin olive oil, divided
1 cup thinly sliced red onion
2 large tomatoes, chopped
1 cup (loosely packed) fresh basil leaves, large leaves torn
⅓ cup fresh lime juice, more as needed
2 Tbsp. chopped fresh thyme
Kosher salt and freshly ground black pepper

Smoky-sweet charred corn kernels, ripe tomatoes, and fragrant basil leaves get a terrific flavor boost from a zingy lime vinaigrette. This can be your go-to salad all summer—it enlivens pretty much anything that comes off the grill.

Build a medium-hot fire in a charcoal grill, or heat a gas grill to high. Brush grill grate with vegetable oil. Rub corn with 1 Tbsp. olive oil. Grill, turning frequently, until corn is charred and heated through, 10 to 12 minutes. Remove from grill; when cool enough to handle, cut kernels from cobs and transfer to a large bowl. **DO AHEAD:** Corn can be made 3 hours ahead. Let stand at room temperature.

Place onion in a strainer and rinse with cold water to mellow its flavor. Drain well. Mix onion, remaining 5 Tbsp. oil, tomatoes, basil, ⅓ cup lime juice, and thyme into corn. Season to taste with salt, pepper, and more lime juice, if desired. **DO AHEAD:** Salad can be assembled 1 hour ahead. Let stand at room temperature.

SUMMER BEAN SALAD
with Walnuts and Pecorino Fresco

6 servings

DRESSING
1 Tbsp. minced shallot
4½ tsp. Sherry vinegar
1 tsp. Dijon mustard
¼ cup extra-virgin olive oil
1 Tbsp. walnut oil
Kosher salt and freshly ground black pepper

SALAD
8 oz. green beans, trimmed
8 oz. yellow wax beans, trimmed
8 oz. haricots verts, trimmed
8 cups (packed) torn frisée leaves
¼ cup chopped toasted walnuts
2 tsp. fresh summer savory leaves or thyme leaves
Freshly ground black pepper
2 oz. semi-firm sheep's-milk cheese (such as Pecorino fresco), shaved with a vegetable peeler

Use a variety of different seasonal beans in this tasty salad. The mild, sweet flavors of the beans are a delicious backdrop to the walnuts and Pecorino cheese. But improvise based on what looks good at the market. You can also substitute any sheep's-milk cheese, such as Manchego, if you prefer.

DRESSING
Whisk shallot, vinegar, and mustard in a small bowl. Gradually whisk in both oils. Season dressing to taste with salt and pepper. **DO AHEAD:** Can be made 1 day ahead. Cover; chill. Bring to room temperature and rewhisk before using.

SALAD
Cook green beans in a large pot of boiling salted water just until crisp-tender, 3 to 4 minutes. Using a slotted spoon, transfer beans to a colander; rinse under cold running water. Cook wax beans and haricots verts separately in same pot of boiling salted water, 3 to 4 minutes for wax beans and 2 to 3 minutes for haricots verts. Transfer to colander; rinse under cold running water. **DO AHEAD:** Can be made 1 day ahead. Wrap green beans, wax beans, and haricots verts separately in paper towels. Enclose in resealable plastic bag and chill.

Combine all beans and frisée in a large bowl. Add dressing; toss to coat. Transfer salad to a serving platter; sprinkle with walnuts and savory and season with pepper. Top with cheese.

GRILLED VEGETABLE SALAD

with Lemon-Mustard Vinaigrette

VINAIGRETTE

- 3 Tbsp. red wine vinegar
- 1 Tbsp. chopped fresh basil
- 1 Tbsp. chopped fresh chives
- 1 Tbsp. chopped fresh dill
- 1 Tbsp. chopped flat-leaf parsley
- 1 Tbsp. Dijon mustard
- 1 Tbsp. fresh lemon juice
- 1 shallot, finely chopped
- 1 garlic clove, minced
- ¾ cup extra-virgin olive oil
  Kosher salt and freshly ground black pepper

VEGETABLES

- 20 asparagus spears, each trimmed to 5-inch length
- 8 scallions, green tops trimmed
- 4 medium zucchini, each cut lengthwise into ¼- to ⅓-inch-thick slices
- 2 large ears of corn, shucked
- 4 medium heads of Belgian endive
- 2 small heads of radicchio, halved through core
- 6 plum tomatoes, halved lengthwise
  Extra-virgin olive oil, for brushing
  Kosher salt and freshly ground black pepper

Consider this your template for a grilled vegetable salad that works every time: Take best-quality vegetables, grill them until they're charred and just tender, and toss with an herbaceous vinaigrette. If you don't have the exact herbs and vegetables on hand, don't sweat it. This dish isn't about precision, it's about embracing summer's bounty.

VINAIGRETTE

Combine first 9 ingredients in a medium bowl. Gradually whisk in oil; season to taste with salt and pepper. **DO AHEAD:** Can be made 2 hours ahead. Let stand at room temperature.

VEGETABLES

Build a medium-hot fire in a charcoal grill, or heat a gas grill to high. Arrange all vegetables on baking sheets. Lightly brush vegetables with oil; season with salt and pepper. Brush grill grate with oil. Grill asparagus, scallions, zucchini, and corn, turning often, until lightly charred and just tender, about 5 minutes for scallions, 8 minutes for asparagus and zucchini, and 10 minutes for corn. Return vegetables to same baking sheets.

Grill endive and radicchio, turning often, until lightly charred, about 8 minutes. Transfer to baking sheets with other vegetables. Place tomatoes, skin side down, on grill and cook until just charred, about 3 minutes. Turn tomatoes; grill until just beginning to soften, about 1 minute longer. Transfer to baking sheets with other vegetables.

Cut asparagus, scallions, and zucchini crosswise into 1-inch pieces; place in a large bowl. Cut corn kernels from cobs; add to bowl. Cut endive in half lengthwise. Remove cores from endive and radicchio. Chop into ½- to ¾-inch pieces; add to bowl. Coarsely chop tomatoes. Using a slotted spoon, add tomatoes to bowl. **DO AHEAD:** Can be made 2 hours ahead. Let stand at room temperature.

Mix vinaigrette into vegetables. Season to taste with salt and pepper.

SUGAR SNAP SALAD

1½ lb. sugar snap peas, trimmed, stringed, cut in half on a diagonal
Kosher salt
3 Tbsp. extra-virgin olive oil
1 Tbsp. fresh lemon juice, more as needed
1 tsp. white wine vinegar
½ tsp. sumac, plus more for garnish (optional)
1 bunch radishes (about 6 oz.), trimmed, thinly sliced
4 oz. feta or ricotta salata, crumbled
Freshly ground black pepper
2 Tbsp. chopped fresh mint

INGREDIENT INFO Sumac is generally sold in ground form and is available at specialty foods stores and Middle Eastern markets.

A bold vinaigrette with Middle Eastern flavors—mint, sumac, lemon, olive oil—livens up crisp, sweet sugar snap peas. Try it as a delicious marinade for grilled chicken. Sumac is a maroon-colored spice with a tart flavor; it's optional but adds a nice piquancy to the salad.

Cook peas in a large pot of boiling salted water until crisp-tender, about 2 minutes. Drain; transfer to a large bowl of ice water; let cool. Drain peas; transfer to a kitchen towel–lined baking sheet to dry.

Whisk oil, 1 Tbsp. lemon juice, vinegar, and ½ tsp. sumac, if using, in a small bowl. Toss peas, radishes, and cheese in a large bowl. **DO AHEAD:** Can be made 1 day ahead. Cover dressing and salad separately and chill.

Add dressing to salad and toss to coat. Season salad with salt, pepper, and more lemon juice, if desired. Sprinkle with mint and sumac, if desired.

SHAVED SUMMER SQUASH SALAD

3 Tbsp. whole almonds
1 lb. summer squash, preferably a mix of green and yellow
2½ Tbsp. extra-virgin olive oil
2 Tbsp. fresh lemon juice
1 garlic clove, minced
Kosher salt
Baby arugula, for serving
Pecorino or Parmesan, for shaving
Freshly ground black pepper

Set the chef's knife aside—the only tool you'll need to make this delightful salad is a vegetable peeler, to shave squash into thin, billowy ribbons. When picking summer squash at the market, choose the small ones; they have fewer seeds and a sweeter flavor.

Preheat oven to 350°F. Roast almonds until toasted, about 8 minutes. Let cool; coarsely crush.

Meanwhile, trim ends off squash. Using a vegetable peeler, thinly slice squash lengthwise into strips and transfer to a large bowl. Whisk oil, lemon juice, and garlic in a small bowl. Season to taste with salt. Pour dressing over squash. Let stand for a few minutes, then add a few handfuls of arugula. Shave a little cheese over squash and toss to combine. Season to taste with salt and pepper. Garnish with almonds.

GRILLED WATERMELON SALAD

1 large sprig basil

⅓ cup plus ½ cup extra-virgin olive oil, plus more for brushing

3 ½-inch-thick slices seedless watermelon, rind removed, each cut into 6 wedges for a total of 18 wedges

¼ cup fresh lime juice

1 Tbsp. honey
Kosher salt and freshly ground black pepper

12 oz. pea sprouts or watercress, with tender stems (about 12 cups)

½ cup crumbled feta or queso fresco (4 oz.)

¼ cup (1 oz.) shelled pumpkin seeds (pepitas), toasted

INGREDIENT INFO Pea sprouts are available at natural foods stores and Asian markets.

Everybody's favorite summer fruit is fantastic on the grill—it caramelizes beautifully, which heightens its natural sugars, and it holds its shape well. Salty feta is the perfect foil to the sweet juiciness of melon. Don't fiddle with it once it's on the grill; just flip the pieces when it's time.

Heat basil and ⅓ cup oil in a small skillet over medium heat until basil begins to bubble. Simmer for 3 minutes. Remove pan from heat. Let cool for 1 hour. Discard basil; set basil oil aside.

Build a medium fire in a charcoal grill, or heat a gas grill to medium-high. Brush grill grate with oil. Grill watermelon until lightly charred, about 2 minutes per side. Set aside.

Whisk remaining ½ cup oil, lime juice, and honey in a large bowl. Season to taste with salt and pepper. Add pea sprouts and toss to coat.

Place 3 pieces of grilled watermelon on each plate. Top with pea sprouts and drizzle basil oil over. Garnish with feta and pumpkin seeds.

BONUS RECIPES: Fresh Tomatoes, 4 Ways

The best way to eat a perfectly ripe summer tomato is in hand, with a sprinkle of sea salt. But to serve them at the table, you should gussy them up a bit. Here are our favorite ways:

SIMPLE SALAD

Toss halved cherry tomatoes with sliced fresh basil and a simple shallot vinaigrette. That's it.

GO GREEK

Chop tomatoes and add to cucumbers, flat-leaf parsley, red onion, black olives, and feta. Toss with a lemon vinaigrette.

QUICK NIÇOISE

Mix tomatoes with cooked white beans and an herb vinaigrette. Top with large chunks of good-quality tuna.

CAPRESE

Arrange sliced tomatoes with fresh mozzarella and basil. Drizzle with extra-virgin olive oil, and add salt liberally.

Pay your respects to tomatoes—**the crown jewels of summer**: Never put them in the refrigerator (it kills their flavor).

DRINKS

YOU DON'T *HAVE* TO DRINK WHILE GRILLING.

But, really, is there ever a better time to crack open a cold one? Friends and/or family are around and you've got a little bit of time to kill while eyeing that rack of ribs cooking on the grill or waiting for some sweet summer corn to blister just so. And unless you're firing up a hibachi in the parking lot of Lambeau Field in November, the weather's probably pretty nice. So why not treat yourself?

This chapter doesn't have rules, per se, because rules go against the spirit of a fun, relaxed time. But we do offer guidelines and advice. Our first tip? Keep it simple. When grilling, you've got your hands full (literally and figuratively). So this isn't the best time to play mixologist and muddle individual Mojitos or shake Martinis. Instead, mix up a batch of cocktails or punches ahead of time—think fruit-infused sangria or spiked lemonade—and let guests serve themselves. And of course, there's never any shame in a cooler or tub filled with beer, wine, soft drinks, and plenty of ice.

CLASSIC DAIQUIRI

2 cups white rum
¾ cup simple syrup (see page 359)
¾ cup fresh lime juice

Like its cousin the Margarita from Mexico, a classic Cuban Daiquiri starts with fresh lime juice. The major difference is that the Daiquiri uses rum and the Margarita contains tequila.

Combine rum, simple syrup, and lime juice in a large pitcher with 5 cups of ice. With a wooden spoon, stir vigorously for about 1 minute until foamy. Strain and divide mixture among 8 coupe glasses.

makes 6

ARNOLD PALMER
with Gin, Tea, and Lemon Fizz

4 tsp. black tea leaves or 4 tea bags (such as Darjeeling)
1 cup thawed frozen lemonade concentrate
1 cup gin
2 cups sparkling water

The Arnold Palmer—equal parts iced tea and lemonade—meets the gin fizz in this bubbly concoction. Usually tea only needs a brief steep before you drink it, but this one has to be good and strong to balance well with the gin and lemon, so we steep it for 15 minutes. To keep the fizz, mix the tea with the lemonade concentrate, gin, and sparkling water just before serving.

Bring 1 cup water to a boil in a small saucepan. Add tea leaves. Remove from heat. Cover and let steep for 15 minutes at room temperature. Chill tea overnight.
    Strain tea through fine-mesh strainer into a pitcher; discard tea leaves or bags. Stir in lemonade concentrate and gin, then add sparkling water to pitcher; stir well. Fill highball glasses with ice. Pour mixture over.

What's our go-to tequila for every Margarita in this chapter? *Tequila blanco*. It has a **peppery kick** that doesn't get lost in the mix.

ULTIMATE MARGARITA

ULTIMATE MARGARITA

photo, left

2 cups tequila blanco
1 cup fresh lime juice
1 cup light agave syrup (nectar)
   Kosher salt
16 lime slices or wedges

INGREDIENT INFO Agave syrup is available at some supermarkets and at natural foods stores.

This version of the classic Margarita calls for agave instead of triple sec. The result is crisp, fresh, and clean. There are two other ingredients that are essential: *Tequila blanco* (a.k.a. silver or white) and maybe the most important element of all, fresh lime juice. To turn it into a frozen Margarita, purée in four batches in a blender, adding 4 cups ice to one-quarter of the mixture at a time. (It's not authentic, but we won't judge.)

Combine tequila, lime juice, and agave syrup in a pitcher. **DO AHEAD:** Can be made 4 hours ahead. Cover and chill.

Pour some salt into a small dish. Rub 1 lime slice over half of the rim of a coupe glass (if you prefer your Margarita up) or an Old-Fashioned glass (if you prefer it on the rocks). Dip rim of glass into salt. Repeat with additional glasses.

Fill pitcher with ice and stir well. Strain Margarita into prepared glasses. Garnish each glass with a lime wedge.

HOW TO: Margarita Mix-Ins

The agave-fueled Margarita recipe (above) is a great base for all kinds of variations. Here are some of our favorites:

FRUITY

Muddle **24 blackberries** with agave syrup in a pitcher until berries are lightly crushed and juices are released. Continue with recipe.

SPICY

Muddle **16 thin jalapeño slices** with some agave syrup in a pitcher until peppers begin to fall apart. For a less spicy version, remove seeds first. Continue with recipe.

BRIGHT

Steep **2 hibiscus tea bags** or **1 teaspoon dried hibiscus flowers** with 8 ounces hot water for 10 minutes. Discard tea bags or strain flowers and let tea cool. Gently spoon some over Margarita, forming a red layer on top.

Sweet, tart, salty, spicy—this Margarita has all the right flavor bases covered.

SPICY GRAPEFRUIT MARGARITA

SPICY GRAPEFRUIT MARGARITA

makes 8

photo, left

2 cups plus 2 Tbsp. tequila blanco

1 or 2 habanero or serrano jalapeño chiles, halved

Kosher salt

6 cups fresh pink grapefruit juice

The longer the tequila is infused with the chiles, the hotter it gets. Grapefruit makes this Margarita a bit sweeter than the classic version, with subtle bitter notes.

Mix tequila and chiles in a large pitcher. Let steep for 3 hours, or longer if a spicier tequila is desired. Discard chiles. **DO AHEAD:** Can be made 1 month ahead. Cover; chill.

Pour water onto a small plate to cover. Pour salt onto another small plate to cover by ¼ inch. Dip rims of 12-oz. glasses into water, then into salt to lightly coat; fill with ice. Add grapefruit juice to pitcher with tequila. Fill with ice; stir until cold. Divide cocktail among glasses.

WATERMELON SUGAR

makes 8

1 jalapeño, halved lengthwise

¾ cup tequila blanco

2 cups ¾-inch cubes seedless watermelon

6 Tbsp. fresh lime juice

6 Tbsp. simple syrup (see page 359)

¼ cup mezcal or gold tequila

This sweet and fiery drink is made with mezcal, tequila's smoky cousin. In this case we recommend that you don't mess around with the cheap stuff.

Scrape stems, seeds, and veins from jalapeño into a small jar (reserve green flesh for another use). Add tequila to jar; cover and let infuse for 15 minutes. Set a fine-mesh strainer over a small bowl. Pour tequila through strainer; discard solids.

Place watermelon cubes in a large pitcher. Using a muddler or potato masher, coarsely crush watermelon. Stir in lime juice, simple syrup, mezcal, and jalapeño tequila. Stir in 2 cups ice. Cover and chill until cold, about 2 hours.

Fill Old-Fashioned glasses with ice. Divide cocktail among glasses.

TANGERINE-GINGER CAIPIRINHAS

makes 6

3 small tangerines or small oranges, unpeeled, seeded, chopped
¼ cup sugar
1 Tbsp. grated peeled ginger
¾ cup fresh tangerine juice
1½ cups cachaça (Brazilian sugarcane liquor) or vodka

The Caipirinha is Brazil's most popular cocktail. It's traditionally made with limes, but this version uses tangerines and ginger, giving it a fresh, somewhat sweeter twist with a touch of heat.

Crush chopped tangerines, sugar, and ginger in the bottom of a pitcher with a muddler or the handle of a wooden spoon. Top with tangerine juice and cachaça; stir well. Fill Old-Fashioned glasses with ice. Divide cocktail among glasses.

RASPBERRY-ROSE GIN RICKEY

makes 4

3 cups fresh raspberries
1 cup gin
½ cup sugar
½ cup fresh lime juice
¼ tsp. (scant) rose water

INGREDIENT INFO Rose water is sold at some supermarkets and at specialty foods stores and Middle Eastern markets.

Crushed fresh raspberries and a few drops of rose water (which enhance the raspberry flavor) transform the gin rickey, traditionally a mix of gin, lime juice, and club soda. Any gin will work, but the cucumber and rose notes of Hendrick's would be particularly good here. You can garnish the drinks with whole fresh raspberries and lime slices.

Mix raspberries, gin, sugar, lime juice, and rose water in a medium bowl. Let stand at room temperature, stirring occasionally and crushing some berries, for 1 hour.
　　Place ¾ cup ice in each highball glass. Divide cocktail among glasses.

ROSEMARY-TANGERINE COOLER

2 Tbsp. raw sugar, more as needed
4 tangerines or small oranges, halved crosswise
16 rosemary sprigs, divided
2 cups white rum

Sugar-coated tangerines seared over rosemary sprigs turn this rum-based refresher into a revelation.

Heat a cast-iron skillet or griddle over high heat or on a grill grate. Pour some raw sugar into a small plate. Dip cut sides of tangerines into sugar. Scatter 8 rosemary sprigs in skillet; add tangerines, cut side down. Cook until sugar caramelizes, about 2 minutes. Let cool.

Quarter tangerines; discard rosemary. Place tangerines in a pitcher, add 2 Tbsp. raw sugar, and muddle to release juices. Add rum and 6 cups ice; stir until pitcher is frosty. Divide among glasses; garnish with remaining 8 rosemary sprigs.

GETTING IT RIGHT: How to Muddle Like a Pro

Muddling is simply crushing herbs or fruit at the bottom of a glass to release flavor into your drinks. But it doesn't mean mashing them to a paste. Here's how to apply the right touch.

IT'S ALL IN THE WRIST

Use the flat-bottomed end of a muddler or the handle of a wooden spoon to **press the mixture gently;** twist your wrist as you press. This extracts the fresh juices and fragrant plant oils from the fruit or herbs.

DON'T GO BONKERS

The idea is to **press the essential oils out of the leaves,** not to mince them or break them apart (you're not making pesto), which would leave annoying bits that get in the way of enjoying a smooth cocktail.

A LITTLE ABRASION

For Mojitos and mint juleps, **combine fresh mint with a bit of sugar** in the bottom of the pitcher—the abrasive granules of sugar help bruise the herbs and coax out the flavors. Needless to say, the sweetness isn't bad, either.

EXTRACT FRUIT JUICES

For Old-Fashioneds and smashes, **crush fruit at the bottom of a glass.** For citrus, or if the drink will be strained, use a little elbow grease to release juices and to press the oils from citrus peel. For other fruit, such as berries, leave some texture (don't mash them into oblivion).

Rosé is our **favorite summer wine**. Here it's paired with iced tea, sangria, and bourbon for a **flavor-packed refresher**.

ROSÉ, BOURBON, AND BLUE

ROSÉ, BOURBON, AND BLUE

photo, left

7 Tbsp. raw sugar
2 cups fresh blueberries, divided
2 cups freshly brewed
  unsweetened black tea
1½ cups fruity rosé
1 cup bourbon
¾ cup fresh lemon juice
8 lemon slices

This patriotic cooler combines two summer favorites—iced tea and sangria—with that all-American spirit, bourbon. For the tea, we like orange pekoe; for the wine, a fruity rosé from Spain's Rioja.

Stir sugar with 7 Tbsp. hot water in a small bowl until sugar is dissolved; transfer to a food processor. Add 1½ cups blueberries and purée until smooth. Set a fine-mesh strainer over a large pitcher. Strain blueberry mixture, pressing on solids to extract as much liquid as possible; discard solids. Add tea, rosé, bourbon, and lemon juice. Chill until cold, about 2 hours.
  Cut remaining ½ cup blueberries in half; add to pitcher. Fill Old-Fashioned glasses with ice. Divide cocktail among glasses. Garnish with lemon slices.

THE BICICLETTA

2½ cups chilled Campari
2 750-ml bottles chilled dry
  white wine
2½ cups chilled club soda
  Lemon slices (optional)

This cocktail—said to be named for the old Italian men who, after indulging in a few, wobble home on their bikes—has made its way around the world in a languorous sort of way. With a pleasant balance of strong and sweet (it's not too much of one or the other), it has a bit of floral fruit to it, a thirst-quenching quality, and just the right amount of bitterness. As a proper aperitif should.

Combine Campari and wine in a large pitcher. Fill wineglasses with ice. Divide Campari mixture among glasses. Top with club soda; stir to mix. Garnish with lemon slices, if desired.

Drinks Wisdom

YOU'VE GOT THE ROSÉ ON ICE, RIGHT? It's versatile, refreshing, and so pretty no matter what kind of glass you serve it in. Two things to remember about rosé: Drink it while it's young (as in, go out right now and buy the vintage from the year before), and choose bottles that come from the Côtes de Provence, which are peachy, fresh, and not too sweet.

MANGO-CUCUMBER WINE COOLER

makes 6

1½ Tbsp. sugar
1 750-ml bottle Sauvignon Blanc
1 hothouse cucumber, peeled, cut into ¼-inch-thick rounds
1 mango, pitted, peeled, finely diced
12 sprigs mint, divided
1 cup ginger ale or ginger beer

Steep cucumber and mango in the wine for 3 hours or longer for maximum flavor. Once the fruit sinks, the wine is ready.

Stir sugar and 1½ Tbsp. hot water in a large pitcher until dissolved. Add wine, cucumber, and mango. Remove leaves from 6 mint sprigs; stir into pitcher. Cover and chill for at least 3 hours and up to 6 hours.

Stir in ginger ale or ginger beer. Fill large wineglasses with ice. Divide wine cooler among glasses. Garnish with remaining 6 mint sprigs.

PISCO PUNCH

makes 12

1 4-lb. pineapple, peeled, halved, cored, cut into 1-inch pieces
1 750-ml bottle pisco
2 cups simple syrup (see page 359)
1½ tsp. finely grated lime zest
1½ tsp. finely grated grapefruit zest
⅔ cup fresh lemon juice
12 pineapple leaves (optional)

Pisco, the clear Peruvian brandy with spicy, exotic flavor, receives a boost from grapefruit and lime zest in this creative punch. The pisco is infused with fresh pineapple for 3 days, so begin preparing it in advance.

Place pineapple pieces in a large jar. Pour pisco over. Cover and chill, shaking occasionally, for 3 days.

Divide simple syrup between 2 bowls. Stir lime zest into 1 bowl and grapefruit zest into the other bowl. Cover and chill both syrups overnight.

Strain pisco through fine-mesh strainer into a pitcher; discard pineapple.

Strain both syrups into pisco. Add lemon juice; stir to blend. Fill small glasses with ice; divide punch among glasses. Garnish with pineapple leaves, if desired.

5

Keys to Sweeten Up SUMMER DRINKS

Want to sweeten up a cocktail, but don't want sugar crystals swirling around the bottom of your glass? Make some simple syrup—and then infuse it with herbs, spices, or citrus zest. Keep batches on hand in your fridge all summer, to sweeten everything from lemonade to Daiquiris. Here's how:

1 MIX IT

Mix **equal parts water** and **sugar** in a jar with a lid, and shake vigorously for 1 minute, or **until sugar is dissolved.** Contrary to popular belief about making simple syrup, we're here to tell you: It's not necessary to heat up the liquid! Unless, that is, you're making an infusion—which is a terrific way to add even more flavor ...

2 INFUSE IT

Bring **equal parts water and sugar to a simmer**; stir until **sugar dissolves.** Add flavorings while syrup is hot (see step 5 for ideas). Steep until it's flavored to your desired strength— anywhere from 15 minutes to 1 hour. Strain and chill in a sealed bottle.

3 SERVE IT UP

At your next cook-out, grab your batch of pre-made syrup from the fridge and **set it out at the drinks station.** Label it clearly, and **encourage guests to experiment.**

4 TAKE A SHORT CUT

If you don't have time to whip up a batch of simple syrup, use **agave nectar.** This thin, sweet, all-natural syrup is made from agave plants and **mixes easily into cold drinks.** Honey diluted with hot water would also do the trick. (Keep in mind, both of these may slightly darken your drinks.)

5 GET CREATIVE

For **iced tea, tonics, Collinses,** and **daiquiris,** add a **citrus** infusion: Add lemon, lime, kumquat, or grape-fruit zest.

For **lemonade, Pimm's Cups,** and **punch,** use **herbs:** Mint and basil (try purple basil—it adds a nice pop of color) are our favorites.

For **sangria** and **Margaritas,** use **whole spices:** Cinnamon sticks, cloves, star anise, or sliced ginger add a nice kick.

Go beyond the beer: **Bubbles pair well** with the sweet, spicy, salty flavors of the grill.

CHAMPAGNE, THE KING OF BARBECUE

SPICED SANGRIA

with Rioja and Albariño

makes 12

1 750-ml bottle Albariño
1 750-ml bottle Rioja
2 cups Grand Marnier or other orange liqueur
1 cup sugar
2 vanilla beans, split lengthwise
2 green apples, quartered, cored, sliced
2 oranges, sliced
2 lemons, sliced
2 limes, sliced
1 pear, quartered lengthwise, cored, sliced
½ pineapple, peeled, quartered lengthwise, cored, sliced crosswise
¼ cup chopped peeled ginger
6 whole star anise
3 cinnamon sticks

INGREDIENT INFO Whole star anise are brown star-shaped seedpods. They are available in the spice section of some supermarkets and at Asian markets and specialty foods stores.

Spain's prized red Rioja and white Albariño wines are steeped overnight with cinnamon, star anise, ginger, and vanilla, along with a good variety of fruit; it results in a slightly sweet sangria with an unexpected depth of flavor and spice.

Mix wines, Grand Marnier, and sugar in a large pitcher; stir until sugar dissolves. Scrape in seeds from vanilla beans; add beans. Mix in apples and remaining ingredients. Cover and chill overnight.

Remove vanilla beans, star anise, and cinnamon sticks from sangria. Fill wineglasses with ice. Divide sangria among glasses.

Drinks Wisdom

CHAMPAGNE, THE KING OF BARBECUE Yes, you read that right. One of our food editors turned us onto the idea of pairing Champagne with barbecue, and we've been sold on this high-low combination ever since. The bubbles open up flavors of thick barbecue sauces. Try it—it's a match made in barbecue heaven.

TUSCAN BELLINI

1½ lb. very ripe peaches (about 6)
2 Tbsp. fresh lemon juice, more as needed
1 Tbsp. sugar, more as needed
1 750-ml bottle chilled Prosecco

Peach purée and prosecco—that's basically all a Bellini is. But peaches vary greatly in how sweet or tart they are. While you're mixing it, taste the purée and adjust with more lemon juice or sugar before you add the Prosecco. You can also substitute store-bought peach purée and just add sparkling wine, if desired.

Bring a large pot of water to a boil. Using the tip of a paring knife, make two 1-inch cuts on the bottom of each peach, forming an X. Add peaches to water and boil just until skin begins to peel back at each X, 30 to 40 seconds. Using a slotted spoon, transfer peaches to a large bowl of ice water; let cool. Peel peaches. (Alternatively, use a vegetable peeler with a serrated blade to peel peaches.)

Halve peaches; discard pits. Chop peaches and transfer to a large bowl. Add 2 Tbsp. lemon juice and 1 Tbsp. sugar; toss to evenly coat. Press plastic wrap against peaches to prevent discoloration. Chill for 20 minutes.

Transfer peach mixture to a blender. Purée until smooth. Strain purée through a fine-mesh sieve into a large pitcher. Season to taste with more lemon juice or sugar (if adding more sugar, be sure to stir until it dissolves). Add Prosecco, then stir slowly to blend (stirring gently will prevent Prosecco from foaming up). Gently divide among Champagne glasses.

VARIATIONS ON A THEME: Bellinis, 6 Ways

When the folks at Harry's Bar in Venice, Italy, invented the Bellini, they had it right: Put a spoonful of peach purée in a glass, then pour in some Prosecco. But there's no need to stop with peaches. All you need is a blender or food processor. Here are a few more spins:

RASPBERRY BELLINIS

Pair puréed fresh raspberries with Champagne and a splash of St-Germain (elderflower liqueur).

STRAWBERRY BELLINIS

Hull fresh strawberries. Purée and mix with sparkling wine and a squeeze of fresh lemon juice.

BLUEBERRY BELLINIS

Match puréed fresh blueberries with sparkling wine and Chambord.

MANGO BELLINIS

Combine puréed fresh mango with lime juice and Prosecco.

BLACKBERRY KIR ROYAL

Mix puréed fresh blackberries with cassis and Champagne.

THE SWEET TOUCH

Add a teaspoon of flavored simple syrup to any of these combinations (see page 359).

STRAWBERRY-ROSÉ SPRITZER

makes 8

1 pint hulled, sliced fresh
   strawberries
1 750-ml bottle rosé
2 cups soda water
⅓ cup Aperol
2 Tbsp. fresh lemon juice
8 lemon twists

This pretty pitcher cocktail—which pairs fresh fruit flavors with rosé and the Italian orange aperitif Aperol—is tailor-made for a dinner of grilled seafood or chicken.

Combine strawberries and wine in a large pitcher; cover and chill for 3 hours to infuse wine.

Strain wine into a large bowl, reserving some strawberries for garnish. Return wine to pitcher. Stir in soda water, Aperol, and lemon juice. Fill glasses with ice and divide mixture among glasses; garnish each with a lemon twist and a few reserved strawberries.

WHITE WINE SANGRIA

Makes 4 to 6

2 plums, thinly sliced, pitted
1 orange, quartered lengthwise,
   thinly sliced
1 cup halved green grapes
¼ cup fresh blueberries
¼ cup Cointreau
1 750-ml bottle crisp white wine

Use a crisp, fruity white wine such as Grüner Veltliner, Sauvignon Blanc, or Pinot Grigio to make our lighter take on the classic red wine Spanish cooler.

Combine plums, orange, grapes, blueberries, and Cointreau in a large pitcher. Mash fruits gently with the back of a wooden spoon to release their juices. Add wine and stir to combine. Cover and refrigerate for at least 8 hours and up to 48 hours (the longer it sits, the fruitier it will be).

Fill wineglasses with ice; divide sangria among glasses.

MICHELADAS

photo, right

2 tsp. hot sauce, more as needed
2 tsp. fresh lime juice
  Coarse salt
8 12-oz. bottles Mexican lager
  Lime wedges

Serve these refreshing beer coolers over ice with lime and some salt—then it's just a matter of adding as many dashes of hot sauce as you can take.

Combine 2 tsp. hot sauce and lime juice in a shallow bowl. Spread out salt on a saucer. Dip rim of pint glasses into hot sauce mixture and then into salt to lightly coat. Fill glasses with ice and pour a bottle of lager into each. Squeeze in lime juice from the wedges, add more hot sauce to taste.

makes 8

JALAPEÑO TEQUILA GIMLET

2 jalapeños, stemmed
2 cups tequila blanco
1 cup fresh lime juice
½ cup light agave syrup (nectar)

INGREDIENT INFO Agave syrup is available at natural foods stores and some supermarkets.

Use this chile-infused tequila in Margaritas and Palomas—salt-rimmed cocktails made with tequila, lime juice, and grapefruit soda.

Grill, broil, or roast jalapeños over a flame, turning frequently, until soft and charred. Stem and chop chiles.
   Transfer chiles and seeds, if using, to a jar. Add tequila and let sit for 1 hour.
   Strain mixture through a fine-mesh sieve into a medium pitcher; discard solids in sieve. Stir in lime juice, agave syrup, and 2 cups ice (to chill and dilute). Let stand, stirring occasionally, until ice is melted. Divide gimlet among chilled glasses.

The Michelada is easy to customize (more **hot sauce**, **lime juice**, or **salt**, anyone?) depending on your taste.

MICHELADAS

WATERMELON–GRAPEFRUIT AGUA FRESCA

makes 8

photo, right (1)

18 cups (about 5 lb.) chopped watermelon (from a 10-lb. watermelon)
1¼ cups fresh grapefruit juice

Mexico has a wonderful variety of sweetened flavored waters known as *agua frescas*, which are sold at street stands and marketplaces everywhere you go throughout the country. They're made from a wide range of ingredients, including citrus juices, melons, and even cucumbers. Here, sweet watermelon balances tart grapefruit juice.

Purée watermelon in a blender until smooth. Pour into a large bowl and let stand for 10 minutes.

Skim foam from surface and discard; strain juice through a fine-mesh sieve lined with cheesecloth into a pitcher (you should have almost 7 cups). Stir in grapefruit juice. Fill glasses with ice; divide agua fresca among glasses.

CANTALOUPE-BASIL AGUA FRESCA

makes 8

photo, right (2)

30 cups (about 10 lb.) chopped cantaloupe (from about 5 cantaloupes)
¾ cup fresh lemon juice
¾ cup (lightly packed) fresh basil leaves

The unexpected combination of melon and fresh basil proves to be incredibly refreshing. Choose cantaloupes that are heavy for their size and have a fresh fragrance, with no sloshing sound when shaken.

Working in batches, purée cantaloupe in a blender until smooth and pour into a large bowl; let stand for 10 minutes.

Skim foam from surface and discard; strain juice through a fine-mesh sieve lined with cheesecloth into a pitcher (you should have about 5 cups). Stir in lemon juice, basil, and 2 cups cold water. Let steep at room temperature for at least 1 hour or up to 8 hours.

Fill glasses with ice; divide agua fresca among glasses.

LIME–CHIA SEED AGUA FRESCA

makes 8

photo, right (3)

2 Tbsp. white chia seeds
2 cups fresh lime juice
1½ cups superfine sugar, more as needed

INGREDIENT INFO Look for chia seeds at some supermarkets and at natural foods stores.

Chia seeds are similar to tiny tapioca pearls and are packed with health benefits. They also give this limeade great texture—and they look cool suspended in the drink.

Whisk chia seeds and 5 cups water in a pitcher; let sit until seeds bloom and become jelly-like, about 10 minutes.

Add lime juice and superfine sugar and stir until sugar dissolves. Add more sugar to taste, if sweeter limeade is desired. Fill glasses with ice; divide limeade among glasses.

Step away from the soda can and try an agua fresca. They're a fun way to **get creative** with **non-alcoholic drinks**.

AGUA FRESCAS

CHERRY SODA

1 lb. fresh cherries, stemmed
   and pitted, or frozen pitted
   cherries, thawed, undrained
1 cup sugar
   Cola or club soda

**Use this quick syrup to make fresh cherry colas or Old-Fashioned cocktails.
It will keep safely for a week in the fridge.**

Using a muddler or potato masher, smash cherries and sugar in a medium
bowl to release juices (it's okay to leave some cherries whole). Stir in ¾ cup hot
water. Let stand, stirring occasionally, until slightly cooled, about 30 minutes.
Cover and chill. **DO AHEAD:** Cherry syrup can be made 1 week ahead. Keep chilled.
   Strain syrup through a fine-sieve into a large pitcher, reserving cherries for
garnish. Fill Collins glasses with ice. Pour 3 to 4 Tbsp. cherry syrup into each
glass. Fill with cola or club soda, garnish with reserved cherries.

makes 8

THE YELLOW JACKET

1 cup pineapple juice
1 cup fresh orange juice
1 cup lemonade
   Generous splash of cranberry
   juice cocktail

SPECIAL EQUIPMENT Paper snow cone
cups (optional)

**This sno cone "cocktail" is so simple that kids can enjoy making it themselves. Blend
equal parts lemonade and pineapple and orange juices, add a splash of cranberry
juice cocktail, and pour the mixture over shaved ice.**

Combine pineapple juice, orange juice, lemonade, and cranberry juice cocktail in
a small pitcher. Chill until cold.
   Working in batches, shave 8 cups ice in a food processor fitted with grating
disk. Using ice cream scoop, pack approximately 1 cup shaved ice into each snow
cone cup or cocktail glass. Drizzle each with juice mixture.

CLASSIC LEMONADE

1 cup sugar
1 cup fresh lemon juice
4 lemon slices

This lightly sweetened and not-too-tart lemonade is a lovely summer refresher. Add fresh summer berries, bright green herbs like mint or basil, or your favorite tea (that makes it an Arnold Palmer)—the possibilities are endless.

Bring sugar and 3 cups water to a simmer in a large saucepan, stirring to dissolve sugar. Place saucepan with simple syrup into an ice water bath. Let cool completely.

Transfer syrup to a large pitcher. Stir in lemon juice. Fill glasses with ice. Pour lemonade over, dividing evenly. Garnish each with a lemon slice.

VARIATIONS ON A THEME: Lemonade Plus...

There are so many ways to revamp this classic—you can add new flavor dimensions with fruits, herbs, and spices, while retaining everything that's refreshing and delicious about lemonade.

RASPBERRY LEMONADE

Crush 1 cup raspberries in a large pitcher with a wooden spoon to a coarse mash and pour prepared lemonade over. Mix to blend. Pour into glasses filled with ice; garnish with whole raspberries.

BASIL LEMONADE

Muddle ½ bunch basil leaves in a large pitcher with a wooden spoon and pour prepared lemonade over. Mix to blend. Pour into glasses filled with ice; garnish with basil leaves.

MATCHA LEMONADE

Mix 2 Tbsp. matcha (green tea powder) and ¼ cup hot water in a small bowl to form a paste. Slowly whisk into prepared lemonade, breaking up any clumps. Pour into glasses filled with ice. Matcha is available at amazon.com and inpursuitoftea.com.

HONEY-GINGER LEMONADE

Bring ¾ cup honey, ½ cup minced peeled ginger, and 3 cups water to a boil in a large saucepan; remove from the heat. Let sit, covered, for 15 minutes. Strain through fine-mesh sieve into a large pitcher and let cool. Stir in 1 cup fresh lemon juice. Pour into glasses filled with ice.

24-HOUR GINGER BEER

1 lb. ginger, peeled, coarsely
   chopped (about 2½ cups)
1 cup (packed) light brown sugar
   or granulated sugar
   Club soda
1 lime, cut into 6 to 8 wedges

Ginger beer contains no beer or alcohol of any kind, just deep, spicy ginger flavor. Most homemade ginger beers are fermented for about 5 days, but this easy version soaks the ginger for only 24 hours. If the ginger heat is too much, tame it with more crushed ice and some club soda.

Bring 6 cups water to a boil in a large saucepan. Finely chop ginger in a food processor. Transfer chopped ginger to a large glass or ceramic bowl; add boiling water and stir to blend. Cover loosely with foil; let ginger mixture stand at room temperature for 24 hours.

Strain ginger liquid through a fine-mesh sieve into a large pitcher; discard solids in strainer. Add sugar to liquid and stir until sugar dissolves. Fill glasses with crushed ice and pour ginger liquid over. Top with club soda to taste. Serve each glass with a lime wedge for squeezing over.

GETTING IT RIGHT: How to Fill Your Cooler

When you're having a cookout, don't skimp on ice. An ice-cold drink is as important to a summer party as the burgers and potato salad, so make sure your cooler is up to the job. Here's how to do it right:

MAKE IT BIG

Get a cooler big enough to hold a lot of ice and a lot of beverages. The last thing you want is to run out of cold drinks.

ICE IT UP

Buy ice. Lots. Don't assume that what's in your freezer is enough. **You need a bunch of bags**, enough to fill up that big cooler.

LAYER IT

Put **beverages in first**, **then a layer of ice**— never the other way around. Repeat until the cooler is full.

CHILL IT QUICK

Need to get it cold in a hurry? Add **a pitcher or two of water** or a handful of salt to create an icy bath.

The grill is hot, and your **drinks need to stay cold.** Get a cooler big enough to hold it all, and load it up with plenty of ice.

SAUCES

...AND RUBS, MARINADES, BRINES & MORE

SOMETIMES YOU NEED AN INFUSION OF FLAVOR.

Maybe that rack of ribs, fish fillet, or chicken cutlet needs more than just a sprinkling of salt and a hot fire. How can you tell? It could depend on what you're grilling (tougher or blander cuts of meat often need some help). Or it could depend on your personal preference—like, say, if you're looking to give a dish an Asian, Mediterranean, or Caribbean spin. This chapter spells out the steps to accomplish these goals.

There are three ways to inject a piece of protein with oomph before it hits the grill:
- **Use a dry rub**—basically salt, pepper, sugar, and a medley of dried spices.
- **Marinate it** using oil, acid, or whatever else you can find in your pantry.
- **Brine it** in a water bath hopped up with sugar, salt, and aromatics.

Once you've mastered each of these techniques, you'll be able to freestyle—creating brines, rubs, and marinades based on whatever ingredients are available to you when you're ready to grill. And if you want to wait till after your piece of meat or fish is off the grill to amp it up, we'll help you out there, too, with a killer chimichurri sauce (page 390), an indispensable pico de gallo (page 400), and more.

THE DRY RUB
The Spice of Grilling Life

The fastest way to deliver intense flavor to grilled food is to coat its surface with a dry rub made with ground spices. A fire's high heat will transform the exterior of spice-rubbed meat or vegetables into a caramelized crust. Bottled ground spices are a fine substitute if you don't have time to grind your own. But rubs are actually pretty easy to assemble at home. We keep a spice mill handy to make them in large batches, so they're ready to whip up at a moment's notice.

THE ULTIMATE DRY RUB

makes about ⅔ cup

photo, page 377

2 tsp. whole black peppercorns
2 tsp. yellow mustard seeds
1 tsp. cumin seeds
3 Tbsp. paprika
2 Tbsp. brown sugar
2 tsp. kosher salt
1 tsp. celery seeds
1 tsp. garlic powder
½ tsp. cayenne pepper

Make a big batch of this tasty all-purpose rub (it'll keep for up to 3 months) and it will pay you back in smoky dividends all summer long.

Stir peppercorns, mustard seeds, and cumin seeds in a small dry skillet over medium heat until toasted, about 2 minutes. Let cool. Put into a spice mill with remaining ingredients and pulse until finely ground. **DO AHEAD:** Store in an airtight container for up to 3 months. If you're using bottled, ground spices, use the same measurements (but you won't need to toast them in a pan).

CHIPOTLE RUB

makes ⅓ cup

1½ dried chipotle chiles, stemmed, seeded, chopped
2 Tbsp. whole pink peppercorns
2 Tbsp. coriander seeds
1 tsp. fennel seeds
¼ tsp. cumin seeds
2 tsp. (packed) dark brown sugar
2 tsp. kosher salt
1 tsp. dry mustard

INGREDIENT INFO Dried chipotle chiles (smoked jalapeños) are available at some specialty foods stores and at Latin markets.

Made with chipotle chiles, this fragrant mix also includes a bit of brown sugar for sweetness and dry mustard for punch. Massage it into your favorite cut of pork or beef (it's great with tri-tip) at least an hour before grilling.

Grind chipotle chiles in a spice mill; transfer to a small bowl. Grind peppercorns, coriander seeds, fennel seeds, and cumin seeds in spice mill; transfer to bowl with chiles. Stir in brown sugar, salt, and dry mustard. Store in an airtight container. **DO AHEAD:** Can be made up to 1 month ahead. Store at room temperature.

CHILEAN SPICE RUB

2 Tbsp. dried guajillo chiles, crushed (about 2 guajillo chiles)
2 tsp. crushed red pepper flakes
1 tsp. smoked paprika
½ tsp. ground coriander
¼ tsp. ground cumin
1 Tbsp. kosher salt

INGREDIENT INFO Guajillo chiles are fairly hot dried chiles that are available at some supermarkets and Latin markets.

A blend of guajillo chiles and crushed red pepper flakes lends the perfect balance of smoky and spicy to this rub. Use it on beef, lamb, pork, or chicken, and for an even deeper flavor, rub this on up to 24 hours before grilling.

Combine all ingredients except salt in a spice mill or mortar and pestle. Grind until a coarse powder is formed. Pour spice blend into a medium bowl and add salt. Mix to blend. **DO AHEAD:** Can be made 1 week ahead. Store at room temperature.

Sprinkle 2 tsp. of spice rub per pound of meat. **DO AHEAD:** Sprinkle on meat and refrigerate at least 1 hour ahead, and up to overnight, before grilling.

TANDOORI RUB

6 Tbsp. paprika
2 Tbsp. ground coriander
2 Tbsp. ground cumin
2 Tbsp. kosher salt
1 Tbsp. freshly ground black pepper
1 Tbsp. sugar
1 Tbsp. ground ginger
1 tsp. ground cinnamon
1 tsp. crumbled saffron threads (optional)
½ tsp. cayenne pepper

This spicy, deeply aromatic blend is made with the same seasonings used to flavor India's clay oven–baked tandoori chicken. Try it rubbed under the skin of a whole chicken, added to a pan sauce for grilled scallops, sprinkled over cauliflower before cooking, or mixed with yogurt as a marinade for leg of lamb.

Whisk all ingredients in a medium bowl. Transfer to an airtight container. **DO AHEAD:** Can be made 1 month ahead. Store at room temperature.

Except for *maybe* a big, expensive rib eye or porterhouse, there's not much that isn't **improved by a good dry rub**.

THE ULTIMATE DRY RUB

YEMENI SPICE RUB

½ cup caraway seeds (generous 1 oz.)
⅓ cup cumin seeds (about 1 oz.)
3 Tbsp. cardamom seeds
    (about ½ oz.)
1 Tbsp. whole black peppercorns
4 whole cloves
3 Tbsp. kosher salt
3 Tbsp. turmeric

This traditional spice blend from Yemen, called *hawayil*, will infuse grilled meats and vegetables with the rich, warm essence of caraway, cumin, and cloves. Try it sprinkled on carrots, or rub some into steaks before they go on the grill. To extract the most flavor from whole spices, toast in a hot, dry skillet before grinding.

Heat a large dry skillet over medium-high heat. Add first 5 ingredients; toast, stirring often, until aromatic and cumin seeds are slightly darker, about 2 minutes. Let cool slightly. Working in batches, finely grind spice mixture and salt in a spice mill. Transfer to a medium bowl. Whisk in turmeric. Transfer to an airtight container. **DO AHEAD:** Can be made 1 month ahead. Store at room temperature.

GETTING IT RIGHT: The Elements of a Dry Rub

SALT

This is the **foundation of every good dry rub**. It carries the flavor of the spices and elevates the flavor of the food you're grilling.

SUGAR

A **pinch of sweetness** is often added to help balance things out. It encourages browning on the grill as the sugar caramelizes.

SPICE

Here's where you can get creative. Keep an arsenal of spices in your pantry: **cumin, peppercorns, paprika, dry mustard, coriander**.

CHILES

Where there's smoke, there should be fire— via everyday incendiary devices like crushed red pepper flakes, ground cayenne, or whole dried chiles de árbol that you grind yourself.

MARINADES
Soaking in Flavor

Put down that bottle of Italian dressing, and make a homemade marinade instead.
From Cuban-inspired, citrusy *mojo* to Southeast Asian mixtures of lemongrass, cilantro, and ginger,
this is the easiest way to up your grilling game.

SRIRACHA MARINADE

makes about 2 cups

1 cup reduced-sodium soy sauce
½ cup fresh orange juice
½ cup light brown sugar
⅓ cup chopped fresh cilantro stems
1 Tbsp. pomegranate molasses
1 Tbsp. Sriracha
4 garlic cloves, thinly sliced
2 whole star anise pods
1 1-inch piece peeled ginger,
   thinly sliced

INGREDIENT INFO Pomegranate
molasses, a thick pomegranate
syrup, is available at some
supermarkets, Middle Eastern
markets, and kalustyans.com.

Sriracha, the hot Asian chili sauce, gives this marinade a hit of spice, which is tempered by sweet, tangy orange juice and a spoonful of syrupy pomegranate molasses. Try it with pork shoulder or lamb.

Combine all ingredients in a medium bowl and whisk until well combined. Store chilled in an airtight container. Add to vinaigrettes, soy- and fish sauce–based sauces, and marinades for a heat boost. **DO AHEAD:** Can be made 1 day ahead.

To use with shrimp, fish, pork, or lamb: Put fish or meat in a glass, ceramic, or stainless-steel dish and marinate for 30 minutes. Remove and pat dry. Brush with oil before grilling.

Fennel seeds and Pernod (the French anise liqueur) **accent this delicate marinade** named after the famous seaport.

MARSEILLES MARINADE

JERK MARINADE

makes 1 cup

6 Tbsp. vegetable oil, divided
¼ cup fresh lime juice
4 scallions, coarsely chopped
4 Scotch bonnet or habanero chiles, stemmed, seeded, coarsely chopped
3 garlic cloves, coarsely chopped
2 Tbsp. fresh thyme leaves
1 Tbsp. minced peeled ginger
1 Tbsp. (packed) dark brown sugar
2 tsp. whole allspice
1 tsp. kosher salt, more as needed
¼ tsp. freshly ground black pepper
2 Tbsp. distilled white vinegar

INGREDIENT INFO Habaneros and Scotch bonnets—small, extremely hot chiles—are available at many supermarkets and at Latin markets.

Jerk chicken or pork—the quintessential Jamaican street food—is typically prepared over hardwood charcoal in jerk pans made from oil drums, but it's just as delicious when cooked on your standard backyard grill. The incendiary wet rub is made with plenty of allspice, thyme, and scorching-hot Scotch bonnet chiles. This recipe yields enough to marinate 2 pounds of chicken (skin-on thighs, legs, or wings) or pork (chops, loin, or boneless shoulder).

Purée 4 Tbsp. oil and the next 10 ingredients in a food processor until smooth. Transfer ¼ cup marinade to a small bowl and make table sauce: Whisk in vinegar and remaining 2 Tbsp. oil and season to taste with salt. Refrigerate sauce; let come to room temperature before using.

To use marinade with chicken or pork: Put chicken or pork in a glass, stainless-steel, or ceramic dish. Toss with remaining marinade. Cover and chill for at least 3 hours or overnight.

Remove meat from marinade, pat dry, and grill. Serve with table sauce.

MARSEILLES MARINADE

makes about 1 cup

photo, left

6 Tbsp. extra-virgin olive oil
6 Tbsp. white wine vinegar
¼ cup Pernod or other anise-flavored liqueur
2 tsp. fennel seeds, crushed
2 large garlic cloves, minced
½ tsp. kosher salt
¼ tsp. freshly ground black pepper

Use half of the recipe to flavor fish, shrimp, scallops, or lobster before grilling. Reserve the other half for passing at the table. The recipe makes enough to marinate 1 pound of seafood.

Whisk all ingredients in a small bowl to blend. Let stand for 15 minutes.
DO AHEAD: Can be made 2 days ahead. Cover and chill. Rewhisk before using.

To use with seafood: Marinate fish or other seafood in half of marinade in refrigerator for 30 minutes. Remove from marinade and grill. Pass remaining half of marinade separately at the table.

SWEET, SALTY, AND SOUR MARINADE

makes about 1 cup

3 oz. palm sugar, chopped, or
  6½ Tbsp. light brown sugar
½ cup fresh lime juice
½ cup fish sauce (such as nam pla
  or nuoc nam)
½ cup coarsely chopped fresh
  cilantro
2 Tbsp. chopped peeled ginger
4 red Thai chiles or 6 Fresno chiles,
  thinly sliced
3 Tbsp. minced lemongrass (from
  peeled bottom 4 inches of
  2 large stalks)

INGREDIENT INFO Palm sugar, fish
sauce, and lemongrass are all available
at Asian markets; lemongrass is also
sold at some supermarkets.

**Redolent of lemongrass, ginger, and chiles, this Vietnamese-accented marinade
starts with a simple syrup made with palm sugar, which gives the dish its subtle,
sweet undertone. This recipe makes enough to marinate 2 pounds of pork
(chops or tenderloin) or fish (oily or white-fleshed; shrimp or scallops). If you like,
after you're done marinating, you can simmer the marinade and the reserved palm
sugar until the mixture reduces to a fragrant glaze, then brush the glaze onto the
pork or fish during the last few minutes of grilling.**

Stir palm sugar and 3 Tbsp. water in a small saucepan over low heat until sugar is
dissolved. Remove from heat.

Combine lime juice, fish sauce, and 3 Tbsp. water in a medium bowl. Whisk in
⅓ cup palm sugar syrup (reserve remaining syrup for another use). Stir in cilantro,
ginger, chiles, and lemongrass.

To use with pork or seafood: Put pork or seafood in a glass, stainless-steel, or
ceramic dish. Toss with marinade. Cover; chill for at least 3 hours or overnight.

Remove pork or seafood from marinade, pat dry, and grill.

MOJO MARINADE

makes about 2½ cups

1½ cups fresh orange juice
½ cup fresh lemon juice
½ cup fresh lime juice
½ cup fresh oregano, coarsely
  chopped
⅓ cup corn or vegetable oil
10 garlic cloves, minced
3 jalapeños, sliced into rounds
1½ tsp. kosher salt

**Inspired by the flavors of Cuba, this tart, citrusy blend for pork or fish is based on
sour Seville oranges, garlic, and oregano. The recipe yields enough to marinate
2 pounds of pork (tenderloin, shoulder, or bone-in chops) or seafood (firm, white-
fleshed fish such as sea bass, or shrimp or scallops). The acid in the marinade will
tenderize the protein, so fish and seafood will need less steeping time than pork.**

Combine all ingredients in a medium bowl and whisk until salt is dissolved.

To use with pork or seafood: Reserve ⅔ cup marinade for sauce at table;
cover and chill. Let come to room temperature before using.

Put pork or seafood in a glass, stainless-steel, or ceramic dish. Toss with
remaining marinade. Cover; chill for 3 to 8 hours.

Remove pork or seafood from marinade, pat dry, and grill. Serve with
reserved sauce.

RED WINE MARINADE

¾ cup Cabernet Sauvignon or other dry red wine
¼ cup balsamic vinegar
3 Tbsp. extra-virgin olive oil
2 Tbsp. mild-flavored (light) molasses
2 Tbsp. chopped fresh thyme or 2 tsp. dried
2 Tbsp. chopped fresh rosemary or 2 tsp. dried
1 Tbsp. crushed juniper berries or 2 Tbsp. gin
3 large garlic cloves, minced
3 2x1-inch strips orange peel (orange part only)
3 2x1-inch strips lemon peel (yellow part only)
8 whole cloves
8 whole black peppercorns
2 bay leaves, broken in half
¾ tsp. kosher salt

This bold, aggressively seasoned marinade calls out for beef or lamb, but it is also excellent with chicken. The dry red wine is key here: It tenderizes the meat and focuses its flavors. Juniper berries and cloves add a piney note, and a touch of sweet molasses balances the blend and helps create that crisp, steakhouse crust.

Mix all ingredients in a medium bowl. **DO AHEAD:** Can be made 2 days ahead. Cover; chill.

To use with beef, lamb, or chicken: Marinate meat for 6 to 12 hours or poultry for 2 to 4 hours in the refrigerator. Drain marinade into a saucepan. Boil for 1 minute. Pat meat or poultry dry. Grill, basting occasionally with marinade.

BUILDING BLOCKS: The Foundation of Marinades

ACID

Vinegars, wines, and citrus juices do double duty: tenderizing proteins and heightening their flavors.

ALLIUMS

Garlic, minced shallots, scallions, or onions are a must-have for a muscular marinade.

CHILES

Heat helps amplify the flavor and bring a marinade to life. After all, where there's smoke there should be fire.

SALT

Whether you're using soy sauce, fish sauce, or kosher salt, salt is the delivery vehicle for flavor. A little bit of salt will ensure that your other ingredients get through the door.

SUGARS AND SYRUPS

Use brown sugar, honey, palm sugar, or agave as a sweetener to balance and mellow out the other intense flavors.

HERBS

Delicate herbs like mint, parsley, and cilantro add subtle flavor, while more potent herbs like oregano, marjoram, and rosemary infuse marinades with stronger oils.

BRINES
The Infusers

Leaner cuts of meat and poultry, such as pork chops and boneless chicken breasts, can use an assist before they hit the dry heat of the grill—that's where brining comes in. At its most basic, a brine is simply a mixture of salt and water that gets a little help from osmosis.

MASTER BRINE

makes 4 cups

3 Tbsp. kosher salt
3 Tbsp. light brown sugar (optional)

The classic brine, with a perfect balance of salty and sweet, can be used as is—or create other flavor combinations by adding herbs, spices, fruit juices, or other flavorings. This recipe will brine 1 pound of pork, chicken, turkey, or freshwater fish.

Whisk salt, sugar, and 4 cups water in a large bowl until dissolved.

APPLE BRINE

makes 4 cups

2 cups apple cider
3 Tbsp. kosher salt
1 Granny Smith apple, cored, chopped
½ cup sliced onion
3 sprigs thyme

The subtle apple flavor in this all-purpose brine pairs well with 1 pound of almost anything—chicken, turkey, pork—particularly when the mercury begins to drop in the fall.

Combine cider, salt, and 2 cups water in a large bowl and stir until salt is dissolved. Stir in remaining ingredients.

Meat soaked in a salt-and-water solution **draws in moisture and flavor**, yielding juicier, tastier results.

SOY-GINGER BRINE

2 Tbsp. kosher salt
2 Tbsp. light brown sugar
6 Tbsp. reduced-sodium soy sauce
3 garlic cloves, smashed
1 2-inch piece ginger, thinly sliced
1 scallion, thinly sliced
1 cinnamon stick

Soy sauce adds deep flavor to this brine, which is great for chicken, turkey, and pork; you could also use it to quick-brine catfish for 30 minutes. The sugar in the brine will help caramelize meat, so grill over medium to medium-high heat to avoid cooking the outside too quickly. This recipe will brine 1 pound of meat or fish.

Combine salt, sugar, and 4 cups water in a large bowl and stir until salt and sugar are dissolved. Stir in remaining ingredients.

makes 4 cups

MOJO BRINE

2 cups fresh orange juice
3 Tbsp. kosher salt
3 garlic cloves, peeled
2 Tbsp. chopped fresh cilantro
2 limes
2 Tbsp. orange zest
1 tsp. crushed cumin seeds

This Cuban-style brine has a pleasant sourness that's just right with pork. Use it with big cuts such as slow-grilled or smoked pork shoulder or with tender, quick-cooking cuts such as pork chops.

Combine orange juice, salt, and 2 cups water in a large bowl and stir until salt is dissolved. Stir in remaining ingredients.

GETTING IT RIGHT: Brining 101

There's no fancy math involved in making a brine, so once you've tried a few of the recipes here, we encourage you to create your own concoction. Here are the basic guidelines:

THE WEIGHT

For every **1 pound of meat, you'll need 1 quart of brine**. You can use all water as the base, or choose a medium- to low-acid liquid—fresh fruit juice, beer, buttermilk—as half of the total liquid.

THE BASIC MIX

Start with **3 Tbsp. kosher salt dissolved in 1 quart of water**. Then add 3 Tbsp. sweetening agent (such as white or brown sugar, honey, or agave) per quart of water to tame the salt.

THE FLAVOR

Add whatever flavoring ingredients you like— **spices like cracked peppercorns, cumin, or cinnamon, dried or fresh herbs** like thyme, rosemary, oregano, or bay leaves.

THE TIME

Brine for **at least 2 hours and up to 24**, depending on the cut and the brine (saltier brines are for shorter soaks). Lean or thin cuts will need less time. Brine whole turkeys overnight.

SAUCES
Layer on the Flavor

For vibrant and fresh relishes, salsas, and sauces, we take cues from grilling cultures around the world, from Mexico to Malaysia to the Mediterranean, that rely on spice-, chile-, and herb-laden sauces that both stand up to and complement charred food and enliven the palate (they look beautiful, too).

D.I.Y. STEAK SAUCE

makes about 1 cup

1 head of garlic, halved horizontally
½ small onion, cut into ¾-inch rounds
2 Fresno chiles or ½ red bell pepper
½ tsp. vegetable oil
Kosher salt and freshly ground black pepper
½ cup Worcestershire sauce
¼ cup red wine vinegar
1 Tbsp. (packed) dark brown sugar
1 tsp. porcini powder

INGREDIENT INFO Porcini powder is available at some supermarkets and from olivenation.com.

You don't find steak sauce like this in a bottle. The secret ingredient? Porcini powder, which adds an earthy, umami quality that perfectly enhances a good steak. Grilling the garlic, onion, and chiles before puréeing brings out their natural sweetness.

Build a medium-hot fire in a charcoal grill, or heat a gas grill to high. Drizzle garlic, onion rounds, and chiles with oil; turn to coat. Season with salt and pepper. Grill, turning often, until golden brown and softened, about 12 minutes for garlic and 8 minutes for onion and chiles. Let cool slightly.

Pop garlic cloves out of skins and reserve. Peel, stem, and seed chiles. Purée garlic, onion, chiles, Worcestershire sauce, and remaining ingredients in a blender until smooth. Strain.

This sweet-and-sour Kansas City–style sauce is **terrific with grilled meats**.

ALL-AMERICAN BARBECUE SAUCE

ALL-AMERICAN BARBECUE SAUCE

makes 1½ cups

photo, left

1 12-oz. can Coca-Cola Classic
1 cup ketchup
¼ cup apple cider vinegar
2 Tbsp. mild-flavored (light) molasses
1 Tbsp. Worcestershire sauce
2 tsp. dry mustard
1 tsp. chili powder
¼ tsp. cayenne pepper

We borrowed a competition barbecue pitmaster's secret weapon—a can of cola—to give this Kansas City–style sauce subtle depth and sweet flavor. The recipe makes enough for grilling a chicken (see our All-American Barbecued Chicken on page 41) and serving extra sauce alongside.

Bring all ingredients to a boil in a large saucepan over medium heat. Reduce heat to low and simmer, stirring often, until thickened and sauce begins to turn dark red, about 20 minutes. Let cool. **DO AHEAD:** Can be made 2 weeks ahead. Cover and chill.

VARIATIONS ON A THEME: Barbecue Sauces

There are three schools of barbecue sauces: sweet, sour, and in-between. We love all of them—at the right time and with the right dishes, of course.

SWEET

Because of their sugar content, sweet sauces are meant to be used at the tail end of the grilling process for caramelizing. Don't add them earlier or they'll burn.

SWEET-AND-SOUR

Like our all-purpose Kansas City–style All-American Barbecue Sauce (above), these sauces work for glazing on the grill and for saucing the meat at the table.

SOUR

Sour sauces, such as the one to be used with the pulled pork sandwich on page 170, rely on vinegar and spice. You can use them during grilling—they won't burn because they contain little sugar.

CHIMICHURRI

½ cup red wine vinegar
1 tsp. kosher salt, more as needed
3 or 4 garlic cloves, thinly sliced or minced
1 shallot, finely chopped
1 Fresno chile or red jalapeño, finely chopped
2 cups minced fresh cilantro
1 cup minced flat-leaf parsley
⅓ cup finely chopped fresh oregano
¾ cup extra-virgin olive oil

This ridiculously addictive, bright green sauce is a staple condiment in Argentina, where they serve it with that country's legendary grilled steaks. The base is a blend of olive oil and fresh herbs like cilantro, parsley, and oregano; garlic, red wine vinegar, and chile pepper add piquancy and a touch of heat. This recipe makes enough to marinate 2 pounds of beef (London broil or skirt, hanger, or flank steaks) or lamb (loin or blade chops) with some left over to serve as a sauce after grilling.

Combine vinegar, 1 tsp. salt, garlic, shallot, and chile in a medium bowl and let stand for 10 minutes. Stir in cilantro, parsley, and oregano. Using a fork, whisk in oil. Transfer ½ cup chimichurri to a small bowl, season with salt to taste, and reserve as sauce.

To use as a marinade with beef or lamb: Put beef or lamb in a glass, stainless-steel, or ceramic dish. Toss with remaining chimichurri. Cover and chill for at least 3 hours or overnight.

Remove meat from marinade, pat dry, and grill. Serve with reserved sauce.

LADOLEMONO

¼ cup fresh lemon juice
¼ cup extra-virgin olive oil
Kosher salt and freshly ground black pepper

This classic Greek vinaigrette gives a flash of brightness to grilled octopus, shrimp, squid, or the smoky, crispy skin of whole fish. Dunk seafood in the citrusy sauce before laying it on the grill, or drizzle it over cooked fish at the table.

Whisk lemon juice and oil in small bowl. Season to taste with salt and pepper.

Sure, you can use a food processor. But we prefer the **integrity of a chimichurri** made from herbs that are **chopped by hand**.

CHIMICHURRI

+

Serve our version of this North African hot sauce with **lamb kebabs** or **grilled shrimp**.

RED HARISSA

RED HARISSA

photo, left

3 large red bell peppers
2½ Tbsp. white wine vinegar
4 garlic cloves, crushed
2 red jalapeños or Fresno chiles, stemmed, seeded, chopped
1 tsp. ground cumin
1 tsp. kosher salt, more as needed
¼ tsp. freshly ground black pepper, more as needed
¼ cup extra-virgin olive oil

In North Africa, *harissa* is like salsa or ketchup—it's everywhere. Roasting your own peppers is a must—it only takes a few minutes but yields a pure, sweet-and-smoky flavor that's key to the bright, spicy purée. To store leftover *harissa*, transfer to a glass jar and top with a ½-inch layer of olive oil. Refrigerate, topping off with more oil after each use.

Roast peppers in broiler or directly over a gas flame, turning occasionally, until charred all over. Transfer to a large bowl, cover, and let stand for 15 minutes. Stem, peel, and seed peppers; coarsely chop.

Place peppers, next 4 ingredients, 1 tsp. salt, and ¼ tsp. black pepper in a food processor. Purée until very smooth. With processor running, gradually add oil. Season to taste with additional salt and black pepper, if desired.

GREEN HARISSA

1 cup chopped fresh cilantro
1 cup chopped spinach
¼ cup extra-virgin olive oil
1 garlic clove, minced
1 serrano chile, seeded, minced
¼ tsp. ground coriander
¼ tsp. ground cumin
  Kosher salt

Sort of like the North African version of *chimichurri*, this vivid green sauce is fragrant with cilantro, garlic, and cumin. Spoon it over grilled chicken, fish, or lamb.

Combine first 7 ingredients in a food processor and purée until smooth. Season harissa to taste with salt. Store in a sealed jar for up to 1 week.

THE ULTIMATE PESTO

Kosher salt
10 cups (loosely packed) fresh basil leaves (about 5 oz., from about 2 bunches)
½ cup finely grated Parmesan, plus more for sprinkling
1½ Tbsp. pine nuts
1 garlic clove, coarsely chopped
½ cup mild extra-virgin olive oil, plus more for drizzling on top

When it comes to pesto, think beyond pasta—brush it over grilled shrimp or fish, use it as a marinade for chicken, and spread it on sandwiches. This "ultimate" version retains the bright green color of the basil via a quick blanch of the leaves, and it offers just the right amount of garlic bite: one clove, no more.

Bring a large pot of lightly salted water to a boil. Set a colander in a large bowl of ice water (this will make it easier to strain the basil later). Working in batches, blanch basil in boiling water for 10 seconds.

Using a large slotted spoon, transfer basil to colander in ice water; let basil cool completely. Set aside ½ cup blanching water.

Drain basil by lifting colander from ice water. Using your hands, squeeze excess water from basil; transfer basil to paper towels. (You should have about ½ cup blanched leaves.)

Pulse basil, ½ cup Parmesan, pine nuts, and garlic in a food processor until well combined, adding blanching water by tablespoonfuls to thin if needed and stopping to scrape down sides as needed, to form a smooth, thick purée, about 1 minute. Transfer basil mixture to a medium bowl. Stir in ½ cup oil. Season pesto to taste with salt.

GETTING IT RIGHT: The Basics of Homemade Pesto

We can't think of a more versatile style of sauce to accompany all kinds of grilled meats, fish, and vegetables. And it's so easy to make your own:

 Pick your herb: basil, cilantro, parsley, sage, mint, or whatever is growing on your windowsill.

 Choose a nut. No need to buy expensive pine nuts. You can use walnuts, pistachios, or even pumpkin seeds.

 Blend with olive oil in a blender or food processor until it forms a coarse purée.

 Stir in ground spices and grated Parmesan, if desired. Spoon pesto onto anything that comes off the grill.

CILANTRO-PEPITA PESTO

1½ tsp. plus ¼ cup extra-virgin olive
    oil, divided
6 Tbsp. shelled pumpkin seeds
    (pepitas)
½ cup (firmly packed) fresh cilantro
½ tsp. cracked coriander seeds
½ garlic clove, coarsely chopped
1 Tbsp. fresh lime juice, more as
    needed
    Kosher salt and freshly ground
    black pepper

Toasted pumpkin seeds and fresh cilantro give this nutty, swoon-worthy pesto a subtle Mexican spin. It pairs particularly well with grilled salmon or chicken thighs, but you're going to want to spoon it over everything, so feel free to make a double batch.

Heat 1½ tsp. oil in a large nonstick skillet over medium-high heat. Add pumpkin seeds; sauté until beginning to brown and pop, about 2 minutes. Transfer seeds to paper towels to drain; let cool. Reserve skillet.

Pulse pumpkin seeds, cilantro, coriander seeds, and garlic in a food processor until coarsely chopped. With machine running, gradually add 1 Tbsp. lime juice, remaining ¼ cup oil, then ¼ cup water, blending until a coarse purée forms. Season pesto to taste with salt, pepper, and more lime juice, if desired.

LEMON TAHINI

6 Tbsp. tahini (sesame seed paste)
2 Tbsp. chopped fresh oregano
1½ Tbsp. fresh lemon juice
    Kosher salt and freshly ground
    black pepper

This tangy, oregano-flecked sauce is delicious with grilled lamb and vegetables. After whisking ingredients together, add water by teaspoonfuls if the sauce is too thick (it should be thin enough to drizzle, but not watery).

Whisk tahini, oregano, lemon juice, and 5 Tbsp. water in a small bowl, adding more water by teaspoonfuls if too thick. Season to taste with salt and pepper. **DO AHEAD:** Can be made 1 day ahead. Cover and chill.

CLASSIC AIOLI

1 large egg yolk
1 small garlic clove, finely grated
¼ tsp. kosher salt, more as needed
¼ cup grapeseed oil
¼ cup extra-virgin olive oil
    Pinch of cayenne pepper
    Fresh lemon juice
    Freshly ground black pepper

Garlicky Provençal mayo is transformed into a magic sauce that begs to be served with grilled fish, meat, vegetables, and bread. The classic uncooked preparation, includes raw egg yolk. To get the emulsification tight, add the oil in a thin drizzle while constantly whisking. To make the whisking easier, stabilize the bowl by putting it inside a towel-lined pot.

Whisk egg yolk, garlic, ¼ tsp. salt, and 2 tsp. water in a small metal bowl. Whisking constantly, slowly drizzle in grapeseed oil, 1 teaspoon at a time, until sauce is thickened and emulsified. Whisking constantly, add olive oil in a slow, steady stream. Stir in cayenne and season to taste with lemon juice, salt, and pepper.

COMPOUND BUTTER
The Instant Sauce

Flavored butter melts into a luscious sauce on top of grilled steaks, pork chops, and vegetables. Make it ahead and store it in your refrigerator or freezer. Customize butters to suit your own taste, or riff on our favorites.

HERB–LEMON ZEST BUTTER

makes about ½ cup

photo, right

¼ cup mixed herbs, such as flat-leaf parsley, chervil, tarragon, and chives, chopped
½ cup (1 stick) unsalted butter, softened
1 teaspoon finely grated lemon zest
  Kosher salt

This versatile butter will become a staple in your grilling repertoire.

Put herbs on a work surface. Add butter and lemon zest. Finely chop together until well combined. Season with salt.

Transfer to a sheet of parchment paper, placing butter on long edge closest to you. Fold paper over and roll into a cylinder, twisting the ends; wrap airtight in foil. Chill until solid. **DO AHEAD:** Butter will keep refrigerated for up to 2 weeks or frozen for up to 3 months.

BACON-BOURBON BUTTER

makes ½ cup

1 slice smoked bacon, finely chopped
½ cup (1 stick) unsalted butter, room temperature
1 Tbsp. bourbon
1 Tbsp. pure maple syrup
1 tsp. (packed) light brown sugar
  Kosher salt

This flavored butter is delicious with grilled pork—and it's pretty great on waffles and pancakes, too.

Cook bacon in a small skillet over medium heat, stirring occasionally, until fat is rendered and bacon is crisp, about 6 minutes. Using a slotted spoon, transfer bacon to paper towels to drain. Reserve 1 tsp. bacon drippings.

Put reserved bacon and drippings into a small bowl; add butter, bourbon, maple syrup, and sugar. Season to taste with salt. Using a fork, vigorously whisk until well combined. Transfer butter mixture to a sheet of parchment paper, waxed paper, or plastic wrap, placing on long edge closest to you. Fold paper over and roll into a cylinder, twisting the ends; wrap airtight in foil. Chill until solid. **DO AHEAD:** Can be made 2 weeks ahead and chilled, or frozen for up to 3 months.

+ This mix of **parsley**, **lemon juice**, and **softened butter** is a divine twist on the classic *beurre maître d'hôtel*.

HERB–LEMON ZEST BUTTER

PORCINI–RED WINE BUTTER

makes ½ cup

½ cup (1 stick) unsalted butter, room temperature
2 Tbsp. finely chopped dried porcini mushrooms
1 Tbsp. red wine
   Kosher salt

INGREDIENT INFO Find dried porcini mushrooms in the produce section of some supermarkets and at specialty foods stores and Italian markets.

Melt coins of this umami-rich butter on grilled steaks, lamb chops, salmon fillets, or chicken breasts.

Spread butter on a work surface and sprinkle with mushrooms. Drizzle with wine. Using a knife, finely chop together until well combined. Season to taste with salt. Transfer butter mixture to a sheet of parchment paper, waxed paper, or plastic wrap, placing on long edge closest to you. Fold paper over and roll into a cylinder, twisting the ends; wrap airtight in foil. Chill until solid. **DO AHEAD:** Can be made 2 weeks ahead and chilled, or frozen for up to 3 months.

ANCHOVY BUTTER

makes about ½ cup

½ cup (1 stick) unsalted butter, room temperature
4 garlic cloves, minced
8 anchovy fillets packed in oil, drained, minced
½ tsp. Hungarian hot paprika
½ tsp. fresh lemon juice
   Kosher salt

Almost any flavored butter will elevate a simply grilled piece of meat or fish, but this umami-rich compound butter goes particularly well with steak. Place a slice of it on top of your favorite cut as it rests.

In a medium bowl, combine butter, garlic, anchovies, paprika, lemon juice, and salt to taste. Mix with a fork until smooth. Transfer butter mixture to a sheet of parchment paper, waxed paper, or plastic wrap, placing on edge closest to you. Fold paper over and roll into a cylinder, twisting the ends; wrap airtight in foil. Chill until solid. **DO AHEAD:** Can be made 2 weeks ahead and chilled, or frozen for up to 1 month.

SALSA
The International Condiment

When we say *salsa,* we're not just talking about *pico de gallo.* It's everything from a chile- and onion-based sauce to a macerated fruit, herb, or vegetable condiment. *Salsa verde* illustrates that versatility. In Mexico, a *salsa verde* is any green sauce, whether made from roasted and puréed tomatillos or cilantro and chiles. In Italy, *salsa verde* is an herb sauce made with parsley and bolstered by anchovies and sometimes garlic and capers.

makes 2½ cups

MEXICAN SALSA VERDE

2 Tbsp. extra-virgin olive oil, plus more for brushing
3 garlic cloves, unpeeled
1 lb. fresh tomatillos, husked, rinsed
1 small onion, quartered through root end
3 to 6 serrano chiles, or 2 to 4 jalapeño
¼ cup chopped fresh cilantro
½ tsp. sugar, more as needed
Kosher salt
1 cup low-salt chicken broth
2 Tbsp. fresh lime juice, more as needed

SPECIAL EQUIPMENT 1 metal skewer

Lightly charred tomatillos give the classic Mexican *salsa verde* a subtle smokiness. This version doesn't hold back on the heat—use fewer chiles for a milder sauce.

Build a medium-hot fire in a charcoal grill, or heat a gas grill to high. Brush grill rack with oil. Thread garlic onto skewer. Grill garlic, tomatillos, onion quarters, and chiles until dark brown spots form on all sides, about 9 minutes for onion, 6 minutes for tomatillos and chiles, and 4 minutes for garlic. Let cool.

Peel garlic. Trim core from onion. Scrape some of burnt skin off chiles; stem. Seed chiles for milder salsa, if desired. Coarsely chop onion, chiles, and garlic. Transfer tomatillos and all vegetables to a blender. Add cilantro and ½ tsp. sugar; purée until smooth. Season to taste with salt.

Heat 2 Tbsp. oil in a large heavy saucepan over high heat. Carefully add tomatillo mixture (juices may splatter). Cook, stirring often, until slightly thickened, about 2 minutes. Add broth and 2 Tbsp. lime juice. Bring to a boil; reduce heat to medium and simmer until mixture measures 2½ cups, about 10 minutes. Season to taste with salt and more sugar and lime juice, if desired.
DO AHEAD: Can be made 1 day ahead. Let cool slightly, then cover and chill.

ITALIAN SALSA VERDE

makes 1½ cups

6 anchovy fillets packed in oil, chopped (optional)
1 garlic clove, chopped
1½ Tbsp. capers, rinsed and chopped
1 Fresno chile or red jalapeño, stemmed, seeded, minced
4 cups loosely packed flat-leaf parsley leaves, finely chopped
2 cups loosely packed fresh mint leaves, finely chopped
1 cup loosely packed fresh cilantro leaves, finely chopped
1 cup plus 2 Tbsp. extra-virgin olive oil
Kosher salt (optional)

You should never be without a jar of *salsa verde*—it's the ketchup of summer. Spoon it on grilled lamb, pork chops, eggplant, or line-caught swordfish. Using a mortar and pestle to grind the ingredients will yield a chunkier sauce.

Combine anchovies, if using, garlic, capers, and chile in a large mortar or food processor. Pound with a pestle or purée until a chunky paste forms. Add herbs and stir to combine. Remove pestle or transfer paste to a bowl. Using a fork, slowly whisk in oil. Season to taste with salt, if desired. Let stand at room temperature for 30 minutes while flavors meld. **DO AHEAD:** Sauce can be made 1 week ahead. Cover and chill. Bring to room temperature and stir before serving.

PICO DE GALLO

makes about 2½ cups

½ medium white onion (about 3 oz.), cut into ¼-inch dice
2 cups diced tomatoes
¼ cup chopped fresh cilantro
1 Tbsp. minced jalapeño (optional)
Kosher salt

This classic tomato-and-onion salsa can be made mild or spicy according to your taste; add the optional jalapeño (and more) if you like the kick, and use the seeds if you want even more heat. Shocking the onion in ice water reduces its bitterness.

Place 1 cup cold water and 2 ice cubes in a medium bowl. Add onion; stir, then discard ice; drain well. Transfer to a medium bowl. Add tomatoes, cilantro, and jalapeño, if using. Season to taste with salt.

TOASTED GUAJILLO CHILE SALSA

makes about 2 cups

4 oz. dried guajillo chiles
6 garlic cloves, unpeeled
3 Tbsp. apple cider vinegar
1½ tsp. kosher salt, more as needed
1 tsp. garlic powder
1 tsp. onion powder

INGREDIENT INFO Guajillo chiles are maroon-colored, fairly hot dried chiles up to 6 inches long and about 1½ inches wide; they are available at some supermarkets and at Latin markets.

Toasting the guajillo chiles adds amazing depth of flavor to this spicy salsa, which is great with grilled beef or pork, and on tacos.

Heat a large dry cast-iron skillet over medium-high heat. Working in batches, toast chiles until slightly puffed and fragrant, 15 to 20 seconds per side (do not allow to burn). Let cool.

Using kitchen scissors and working over a medium bowl, cut chiles into thin rings, reserving seeds. Cover with 2 cups very hot water and let soak for 10 minutes.

Meanwhile, heat the same skillet over medium-high heat. Add garlic; cook, turning often, until tender and skin is lightly charred, about 8 minutes. Let cool. Peel; trim ends.

Transfer chiles with seeds and liquid to a blender; add roasted garlic, vinegar, 1½ tsp. salt, and remaining ingredients. Pulse until a thick, coarse purée forms. Season to taste with salt.

Bonus Recipe
TOMATO, CORN, AND AVOCADO SALSA

This fresh and simple salsa is a great complement to grilled chicken breasts or grilled fish. Dice ripe tomatoes and combine with grilled or raw corn kernels, diced avocado, chopped cilantro, and fresh lime juice. Add minced serrano chile for a little heat. Season with salt and more lime juice.

ACKNOWLEDGMENTS

Four hundred and thirty-two pages, 380 recipes, 100 photos, 36 illustrations, and over 100,000 words. Over the past year, we here at *Bon Appétit* learned that it takes a lot of hard work and, more specifically, a lot of contributors to make a book of this size. It's time they get the credit they deserve.

First up, big thanks to Kirsty Melville, Tim Lynch, Jean Lucas, and the gang at Andrews McMeel for patiently guiding us through the process of getting a book published (we monthly magazine folks are used to a different grind). And thanks to agent David Black for hammering out the deal.

The meat of this book, so to speak, is its recipes. Former *Bon Appétit* food editor Hunter Lewis and deputy food editor Janet McCracken (with ample help from the entire *Bon Appétit* kitchen crew) tested and retested the recipes, edited them, wrote and rewrote them—a tremendous undertaking. They are the foundation of both *Bon Appétit* the magazine and this book.

Of course, if there aren't gorgeous photos of the food, who's going to cook all those recipes? The photography duo Peden & Munk (Taylor Peden and Jen Munkvold), along with food stylist Rebecca Jurkevich, stepped up big time, embracing this ambitious project and supplying us with imagery that's as strikingly beautiful as it is authentically real. They are straight-up awesome.

Back in the *Bon Appétit* offices, several editors worked tirelessly (above and beyond their already taxing daily duties) to make this book happen. Creative director Alex Grossman and art director Elizabeth Spiridakis poured their artistic hearts into the book, ensuring that it looks every bit as beautiful as the monthly magazine, while still carving out its own unique identity. Photo director Alex Pollack and her team undertook the difficult task of coordinating and executing the book's week-long photo shoot in Connecticut—locking in the location, the food stylist, and the travel accommodations, not to mention the countless bags of charcoal, pounds of quality dry-aged steak, farm-fresh heirloom tomatoes, sides of wild salmon, stylish serving platters, and all the other things, big and small, that go into a shoot of this scale.

Deputy editor Meghan Sutherland edited every last word in this book, long after the rest of us had gone home for the night, and made sure that all the moving parts involved in this project moved in sync. As difficult a task as there is in this game.

Oh, and I can't forget my former assistant, Rachel Sanders, who did all those little things that end up making a huge difference, and for generally putting up with me when things got just a little hectic.

Of course, we needed plenty of help from outside our office to bring this book to fruition. Susan Champlin served as our project coordinator, our steady hand. She oversaw the edit for each chapter from the very beginning all the way through to the last copyedit, corralling the work of the numerous contributing writers and gently, but firmly, prodding us to keep things moving. A pleasure to work with.

Designer Joe Shouldice worked (and worked, and worked) with us to give us a book that's both easy to cook with and a joy to look at, that feels modern while still capturing the primal and timeless appeal of grilling. Joe's a champ. And the other Joe—McKendry—created the crystal-clear illustrations that guide you through the necessary techniques.

Finally, I need to thank the entire editorial staff of *Bon Appétit*, who work their tails off each month to make a magazine and website with voice, attitude, passion, and beauty. Without those daily and monthly iterations of *Bon Appétit*, this book wouldn't exist.

ADAM RAPOPORT

RECIPE CONTRIBUTORS

The recipes in this book were tested and developed by the Bon Appétit Test Kitchen but in many cases started out from a chef or cook outside of our offices. To them, we're thankful.

A
Bruce Aidells
Americano, *San Francisco*
Pam Anderson
Nate Appleman
John Ash
Ayung Terrace, Four Seasons Resort Bali at Sayan, *Indonesia*

B
Ben and Karen Baker, Magnolia Grill, *Durham, North Carolina*
Melanie Barnard
Scott Beatie
Beti-Jai Restaurant, *Donostia-San Sebastian, Spain*
Lena Cederham Birnbaum
Emily and Dick Boenning
Jimmy Bradley
Georgeanne Brennan
Rick Browne
Virginia Burke
Buzzards Restaurant, *Calgary, Alberta, Canada*

C
Kenny Callaghan, Blue Smoke, *New York*
Bryan Caswell
Jeff Cerciello, Farmshop, *Santa Monica*
Adel Chagar
Kay Chun

Melissa Clark
Jenna Clemens
Cristina Ceccatelli Cook
Cat Cora

D
Lori De Mori
Sara Dickerman
Brooke Dojny
Jill Dupleix
Dagny and Tim Du Val

E
Jan Esterly, *Pittsburgh, Pennsylvania*

F
Judith Fertig
Amy Finely
Bobby Flay
Janet Fletcher
Sara Foster
The Franklin Café, *Boston*
Gianni Franzi, *Vernazza, Italy*
Clark Frasier and Mark Gaier

G
Paul Gayler, The Lanesborough, *London*
Thomas Goetz
Suzanne Goin
Rozanne Gold
Bill Granger
Dorie Greenspan
Sophie Grigson
Kathy Gunst

H
Melissa Hamilton and Christopher Hersheimer
Mary-Frances Heck
Susanna Hoffman

Charlie Hollowell
Jill Hough
Helen Hull and David Hardee

J
Cheryl Alters Jamison and Bill Jamison
Jasper's, *Plano, Texas*

K
Zov Karamardian
Elizabeth Karmel
Jeanne Kelley
Kristine Kidd
Paul Kirk
Dan Kluger
Ian Knauer
Andrew Knowlton

L
Matt Lee and Ted Lee
Le Palanquin, *Paris*
Amber Levinson
Hannah Levitz
Hunter Lewis
David Lynch

M
Malibu Seafood, *Malibu, California*
John Malik
Francine Maroukian
Daisy Martinez
Janet Taylor McCracken
Michael McLaughlin
Metrazur, *New York*
Chris Morocco
Selma Brown Morrow
Dave Mueller

O
Nancy Oakes
Katie O'Kennedy

Old House Restaurant, *Santa Fe, New Mexico*
Old Mexico Grill, *Santa Fe, New Mexico*
Sri Owen

P
Alex Palermo
Zakary Pelaccio
The Peninsula, *Beverly Hills*
Poppies Bistro Café, *Aspen, Colorado*
Michael Presnal, The Federal Restaurant, *Agawam, Massachusetts*
Jamie Purviance

R
Steven Raichlen
Ted Reader
Andrea Reusing
Tori Ritchie
Chad Robertson
Claudia Roden
Rick Rodgers
Betty Rosbottom
Tony Rosenfeld
Jenny Rosenstrach and Andy Ward
Judy Ross
Silvena Rowe
Jennifer Rubell

S
Adam Sachs
Roberto Santibañez
Pascal Sauton
Richard Sax
Andrew Schloss
Ben Schneider and Sohui Kim, The Good Fork, *Brooklyn*
Barbara Scott-Goodman
Scylla, *Chicago*

Shadowbrook Restaurant, *Capitola, California*
Sam Sifton
Marie Simmons
Maria Helm Sinskey
Snake River Grill, *Jackson Hole, Wyoming*
Spago, *Las Vegas*
Susan Spicer, *Mondo, New Orleans*
Marlena Spieler
Steak & Sticks, *Sedona, Arizona*
Romney Steele
Molly Stevens
Oliver Strand

T
Sarah Tenaglia
Cynthia and Dwayne Thomas

Fred Thompson
Cabell Tomlinson, Frankies 570 Spuntino, *New York*
Tommy's Mexican Restaurant, *San Francisco*
Charlie Trotter
Jo Tunnell
Two, *San Francisco*

V
Jean-Georges Vongerichten

W
Robb Walsh
Philip Ward, Mayahuel, *New York*
Walt's Wharf, *Seal Beach, California*
Joanne Weir

Eric Werner
Kevin West
Arnold West and Nadine Francis West
John Willingham
Diane Rossen Worthington

WE'D ALSO LIKE TO THANK...

Kerry Acker
Zoe Alexander
Maria Benetos
Cameron Berkman
Lena Cederham Birnbaum
Frederika Brookfield
Elizabeth Brownfield
Caroline Campion
Kay Chun
Carol Coe
Liesel Davis
Laura K. DePalma
Zinzi Edmundson
Emily Farris
Susan Getzendanner
Jim Gomez

Gaylen Ducker Grody
Kirsten Hageleit
Lonnee Hamilton
Colu Henry
Jennifer Hoche
Anya Hoffman
Alexandra Horton
Dorothy Irwin
Julie Jamerson
Andrew Knowlton
Yewande Komolafe
Barbara Kroells
Jean Lucas
Tim Lynch
Marcy MacDonald
Timothy McSweeney

Chris Morocco
Selma Brown Morrow
Faye Chiu Mosley
Jennifer Murray
Carla Lalli Music
Rachel Ng
Tricia Callas O'Donnell
Rochelle Palermo
Stacey C. Rivera
Roberto Rodriguez
Alison Roman
Meryl Rothstein
Christine Schuchart
Joanna Sciarrino
David Shaw
Hank Shaw

Lucy Silberman
Victoria Spencer
Amy Steinberg
Alaina Sullivan
Victoria von Biel
Leslie Anne Wiggins
Brooke Wolin
Amy Worley

METRIC EQUIVALENTS AND CONVERSIONS

APPROXIMATE METRIC EQUIVALENTS

Volume

¼ teaspoon	1 milliliter
½ teaspoon	2.5 milliliters
¾ teaspoon	4 milliliters
1 teaspoon	5 milliliters
1¼ teaspoons	6 milliliters
1½ teaspoons	7.5 milliliters
1¾ teaspoons	8.5 milliliters
2 teaspoons	10 milliliters
1 tablespoon (½ fluid ounce)	15 milliliters
2 tablespoons (1 fluid ounce)	30 milliliters
¼ cup	60 milliliters
⅓ cup	80 milliliters
½ cup (4 fluid ounces)	120 milliliters
⅔ cup	160 milliliters
¾ cup	180 milliliters
1 cup (8 fluid ounces)	240 milliliters
1¼ cups	300 milliliters
1½ cups (12 fluid ounces)	360 milliliters
1⅔ cups	400 milliliters
2 cups (1 pint)	460 milliliters
3 cups	700 milliliters
4 cups (1 quart)	0.95 liter
1 quart plus ¼ cup	1 liter
4 quarts (1 gallon)	3.8 liters

Weight

¼ ounce	7 grams
½ ounce	14 grams
¾ ounce	21 grams
1 ounce	28 grams
1¼ ounces	35 grams
1½ ounces	42.5 grams
1⅔ ounces	45 grams
2 ounces	57 grams
3 ounces	85 grams
4 ounces (¼ pound)	113 grams
5 ounces	142 grams
6 ounces	170 grams
7 ounces	198 grams
8 ounces (½ pound)	227 grams
16 ounces (1 pound)	454 grams
35.25 ounces (2.2 pounds)	1 kilogram

Length

⅛ inch	3 millimeters
¼ inch	6 millimeters
½ inch	1¼ centimeters
1 inch	2½ centimeters
2 inches	5 centimeters
2½ inches	6 centimeters
4 inches	10 centimeters
5 inches	13 centimeters
6 inches	15¼ centimeters
12 inches (1 foot)	30 centimeters

METRIC CONVERSION FORMULAS

To Convert	Multiply
Ounces to grams	Ounces by 28.35
Pounds to kilograms	Pounds by 454
Teaspoons to milliliters	Teaspoons by 4.93
Tablespoons to milliliters	Tablespoons by 14.79
Fluid ounces to milliliters	Fluid ounces by 29.57
Cups to milliliters	Cups by 236.59
Cups to liters	Cups by .236
Pints to liters	Pints by .473
Quarts to liters	Quarts by .946
Gallons to liters	Gallons by 3.785
Inches to centimeters	Inches by 2.54

OVEN TEMPERATURES

To convert Fahrenheit to Celsius, subtract 32 from Fahrenheit, multiply the result by 5, then divide by 9.

Description	Fahrenheit	Celsius	British Gas Mark
Very cool	200°	95°	0
Very cool	225°	110°	¼
Very cool	250°	120°	½
Cool	275°	135°	1
Cool	300°	150°	2
Warm	325°	165°	3
Moderate	350°	175°	4
Moderately hot	375°	190°	5
Fairly hot	400°	200°	6
Hot	425°	220°	7
Very hot	450°	230°	8
Very hot	475°	245°	9

COMMON INGREDIENTS AND THEIR APPROXIMATE EQUIVALENTS

1 cup uncooked white rice = 185 grams
1 cup all-purpose flour = 140 grams
1 stick butter (4 ounces • ½ cup • 8 tablespoons) = 110 grams
1 cup butter (8 ounces • 2 sticks • 16 tablespoons) = 220 grams
1 cup brown sugar, firmly packed = 225 grams
1 cup granulated sugar = 200 grams

Information compiled from a variety of sources, including *Recipes into Type* by Joan Whitman and Dolores Simon (Newton, MA: Biscuit Books, 2000); *The New Food Lover's Companion* by Sharon Tyler Herbst (Hauppauge, NY: Barron's, 1995); and *Rosemary Brown's Big Kitchen Instruction Book* (Kansas City, MO: Andrews McMeel, 1998).

INDEX